THE COMPLETE REPUBLIC OF IRELAND FC 1926-2020

Dirk Karsdorp

British Library Cataloguing in Publication Data
A catalogue record for this book is available from the British Library

ISBN 978-1-86223-445-1

Copyright © 2020, SOCCER BOOKS LIMITED. (01472 696226)
72 St. Peter's Avenue, Cleethorpes, N.E. Lincolnshire, DN35 8HU, England

All rights are reserved. No part of this publication may be reproduced, stored in a retrieval system or transmitted, in any form or by any means, electronic, mechanical, photocopying, recording, or otherwise, without the prior written permission of Soccer Books Limited.

Printed in the UK by Severn

FOREWORD

This book contains statistics for all of the officially-recognised full international games played by the Republic of Ireland from their first ever game (played as the Irish Free State) against Italy in 1926 through to the end of 2020. Readers should note that for consistency in the statistics in this book, we always list Ireland under the name, 'Republic of Ireland', despite the fact that the country itself did not become a Republic until 1937!

Other titles in this series updated to 2020 are also available covering the matches played by England, Scotland, Wales and Northern Ireland. We have also published new books containing complete statistics for the international matches of Belgium, Italy and the Netherlands.

Although we have endeavoured to include statistics which are as complete as possible, inevitably there are omissions with one or two small pieces of information missing for some games. Most notably, the times at which goals were scored were not recorded for a few of the earliest games. In such cases, the following symbol has been used to indicate that the time of the goal is not known: "#". Additionally, the referee's names or attendances are also not recorded for a handful of games and this is also noted in the text. Finally, the team line-ups of Ireland's opponents are not recorded for the games played against Trinidad & Tobago in 1982 and against China in 1984 as it has proved impossible to discover this information.

1. 21.03.1926
ITALY v REPUBLIC OF IRELAND 3-0 (3-0)
Campo Juventus FC, Torino

Referee: Paul Ruoff (Switzerland)   Attendance: 20,000

ITALY: Giovanni De Pra', Virginio Rosetta, Umberto Caligaris, Antonio Janni, Fulvio Bernardini, Carlo Bigatto, Leopoldo Conti, Adolfo Baloncieri (Cap), Giuseppe Della Valle, Mario Magnozzi, Mariano Tansini.   Trainer: Augusto Rangone.

REPUBLIC OF IRELAND: Harold Cannon, Francis Brady, John McCarthy, Michael Foley (Cap), Denis Doyle, James Connolly, John Joseph Flood, Joseph Grace, Francis Watters, Robert P. Fullam, John Fagan.

Goals: Adolfo Baloncieri (13), Mario Magnozzi (36), Fulvio Bernardini (44)

2. 24.04.1927
REPUBLIC OF IRELAND v ITALY "B" 1-2 (1-0)
Lansdowne Road, Dublin

Referee: John Langenus (Belgium)   Attendance: 20,000

REPUBLIC OF IRELAND: Frank Collins, Alexander Kirkland, Francis Brady (Cap), William Glen, Michael Terence O'Brien, Thomas Muldoon, William Lacey, Henry Anthony Duggan, Christopher Martin, Robert P. Fullam, Joseph Kendrick.

ITALY: Mario Gianni, Mario Zanello, Delfo Bellini, Pietro Genovesi, Luigi Burlando, Alberto Giordani, Federico Munerati, Antonio Vojak, Pietro Pastore, Enrico Rivolta, Luigi Cevenini III.

Goals: Robert P. Fullam (6) / Federico Munerati (#, #)

3. 12.02.1928
BELGIUM v REPUBLIC OF IRELAND 2-4 (2-0)
Sclessin, Liège

Referee: Arthur H. Kingscott (England)   Attendance: 25,000

BELGIUM: Louis Vandenbergh, Armand Swartenbroeks, Nikolaas Hoydonckx, Henri Van Averbeke, Florimond Van Halme, Gustave Boesman, Cornelius Elst, Pierre Braine, Raymond Braine, François Ledent, Jan Diddens.
Trainer: William Sturrock Maxwell (Scotland).

REPUBLIC OF IRELAND: Harold Cannon, Jeremiah Robinson, John McCarthy (Cap), Joseph Kinsella, John Byrne, Patrick Barry, John O'Sullivan, William Lacey, John Joseph White, Charles Dowdall, Joseph Golding.

Goals: Raymond Braine (38), François Ledent (41) / John Joseph White (55, 73), William Lacey (59), John O'Sullivan (77 pen)

4. 20.04.1929
REPUBLIC OF IRELAND v BELGIUM 4-0 (1-0)
Dalymount Park, Dublin

Referee: Stanley Frederick Rous (England)   Att: 12,000

REPUBLIC OF IRELAND: Thomas George Farquharson, James Maguire, John Burke (Cap), William Glen, Michael Terence O'Brien, Patrick Barry, James Bermingham, John Joseph Flood, David Byrne, Charles Dowdall, Robert Egan.

BELGIUM: Louis Somers, Theodoor Nouwens, Nikolaas Hoydonckx, Henri Van Averbeke, Florimond Van Halme, Gustave Boesman, Pierre Braine, Michel Vanderbauwhede, Raymond Braine, Jacques Moeschal, Jan Diddens.
Trainer: Viktor Löwenfeld (Austria).

Goals: John Joseph Flood (32, 80, 89), David Byrne (73)

5. 11.05.1930
BELGIUM v REPUBLIC OF IRELAND 1-3 (1-1)
"Charles Malis", Bruxelles

Referee: Ramón Melcón (Spain)   Attendance: 18,000

BELGIUM: Arnold Badjou, Theodoor Nouwens, Nikolaas Hoydonckx, Pierre Braine, August Hellemans, Jean De Clercq, Louis Versijp, Ferdinand Adams, Michel Vanderbauwhede, Jacques Moeschal, Désiré Bastin.
Trainer: Viktor Löwenfeld (Austria).

REPUBLIC OF IRELAND: Thomas George Farquharson, William Lacey, John McCarthy, William Glen, Michael Terence O'Brien (Cap), Francis McLoughlin, Henry Anthony Duggan, John Joseph Flood, James Dunne, Alfred Horlacher, Joseph Golding.

Goals: Désiré Bastin (20) / James Dunne (33, 57), John Joseph Flood (77)

6. 26.04.1931
SPAIN v REPUBLIC OF IRELAND 1-1 (1-1)
Montjuich, Barcelona

Referee: Silvestre Romanhino (Portugal)   Att: 35,000

SPAIN: Ricardo Zamora Martínez (Cap), Ciriaco Errasti Siunaga, Jacinto Fernández y López de Quincoce "Quincoces I", Cristóbal Martí Batalla, Pedro Solé Junoy, José Castillo, Vicente Piera Paniella, Severino Goiburu Lopetegui, José Samitier Vilalta, Ángel Arocha Guillén, Guillermo Gorostiza Paredes.   Trainer: José María Mateos Larrucea.

REPUBLIC OF IRELAND: Thomas George Farquharson, George Lennox, Patrick Byrne, Jeremiah Robinson, James Harold Chatton, Sean Byrne, John Joseph Flood (Cap), Charles Dowdall, Patrick J. Moore, Charles Reid, Peter J. Kavanagh.

Goals: Ángel Arocha Guillén (38) / Patrick J. Moore (35)

7. 13.12.1931
REPUBLIC OF IRELAND v SPAIN 0-5 (0-3)
Dalymount Park, Dublin

Referee: John Langenus (Belgium)   Attendance: 31,000

REPUBLIC OF IRELAND: Thomas George Farquharson, George Lennox, Laurence Doyle, William Glen, James Harold Chatton (Cap), Francis McLoughlin, John Joseph Flood, Patrick Gallagher, David Byrne, Alfred Horlacher, Peter J. Kavanagh.

SPAIN: Gregorio Blasco Sánchez, Ciriaco Errasti Siunaga, Ramón Zabalo Zubiarre, José León Amador "Leoncito", Francisco Gamborena Hernández, Roberto Roberto Etxebarría Arruti, Martín Ventolrà, Luis Regueiro Pagola, José Samitier Vilalta (Cap), Ángel Arocha Guillén, Guillermo Gorostiza Paredes.   Trainer: José María Mateos Larrucea.

Goals: Luis Regueiro Pagola (4, 28), Ángel Guillén (35), José Samitier Vilalta (70), Martín Ventolrà (89)

8. 08.05.1932
HOLLAND v REPUBLIC OF IRELAND 0-2 (0-1)
Olympisch, Amsterdam

Referee: John Langenus (Belgium)   Attendance: 30,000

HOLLAND: Ageaus Yme van der Meulen (Cap), Bartholomeus Marius Weber, Josephus Franciscus Johannes Antonius van Run, Bastiaan Jacob Paauwe, Willem Gerardus Anderiesen, Gerardus Henricus van Heel, Frank Wels, Willem Frederick Volkers, Willem Lagendaal, Jacob Mol, Johannes Cornelis van Nellen.   Trainer: Robert Glendenning.

REPUBLIC OF IRELAND: Michael McCarthy, James Daly, Patrick Byrne, Joseph O'Reilly, Michael Terence O'Brien (Cap), Owen Kinsella, William Kennedy, Alexander Ernest Stevenson, Patrick J. Moore, Alfred Horlacher, James Kelly.

Goals: Patrick J. Moore (20, 51)

9. 25.02.1934   2nd World Cup Qualifiers
REPUBLIC OF IRELAND v BELGIUM 4-4 (1-2)
Dalymount Park, Dublin

Referee: Thomas Crew (England)   Attendance: 28,000

REPUBLIC OF IRELAND: James Foley, Jeremiah Lynch, Thomas Burke, Patrick Gaskins (Cap), Joseph O'Reilly, Joseph Kendrick, William Kennedy, David Byrne, Patrick J. Moore, Timothy O'Keefe, James Kelly.

BELGIUM: André Vandeweyer, Jules Pappaert, Philibert Smellinckx, Joseph Van Ingelghem, Félix Welkenhuyzen, Désiré Bourgeois, Louis Versijp, Jean Brichaut, Jean Capelle, André Saeys, Stanley Vanden Eynde (35 François Vanden Eynden).   Trainer: Hector Goetinck.

Goals: Patrick J. Moore (27, 48, 59, 75) / Jean Capelle (15), Stanley Vanden Eynde (25), François Vanden Eynden (47, 60)

10. 08.04.1934   2nd World Cup Qualifiers
HOLLAND v REPUBLIC OF IRELAND 5-2 (1-1)
Olympisch, Amsterdam

Referee: Otto Ohlsson (Sweden)   Attendance: 38,000

HOLLAND: Adriaanus van Male, Bartholomeus Marius Weber, Josephus Franciscus Johannes Antonius van Run, Hendrikus Adrianus Pellikaan, Willem Gerardus Anderiesen, Gerardus Henricus van Heel (Cap), Frank Wels, Leendert Roedolf Johan Vente, Eberhard Elisa Hendrik Bakhuys, Johannes Chrysostomus Smit, Cornelis Lambertus Mijnders.   Trainer: Robert Glendenning.

REPUBLIC OF IRELAND: James Foley, Patrick Gaskins (Cap), Patrick Byrne, Joseph O'Reilly, James Harold Chatton, Joseph Kendrick, William Kennedy, John Squires, Patrick J. Moore, William Jordan (42 Alfred Horlacher), Patrick Meehan.   Trainer: William Lacey.

Goals: Johannes Chrysostomus Smit (41), Eberhard Elisa Hendrik Bakhuys (67, 78), Leendert Roedolf Johan Vente (83), Johannes Chrysostomus Smit (85) / John Squires (44), Patrick J. Moore (57)

11. 16.12.1934
REPUBLIC OF IRELAND v HUNGARY 2-4 (1-2)
Dalymount Park, Dublin

Referee: John Langenus (Belgium)   Attendance: 25,000

REPUBLIC OF IRELAND: James Foley, Patrick Gaskins (Cap), Patrick Bermingham, Patrick O'Kane, Charles Lennon, Alfred Horlacher, Robert Griffiths, John Donnelly, Alfred Rigby, Patrick J. Moore, William Fallon.

HUNGARY: József Háda (46 Antal Szabó), József Vágó, László Sternberg, Gyula Seres (46 József Győri II), György Szűcs, Antal Szalay, Imre Markos, Jenő Vincze, István Avar, László Cseh II, Pál Titkos.   Trainer: Dr. Károly Dietz.

Goals: John Donnelly (36), Patrick Bermingham (62 pen) / István Avar (19, 85), Jenő Vincze (30), Imre Markos (86)

12. 05.05.1935
SWITZERLAND v REPUBLIC OF IRELAND 1-0 (0-0)
Rankhof, Basel

Referee: Alois Beranek (Austria)   Attendance: 23,000

SWITZERLAND: Renato Bizzozero, Severino Minelli, Louis Gobet, Francis Defago, Walter Weiler II, Eduard Müller, Lauro Amadò, Aldo Poretti III, Leopold Kielholz, Engelbert Bösch, Alfred Jaeck.   Trainer: Henry Müller.

REPUBLIC OF IRELAND: James Foley, Patrick Gaskins (Cap), Leo Dunne, Patrick O'Kane, Charles Lennon, Frederick Hutchinson, James Daly, Plev Ellis, Alfred Rigby, John Donnelly, Patrick Monahan.   Trainer: William Lacey.

Goal: Walter Weiler II (62 pen)

13. 08.05.1935
GERMANY v REPUBLIC OF IRELAND 3-1 (1-1)
Rote Erde, Dortmund
Referee: Gustav Krist (Czechoslovakia)   Attendance: 35,000
GERMANY: Fritz Buchloh (Cap), Paul Janes, Willi Tiefel, Paul Zielinski, Ludwig Goldbrunner, Jakob Bender, Ernst Lehner, Otto Siffling, August Lenz, Ludwig Damminger, Josef Fath. Trainer: Prof Dr. Otto Nerz.
REPUBLIC OF IRELAND: James Foley, Patrick Gaskins (Cap), Leo Dunne, Patrick O'Kane, Charles Lennon, Frederick Hutchinson, Plev Ellis, Patrick J. Moore, Alfred Rigby, John Donnelly, Patrick Monahan. Trainer: William Lacey.
Goals: Ludwig Damminger (32, 47), Ernst Lehner (88) / Patrick Gaskins (19)

14. 08.12.1935
REPUBLIC OF IRELAND v HOLLAND 3-5 (3-2)
Dalymount Park, Dublin
Referee: Dr. Peco J. Bauwens (Germany)   Att: 35,000
REPUBLIC OF IRELAND: William Harrington, William O'Neill, William McGuire, William Glen (Cap), Patrick Andrews, Joseph O'Reilly, Plev Ellis, John Donnelly, Patrick J. Moore, Alfred Horlacher, Joseph Kendrick.
HOLLAND: Leonard Herman Gerrit Halle, Bartholomeus Marius Weber, Bernardus Johannes Caldenhove, Bastiaan Jacob Paauwe, Willem Gerardus Anderiesen, Gerardus Henricus van Heel (Cap), Frank Wels, David Drok, Eberhard Elisa Hendrik Bakhuys, Johannes Chrysostomus Smit, Johannes Cornelis van Nellen. Trainer: Robert Glendenning.
Goals: Plev Ellis (13), Alfred Horlacher (31, 34) / Eberhard Elisa Hendrik Bakhuys (1), Johannes Cornelis van Nellen (14, 47), David Drok (67), Johannes Chrysostomus Smit (87)

15. 17.03.1936
REPUBLIC OF IRELAND v SWITZERLAND 1-0 (1-0)
Dalymount Park, Dublin
Referee: John Langenus (Belgium)   Attendance: 32,000
REPUBLIC OF IRELAND: William Harrington, William O'Neill, William Charles Gorman, William Glen (Cap), Charles Turner, Joseph O'Reilly, Plev Ellis, John Donnelly, James Dunne, Alfred Horlacher, James Kelly.
SWITZERLAND: Gustav Schlegel, Severino Minelli, Walter Weiler II, Francis Defago, Fernand Jaccard, Eduard Müller, Eugen Diebold, Leopold Kielholz, Alessandro Frigerio, Jacques Spagnoli, Georges Aeby. Trainer: Henry Müller.
Goal: James Dunne (34)

16. 03.05.1936
HUNGARY v REPUBLIC OF IRELAND 3-3 (2-1)
Hungária út, Budapest
Referee: Dr. Brüll (Czechoslovakia)   Attendance: 15,000
REPUBLIC OF IRELAND: William Harrington, William O'Neill, William Charles Gorman, William Glen (Cap), Cornelius Moulson, Joseph O'Reilly, Henry Anthony Duggan, John Donnelly, James Dunne, Owen Madden, William Fallon.
HUNGARY: Antal Szabó (69 György Hóri), Gyula Futó, Sándor Bíró, Béla Magda, József Turay, János Dudás, Ferenc Sas, Jenő Vincze, György Sárosi dr., László Cseh II, Tibor Kemény. Trainer: Dr. Károly Dietz.
Goals: György Sárosi dr. (6, 47 pen), Ferenc Sas (73) / James Dunne (11, 20), Owen Madden (68)

17. 09.05.1936
LUXEMBOURG v REPUBLIC OF IRELAND 1-5 (0-1)
Municipal, Luxembourg
Referee: Dr. Peco J. Bauwens (Germany)   Attendance: 8,000
LUXEMBOURG: Jean-Pierre Hoscheid, Jean-Pierre Frisch, Victor Majerus, Jean Schmit, Alfred Kieffer, Joseph Fischer (Cap), Oscar Stamet, André Schmit, Léon Mart, Robert Geib, Théophile Speicher.
REPUBLIC OF IRELAND: William Harrington, William O'Neill, William Charles Gorman, William Glen (Cap), Cornelius Moulson, Joseph O'Reilly, Plev Ellis, Henry Anthony Duggan, James Dunne, John Donnelly, James Kelly. Trainer: William Lacey.
Goals: Léon Mart (59 pen) / James Dunne (9, 86), John Donnelly (65), James Kelly (71, 87)

18. 17.10.1936
REPUBLIC OF IRELAND v GERMANY 5-2 (2-2)
Dalymount Park, Dublin
Referee: William Webb (Scotland)   Attendance: 27,109
REPUBLIC OF IRELAND: James Foley, William O'Neill, William Charles Gorman, Joseph O'Reilly, Charles Turner (Cap), Hugh Connolly, Plev Ellis, John Donnelly, Thomas Lawrence Davis, Patrick J. Moore, Matthew Geoghegan.
GERMANY: Hans Jakob, Reinhold Münzenberg, Andreas Munkert, Josef Rodzinski, Ludwig Goldbrunner, Albin Kitzinger, Ernst Lehner, Otto Siffling, Karl Hohmann, Fritz Szepan (Cap), Stanislaus Kobierski.
Trainer: Josef Herberger.
Goals: John Donnelly (25, 71), Thomas Davis (35 pen, 76), Matthew Geoghegan (59) / Stanislaus Kobierski (25), Fritz Szepan (32)

19. 06.12.1936
REPUBLIC OF IRELAND v HUNGARY 2-3 (1-2)
Dalymount Park, Dublin
Referee: H. Nattrass (England)   Attendance: 30,000
REPUBLIC OF IRELAND: James Foley, William O'Neill, William Charles Gorman, Joseph O'Reilly, Charles Turner (Cap), Cornelius Moulson, Plev Ellis, John Donnelly, Thomas Lawrence Davis, Patrick J. Moore, William Fallon.
HUNGARY: József Pálinkás dr. (66 Antal Szabó), Gyula Polgár, József Vágó, József Turay, György Szűcs, János Dudás, László Cseh II, Jenő Vincze, György Sárosi dr., Géza Toldi, Pál Titkos.   Trainer: Dr. Károly Dietz.
Goals: William Fallon (21), Thomas Lawrence Davis (72 pen) / Pál Titkos (37), László Cseh II (38), Géza Toldi (48).

20. 17.05.1937
**SWITZERLAND
v REPUBLIC OF IRELAND 0-1** (0-1)
Wankdorf, Bern
Referee: Walter Lewington (England)   Attendance: 16,000
REPUBLIC OF IRELAND: Thomas Breen, William O'Neill, John Feenan, Joseph O'Reilly, Charles Turner (Cap), Cornelius Moulson, John Brown, David Jordan, James Dunne, Patrick Farrell, William Fallon.
SWITZERLAND: Renato Bizzozero, Severino Minelli, August Lehmann, Hans Liniger, Sirio Vernati, Ernest Lörtscher, Alfred Bickel, Paul Aebi, Eugen Rupf, Willy Karcher, Georges Aeby. Trainer: Henry Müller.
Goal: James Dunne (30)

21. 23.05.1937
FRANCE v REPUBLIC OF IRELAND 0-2 (0-0)
Yves du Manoir, Colombes, Paris
Referee: Gustav Krist (Czechoslovakia)   Attendance: 16,688
FRANCE: Laurent Di Lorto, Abdelkader Ben Bouali, Raoul Diagne, François Bourbotte, Georges Meuris, Edmond Delfour (Cap), Michel Lauri, Kowalczyk Ignace, Roger Courtois, Michel Frutuoso, Alfred Aston.
REPUBLIC OF IRELAND: Thomas Breen, William O'Neill, John Feenan, Joseph O'Reilly, Charles Turner (Cap), Cornelius Moulson, John Brown, David Jordan, James Dunne, Patrick Farrell, William Fallon.   Trainer: William Lacey.
Goals: David Jordan (51), John Brown (58)

22. 10.10.1937   3rd World Cup Qualifiers
NORWAY v REPUBLIC OF IRELAND 3-2 (1-1)
Ullevaal, Oslo
Referee: Dr. Peco J. Bauwens (Germany)   Att: 19,000
NORWAY: Tom Blohm, Rolf Johannessen, Øivind Holmsen, Frithjof Ulleberg, Nils Eriksen, Rolf Holmberg, Odd Frantzen, Reidar Kvammen, Alf Martinsen, Magnar Isaksen, Arne Brustad.   Trainer: Asbjørn Halvorsen.
REPUBLIC OF IRELAND: George McKenzie, Joseph Williams, Michael Hoy, Joseph O'Reilly, Charles Turner (Cap), Owen Kinsella, Thomas Donnelly, John Donnelly, James Dunne, William Jordan, Matthew Geoghegan.
Goals: Reidar Kvammen (30, 61), Alf Martinsen (78) / Matthew Geoghegan (37), James Dunne (49)

23. 07.11.1937   3rd World Cup Qualifiers
REPUBLIC OF IRELAND v NORWAY 3-3 (1-2)
Dalymount Park, Dublin
Referee: T. Gibbs (England)   Attendance: 27,000
REPUBLIC OF IRELAND: George McKenzie, William O'Neill, William Charles Gorman, Joseph O'Reilly, Charles Turner (Cap), Thomas Arrigan, Kevin Patrick O'Flanagan, Henry Anthony Duggan, James Dunne, John James Carey, Thomas Foy.
NORWAY: Sverre Nordby, Rolf Johannessen, Øivind Holmsen, Kristian Henriksen, Nils Eriksen, Rolf Holmberg, Kjell Eeg, Reidar Kvammen, Alf Martinsen, Odd Frantzen, Jørgen Hval.   Trainer: Asbjørn Halvorsen.
Goals: James Dunne (10), Henry Anthony Duggan (62), Kevin Patrick O'Flanagan (88) / Reidar Kvammen (16, 33), Alf Martinsen (49)

24. 18.05.1938
**CZECHOSLOVAKIA
v REPUBLIC OF IRELAND 2-2** (1-1)
Sparta, Praha
Referee: John Langenus (Belgium)   Attendance: 17,000
CZECHOSLOVAKIA: František Plánička (Cap), Jaroslav Burgr, Ferdinand Daučik, Josef Košťálek, Jaroslav Bouček, Vlastimil Kopecký, Jan Říha, Ladislav Šimůnek, Vojtěch Bradáč, Josef Ludl, Oldřich Nejedlý.
Trainer: Dr. Václav Meissner.
REPUBLIC OF IRELAND: George McKenzie, Patrick Gaskins, William Charles Gorman, Joseph O'Reilly, Matthew Augustine O'Mahoney, Charles Turner (Cap), Kevin Patrick O'Flanagan, Thomas Lawrence Davis, James Dunne, John James Carey, Timothy O'Keefe.
Goals: Oldřich Nejedlý (3 pen, 46) / Thomas Lawrence Davis (53), James Dunne (89)

25. 22.05.1938
POLAND v REPUBLIC OF IRELAND 6-0 (3-0)

Wojska Polskiego, Warszawa

Referee: Ferenc Majorszky (Hungary)   Attendance: 25,000

POLAND: Edward Madejski, Władysław Szczepaniak (Cap), Antoni Gałecki, Wilhelm Góra, Jan Wasiewicz, Edward Dytko, Ryszard Piec I, Leonard Piątek, Fryderyk Scherfke, Ernest Wilimowski, Gerard Wodarz.   Trainer: Józef Kaluza.

REPUBLIC OF IRELAND: George McKenzie (69 William Harrington), Patrick Gaskins, William Charles Gorman, Joseph O'Reilly, Matthew Augustine O'Mahoney, Charles Turner (Cap), Kevin Patrick O'Flanagan, James Dunne, Thomas Lawrence Davis, John James Carey, Timothy O'Keefe.

Goals: Jan Wasiewicz (12), Gerard Wodarz (21, 78), Leonard Piątek (43, 52), Ernest Wilimowski (58)

26. 18.09.1938
REPUBLIC OF IRELAND v SWITZERLAND 4-0 (3-0)

Dalymount Park, Dublin

Referee: Herbert Mortimer (England)   Attendance: 31,000

REPUBLIC OF IRELAND: George McKenzie, William Charles Gorman, Michael Hoy, Joseph O'Reilly, Matthew Augustine O'Mahoney, Richard Lunn, Thomas Donnelly, James Dunne (Cap), Patrick Bradshaw, John James Carey, William Fallon.

SWITZERLAND: Willy Huber, Severino Minelli, August Lehmann, Hermann Springer, Sirio Vernati, Ernest Lörtscher, Alfred Bickel, André Abegglen III, Lauro Amadò, Eugène Walaschek, Georges Aeby.   Trainer: Henry Müller.

Goals: Patrick Bradshaw (#, #), James Dunne (#), Thomas Donnelly (#)

27. 13.11.1938
REPUBLIC OF IRELAND v POLAND 3-2 (2-1)

Dalymount Park, Dublin

Referee: John Langenus (Belgium)   Attendance: 35,000

REPUBLIC OF IRELAND: George McKenzie, William Charles Gorman, Michael Hoy, Joseph O'Reilly, Matthew Augustine O'Mahoney, Richard Lunn, Kevin Patrick O'Flanagan, James Dunne (Cap), Patrick Bradshaw, John James Carey, William Fallon.

POLAND: Edward Madejski (14-47 Roman Mrugała), Władysław Szczepaniak (Cap), Antoni Gałecki, Wilhelm Góra, Edward Nyc, Edward Dytko, Ryszard Piec I, Leonard Piątek, Jerzy Wostal, Ernest Wilimowski, Gerard Wodarz.   Trainer: Józef Kaluza.

Goals: William Fallon (10), John James Carey (12), James Dunne (67) / Ernest Wilimowski (17), Leonard Piątek (83)

28. 19.03.1939
REPUBLIC OF IRELAND v HUNGARY 2-2 (1-1)

The Mardyke, Cork

Referee: H. Nattrass (England)   Attendance: 12,000

REPUBLIC OF IRELAND: George McKenzie, William Charles Gorman, Michael Hoy, Joseph O'Reilly, Charles Turner, Edward Weir, Kevin Patrick O'Flanagan, James Dunne (Cap), Patrick Bradshaw, John James Carey, Thomas Foy.

HUNGARY: Antal Szabó, Lajos Korányi I, Sándor Bíró, Gyula Lázár, Béla Sárosi III, István Balogh I, Sándor Ádám, Gyula Zsengellér, Ferenc Kolláth II, István Kiszely, László Gyetvai.   Trainer: Dr. Károly Dietz.

Goals: Patrick Bradshaw (14), John James Carey (88) / Gyula Zsengellér (38), Ferenc Kolláth II (50)

29. 18.05.1939
HUNGARY v REPUBLIC OF IRELAND 2-2 (1-0)

Hungária út, Budapest

Referee: Dr. Peco J. Bauwens (Germany)   Att: 15,000

HUNGARY: Antal Szabó, Károly Kis, Sándor Bíró, Antal Szalay, György Szűcs, István Balogh I, József Szántó, György Sárosi dr., Ferenc Kolláth II, István Kiszely, Antal Nagy.   Trainer: Dr. Károly Dietz.

REPUBLIC OF IRELAND: George McKenzie, William O'Neill, Michael Hoy, Joseph O'Reilly, Matthew Augustine O'Mahoney, Edward Weir, Kevin Patrick O'Flanagan, James Dunne (Cap), Patrick Bradshaw, John James Carey, William Fallon.

Goals: Ferenc Kolláth II (39, 84) / Kevin O'Flanagan (52, 77)

30. 23.05.1939
GERMANY v REPUBLIC OF IRELAND 1-1 (1-0)

Weser, Bremen

Referee: Dr. Otto Remke (Denmark)   Attendance: 35,000

GERMANY: Hans Jakob, Paul Janes (Cap), Jakob Streitle, Andreas Kupfer, Hans Rohde, Albin Kitzinger, Ernst Lehner, Wilhelm Hahnemann, Josef Gauchel, Helmut Schön, Willi Arlt.   Trainer: Josef Herberger.

REPUBLIC OF IRELAND: George McKenzie, William O'Neill, Michael Hoy, Joseph O'Reilly, Matthew Augustine O'Mahoney, Edward Weir, Kevin Patrick O'Flanagan, James Dunne (Cap), Patrick Bradshaw, John James Carey, William Fallon.

Goals: Helmut Schön (39) / Patrick Bradshaw (68)

31. 16.06.1946
PORTUGAL v REPUBLIC OF IRELAND 3-1 (3-0)
Nacional, Lisboa

Referee: Von Wartburg (Switzerland)   Attendance: 50,000

PORTUGAL: João Mendonça Azevedo, Álvaro Cardoso da Silva (Cap), Serafim das Neves, Mariano Rodrigues Amaro, António Feliciano, Francisco Ferreira, Miguel Lourenço, António de Araújo, Fernando Baptista de Seixas Peyroteo de Vasconcelos, Fernando Augusto Amoral Caiado, Rogério Lantres de Carvalho "Pipi" (43 António da Deus Costa de Matos Bentes de Oliveira).   Trainer: Tavares da Silva.

REPUBLIC OF IRELAND: Edward Courtney (3 Cornelius Joseph Martin), William McMillan, Thomas Aherne, John James Carey, John Joseph Vernon, Peter Desmond Farrell (Cap), Jack O'Reilly II, Joseph Walter Sloan, David John Walsh, James McAlinden, Thomas Joseph Eglington.

Goals: António de Araújo (7), Rogério Lantres de Carvalho "Pipi" (15), Fernando Baptista de Seixas Peyroteo de Vasconcelos (24) / Jack O'Reilly II (53)

32. 23.06.1946
SPAIN v REPUBLIC OF IRELAND 0-1 (0-1)
Metropolitano, Madrid

Referee: Von Wartburg (Switzerland)   Attendance: 35,000

SPAIN: Ignacio Eizaguirre Arregui, Juan Jugo Larráuri, Alfonso Aparicio Guttiérez, Mariano Gonzalvo (III) Falcón, Juan Antonio Ipiña Iza (Cap), Félix Huete Pineño, Rafael Iriondo Aurtenechea, José Luis López Panizo, Mariano Martín Alonso (35 Telmo Zarraonaindía Montoya "Zarra"), César Rodríguez Alvarez, Agustín Gaínza Vicandi.   Trainer: Luis Casas Pasarín.

REPUBLIC OF IRELAND: Cornelius Joseph Martin, William McMillan, Thomas Aherne, John James Carey, John Joseph Vernon, Peter Desmond Farrell (Cap), Jack O'Reilly II, Joseph Walter Sloan, David John Walsh, James McAlinden, Thomas Joseph Eglington.

Goal: Joseph Walter Sloan (37)

33. 30.09.1946
REPUBLIC OF IRELAND v ENGLAND 0-1 (0-0)
Dalymount Park, Dublin

Referee: William Webb (Scotland)   Attendance: 32,000

REPUBLIC OF IRELAND: Thomas Breen, William Charles Gorman, William Edward Hayes, John James Carey (Cap), Cornelius Joseph Martin, William Walsh, Kevin Patrick O'Flanagan, Patrick Coad, Michael O'Flanagan, Alexander Ernest Stevenson, Thomas Joseph Eglington.

ENGLAND: Frank Victor Swift, Lawrence Scott, George Francis Moutry Hardwick (Cap), William Ambrose Wright, Cornelius "Neil" Franklin, Henry Cockburn, Thomas Finney, Horatio Stratton Carter, Thomas Lawton, Wilfred Mannion, Robert Langton.   Manager: Walter Winterbottom.

Goal: Thomas Finney (82)

34. 02.03.1947
REPUBLIC OF IRELAND v SPAIN 3-2 (2-1)
Dalymount Park, Dublin

Referee: Cecil John Barrick (England)   Attendance: 42,102

REPUBLIC OF IRELAND: Thomas Breen, John McGowan, John James Carey (Cap), Peter Desmond Farrell, Cornelius Joseph Martin, William Walsh, Kevin Patrick O'Flanagan, Patrick Coad, David John Walsh, Alexander Ernest Stevenson, Thomas Joseph Eglington.

SPAIN: Ignacio Eizaguirre Arregui, José María Querejeta Alberro, José Puig Puig "Curta", Mariano Gonzalvo (III) Falcón, Juan Sans Alsina, Fernando González Valenciaga "Nando", Epifanio Fernández Berridi "Epi", Juan Arza Iñigo, Telmo Zarraonaindía Montoya "Zarra", Eduardo Herrera Bueno "Herrerita" (Cap), Agustín Gaínza Vicandi.   Trainer: Pablo Hernández Coronado.

Goals: William Walsh (17, 77), Patrick Coad (22) / Telmo Zarraonaindía Montoya "Zarra" (25, 60)

35. 04.05.1947
REPUBLIC OF IRELAND v PORTUGAL 0-2 (0-2)
Dalymount Park, Dublin

Referee: W. Pearce (England)   Attendance: 31,618

REPUBLIC OF IRELAND: Thomas Breen, William Charles Gorman, William Edward Hayes, William Walsh, John James Carey (Cap), Peter Desmond Farrell, Kevin Patrick O'Flanagan, Patrick Coad, David John Walsh, Alexander Ernest Stevenson, Thomas Joseph Eglington.

PORTUGAL: João Mendonça Azevedo, Álvaro Cardoso da Silva (Cap), Francisco Ferreira, Mariano Rodrigues Amaro, António Feliciano, Francisco Moreira, António Jesus Correia, António de Araújo, Fernando Baptista de Seixas Peyroteo de Vasconcelos, José António Barreto Travaços, Rogério Lantres de Carvalho "Pipi".   Trainer: Tavares da Silva.

Goals: António Jesus Correia (13), António de Araújo (33)

36. 23.05.1948
PORTUGAL v REPUBLIC OF IRELAND 2-0 (2-0)
Nacional, Lisboa

Referee: Generoso Dattilo (Italy)   Attendance: 50,000

PORTUGAL: Frederico Barrigana, Serafim das Neves, Alberto Ferreira de Jesus, Carlos Augusto Ribeiro Canário (39 Joaquim Machado), António Feliciano, Francisco Ferreira (Cap), António Jesus Correia, Manuel Vasques, Fernando Baptista de Seixas Peyroteo de Vasconcelos, José António Barreto Travaços, Albano Narciso Pereira.
Trainer: Virgílio Paula.

REPUBLIC OF IRELAND: George Bernard Moulson, John James Carey (Cap), Cornelius Joseph Martin, William Walsh, Patrick Kevin Noel Clarke, Peter Desmond Farrell, Benjamin Henderson, Patrick Coad, David John Walsh, Alexander Ernest Stevenson, Thomas Joseph Eglington.

Goals: Fernando Baptista de Seixas Peyroteo de Vasconcelos (20), Albano Narciso Pereira (23)

37. 30.05.1948
SPAIN v REPUBLIC OF IRELAND 2-1 (1-1)
Monjuic, Barcelona

Referee: Sdez (France)   Attendance: 65,000

SPAIN: Ignacio Eizaguirre Arregui, Gabriel Alonso Aristiaguirre, Alfonso Aparicio Guttiérez, José Gonzalvo (II) Falcón, Pedro Alconero Arzagoitia, Fernando González Valenciaga "Nando", José Juncosa Ballmunt (31 Emilio Aldecoa Gómez), José Luis López Panizo, César Rodríguez Alvarez, Silvestre Igoa Garciandía, Epifanio Fernández Berridi "Epi" (Cap).   Trainer: Guillermo Eizaguirre Olmos.

REPUBLIC OF IRELAND: George Bernard Moulson, John James Carey (Cap), Cornelius Joseph Martin, William Walsh, Patrick Kevin Noel Clarke, Peter Desmond Farrell, Alexander Ernest Stevenson, Patrick Coad, David John Walsh, Thomas Moroney, Benjamin Henderson.

Goals: Silvestre Igoa Garciandía (36, 72) / Thomas Moroney (24)

38. 05.12.1948
REPUBLIC OF IRELAND v SWITZERLAND 0-1 (0-0)
Dalymount Park, Dublin

Referee: George A. Reader (England)   Attendance: 25,563

REPUBLIC OF IRELAND: George Bernard Moulson, John James Carey (Cap), Thomas Roderick Keane, Edward Gannon, Cornelius Joseph Martin, Peter Desmond Farrell, John Francis O'Driscoll, Patrick Coad, David John Walsh, Alexander Ernest Stevenson, Thomas Joseph Eglington.

SWITZERLAND: Fritz Jucker, Rudolf Gyger, André Neury, Bernard Lanz, Oliver Eggimann, Roger Bocquet, Charles Antenen, Jean Tamini, Alfred Bickel, René Maillard II, Lauro Amadò.   Trainer: Karl Rappan (Austria).

Goal: Alfred Bickel (53)

39. 24.04.1949
REPUBLIC OF IRELAND v BELGIUM 0-2 (0-0)
Dalymount Park, Dublin

Referee: Sdez (France)   Attendance: 40,000

REPUBLIC OF IRELAND: William John Hayes, John James Carey (Cap), Larry O'Byrne, Edward Gannon, Cornelius Joseph Martin, William Walsh, John Francis O'Driscoll, John Christopher Lawlor, Brendan Carroll, Patrick Coad, Gerard Malone.

BELGIUM: Henri Meert, Léon Aernaudts, René Gillard, Jan Van der Auwera, Jules Henriet, Victor Mees, Victor Lemberechts, Henri Coppens, Joseph Mermans, Frédéric Chavès D'Aguilar, René Thirifays.
Trainer: William Gormlie (England)

Goals: Victor Lemberechts (54), Joseph Mermans (84)

40. 22.05.1949
REPUBLIC OF IRELAND v PORTUGAL 1-0 (1-0)
Dalymount Park, Dublin

Referee: Le Foll (France)   Attendance: 28,108

REPUBLIC OF IRELAND: Thomas Fergus Godwin, John James Carey (Cap), Thomas Roderick Keane, Edward Gannon, Cornelius Joseph Martin, Thomas Moroney, Peter Joseph Corr, Patrick Coad, David John Walsh (35 Peter Desmond Farrell), Daniel McGowan, Thomas Joseph Eglington.

PORTUGAL: Frederico Barrigana, Virgílio Marques Mendes, Serafim das Neves, Carlos Augusto Ribeiro Canário, Félix Assunção Antunes, Francisco Ferreira, Armando Félix Ferreira (Cap), Manuel Vasques, José Mota, José António Barreto Travaços, Rogério Lantres de Carvalho "Pipi".
Trainer: Armando Sampaio.

Goal: Patrick Coad (42 pen)

41. 02.06.1949   4th World Cup Qualifiers
SWEDEN v REPUBLIC OF IRELAND 3-1 (2-1)
Råsunda, Stockholm

Referee: Louis Baert (Belgium)   Attendance: 38,000

SWEDEN: Karl Svensson, Karl-Erik Andersson, Erik Nilsson (Cap), Kjell Rosén, Knut Nordahl, Sune Andersson, Egon Johnsson, Gunnar Gren, Hans Jeppson, Henry Carlsson, Nils Liedholm.   Trainer: Rudolf Kock.

REPUBLIC OF IRELAND: Thomas Fergus Godwin, John James Carey (Cap), Thomas Roderick Keane, Edward Gannon, Cornelius Joseph Martin, Thomas Moroney, John Francis O'Driscoll, Patrick Coad, David John Walsh, Daniel McGowan, Thomas Joseph Eglington.

Goals: Sune Andersson (18 pen), Hans Jeppson (38), Nils Liedholm (69) / David John Walsh (9)

42.　12.06.1949
REPUBLIC OF IRELAND v SPAIN 1-4 (1-3)
Dalymount Park, Dublin
Referee: Arthur Edward Ellis (England)　　Att: 30,171
REPUBLIC OF IRELAND: Thomas Fergus Godwin, John James Carey (Cap), Thomas Roderick Keane, Peter Desmond Farrell, Cornelius Joseph Martin, Thomas Moroney, Peter Joseph Corr, Edward Gannon, David John Walsh, Daniel McGowan, James Benedict Hartnett.
SPAIN: Ignacio Eizaguirre Arregui (Cap), Vicente Asensi Albentosa, Francisco Antúnez Espada, Diego Lozano Rodríguez, Mariano Gonzalvo (III) Falcón, Antonio Puchades Casanova, Estanislao Basora Brunet, Venancio Pérez García, Telmo Zarraonaindía Montoya "Zarra", José Artigas Morrajas (39 Silvestre Igoa Garciandía), Agustín Gaínza Vicandi. Trainer: Guillermo Eizaguirre Olmos.

Goal: Cornelius Joseph Martin (13 pen) / Telmo Zarraonaindía Montoya "Zarra" (29, 34), Estanislao Basora Brunet (33), Silvestre Igoa Garciandía (85)

43.　08.09.1949　　4th World Cup Qualifiers
REPUBLIC OF IRELAND v FINLAND 3-0 (2-0)
Dalymount Park, Dublin
Referee: W.H. Evans (England)　　Attendance: 22,479
REPUBLIC OF IRELAND: Thomas Fergus Godwin, John James Carey (Cap), Thomas Aherne, Edward Gannon, Cornelius Joseph Martin, Thomas Moroney, John Thomas Gavin, Arthur Gerard Fitzsimons, Brendan Carroll (25 Patrick Daly), Peter Desmond, Thomas O'Connor.
FINLAND: Thure Sarnola, Kurt Martin, Eero Saarnio, Veikko Asikainen, Tapio Pylkkönen, Erik Beijar, Helge Svahn, Stig-Göran Myntti, Aulis Rytkönen, Jorma Vaihela, Kalevi Lehtovirta. Trainer: Aatos Lehtonen.

Goals: John Gavin (36), Cornelius Joseph Martin (44 pen, 68)

44.　21.09.1949
ENGLAND v REPUBLIC OF IRELAND 0-2 (0-1)
Goodison Park, Liverpool
Referee: John Mowatt (Scotland)　　Attendance: 51,487
ENGLAND: Bert Frederick Williams, Bertram Mozley, John Aston, William Ambrose Wright (Cap), Cornelius "Neil" Franklin, James William Dickinson, Peter Philip Harris, John Morris, Jesse Pye, Wilfred Mannion, Thomas Finney. Manager: Walter Winterbottom.
REPUBLIC OF IRELAND: Thomas Fergus Godwin, Cornelius Joseph Martin, Thomas Aherne, Thomas Moroney, David John Walsh, Peter Joseph Corr, Thomas O'Connor, John James Carey (Cap), Peter Desmond, Peter Desmond Farrell, William Walsh.

Goals: Cornelius Martin (33 pen), Peter Farrell (85)

45.　09.10.1949　　4th World Cup Qualifiers
FINLAND v REPUBLIC OF IRELAND 1-1 (0-1)
Olympiastadion, Helsinki
Referee: Just Bronkhorst (Holland)　　Attendance: 13,437
FINLAND: Olavi Laaksonen, Kurt Martin, Eero Saarnio, Veikko Asikainen, Tapio Pylkkönen, Erik Beijar, Jorma Vaihela, Stig-Göran Myntti, Yrjö Asikainen, Urho Teräs, Helge Saarinen. Trainer: Aatos Lehtonen.
REPUBLIC OF IRELAND: Thomas Fergus Godwin, John James Carey (Cap), Thomas Aherne, Tim Coffey, Cornelius Joseph Martin, Thomas Moroney, John Thomas Gavin, Peter Desmond Farrell, David John Walsh, Peter Desmond, Thomas O'Connor.

Goals: Jorma Vaihela (89) / Peter Desmond Farrell (72)

46.　13.11.1949　　4th World Cup Qualifiers
REPUBLIC OF IRELAND v SWEDEN 1-3 (0-2)
Dalymount Park, Dublin
Referee: William Ling (England)　　Attendance: 41,031
REPUBLIC OF IRELAND: Thomas Fergus Godwin, John James Carey (Cap), Thomas Aherne, William Walsh, Cornelius Joseph Martin, Reginald Alphonso Ryan, Peter Joseph Corr, Peter Desmond Farrell, David John Walsh, Peter Desmond, Thomas O'Connor.
SWEDEN: Torsten Lindberg, Karl-Erik Andersson, Erik Nilsson (Cap), Olle Åhlund, Knut Nordahl, Kjell Rosén, Egon Jönsson, Carl-Erik Palmér, Hans Jeppson, Sune Andersson, Stig Sundkvist. Trainer: Rudolf Kock.

Goals: Cornelius Joseph Martin (75 pen) / Carl-Erik Palmér (4, 40, 68)

47.　10.05.1950
BELGIUM v REPUBLIC OF IRELAND 5-1 (3-0)
Heysel, Bruxelles
Referee: Just Bronkhorst (Holland)　　Attendance: 24,083
BELGIUM: Henri Meert, Arsène Vaillant, Léopold Anoul, Jan Van der Auwera, Louis Carré, Victor Mees, Rik Coppens, Frédéric Chavès D'Aguilar, Joseph Mermans, Albert De Hert, Georges Mordant. Trainer: William Gormlie (England).
REPUBLIC OF IRELAND: Thomas Fergus Godwin, Matthew Clarke, Thomas Aherne, William Walsh, Cornelius Joseph Martin (Cap), Thomas Moroney, Terence Murray, Arthur Gerard Fitzsimons, Robert Duffy, Reginald Alphonso Ryan, Martin Colfer.

Goals: Joseph Mermans (3, 33, 84), Albert De Hert (19), Frédéric Chavès D'Aguilar (56) / Robert Duffy (72)

48. 26.11.1950
REPUBLIC OF IRELAND v NORWAY 2-2 (1-2)
Dalymount Park, Dublin
Referee: W. Pearce (England)   Attendance: 30,215
REPUBLIC OF IRELAND: Thomas Fergus Godwin, Sean Fallon, Thomas Aherne, Edward Gannon, John James Carey (Cap), Thomas Moroney, Christopher Joseph Giles, John Christopher Lawlor, David John Walsh, Reginald Alphonso Ryan, Thomas Joseph Eglington.

NORWAY: Torgeir Torgersen, Bjørn Spydevold, Harry Boye Karlsen, Gunnar Hansen, Thorbjørn Svenssen, Thorleif Olsen, Gunnar Thoresen, Per Bredesen, Willy Andresen, Ragnar Hvidsten, Wilhelm Olsen.

Goals: John James Carey (24 pen), David John Walsh (61) / Per Bredesen (6), Willy Andresen (11)

49. 13.05.1951
REPUBLIC OF IRELAND v ARGENTINA 0-1 (0-0)
Dalymount Park, Dublin
Referee: Reginald J. Leafe (England)
REPUBLIC OF IRELAND: Frederick William Kiernan, John James Carey (Cap), Thomas Aherne, Reginald Alphonso Ryan, Cornelius Joseph Martin, Peter Desmond Farrell, Alfred Ringstead, James Higgins, David John Walsh, John Christopher Lawlor, Thomas Joseph Eglington.
Trainer: Dougall Livingstone (Scotland).

ARGENTINA: Miguel Ángel Rugilo, Ángel Natalio Allegri, Juan Manuel Filgueiras (39 José M. García Pérez), Norberto Antonio Yácono (Cap), Ubaldo Faina, Ernesto Gutiérrez, Mario Emilio Heriberto Boyé, Norberto Doroteo Méndez, Juan Armando Benavídez, Ángel Amadeo Labruna, Félix Loustau.
Trainer: Guillermo Stábile.

Goal: Ángel Amadeo Labruna (53)

50. 30.05.1951
NORWAY v REPUBLIC OF IRELAND 2-3 (1-1)
Ullevaal, Oslo
Referee: Carl Frederik Jørgensen (Denmark)   Att: 20,900
NORWAY: Evald Kihle, Bjørn Spydevold, Harry Boye Karlsen, Thorleif Olsen, Thorbjørn Svenssen, Egil Lærum, Ragnar Hvidsten, Per Bredesen, Gunnar Dybwad, Odd Wang Sørensen, Karl Skifjeld.

REPUBLIC OF IRELAND: Frederick William Kiernan, Thomas Joseph Clinton, Thomas Aherne, Reginald Alphonso Ryan, John James Carey (Cap), Thomas Moroney, Alfred Ringstead, Tim Cunneen (42 Patrick Coad), David John Walsh, Peter Desmond Farrell, Martin Colfer.
Trainer: Dougall Livingstone (Scotland).

Goals: Odd Wang Sørensen (14), Ragnar Hvidsten (55) / Peter Desmond Farrell (17), Alfred Ringstead (67), Patrick Coad (82)

51. 17.10.1951
REPUBLIC OF IRELAND v WEST GERMANY 3-2 (2-0)
Dalymount Park, Dublin
Referee: William Ling (England)   Attendance: 31,000
REPUBLIC OF IRELAND: Frederick William Kiernan, Sean Fallon, Thomas Aherne, Thomas Moroney, Florrie Burke, Peter Desmond Farrell (Cap), Alfred Ringstead, Arthur Gerard Fitzsimons, Desmond Glynn, Reginald Alphonso Ryan, Thomas Joseph Eglington.
Trainer: Dougall Livingstone (Scotland).

GERMANY: Anton Turek, Jakob Streitle, Werner Kohlmeyer, Paul Mebus, Josef Posipal, Erich Schanko, Felix Gerritzen, Alfred Preißler, Max Morlock, Fritz Walter (Cap), Richard Herrmann.   Trainer: Josef Herberger.

Goals: Josef Posipal (9 own goal), Arthur Fitzsimons (39), Desmond Glynn (84) / Max Morlock (62), Fritz Walter (75)

52. 04.05.1952
WEST GERMANY v REPUBLIC OF IRELAND 3-0 (1-0)
Müngersdorfer, Köln
Referee: Arthur Edward Ellis (England)   Att: 75,000
GERMANY: Karl Adam, Erich Retter, Werner Kohlmeyer, Josef Posipal, Jakob Streitle (Cap), Erich Schanko, Bernhard Klodt, Josef Röhrig, Ottmar Walter, Richard Herrmann (43 Georg Stollenwerk), Bernhard Termath.
Trainer: Josef Herberger.

REPUBLIC OF IRELAND: Frederick William Kiernan, Thomas Aherne, Sean Fallon, Edward Gannon, Cornelius Joseph Martin, Peter Desmond Farrell (Cap), Alfred Ringstead, Arthur Gerard Fitzsimons, Seamus Gibbons, Reginald Alphonso Ryan, Thomas Joseph Eglington.
Trainer: Dougall Livingstone (Scotland).

Goals: Josef Posipal (31), Ottmar Walter (77), Bernhard Termath (88)

53. 07.05.1952
AUSTRIA v REPUBLIC OF IRELAND 6-0 (4-0)
Prater, Wien
Referee: Reinhardt (West Germany)   Attendance: 60,000
AUSTRIA: Josef Musil, Rudolf Röckl, Ernst Happel, Gerhard Hanappi, Ernst Ocwirk, Karl Koller, Ernst Melchior, Karl Decker, Robert Dienst, Adolf Huber, Walter Haummer.
Trainer: Walter Nausch.

REPUBLIC OF IRELAND: Frederick William Kiernan, Sean Fallon, Thomas Aherne, Edward Gannon, Cornelius Joseph Martin, Francis O'Farrell, Alfred Ringstead, Arthur Gerard Fitzsimons, Reginald Alphonso Ryan, Peter Desmond Farrell (Cap), Thomas Joseph Eglington.
Trainer: Dougall Livingstone (Scotland).

Goals: Adolf Huber (22, 24, 26), Walter Haummer (36), Robert Dienst (58, 81)

54. 01.06.1952
SPAIN v REPUBLIC OF IRELAND 6-0 (4-0)
Chamartin, Madrid

Referee: Reginald J. Leafe (England)   Attendance: 75,000

SPAIN: Antonio Ramallets Simón, José María Martín Rodríguez, Gustavo Biosca Pagés, José Seguer Sans, Miguel Muñoz Mozún, Antonio Puchades Casanova, Estanislao Basora Brunet, Gerardo Coque Benavente, César Rodríguez Alvarez, José Luis López Panizo, Agustín Gaínza Vicandi (Cap).   Trainer: Ricardo Zamora Martínez.

REPUBLIC OF IRELAND: James Anthony O'Neill, Sean Fallon, Thomas Aherne, Peter Desmond Farrell (Cap), Cornelius Joseph Martin, Reginald Alphonso Ryan, Alfred Ringstead, Patrick Coad, David John Walsh, Arthur Gerard Fitzsimons, Thomas Joseph Eglington.
Trainer: Dougall Livingstone (Scotland).

Goals: Gerardo Coque Benavente (2), Agustín Gaínza Vicandi (9), César Rodríguez Alvarez (14), Estanislao Basora Brunet (43, 68), José Luis López Panizo (53)

55. 16.11.1952
REPUBLIC OF IRELAND v FRANCE 1-1 (1-0)
Dalymount Park, Dublin

Referee: Albert Alsteen (Belgium)   Attendance: 40,000

REPUBLIC OF IRELAND: James Anthony O'Neill, Seamus Dunne, Thomas Aherne, Peter Desmond Farrell, John James Carey (Cap), Sean Cusack, John Thomas Gavin, Arthur Gerard Fitzsimons, Sean Fallon, Reginald Alphonso Ryan, Thomas Joseph Eglington.   Trainer: Dougall Livingstone (Scotland).

FRANCE: Jean Ruminski, Lazare Gianessi, Robert Jonquet, Roger Marche (Cap), Ferenc Koczur "Ferry", Armand Penverne, Joseph Ujlaki, Roger Piantoni, Raymond Kopa, André Strappe, Stanislas Curyl.

Goals: Sean Fallon (19) / Roger Piantoni (67)

56. 25.03.1953
REPUBLIC OF IRELAND v AUSTRIA 4-0 (0-0)
Dalymount Park, Dublin

Referee: Arthur Edward Ellis (England)   Att: 40,000

REPUBLIC OF IRELAND: James Anthony O'Neill, Seamus Dunne, Joseph Frederick Lawler, Peter Desmond Farrell, John James Carey (Cap), Francis O'Farrell, Alfred Ringstead, Arthur Gerard Fitzsimons, David John Walsh, Reginald Alphonso Ryan, Thomas Joseph Eglington.
Trainer: Dougall Livingstone (Scotland).

AUSTRIA: Paul Schweda (35 Franz Pelikan), Karl Stotz, Karl Kowanz, Gerhard Hanappi, Ernst Ocwirk, Karl Koller, Friedrich Kominek, Theodor Wagner, Adolf Huber (36 Paul Halla), Ernst Stojaspal, Ferdinand Zechmeister.
Trainer: Walter Nausch.

Goals: Alfred Ringstead (47, 54), Thomas Eglington (73), Francis O'Farrell (82)

57. 04.10.1953   5th World Cup Qualifiers
REPUBLIC OF IRELAND v FRANCE 3-5 (0-2)
Dalymount Park, Dublin

Referee: Laurent Franken (Belgium)   Attendance: 45,000

REPUBLIC OF IRELAND: James Anthony O'Neill, Seamus Dunne, Thomas Aherne, Peter Desmond Farrell (Cap), Cornelius Joseph Martin, Francis O'Farrell, Arthur Gerard Fitzsimons, Thomas Moroney, David John Walsh, Reginald Alphonso Ryan, Thomas Joseph Eglington.

FRANCE: René Vignal, Lazare Gianessi, Robert Jonquet, Roger Marche (Cap), Armand Penverne, Jean-Jacques Marcel, Léon Glovacki, Pierre Flamion, Joseph Ujlaki, Raymond Kopa, Roger Piantoni.

Goals: Reginald Alphonso Ryan (58), David John Walsh (83), Francis O'Farrell (88) /
Léon Glovacki (23), Armand Penverne (40), Joseph Ujlaki (50, 69), Pierre Flamion (72)

58. 28.10.1953   5th World Cup Qualifiers
REPUBLIC OF IRELAND v LUXEMBOURG 4-0 (1-0)
Dalymount Park, Dublin

Referee: Alfred Bond (England)   Attendance: 20,000

REPUBLIC OF IRELAND: James Anthony O'Neill, Seamus Dunne, Joseph Frederick Lawler, Edward Gannon, Noel Euchuria Cornelius Cantwell, Reginald Alphonso Ryan, Liam Munroe, George Patrick Cummins, Seamus Gibbons, Arthur Gerard Fitzsimons, Thomas Joseph Eglington (Cap).

LUXEMBOURG: Paul Steffen, Jacques Speck, Camille Wagner (Cap), Roger Lorang, Léon Spartz, Nicolas May, Jules Meurisse, Henri Fickinger, Antoine Kohn, Roger Weydert, Paul Kemp.

Goals: Arthur Fitzsimons (20, 75), Reginald Ryan (47 pen), Thomas Joseph Eglington (62)

59. 25.11.1953   5th World Cup Qualifiers
FRANCE v REPUBLIC OF IRELAND 1-0 (0-0)
Parc des Princes, Paris

Referee: Lucien Van Nuffel (Belgium)   Attendance: 32,265

FRANCE: François Remetter, Ahmed Mihoubi, Lazare Gianessi, Roger Marche (Cap), Antoine Cuissard, Jean-Jacques Marcel, André Strappe, Roger Piantoni, Joseph Ujlaki, Ben Mohammed Abdesselem, Léon Deladerrière.

REPUBLIC OF IRELAND: James Anthony O'Neill, Thomas Joseph Clinton, Joseph Frederick Lawler, Edward Gannon, Cornelius Joseph Martin, Peter Desmond Farrell, Alfred Ringstead, Reginald Alphonso Ryan, David John Walsh, Arthur Gerard Fitzsimons, Thomas Joseph Eglington (Cap).

Goal: Roger Piantoni (73)

60. 07.03.1954   5th World Cup Qualifiers
**LUXEMBOURG
v REPUBLIC OF IRELAND 0-1** (0-0)
Municipal, Luxembourg

Referee: J. Aussum (Holland)   Attendance: 20,000

REPUBLIC OF IRELAND: Thomas Scannell, Thomas Joseph Clinton, Thomas Joseph Traynor, Matthew Gallagher, Cornelius Joseph Martin (Cap), Patrick Saward, John Thomas Gavin, Noel Kelly, Frederick Thomas Kearns, George Patrick Cummins, James Benedict Hartnett.

LUXEMBOURG: Paul Steffen, Josy Mosar, Nicolas May (Cap), Secondo Caldarelli, Camille Wagner, Michel Reuter, Jules Meurisse, Guillaume Peiffer, Antoine Kohn, Roger Weydert, Lucien Karier.

Goal: George Patrick Cummins (62)

61. 07.11.1954
REPUBLIC OF IRELAND v NORWAY 2-1 (0-1)
Dalymount Park, Dublin

Referee: John Harold Clough (England)   Att: 35,000

REPUBLIC OF IRELAND: James Anthony O'Neill, Daniel Christopher Donovan, Joseph Frederick Lawler, Edward Gannon, Cornelius Joseph Martin, Peter Desmond Farrell (Cap), Fionan Fagan, Reginald Alphonso Ryan, Patrick Ambrose, George Patrick Cummins, Thomas Joseph Eglington.

NORWAY: Willy Aronsen, Arne Bakker, Harry Boye Karlsen, Ragnar Rygel, Thorbjørn Svenssen, Thor Hernes, Petter Fauchland, Ragnar Hvidsten, Ragnar Larsen, Harald Hennum, Wilhelm Olsen.   Trainer: Willibald Hahn (Austria).

Goals: Cornelius Joseph Martin (59), Reginald Ryan (66 pen) / Wilhelm Olsen (13)

62. 01.05.1955
REPUBLIC OF IRELAND v HOLLAND 1-0 (0-0)
Dalymount Park, Dublin

Referee: Archer Luty (England)   Attendance: 28,000

REPUBLIC OF IRELAND: James Anthony O'Neill, Daniel Christopher Donovan, Joseph Frederick Lawler, Peter Desmond Farrell (Cap), Cornelius Joseph Martin, Francis O'Farrell, John Thomas Gavin, Patrick Ambrose, F. Jack Fitzgerald, Arthur Gerard Fitzsimons, Thomas Joseph Eglington.

HOLLAND: Willem Landman, Roelof Wiersma, Cornelis Johannes Kuys, Cornelius van der Hart, Pieter Steenbergen (Cap), Jean Anna Klaassens, Henrikus Schouten, Servaas Wilkes, Cornelis van der Gijp (13 Michael Christinus de Bruyckere), Theodorus Ludovicus Timmermans, Peet Geel.   Trainer: Maximilian Merkel (Austria).

Goal: F. Jack Fitzgerald (77)

63. 25.05.1955
NORWAY v REPUBLIC OF IRELAND 1-3 (1-1)
Bislett, Oslo

Referee: Walter Meissner (West Germany)   Att: 18,574

NORWAY: Willy Aronsen, Arne Bakker, Ragnar Berge, Thorleif Olsen, Thorbjørn Svenssen, Thor Hernes, Ragnar Hvidsten, Reidar Kristiansen, Arne Kotte, Odd Wang Sørensen, Wilhelm Olsen.   Trainer: Willibald Hahn (Austria).

REPUBLIC OF IRELAND: James Anthony O'Neill, Daniel Christopher Donovan, Joseph Frederick Lawler, Edward Gannon, Cornelius Joseph Martin (Cap), Francis O'Farrell, Alfred Ringstead, George Patrick Cummins, Sean Fallon, Arthur Gerard Fitzsimons, Desmond Glynn.

Goals: Arne Kotte (39) / George Patrick Cummins (17, 70), Arthur Gerard Fitzsimons (80)

64. 28.05.1955
**WEST GERMANY
v REPUBLIC OF IRELAND 2-1** (1-0)
Volkspark, Hamburg

Referee: Karel van der Meer (Holland)   Attendance: 50,000

GERMANY: Heinz Kubsch, Erich Retter, Herbert Erhardt, Robert Schlienz, Rudolf Hoffmann, Karl Mai, Erwin Waldner, Hans Weilbächer, Ulrich Biesinger, Josef Röhrig (Cap), Hans Schäfer.   Trainer: Josef Herberger.

REPUBLIC OF IRELAND: James Anthony O'Neill, Daniel Christopher Donovan, Joseph Frederick Lawler, Edward Gannon, Cornelius Joseph Martin (Cap), Peter Desmond Farrell, John Thomas Gavin, Sean Fallon, Arthur Gerard Fitzsimons, George Patrick Cummins, Thomas Joseph Eglington.

Goals: Erwin Waldner (13), Karl Mai (63) / Sean Fallon (67)

65. 19.10.1955
**REPUBLIC OF IRELAND
v YUGOSLAVIA 1-4** (1-3)
Dalymount Park, Dublin

Referee: Murdock (England)   Attendance: 22,000

REPUBLIC OF IRELAND: James Anthony O'Neill, Albert Murphy, Joseph Frederick Lawler, Peter Desmond Farrell (Cap), Cornelius Joseph Martin, Francis O'Farrell, Alfred Ringstead, Arthur Gerard Fitzsimons, Seamus Gibbons, George Patrick Cummins, William Tuohy.

YUGOSLAVIA: Vladimir Beara (85 Branko Kralj), Bruno Belin, Milan Zeković, Dobrosav Krstić, Tomislav Crnković, Vujadin Boškov, Zdravko Rajkov, Miloš Milutinović, Bernard Vukas (Cap), Todor Veselinović, Branko Zebec.   Trainer: Aleksandar Tirnanić.

Goals: Arthur Gerard Fitzsimons (33) / Miloš Milutinović (10, 14, 44), Todor Veselinović (77)

66. 27.11.1955
REPUBLIC OF IRELAND v SPAIN 2-2 (1-2)
Dalymount Park, Dublin

Referee: Arthur Edward Ellis (England)   Att: 35,000

REPUBLIC OF IRELAND: James Anthony O'Neill, Seamus Dunne, Noel Euchuria Cornelius Cantwell, Peter Desmond Farrell (Cap), Cornelius Joseph Martin, Reginald Alphonso Ryan, Alfred Ringstead, Arthur Gerard Fitzsimons, Seamus Gibbons, George Patrick Cummins, Thomas Joseph Eglington.

SPAIN: Carmelo Cedrún Ochandategui, Guillamón, Jesús Garay Vecino, Marcelino Vaquero González "Campanal II", Mauricio Ugartemendia Lauzirica "Mauri", Segarra, Miguel González Pérez, Manuel Doménech Pinto (38 José Luis Arteche Mugueri), Manuel Fernández Fernández "Pahíño" (Cap), José María Maguregui Ibarguchi, Enrique Collar Monterrubio.   Trainer: Guillermo Eizaguirre Olmos.

Goals: Arthur Gerard Fitzsimons (8), Alfred Ringstead (76) / Manuel Fernández Fernández "Pahíño" (25, 44)

67. 10.05.1956
HOLLAND v REPUBLIC OF IRELAND 1-4 (0-0)
Feijenoord, Rotterdam

Referee: Pennig (West Germany)   Attendance: 65,000

HOLLAND: Frans de Munck, Roelof Wiersma, Johannes Bernardus Odenthal, Johannes Cornelis Brooijmans, Cornelius van der Hart, Jean Anna Klaassens (Cap), Abraham Leonardus Appel, Martinus Bosselaar, Cornelis Jan Marinus Koopal, Abe Lenstra, Coenraad Moulijn.
Trainer: Maximilian Merkel (Austria).

REPUBLIC OF IRELAND: Thomas Fergus Godwin, Seamus Dunne, Noel Euchuria Cornelius Cantwell, Thomas James Patrick Dunne, Cornelius Joseph Martin (Cap), Francis O'Farrell, Alfred Ringstead, Arthur Gerard Fitzsimons, F. Jack Fitzgerald, William Augustine Whelan, Joseph Haverty.

Goals: Abraham Leonardus Appel (77) / Arthur Gerard Fitzsimons (52, 67), Joseph Haverty (59), Alfred Ringstead (71)

68. 03.10.1956   6th World Cup Qualifiers
REPUBLIC OF IRELAND v DENMARK 2-1 (2-0)
Dalymount Park, Dublin

Referee: Alfred Bond (England)   Attendance: 35,000

REPUBLIC OF IRELAND: James Anthony O'Neill, Seamus Dunne (Cap), Noel Euchuria Cornelius Cantwell, Thomas James Patrick Dunne, Gerry Mackey, Ronald Nolan, John Thomas Gavin, William Augustine Whelan, Dermot Patrick Curtis, Arthur Gerard Fitzsimons, Joseph Haverty.

DENMARK: Kaj Jørgensen, Erling Linde Larsen, Verner Nielsen, Erik Pondal Jensen, Ove Hansen, Jørgen Olesen, Jørgen Hansen, Knud Lundberg (Cap), Ove Andersen, Aage Rou Jensen, Ove Bech Nielsen.   Trainer: Alf Young (England)

Goals: Dermot Curtis (30), John Thomas Gavin (45 pen) / Aage Rou Jensen (85)

69. 25.11.1956
REPUBLIC OF IRELAND v WEST GERMANY 3-0 (0-0)
Dalymount Park, Dublin

Referee: Murdock (England)   Attendance: 40,000

REPUBLIC OF IRELAND: Alan James Alexander Kelly, Seamus Dunne, Noel Euchuria Cornelius Cantwell, Thomas James Patrick Dunne, Gerry Mackey (Cap), Ronald Nolan, James McCann, Noel Peyton, Dermot Patrick Curtis, Arthur Gerard Fitzsimons, Joseph Haverty.

GERMANY: Heinz Kwiatkowski, Herbert Erhardt, Erich Juskowiak, Elwin Schlebrowski, Heinz Wewers, Karl Mai, Helmut Rahn, Max Morlock (Cap), Jakob Miltz, Hans Schäfer (10 Horst Eckel), Heinz Vollmar.   Trainer: Josef Herberger.

Goals: Noel Euchuria Cornelius Cantwell (63 pen), Joseph Haverty (87), James McCann (89)

70. 08.05.1957   6th World Cup Qualifiers
ENGLAND v REPUBLIC OF IRELAND 5-1 (4-0)
Wembley, London

Referee: Hugh Phillips (Scotland)   Attendance: 52,000

ENGLAND: Alan Hodgkinson, Jeffrey James Hall, Roger William Byrne, Ronald Clayton, William Ambrose Wright (Cap), Duncan Edwards, Stanley Matthews, Peter John Walter Atyeo, Thomas Taylor, John Norman Haynes, Thomas Finney.   Manager: Walter Winterbottom.

REPUBLIC OF IRELAND: Alan James Alexander Kelly, Daniel Christopher Donovan, Noel Euchuria Cornelius Cantwell, Peter Desmond Farrell (Cap), Gerry Mackey, Patrick Saward, Alfred Ringstead, William Augustine Whelan, Dermot Patrick Curtis, Arthur Gerard Fitzsimons, Joseph Haverty.

Goals: Thomas Taylor (9, 18, 40), Peter Atyeo (38, 89) / Dermot Patrick Curtis (55)

71. 19.05.1957   6th World Cup Qualifiers
REPUBLIC OF IRELAND v ENGLAND 1-1 (1-0)
Dalymount Park, Dublin

Referee: Hugh Phillips (Scotland)   Attendance: 47,000

REPUBLIC OF IRELAND: Thomas Fergus Godwin, Seamus Dunne, Noel Euchuria Cornelius Cantwell (Cap), Patrick Saward, Ronald Nolan, Charles John Hurley, Alfred Ringstead, William Augustine Whelan, Dermot Patrick Curtis, Arthur Gerard Fitzsimons, Joseph Haverty.

ENGLAND: Alan Hodgkinson, Jeffrey James Hall, Roger William Byrne, Ronald Clayton, William Ambrose Wright (Cap), Duncan Edwards, Thomas Finney, Peter John Walter Atyeo, Thomas Taylor, John Norman Haynes, David Pegg.   Manager: Walter Winterbottom.

Goals: Alfred Ringstead (3) / Peter John Walter Atyeo (89)

72. 02.10.1957   6th World Cup Qualifiers
DENMARK v REPUBLIC OF IRELAND 0-2 (0-0)

Idrætsparken, København

Referee: Gerhard Schulz (East Germany)   Att: 28,000

DENMARK: Henry From, Erling Linde Larsen, Verner Nielsen, Flemming Nielsen, Poul Andersen (Cap), Jørgen Olesen, Poul Pedersen, Egon Jensen, Alfred Finn Hansen, Kristian Mosegaard, Peder Kjær-Andersen. Trainer: Arne Sørensen.

REPUBLIC OF IRELAND: Thomas Fergus Godwin, Seamus Dunne, Noel Euchuria Cornelius Cantwell (Cap), Patrick Saward, Charles John Hurley, Francis O'Farrell, Alfred Ringstead, Arthur Gerard Fitzsimons, Dermot Patrick Curtis, George Patrick Cummins, Joseph Haverty.

Goals: George Cummins (53), Dermot Patrick Curtis (60)

73. 11.05.1958
POLAND v REPUBLIC OF IRELAND 2-2 (1-1)

Śląski, Chorzów

Referee: Rudolf Roman (Austria)   Attendance: 80,000

POLAND: Edward Szymkowiak, Stefan Florenski, Roman Korynt, Jerzy Woźniak, Ginter Gawlik (39 Czesław Suszczyk), Edmund Zientara, Leszek Jezierski, Edward Jankowski, Gerard Cieślik (Cap), Władysław Soporek, Roman Lentner. Trainers: Henryk Reyman, Feliks Dyrda & Stanisław Szymaniak.

REPUBLIC OF IRELAND: Thomas Fergus Godwin, Seamus Dunne, Noel Euchuria Cornelius Cantwell (Cap), Ronald Nolan, Charles John Hurley, Patrick Saward, Alfred Ringstead, George Patrick Cummins, Dermot Patrick Curtis, Arthur Gerard Fitzsimons, Joseph Haverty.

Goals: Gerard Cieślik (25), Edmund Zientara (75) / Dermot Patrick Curtis (13), George Patrick Cummins (49)

74. 14.05.1958
AUSTRIA v REPUBLIC OF IRELAND 3-1 (1-0)

Prater, Wien

Referee: Paul Wyssling (Switzerland)   Attendance: 35,000

AUSTRIA: Rudolf Szanwald, Paul Halla, Franz Swoboda, Gerhard Hanappi, Ernst Happel, Karl Koller, Walter Horak, Helmut Senekowitsch, Johann Buzek, Alfred Körner II, Josef Hamerl.   Trainer: Josef Argauer.

REPUBLIC OF IRELAND: James Anthony O'Neill, Seamus Dunne, Noel Euchuria Cornelius Cantwell (Cap), Michael McGrath, Charles John Hurley, Patrick Saward, Alfred Ringstead, George Patrick Cummins, Dermot Patrick Curtis, Arthur Gerard Fitzsimons, Joseph Haverty.

Goals: Alfred Körner II (18), Johann Buzek (58), Josef Hamerl (77) / Dermot Patrick Curtis (70)

75. 05.10.1958
REPUBLIC OF IRELAND v POLAND 2-2 (2-2)

Dalymount Park, Dublin

Referee: John Harold Clough (England)   Att: 35,000

REPUBLIC OF IRELAND: James Anthony O'Neill (68 Thomas Taylor), Seamus Dunne, Noel Euchuria Cornelius Cantwell (Cap), Michael McGrath, Seamus Keogh, Patrick Saward, Alfred Ringstead, Arthur Gerard Fitzsimons, Dermot Patrick Curtis, George Patrick Cummins, Joseph Haverty.

POLAND: Edward Szymkowiak, Stefan Florenski, Roman Korynt, Jerzy Woźniak, Ginter Gawlik, Edmund Zientara (Cap), Witold Majewski, Ernest Pol, Stanisław Hachorek, Marian Norkowski, Krzysztof Baszkiewicz. Trainers: Henryk Reyman, Feliks Dyrda & Stanisław Szymaniak.

Goals: Noel Euchuria Cornelius Cantwell (27 pen, 32) / Ernest Pol (17, 20)

76. 05.04.1959   1st European Champs, 1st Round
REPUBLIC OF IRELAND v CZECHOSLOVAKIA 2-0 (2-0)

Dalymount Park, Dublin

Referee: Lucien Van Nuffel (Belgium)   Attendance: 42,000

REPUBLIC OF IRELAND: James Anthony O'Neill, John Brendan McNally, Noel Euchuria Cornelius Cantwell (Cap), Michael McGrath, Charles John Hurley, Patrick Saward, Alfred Ringstead, Thomas Hamilton, Christopher Doyle, George Patrick Cummins, William Tuohy.

CZECHOSLOVAKIA: Imrich Stacho, Jiří Tichý, Ján Popluhár, Gustáv Mráz (23 Jiří Hildebrandt), Svatopluk Pluskal (Cap), Titus Buberník, Jan Brumovský, Anton Moravčík, Ladislav Kačáni, Pavol Molnár, Tadeáš Kraus.   Trainer: Rudolf Vytlačil

Goals: William Tuohy (22), Noel Cantwell (42 pen)

77. 10.05.1959   1st European Champs, 1st Round
CZECHOSLOVAKIA v REPUBLIC OF IRELAND 4-0 (1-0)

Tehelné pole, Bratislava

Referee: Joseph Barberan (France)   Attendance: 60,000

CZECHOSLOVAKIA: Imrich Stacho, Jiří Tichý, Ján Popluhár, Ladislav Novák (Cap), Štefan Matlák, Titus Buberník, Ladislav Pavlovič, Adolf Scherer, Vlastimil Bubník, Ladislav Kačáni, Milan Dolinský.   Trainer: Rudolf Vytlačil.

REPUBLIC OF IRELAND: James Anthony O'Neill, Richard Whittaker, Noel Euchuria Cornelius Cantwell (Cap), Francis O'Farrell, Charles John Hurley, Michael McGrath, Alfred Ringstead, Thomas Hamilton, Arthur Gerard Fitzsimons, George Patrick Cummins, William Tuohy.

Goals: Imrich Stacho (3 pen), Titus Buberník (57), Ladislav Pavlovič (67), Milan Dolinský (75)

78. 01.11.1959
REPUBLIC OF IRELAND v SWEDEN 3-2 (2-2)
Dalymount Park, Dublin
Referee: Arthur Holland (England)   Attendance: 40,250
REPUBLIC OF IRELAND: Noel Michael Dwyer, Joseph Francis Carolan, Noel Euchuria Cornelius Cantwell (Cap), Michael McGrath, Charles John Hurley, Patrick Saward, Fionan Fagan, John Michael Giles, Dermot Patrick Curtis, George Patrick Cummins, Joseph Haverty.
SWEDEN: Bengt Nyholm, Orvar Bergmark (Cap), Sven Axbom, Torbjörn Jonsson, Åke Johansson, Sigvard Parling, Bengt Berndtsson, Henry Thillberg, Agne Simonsson, Rune Börjesson, Bengt Salomonsson.   Trainer: Eric Persson.
Goals: John Giles (16), Dermot Patrick Curtis (24, 53) / Rune Börjesson (7), Bengt Berndtsson (13)

79. 30.03.1960
REPUBLIC OF IRELAND v CHILE 2-0 (1-0)
Dalymount Park, Dublin
Referee: Kenneth Aston (England)   Attendance: 17,000
REPUBLIC OF IRELAND: Noel Michael Dwyer, Joseph Francis Carolan, Noel Euchuria Cornelius Cantwell (Cap), Ronald Nolan, Charles John Hurley, Patrick Saward, Fionan Fagan, John Michael Giles, Dermot Patrick Curtis, George Patrick Cummins, Joseph Haverty.
CHILE: Raúl Coloma, Luis Armando Eyzaguirre, Sergio Navarro, Jorge Luco, Raúl Sánchez, Hernán Rodríguez, Mario Moreno, Alberto Fouilloux, Juan Soto Mura, Leonel Sánchez, Braulio Musso.   Trainer: Fernando Riera.
Goals: Noel Euchuria Cornelius Cantwell (16 pen), Dermot Patrick Curtis (80)

80. 11.05.1960
**WEST GERMANY
v REPUBLIC OF IRELAND 0-1** (0-1)
Rhein, Düsseldorf
Referee: Arthur Edward Ellis (England)   Att: 51,000
GERMANY: Günter Sawitzki, Willi Giesemann, Herbert Erhardt (Cap), Willi Schulz, Ferdinand Wenauer, Ingo Porges, Bernhard Steffen, Alfred Schmidt, Albert Brülls, Helmut Haller, Heinz Vollmar.   Trainer: Josef Herberger.
REPUBLIC OF IRELAND: Noel Michael Dwyer, Seamus Dunne, Ronald Nolan, Michael McGrath, Charles John Hurley, Patrick Saward (Cap), Ambrose Gerald Fogarty, Noel Peyton, Dermot Patrick Curtis, George Patrick Cummins, Fionan Fagan.
Goal: Fionan Fagan (30)

81. 18.05.1960
SWEDEN v REPUBLIC OF IRELAND 4-1 (1-1)
Malmö Stadion, Malmö
Referee: Just Bronkhorst (Holland)   Attendance: 20,546
SWEDEN: Bengt Nyholm, Orvar Bergmark (Cap), Hans Mild, Torbjörn Jonsson, Åke Johansson, Sigvard Parling, Bengt Berndtsson, Owe Ohlsson, Agne Simonsson, Rune Börjesson, Lennart Backman.   Trainer: Eric Persson.
REPUBLIC OF IRELAND: Noel Michael Dwyer (46 Maurice Michael George Swan), Seamus Dunne, Ronald Nolan, Michael McGrath, Charles John Hurley, Patrick Saward, Ambrose Gerald Fogarty, Noel Euchuria Cornelius Cantwell (Cap) (43 Noel Peyton), Dermot Patrick Curtis, George Patrick Cummins, Fionan Fagan.
Goals: Agne Simonsson (25, 30), Seamus Dunne (43 own goal), Rune Börjesson (89) / Fionan Fagan (77 pen)

82. 28.09.1960
REPUBLIC OF IRELAND v WALES 2-3 (1-1)
Dalymount Park, Dublin
Referee: Best (United States)   Attendance: 20,000
REPUBLIC OF IRELAND: Noel Michael Dwyer, James Philip Vincent Kelly, John O'Neill, Michael McGrath, Charles John Hurley, Patrick Saward (Cap), Fionan Fagan, John Michael Giles, Peter Joseph Fitzgerald, Noel Peyton, Joseph Haverty.
WALES: Graham Vearncombe, Stuart Grenville Williams, Graham Evan Williams, Victor Herbert Crowe, Melvyn Tudor George Nurse, Colin Walter Baker, Terence Cameron Medwin, Philip Abraham Woosnam, Graham Moore, Thomas Royston Vernon, Clifford William Jones.
Manager: James Patrick Murphy.
Goals: Fionan Fagan (28, 72 pen) / Clifford Jones (26, 53), Philip Abraham Woosnam (65)

83. 06.11.1960
REPUBLIC OF IRELAND v NORWAY 3-1 (2-1)
Dalymount Park, Dublin
Referee: Gilbert Bowman (Scotland)   Attendance: 26,000
REPUBLIC OF IRELAND: Noel Michael Dwyer, James Philip Vincent Kelly, Noel Euchuria Cornelius Cantwell (Cap), John Rowan Fullam, Charles John Hurley, Patrick Saward, Fionan Fagan, John Michael Giles, Peter Joseph Fitzgerald, Dermot Patrick Curtis, Joseph Haverty.
NORWAY: Asbjørn Hammer, Arne Bakker, Jack Kramer, Arne Natland, Hans Jacob Mathisen, Roar Johansen, Bjørn Borgen, Roald Jensen, Harald Hennum, Rolf Birger Pedersen, Axel Berg.   Trainer: Wilhelm Kment (Austria).
Goals: Fionan Fagan (28), Peter Joseph Fitzgerald (39, 83) / Harald Hennum (3)

84.   03.05.1961   7th World Cup Qualifiers
SCOTLAND v REPUBLIC OF IRELAND 4-1 (2-0)
Hampden Park, Glasgow
Referee: Maurice Guigue (France)   Attendance: 46,696
SCOTLAND: Lawrence Grant Leslie, Robert Shearer, Eric Caldow (Cap), Patrick Timothy Crerand, William McNeill, James Curran Baxter, John Murdoch MacLeod, Patrick Quinn, David George Herd, Ralph Laidlaw Brand, David Wilson. Manager: John Miller McColl.

REPUBLIC OF IRELAND: Noel Michael Dwyer, John Brendan McNally, Noel Euchuria Cornelius Cantwell (Cap), Matthew Andrew McEvoy, Charles John Hurley, Patrick Saward, John Michael Giles, Ambrose Gerald Fogarty, Dermot Patrick Curtis, George Patrick Cummins, Joseph Haverty.

Goals: Ralph Laidlaw Brand (14, 40), David Herd (59, 85) / Joseph Haverty (52)

85.   07.05.1961   7th World Cup Qualifiers
REPUBLIC OF IRELAND v SCOTLAND 0-3 (0-2)
Dalymount Park, Dublin
Referee: Gaston Grandain (Belgium)   Attendance: 45,000
REPUBLIC OF IRELAND: Noel Michael Dwyer, James Philip Vincent Kelly, Noel Euchuria Cornelius Cantwell (Cap), Matthew Andrew McEvoy, Charles John Hurley, Michael Kevin Meagan, Fionan Fagan, John Michael Giles, Peter Joseph Fitzgerald, George Patrick Cummins, Joseph Haverty.

SCOTLAND: Lawrence Grant Leslie, Robert Shearer, Eric Caldow (Cap), Patrick Timothy Crerand, William McNeill, James Curran Baxter, John Murdoch MacLeod, Patrick Quinn, Alexander Young, Ralph Laidlaw Brand, David Wilson. Manager: John Miller McColl.

Goals: Alexander Young (4, 16), Ralph Laidlaw Brand (86)

86.   08.10.1961   7th World Cup Qualifiers
REPUBLIC OF IRELAND v CZECHOSLOVAKIA 1-3 (1-1)
Dalymount Park, Dublin
Referee: Arthur Holland (England)   Attendance: 30,000
REPUBLIC OF IRELAND: Noel Michael Dwyer, James Philip Vincent Kelly, Noel Euchuria Cornelius Cantwell (Cap), Michael McGrath, Charles John Hurley, Ronald Nolan, Ambrose Gerald Fogarty, John Michael Giles, Peter Joseph Fitzgerald, Frank Simon O'Neill, Joseph Haverty.

CZECHOSLOVAKIA: Viliam Schrojf, Jiří Tichý (Cap), Ján Popluhár, Jiří Hledík, Svatopluk Pluskal, Josef Masopust, Tomáš Pospíchal, Adolf Scherer, Rudolf Kučera, Andrej Kvašňák, Václav Mašek.   Trainer: Rudolf Vytlačil.

Goals: John Michael Giles (40) / Adolf Scherer (3), Andrej Kvašňák (61, 69)

87.   29.10.1961   7th World Cup Qualifiers
CZECHOSLOVAKIA v REPUBLIC OF IRELAND 7-1 (4-0)
Strahov, Praha
Referee: Bengt Lundell (Sweden)   Attendance: 30,000
CZECHOSLOVAKIA: Viliam Schrojf, Jiří Hledík, Ján Popluhár, Jiří Tichý, Svatopluk Pluskal (Cap), Josef Masopust, Tomáš Pospíchal, Adolf Scherer, Andrej Kvašňák, Jozef Adamec, Josef Jelínek II.   Trainer: Rudolf Vytlačil.

REPUBLIC OF IRELAND: Noel Michael Dwyer, James Philip Vincent Kelly, Noel Euchuria Cornelius Cantwell (Cap), Ronald Nolan, Charles John Hurley, Michael McGrath, Frank Simon O'Neill, Ambrose Gerald Fogarty, Peter Joseph Fitzgerald, John Michael Giles, Joseph Haverty.

Goals: Andrej Kvašňák (8, 36), Adolf Scherer (24, 74), Josef Jelínek II (30), Tomáš Pospíchal (59), Josef Masopust (61) / Ambrose Gerald Fogarty (57)

88.   08.04.1962
REPUBLIC OF IRELAND v AUSTRIA 2-3 (0-1)
Dalymount Park, Dublin
Referee: Josef Gulde (Switzerland)   Attendance: 35,000
REPUBLIC OF IRELAND: Alan James Alexander Kelly (34 Dinny Lowry), Anthony Peter Dunne, Thomas Joseph Traynor, Patrick Saward, Charles John Hurley (Cap), Michael Kevin Meagan, Alfred Hale, John Michael Giles, Noel Euchuria Cornelius Cantwell, Dermot Patrick Curtis, William Tuohy.

AUSTRIA: Gernot Fraydl, Johann Windisch, Erich Strobl, Ignaz Puschnik, Karl Stotz, Karl Koller, Horst Hirnschrodt (59 Friedrich Rafreider), Adolf Knoll, Johann Buzek, Erich Hof, Rudolf Flögel.   Trainer: Karl Decker.

Goals: Noel Euchuria Cornelius Cantwell (47), William Tuohy (58) / Johann Buzek (43), Horst Hirnschrodt (57), Erich Hof (63)

89.   12.08.1962   2nd European Champs, 1st Round
REPUBLIC OF IRELAND v ICELAND 4-2 (2-1)
Lansdowne Road, Dublin
Referee: Robert Ernest Smith (Wales)   Attendance: 19,848
REPUBLIC OF IRELAND: Alan James Alexander Kelly, Anthony Peter Dunne, Thomas Joseph Traynor, Patrick Saward, Charles John Hurley (Cap), Michael Kevin Meagan, Alfred Hale, John Michael Giles, Noel Euchuria Cornelius Cantwell, Ambrose Gerald Fogarty, William Tuohy.

ICELAND: Helgi Daníelsson, Árni Njálsson, Bjarni Felixson, Garðar Árnason, Hörður Felixson, Sveinn Jónsson, Skúli Ágústsson, Þórólfur Beck, Ríkharður Jónsson (Cap), Ellert B. Schram, Þórður Jónsson.
Trainers: Karl Guðmundsson & Ríkharður Jónsson.

Goals: William Tuohy (11), Ambrose Gerald Fogarty (41), Noel Euchuria Cornelius Cantwell (65, 76) / Ríkharður Jónsson (37, 86)

90. 02.09.1962   2nd European Champs, 1st Round
ICELAND v REPUBLIC OF IRELAND 1-1 (0-1)
Laugardalsvöllur, Reykjavík
Referee: Arnold Nielsen (Norway)   Attendance: 9,014
ICELAND: Helgi Daníelsson, Árni Njálsson, Bjarni Felixson, Garðar Árnason, Jón Stefánsson, Sveinn Jónsson, Skúli Ágústsson, Þórólfur Beck, Ríkharður Jónsson (Cap), Ellert B. Schram, Sigurþór Jakobsson.
Trainers: Karl Guðmundsson & Ríkharður Jónsson.
REPUBLIC OF IRELAND: Alan James Alexander Kelly, John Brendan McNally, Thomas Joseph Traynor, Ronald Nolan, Charles John Hurley (Cap), Patrick Saward, Dermot Patrick Curtis, Ambrose Gerald Fogarty, Noel Euchuria Cornelius Cantwell, Noel Peyton, William Tuohy.
Goals: Garðar Árnason (57) / William Tuohy (38)

91. 09.06.1963
REPUBLIC OF IRELAND v SCOTLAND 1-0 (1-0)
Dalymount Park, Dublin
Referee: Kevin Howley (England)   Attendance: 30,000
REPUBLIC OF IRELAND: Alan James Alexander Kelly, Anthony Peter Dunne, Thomas Joseph Traynor, Matthew Andrew McEvoy, Charles John Hurley, Michael McGrath, John Michael Giles, Patrick Turner, Noel Euchuria Cornelius Cantwell (Cap), Noel Peyton (44 Ambrose Gerald Fogarty), Joseph Haverty.
SCOTLAND: Thomas Johnstone Lawrence, Alexander William Hamilton, David Duff Holt, Francis McLintock, William McNeill, James Curran Baxter, William Henderson, David Wedderburn Gibson, James Millar, Denis Law (Cap), David Wilson (44 Ian St. John).
Manager: John Miller McColl.
Goal: Noel Euchuria Cornelius Cantwell (6)

92. 25.09.1963   2nd European Champs, 2nd Round
AUSTRIA v REPUBLIC OF IRELAND 0-0
Prater, Wien
Referee: Gyula Gere (Hungary)   Attendance: 26,741
AUSTRIA: Gernot Fraydl, Peter Vargo, Erich Hasenkopf, Rudolf Oslansky, Walter Glechner, Karl Koller, Rudolf Flögel, Erich Hof, Horst Nemec, Ernst Fiala, Johann Hörmayer.
Trainer: Karl Decker.
REPUBLIC OF IRELAND: Alan James Alexander Kelly, William Browne, Thomas Joseph Traynor, Thomas Raymond Brady, Charles John Hurley (Cap), Michael McGrath, John Michael Giles, Ronald Whelan, Dermot Patrick Curtis, Ambrose Gerald Fogarty, William Tuohy.

93. 13.10.1963   2nd European Champs, 2nd Round
REPUBLIC OF IRELAND v AUSTRIA 3-2 (1-1)
Dalymount Park, Dublin
Referee: Åge Poulsen (Denmark)   Attendance: 39,963
REPUBLIC OF IRELAND: Alan James Alexander Kelly, Anthony Peter Dunne, Thomas Joseph Traynor, Thomas Raymond Brady, Charles John Hurley (Cap), Michael McGrath, John Michael Giles, Matthew Andrew McEvoy, Noel Euchuria Cornelius Cantwell, Ambrose Gerald Fogarty, Joseph Haverty.
AUSTRIA: Gernot Fraydl, Peter Vargo, Erich Hasenkopf, Johann Frank, Walter Glechner, Karl Koller, Walter Koleznik, Johannes Jank, Johann Buzek, Horst Nemec, Rudolf Flögel.
Trainer: Karl Decker.
Goals: Noel Euchuria Cornelius Cantwell (45, 88 pen), Ambrose Gerald Fogarty (66) / Walter Koleznik (38), Rudolf Flögel (82)

94. 11.03.1964   2nd Euro Champs, Quarter-Finals
SPAIN v REPUBLIC OF IRELAND 5-1 (4-1)
"Ramón Sánchez Pizjuán", Sevilla
Referee: Lucien Van Nuffel (Belgium)   Attendance: 27,200
SPAIN: José Ángel Iribar Cortajarena, Feliciano Ruiz Muñoz Rivilla, Fernando Olivella Pons (Cap), Isacio Calleja García Monferoni, Ignacio Zoco Esparza, José María Fusté Blanch, Amancio Amaro Varela, Jesús María Pereda Ruiz de Temiño, Marcelino Martínez Cao, Juan Manuel Villa Gutiérrez, Carlos Lapetra Coarasa. Trainer: José Luis Villalonga.
REPUBLIC OF IRELAND: Alan James Alexander Kelly, Theodore Cornelius Foley, Thomas Joseph Traynor, Thomas Raymond Brady, Charles John Hurley (Cap), Michael Kevin Meagan, John Michael Giles, Matthew Andrew McEvoy, Alfred Hale, Ambrose Gerald Fogarty, Joseph Haverty.
Goals: Amancio Amaro Varela (5, 29), José María Fusté Blanch (12), Marcelino Martínez Cao (33, 89) / Matthew Andrew McEvoy (18)

95. 08.04.1964   2nd Euro Champs, Quarter-Finals
REPUBLIC OF IRELAND v SPAIN 0-2 (0-1)
Dalymount Park, Dublin
Referee: Gérard Versyp (Belgium)   Attendance: 38,100
REPUBLIC OF IRELAND: Alan James Alexander Kelly, Anthony Peter Dunne, William Browne, Thomas Raymond Brady, Charles John Hurley (Cap), John Rowan Fullam, John Michael Giles, Matthew Andrew McEvoy, Noel Euchuria Cornelius Cantwell, Patrick Turner, Alfred Hale.
SPAIN: José Ángel Iribar Cortajarena, Feliciano Ruiz Muñoz Rivilla, Fernando Olivella Pons (Cap), Isacio Calleja García Monferoni, Ignacio Zoco Esparza, José María Fusté Blanch, Jesús María Pereda Ruiz de Temiño, Marcelino Martínez Cao, Pedro Zaballa Barquín Marín, Juan Manuel Villa Gutiérrez, Carlos Lapetra Coarasa.   Trainer: José Luis Villalonga.
Goals: Pedro Zaballa Barquín Marín (25, 88)

96. 10.05.1964
POLAND v REPUBLIC OF IRELAND 3-1 (1-0)
Wisła, Kraków

Referee: Karl Kainer (Austria)   Attendance: 35,000

POLAND: Konrad Kornek, Henryk Szczepański (Cap), Stanisław Oślizło, Roman Bazan, Alojzy Łysko, Antoni Nieroba, Zygfryd Szołtysik, Eugeniusz Faber, Władysław Gzel (33 Jerzy Wilim I), Jerzy Musiałek, Roman Lentner. Trainers: Wiesław Motoczyński, Tadeusz Foryś & Wiesław Pegza.

REPUBLIC OF IRELAND: Alan James Alexander Kelly (55 Noel Michael Dwyer), Theodore Cornelius Foley, Anthony Peter Dunne, Thomas Raymond Brady, Charles John Hurley (Cap), Frederick Strahan, John Michael Giles, Matthew Andrew McEvoy, Patrick Ambrose, John Rowan Fullam, Joseph Haverty.

Goals: Eugeniusz Faber (25), Jerzy Wilim I (64), Zygfryd Szołtysik (76) / Patrick Ambrose (35)

97. 13.05.1964
NORWAY v REPUBLIC OF IRELAND 1-4 (0-2)
Ullevaal, Oslo

Referee: Johannes Malka (West Germany)   Att: 14,354

NORWAY: Sverre Andersen II, Erik Hagen, Edgar Stakset, Roar Johansen, Finn Thorsen, Trygve Andersen, Bjørn Borgen, Arne Pedersen, Per Kristoffersen, Olav Nilsen, Roald Jensen (46 Leif Eriksen II).   Trainer: Ragnar Nikolay Larsen.

REPUBLIC OF IRELAND: Noel Michael Dwyer, Theodore Cornelius Foley, Anthony Peter Dunne, Thomas Raymond Brady, Frederick Strahan, John Rowan Fullam, John Michael Giles, Matthew Andrew McEvoy, Charles John Hurley (Cap), Patrick Ambrose, Joseph Haverty.

Goals: Leif Eriksen (53) / Charles John Hurley (3, 63), John Michael Giles (10), Matthew Andrew McEvoy (77)

98. 24.05.1964
REPUBLIC OF IRELAND v ENGLAND 1-3 (1-2)
Dalymount Park, Dublin

Referee: Robert Holley Davidson (Scotland)   Att: 45,000

REPUBLIC OF IRELAND: Noel Michael Dwyer, Anthony Peter Dunne, Noel Euchuria Cornelius Cantwell (Cap), Frederick Strahan, William Browne, Michael McGrath, John Michael Giles, Matthew Andrew McEvoy, Edward Bailham, Patrick Ambrose, Joseph Haverty (5 Ronald Whelan).

ENGLAND: Anthony Keith Waiters, George Reginald Cohen, Ramon Wilson, Gordon Milne, Ronald Flowers, Robert Frederick Moore (Cap), Peter Thompson, James Peter Greaves, John Joseph Byrne, George Edward Eastham, Robert Charlton. Manager: Alfred Ernest Ramsey.

Goal: Frederick Strahan (41) / George Edward Eastham (9), John Joseph Byrne (22), James Peter Greaves (55)

99. 25.10.1964
REPUBLIC OF IRELAND v POLAND 3-2 (1-2)
Dalymount Park, Dublin

Referee: William Clements (England)   Attendance: 42,000

REPUBLIC OF IRELAND: Noel Michael Dwyer, Theodore Cornelius Foley, Anthony Peter Dunne, Frederick Strahan, Noel Euchuria Cornelius Cantwell (Cap), Michael McGrath, Frank Simon O'Neill, Matthew Andrew McEvoy, James Mooney, John Hennessy, Joseph Haverty.

POLAND: Konrad Kornek (54 Stanislaw Fołtyn), Henryk Szczepański (Cap), Paweł Orzechowski, Stanisław Oślizło, Roman Bazan, Ryszard Grzegorczyk, Ernest Pol, Jan Banaś, Lucjan Brychczy, Włodzimierz Lubański, Eugeniusz Faber. Trainers: Wiesław Motoczyński, Ryszard Koncewicz & Karol Krawczyk.

Goals: Matthew McEvoy (25, 82), James Mooney (84) / Włodzimierz Lubański (19), Ernest Pol (21)

100. 24.03.1965
REPUBLIC OF IRELAND v BELGIUM 0-2 (0-1)
Dalymount Park, Dublin

Referee: Albert Boogaerts (Holland)   Attendance: 30,000

REPUBLIC OF IRELAND: Alan James Alexander Kelly (Cap), Theodore Cornelius Foley, Michael Kevin Meagan, Michael McGrath, Francis Brennan, John Hennessy, Frank Simon O'Neill, Oliver Martin Conmy, James Mooney, Matthew Andrew McEvoy, William Tuohy.

BELGIUM: Jean Nicolay, Georges Heylens, Robert Willems, Albert Sulon, Jean Cornelis, Gérard Sulon, Joseph Jurion, Jan Verheyen, Paul Van Himst, Frans Vermeyen, Wilfried Puis. Trainer: Arthur Ceeulers.

Goals: Matthew Andrew McEvoy (15 own goal), Joseph Jurion (59)

101. 05.05.1965   8th World Cup Qualifiers
REPUBLIC OF IRELAND v SPAIN 1-0 (0-0)
Dalymount Park, Dublin

Referee: Leo Callaghan (Wales)   Attendance: 40,772

REPUBLIC OF IRELAND: Patrick Anthony Joseph Dunne, James Seamus Anthony Brennan, Anthony Peter Dunne, Michael McGrath, Charles John Hurley, John Hennessy, Frank Simon O'Neill, John Michael Giles, Noel Euchuria Cornelius Cantwell (Cap), Matthew Andrew McEvoy, Joseph Haverty.

SPAIN: José Ángel Iribar Cortajarena, Feliciano Ruiz Muñoz Rivilla, Fernando Olivella Pons (Cap), Severino Reija Vásquez, Jesús Glaría Roldán, Ignacio Zoco Esparza, José Armando Ufarte Ventoso "Luego Ufarte", Vicente Guillot Fabián, Marcelino Martínez Cao, Adelardo Rodríguez Sánchez, Carlos Lapetra Coarasa.   Trainer: José Luis Villalonga.

Goal: José Ángel Iribar Cortajarena (61 own goal)

102. 27.10.1965   8th World Cup Qualifiers
SPAIN v REPUBLIC OF IRELAND 4-1 (2-1)
"Ramón Sánchez Pizjuán", Sevilla

Referee: Dr. Decio de Freitas (Portugal)   Attendance: 29,452

SPAIN: Antonio Betancort Barrera, Feliciano Ruiz Muñoz Rivilla, Fernando Olivella Pons (Cap), Severino Reija Vásquez, Jesús Glaría Roldán, Ignacio Zoco Esparza, José Armando Ufarte Ventoso "Luego Ufarte", Jesús María Pereda Ruiz de Temiño, Marcelino Martínez Cao, Luis Suárez Miramónte, Carlos Lapetra Coarasa.   Trainer: José Luis Villalonga.

REPUBLIC OF IRELAND: Patrick Anthony Joseph Dunne, Theodore Cornelius Foley, Anthony Peter Dunne, Michael McGrath, Noel Euchuria Cornelius Cantwell (Cap), Michael Kevin Meagan, Frank Simon O'Neill, Matthew Andrew McEvoy, Eric Barber, John Michael Giles, Joseph Haverty.

Goals: Jesús María Pereda Ruiz de Temiño (40, 43, 58), Carlos Lapetra Coarasa (63) / Matthew Andrew McEvoy (26)

103. 10.11.1965   8th World Cup Qualifiers, Play-Offs
REPUBLIC OF IRELAND v SPAIN 0-1 (0-0)
Parc des Princes, Paris

Referee: Pierre Schwinte (France)   Attendance: 35,371

REPUBLIC OF IRELAND: Patrick Anthony Joseph Dunne, James Seamus Anthony Brennan, Anthony Peter Dunne, Theodore Cornelius Foley, Noel Euchuria Cornelius Cantwell (Cap), Michael Kevin Meagan, Frank Simon O'Neill, Eamonn Martin Dunphy, Matthew Andrew McEvoy, John Michael Giles, Joseph Haverty.

SPAIN: Antonio Betancort Barrera, Feliciano Ruiz Muñoz Rivilla, Fernando Olivella Pons (Cap), Severino Reija Vásquez, Jesús Glaría Roldán, Ignacio Zoco Esparza, José Armando Ufarte Ventoso "Luego Ufarte", Jesús María Pereda Ruiz de Temiño, Marcelino Martínez Cao, Luis Suárez Miramónte, Carlos Lapetra Coarasa.   Trainer: José Luis Villalonga.

Goal: José Armando Ufarte Ventoso "Luego Ufarte" (80)

104. 04.05.1966
**REPUBLIC OF IRELAND
v WEST GERMANY 0-4** (0-2)
Dalymount Park, Dublin

Referee: William Joseph Mullan (Scotland)   Att: 16,091

REPUBLIC OF IRELAND: Patrick Anthony Joseph Dunne, Theodore Cornelius Foley (10 John Keogh), Frederick Strahan, Michael McGrath, Charles John Hurley (Cap), John Hennessy, Frank Simon O'Neill, Raymond Christopher Patrick Treacy, Robert Gilbert, Eamonn Martin Dunphy, Joseph Haverty.

GERMANY: Josef Maier, Friedel Lutz, Andreas Kurbjuhn, Franz Beckenbauer, Willi Schulz, Horst-Dieter Höttges, Jürgen Grabowski, Helmut Haller, Uwe Seeler (Cap), Wolfgang Overath, Heinz Hornig.   Trainer: Helmut Schön.

Goals: Helmut Haller (5), Franz Beckenbauer (18), Wolfgang Overath (57, 74)

105. 22.05.1966
AUSTRIA v REPUBLIC OF IRELAND 1-0 (0-0)
Prater, Wien

Referee: Gyula Gere (Hungary)   Attendance: 50,000

AUSTRIA: Roman Pichler, Walter Gebhardt, Walter Glechner, Walter Stamm, Walter Ludescher, Walter Skocik, Ewald Ullmann, Horst Hirnschrodt (55 Thomas Parits), Walter Seitl, Rudolf Flögel, Adolf Macek.   Trainer: Eduard Frühwirth.

REPUBLIC OF IRELAND: Alan James Alexander Kelly, James Seamus Anthony Brennan, Anthony Peter Dunne, Michael McGrath, Charles John Hurley (Cap), Michael Kevin Meagan, Frank Simon O'Neill, John Rowan Fullam, Noel Euchuria Cornelius Cantwell, John Michael Giles, Joseph Haverty.

Goal: Walter Seitl (76)

106. 25.05.1966
BELGIUM v REPUBLIC OF IRELAND 2-3 (2-1)
Sclessin, Liège

Referee: Pierre Schwinte (France)   Attendance: 2,445

BELGIUM: Jean Trappeniers, Georges Heylens, Jean Plaskie, Marcel Lemoine, Jean Cornelis, Joseph Jurion, Godfried Vandeboer, Léon Semmeling, Jacques Stockman, Paul Van Himst, Wilfried Puis.   Trainer: Raymond Goethals.

REPUBLIC OF IRELAND: Alan James Alexander Kelly, James Seamus Anthony Brennan, Anthony Peter Dunne, Michael McGrath, Charles John Hurley (Cap), Michael Kevin Meagan, Eric Barber, John Rowan Fullam, Noel Euchuria Cornelius Cantwell, John Michael Giles, Joseph Haverty.

Goals: Paul Van Himst (5), Godfried Vandeboer (25) / Noel Euchuria Cornelius Cantwell (20, 46), John Rowan Fullam (69)

107. 23.10.1966   3rd European Champs Qualifiers
REPUBLIC OF IRELAND v SPAIN 0-0
Dalymount Park, Dublin

Referee: Hans Carlsson (Sweden)   Attendance: 37,000

REPUBLIC OF IRELAND: Alan James Alexander Kelly, James Seamus Anthony Brennan, Anthony Peter Dunne, James Patrick Conway, Noel Euchuria Cornelius Cantwell (Cap), Michael Kevin Meagan, Frank Simon O'Neill, Matthew Andrew McEvoy, Raymond Christopher Patrick Treacy, John Michael Giles, Anthony O'Connell.

SPAIN: José Ángel Iribar Cortajarena, Manuel Sanchis Martínez, Francisco Santamaría Mirones, Severino Reija Vásquez (Cap), Jesús Glaría Roldán, José Luis Violeta Lajusticia, Luciano Sánchez Rodríguez "Vavá", Fernando Ansola Sanmartín, José Luis Aragonés Suárez, Marcial Manuel Pina Morales, Francisco García Gómez "Paquito".   Trainer: Domingo Balmanya Perera.

108. 16.11.1966   3rd European Champs Qualifiers
REPUBLIC OF IRELAND v TURKEY 2-1 (0-0)
Dalymount Park, Dublin
Referee: Tage Sørensen (Denmark)   Attendance: 22,300
REPUBLIC OF IRELAND: Patrick Anthony Joseph Dunne, James Seamus Anthony Brennan, Anthony Peter Dunne, James Patrick Conway, Charles John Hurley (Cap), Michael Kevin Meagan, Frank Simon O'Neill, Eamonn Martin Dunphy, Matthew Andrew McEvoy, John Michael Giles, Joseph Haverty.
TURKEY: Ali Artuner, Talat Özkarslı, Yılmaz Şen, Ercan Aktuna, Fehmi Sağınoğlu, Ayhan Elmastaşoğlu, Şeref Has, Nevzat Güzelırmak, Ogün Altıparmak, Fevzi Zemzem, Faruk Karadoğan.   Trainer: Adnan Suvari.
Goals: Frank Simon O'Neill (60), Matthew McEvoy (74) / Ogün Altıparmak (88)

109. 07.12.1966   3rd European Champs Qualifiers
SPAIN v REPUBLIC OF IRELAND 2-0 (2-0)
Mestalla, Valencia
Referee: Pieter Paulus Roomer (Holland)   Att: 25,000
SPAIN: José Ángel Iribar Cortajarena, Manuel Sanchis Martínez, Francisco Fernández Rodríguez "Gallego", Severino Reija Vásquez (Cap), José Luis Violeta Lajusticia, Francisco García Gómez "Paquito", Vicente Anastasio Jara Segovia, José Martínez Sánchez "Pirri", Fernando Ansola Sanmartín, José Luis Aragonés Suárez, José María García La Villa.   Trainer: Domingo Balmanya Perera.
REPUBLIC OF IRELAND: Alan James Alexander Kelly, James Seamus Anthony Brennan, Anthony Peter Dunne, John Thomas Dempsey, Charles John Hurley (Cap), Michael Kevin Meagan, Frank Simon O'Neill, James Patrick Conway, Alfred Hale, Eamonn Martin Dunphy, Joseph Haverty.
Goals: José María García La Villa (20), José Martínez Sánchez "Pirri" (35)

110. 22.02.1967   3rd European Champs Qualifiers
TURKEY v REPUBLIC OF IRELAND 2-1 (1-0)
19 Mayis, Ankara
Referee: Dimitar Rumenchev (Bulgaria)   Att: 31,063
TURKEY: Ali Artuner, Şükrü Birant, Talat Özkarslı, Ercan Aktuna, Fehmi Sağınoğlu, Ayhan Elmastaşoğlu, Şeref Has, Ergün Acuner, Ogün Altıparmak, Abdullah Çevrim, Faruk Karadoğan.   Trainer: Adnan Suvari.
REPUBLIC OF IRELAND: Alan James Alexander Kelly, Joseph Patrick Kinnear, Michael Kevin Meagan, Alfred Finucane, Charles John Hurley (Cap), Michael McGrath, Frank Simon O'Neill, Charles Gallagher, Noel Euchuria Cornelius Cantwell, John Michael Giles, Eamonn Martin Dunphy.
Goals: Ayhan Elmastaşoğlu (35), Ogün Altıparmak (78) / Noel Euchuria Cornelius Cantwell (89)

111. 21.05.1967   3rd European Champs Qualifiers
REPUBLIC OF IRELAND v CZECHOSLOVAKIA 0-2 (0-1)
Dalymount Park, Dublin
Referee: Dittmar Huber (Switzerland)   Attendance: 6,257
REPUBLIC OF IRELAND: Alan James Alexander Kelly, Theodore Cornelius Foley, John Thomas Dempsey, Alfred Finucane, Charles John Hurley (Cap), Michael Kevin Meagan, Charles Gallagher, Matthew Andrew McEvoy, Raymond Christopher Patrick Treacy, Eamonn Martin Dunphy, Oliver Martin Conmy.
CZECHOSLOVAKIA: Ivo Viktor, Jan Lála, Kamil Majerník, Ján Popluhár (Cap), Vladimír Táborský, Ján Geleta, Andrej Kvašňák, Juraj Szikora, Vojtěch Masný, Jozef Adamec, Dušan Kabát.   Trainer: Josef Marko.
Goals: Juraj Szikora (16), Vojtěch Masný (47)

112. 22.11.1967   3rd European Champs Qualifiers
CZECHOSLOVAKIA v REPUBLIC OF IRELAND 1-2 (0-0)
Slavia, Praha
Referee: Erwin Vetter (East Germany)   Attendance: 7,615
CZECHOSLOVAKIA: Antonín Kramerius, Jan Lála, Alexander Horváth, Ján Popluhár (Cap), Vladimír Táborský, Ján Geleta, Ladislav Kuna, Jozef Levický, Juraj Szikora, Josef Jurkanin, Václav Vrána.   Trainer: Josef Marko.
REPUBLIC OF IRELAND: Alan James Alexander Kelly, Joseph Patrick Kinnear, Michael Kevin Meagan, John Thomas Dempsey, Charles John Hurley (Cap), James Patrick Conway, Edward Eamonn Rogers, Eamonn Martin Dunphy, Oliver Martin Conmy, Raymond Christopher Patrick Treacy, Turlough O'Connor.
Goals: John Thomas Dempsey (57 own goal) / Raymond Treacy (65), Turlough O'Connor (86)

113. 15.05.1968
REPUBLIC OF IRELAND v POLAND 2-2 (0-2)
Dalymount Park, Dublin
Referee: Eric Jennings (England)   Attendance: 25,000
REPUBLIC OF IRELAND: Alan James Alexander Kelly, Joseph Patrick Kinnear, Thomas Roger Carroll, John Rowan Fullam, Charles John Hurley (Cap), Michael Kevin Meagan, Oliver Martin Conmy, Raymond Christopher Patrick Treacy, John Thomas Dempsey, Eamonn Martin Dunphy, Edward Eamonn Rogers (71 Alfred Hale).
POLAND: Hubert Kostka, Roman Bazan, Jacek Gmoch, Stanisław Oślizło (Cap), Henryk Latocha, Walter Winkler, Bronisław Bula, Janusz Żmijewski, Andrzej Jarosik, Włodzimierz Lubański, Eugeniusz Faber.   Trainer: Ryszard Konczewicz.
Goals: John Thomas Dempsey (51), Alfred Hale (86) / Włodzimierz Lubański (5 pen), Andrzej Jarosik (24)

114. 30.10.1968
POLAND v REPUBLIC OF IRELAND 1-0 (0-0)
Śląski, Chorzów
Referee: Bo Nilsson (Sweden)   Attendance: 18,000
POLAND: Hubert Kostka (Cap), Jan Rudnow, Stefan Florenski, Walter Winkler, Adam Musiał, Erwin Wilczek, Bernard Blaut, Jerzy Sadek, Janusz Żmijewski, Włodzimierz Lubański, Robert Gadocha.   Trainer: Ryszard Konczewicz.
REPUBLIC OF IRELAND: Alan James Alexander Kelly (61 Michael Smyth), Thomas Roger Carroll, Anthony Peter Dunne, John Rowan Fullam, Charles John Hurley (Cap), John Thomas Dempsey, Frank Simon O'Neill, Raymond Christopher Patrick Treacy, Alfred Hale, Eamonn Martin Dunphy, Edward Eamonn Rogers.
Goal: Włodzimierz Lubański (61)

115. 10.11.1968
REPUBLIC OF IRELAND v AUSTRIA 2-2 (0-1)
Dalymount Park, Dublin
Referee: Robert Holley Davidson (Scotland)   Att: 20,000
REPUBLIC OF IRELAND: Alan James Alexander Kelly, Joseph Patrick Kinnear, Thomas Roger Carroll, John Rowan Fullam, John Thomas Dempsey, John Hennessy (54 James Patrick Conway), Frank Simon O'Neill, Eamonn Martin Dunphy, Alfred Hale, John Michael Giles (Cap), Edward Eamonn Rogers.
AUSTRIA: Gerald Fuchsbichler (8 Wilhelm Harreither), Walter Gebhardt, Gerhard Sturmberger, Johann Eigenstiller, Heinz Russ, Rudolf Horvath, Erich Hof, Johann Ettmayer, Anton Fritsch, Helmut Köglberger (78 Helmut Mätzler), Helmut Redl.   Trainer: Leopold Stastny.
Goals: Edward Eamonn Rogers (82), Alfred Hale (87) / Helmut Redl (15), Erich Hof (50)

116. 04.12.1968   9th World Cup Qualifiers
REPUBLIC OF IRELAND v DENMARK 1-1 (1-0)*
Dalymount Park, Dublin
Referee: William Syme (Scotland)   Attendance: 23,555
REPUBLIC OF IRELAND: Alan James Alexander Kelly, Thomas Roger Carroll, Anthony Peter Dunne, John Thomas Dempsey, Charles John Hurley, John Rowan Fullam, Frank Simon O'Neill, Eamonn Martin Dunphy, Alfred Hale, John Michael Giles (Cap), Edward Eamonn Rogers.
DENMARK: Knud Engedal, Jan Larsen, Hans Jørgen Christiansen, Leif Sørensen (Cap), Henning Munk Jensen, Erik Sandvad, Kurt Præst, Bent Jensen, Niels-Christian Holmstrøm, Finn Wiberg, Ulrik Le Fevre.
Goals: John Michael Giles (40 pen) / Finn Wiberg (18)
* The match was abandoned after 51 minutes due to fog.

117. 04.05.1969   9th World Cup Qualifiers
REPUBLIC OF IRELAND v CZECHOSLOVAKIA 1-2 (1-0)
Dalymount Park, Dublin
Referee: Antonio Ribeiro Saldaña (Portugal)   Att: 32,002
REPUBLIC OF IRELAND: Alan James Alexander Kelly, James Seamus Anthony Brennan, Patrick Martin Mulligan, Alfred Finucane, Charles John Hurley (Cap), John Thomas Dempsey, Frank Simon O'Neill, Michael Leech (44 Eoin Kevin Joseph Colin Hand), Raymond Christopher Patrick Treacy, John Michael Giles, Edward Eamonn Rogers.
CZECHOSLOVAKIA: Alexander Vencel, Karel Dobiaš. František Plass, Alexander Horváth (Cap), Vladimír Hagara, Juraj Szikora (85 Ivan Hrdlička), Andrej Kvašňák, Bohumil Veselý, Josef Jurkanin, Jozef Adamec, Dušan Kabát.   Trainer: Josef Marko.
Goals: Edward Eamonn Rogers (15) / Dušan Kabát (51), Jozef Adamec (70)

118. 27.05.1969   9th World Cup Qualifiers
DENMARK v REPUBLIC OF IRELAND 2-0 (1-0)
Idrætsparken, København
Referee: Sergey Arkhipov (Soviet Union)   Att: 26,195
DENMARK: Knud Engedal, Jan Larsen, Torben Nielsen, Christian Andersen, Henning Munk Jensen, Niels Møller, Bent Jensen, Ole Sørensen, Ole Madsen, Leif Sørensen, Ulrik Le Fevre (Cap).
REPUBLIC OF IRELAND: Alan James Alexander Kelly, James Seamus Anthony Brennan, Patrick Martin Mulligan, Alfred Finucane, John Thomas Dempsey (Cap), William Newman (55 Frank Simon O'Neill), Michael Leech, Daniel Joseph Givens, Eamonn Martin Dunphy, Raymond Christopher Patrick Treacy, Edward Eamonn Rogers.
Goals: Ole Sørensen (35, 67)

119. 08.06.1969   9th World Cup Qualifiers
REPUBLIC OF IRELAND v HUNGARY 1-2 (0-1)
Dalymount Park, Dublin
Referee: Vital Loraux (Belgium)   Attendance: 17,286
REPUBLIC OF IRELAND: Alan James Alexander Kelly, James Seamus Anthony Brennan, Anthony Peter Dunne, James Patrick Conway, Patrick Martin Mulligan, Alfred Finucane, Eamonn Martin Dunphy, Michael Leech, Charles John Hurley (Cap) (46 Frank Simon O'Neill), Edward Eamonn Rogers, Daniel Joseph Givens.
HUNGARY: Antal Szentmihályi, Benő Káposzta, Kálmán Mészöly, Lajos Szűcs, Kálmán Ihász, János Göröcs, Flórián Albert, Sándor Zámbó, Ferenc Bene, Antal Dunai II, Mihály Kozma (70 János Farkas).   Trainer: Károly Sós.
Goals: Daniel Joseph Givens (60) / Antal Dunai II (24), Ferenc Bene (80)

120. 21.09.1969
REPUBLIC OF IRELAND v SCOTLAND 1-1 (1-1)
Dalymount Park, Dublin
Referee: Norman Burtenshaw (England)   Att: 27,000
REPUBLIC OF IRELAND: Alan James Alexander Kelly, James Seamus Anthony Brennan, Michael Kevin Meagan (Cap), Alfred Finucane, Patrick Martin Mulligan, James Patrick Conway, Edward Eamonn Rogers, John Michael Giles, Daniel Joseph Givens, Alfred Hale, Raymond Christopher Patrick Treacy.   Trainer: Michael Kevin Meagan.
SCOTLAND: Ernest McGarr (24 James Herriot), John Greig, Thomas Gemmell (46 William Thomas Callaghan), Patrick Gordon Stanton, Ronald McKinnon, Robert Moncur, William Henderson, William John Bremner (Cap), Colin Anderson Stein, Peter Barr Cormack, John Hughes.
Manager: Robert Brown.
Goals: Daniel Joseph Givens (27) / Colin Anderson Stein (8)

121. 07.10.1969   9th World Cup Qualifiers
**CZECHOSLOVAKIA
v REPUBLIC OF IRELAND 3-0 (3-0)**
Sparta, Praha
Referee: Concetto Lo Bello (Italy)   Attendance: 32,879
CZECHOSLOVAKIA: Ivo Viktor, Jan Pivarník, Václav Migas (76 Vladimír Hrivnák), Alexander Horváth (Cap), Vladimír Hagara, Andrej Kvašňák, Ladislav Kuna, Bohumil Veselý, Josef Jurkanin (71 Karol Jokl), Jozef Adamec, Dušan Kabát.   Trainer: Josef Marko.
REPUBLIC OF IRELAND: Kevin Fitzpatrick, James Seamus Anthony Brennan (Cap), Thomas Roger Carroll, Alfred Finucane, Patrick Martin Mulligan, Joseph Patrick Kinnear, James Patrick Conway, Gerard Anthony Francis Conroy, Daniel Joseph Givens (46 John Rowan Fullam), Alfred Hale, Oliver Martin Conmy.   Trainer: Michael Kevin Meagan.
Goals: Jozef Adamec (8, 36, 45)

122. 15.10.1969   9th World Cup Qualifiers
REPUBLIC OF IRELAND v DENMARK 1-1 (1-0)
Dalymount Park, Dublin
Referee: John Patterson (Scotland)   Attendance: 26,108
REPUBLIC OF IRELAND: Alan James Alexander Kelly, Joseph Patrick Kinnear, James Seamus Anthony Brennan (Cap), Patrick Martin Mulligan, Anthony Brendan Byrne, James Patrick Conway, Eamonn Martin Dunphy, Edward Eamonn Rogers, Gerard Anthony Francis Conroy, Daniel Joseph Givens, Raymond Christopher Patrick Treacy.   Trainer: Michael Kevin Meagan.
DENMARK: Kaj Paulsen, Jan Larsen, Erik Nielsen II, Kjeld Thorst, Henning Munk Jensen, Niels Møller (Cap), Kurt Præst, Allan Michaelsen, Bent Jensen, Jan Andersen, Steen Rømer Larsen (Per Madsen).
Goals: Daniel Joseph Givens (8) / Bent Jensen (84 pen)

123. 05.11.1969   9th World Cup Qualifiers
HUNGARY v REPUBLIC OF IRELAND 4-0 (1-0)
Népstadion, Budapest
Referee: Vlado Jakse (Yugoslavia)   Attendance: 30,000
HUNGARY: Gyula Tamás, József Kelemen, Miklós Páncsics, Lajos Szűcs, Kálmán Ihász, Zoltán Halmosi, János Göröcs (58 Lajos Kocsis), László Fazekas, Ferenc Bene, Antal Dunai II (46 Lajos Puskás dr.), Sándor Zámbó.   Trainer: Károly Sós.
REPUBLIC OF IRELAND: Alan James Alexander Kelly, James Seamus Anthony Brennan, Anthony Peter Dunne (Cap), Patrick Martin Mulligan, John Thomas Dempsey, Joseph Patrick Kinnear, Gerard Anthony Francis Conroy (40 Raymond Christopher Patrick Treacy), James Patrick Conway, Daniel Joseph Givens, Eamonn Martin Dunphy, Edward Eamonn Rogers.   Trainer: Michael Kevin Meagan.
Sent off: John Thomas Dempsey (84), Lajos Szűcs (90)
Goals: Zoltán Halmosi (30), Ferenc Bene (50), Lajos Puskás dr. (68), Lajos Kocsis (84)

124. 06.05.1970
POLAND v REPUBLIC OF IRELAND 2-1 (2-0)
Warta, Poznań
Referee: Vladimir Tolchinski (Soviet Union)   Att: 52,000
POLAND: Hubert Kostka, Henryk Latocha, Roman Strzałkowski, Stanisław Oślizło (Cap) (46 Walter Winkler), Zygmunt Anczok, Lesław Ćmikiewicz (46 Alfred Olek), Zygfryd Szołtysik, Bronisław Bula, Marian Kozerski, Włodzimierz Lubański, Andrzej Jarosik.
Trainer: Ryszard Konczewicz.
REPUBLIC OF IRELAND: Alan James Alexander Kelly, Joseph Patrick Kinnear, Thomas Roger Carroll (46 James Seamus Anthony Brennan), Eoin Kevin Joseph Colin Hand, Patrick Martin Mulligan, Anthony Brendan Byrne, Eamonn Martin Dunphy, John Michael Giles (Cap), James Patrick Conway (46 Raymond Christopher Patrick Treacy), Gerard Anthony Francis Conroy, Daniel Joseph Givens.   Trainer: Michael Kevin Meagan.
Goals: Marian Kozerski (9), Zygfryd Szołtysik (25) / Daniel Joseph Givens (84)

125. 09.05.1970
WEST GERMANY v REPUBLIC OF IRELAND 2-1 (1-0)
Olympia, West-Berlin

Referee: Einar Boström (Sweden)   Attendance: 70,000

GERMANY: Horst Wolter, Bernd Patzke, Hans-Hubert Vogts, Franz Beckenbauer, Willi Schulz, Wolfgang Weber, Jürgen Grabowski (46 Peter Dietrich), Uwe Seeler (Cap), Gerhard Müller, Wolfgang Overath (76 Siegfried Held), Johannes Löhr. Trainer: Helmut Schön.

REPUBLIC OF IRELAND: Alan James Alexander Kelly, James Seamus Anthony Brennan, Thomas Roger Carroll, Eoin Kevin Joseph Colin Hand, John Thomas Dempsey, Patrick Martin Mulligan, James Patrick Conway (59 Eamonn Martin Dunphy), John Michael Giles (Cap), Daniel Joseph Givens (87 Raymond Christopher Patrick Treacy), Anthony Brendan Byrne, Gerard Anthony Francis Conroy. Trainer: Michael Kevin Meagan.

Goals: Uwe Seeler (17), Johannes Löhr (82) / Patrick Martin Mulligan (86)

126. 23.09.1970
REPUBLIC OF IRELAND v POLAND 0-2 (0-2)
Dalymount Park, Dublin

Referee: Daniel Lyden (England)   Attendance: 20,000

REPUBLIC OF IRELAND: Alan James Alexander Kelly (76 Michael Kearns), James Seamus Anthony Brennan (Cap), Anthony Brendan Byrne, Eoin Kevin Joseph Colin Hand, John Thomas Dempsey, Patrick Martin Mulligan, Gerard Anthony Francis Conroy, Eamonn Martin Dunphy, Raymond Christopher Patrick Treacy, Michael Lawlor (46 Anthony O'Connell), Stephen Derek Heighway (85 Alfred Hale). Trainer: Michael Kevin Meagan.

POLAND: Władysław Grotyński, Władysław Stachurski, Jerzy Wyrobek, Jerzy Gorgoń, Adam Musiał, Lesław Ćmikiewicz, Zygfryd Szołtysik, Bernard Blaut (Cap), Joachim Marx, Włodzimierz Lubański, Robert Gadocha. Trainer: Ryszard Konczewicz.

Goals: Władysław Stachurski (26), Zygfryd Szołtysik (36)

127. 14.10.1970   4th European Champs Qualifiers
REPUBLIC OF IRELAND v SWEDEN 1-1 (1-0)
Dalymount Park, Dublin

Referee: Robert Helies (France)   Attendance: 28,194

REPUBLIC OF IRELAND: Alan James Alexander Kelly, Thomas Roger Carroll (70 Joseph Patrick Kinnear), Anthony Peter Dunne (Cap), Patrick Martin Mulligan, John Thomas Dempsey, Anthony Brendan Byrne, Gerard Anthony Francis Conroy, Eamonn Martin Dunphy, Daniel Joseph Givens (83 Raymond Christopher Patrick Treacy), Michael Lawlor, Stephen Derek Heighway. Trainer: Michael Kevin Meagan.

SWEDEN: Sven-Gunnar Larsson, Hans Selander, Krister Kristensson, Björn Nordqvist, Roland Grip, Tommy Svensson, Jan Olsson I, Bo Göran Larsson, Leif Eriksson, Inge Danielsson (46 Dan Brzokoupil), Ove Grahn. Trainer: Orvar Bergmark.

Goals: Thomas Roger Carroll (44 pen) / Dan Brzokoupil (61)

128. 28.10.1970   4th European Champs Qualifiers
SWEDEN v REPUBLIC OF IRELAND 1-0 (0-0)
Råsunda, Stockholm

Referee: Pavel Kazakov (Soviet Union)   Attendance: 11,922

SWEDEN: Ronnie Carl Hellström, Hans Selander, Krister Kristensson, Björn Nordqvist, Roland Grip (65 Claes Cronqvist), Tommy Svensson, Bo Göran Larsson, Jan Olsson I, Ove Grahn, Leif Eriksson, Dan Brzokoupil (61 Tom Turesson). Trainer: Orvar Bergmark.

REPUBLIC OF IRELAND: Alan James Alexander Kelly, James Seamus Anthony Brennan (Cap), John Thomas Dempsey, Patrick Dunning, Anthony Brendan Byrne, Eamonn Martin Dunphy, Alfred Finucane, Michael Lawlor, Gerard Anthony Francis Conroy, Raymond Christopher Patrick Treacy, Stephen Derek Heighway. Trainer: Michael Kevin Meagan.

Goal: Tom Turesson (74)

129. 08.12.1970   4th European Champs Qualifiers
ITALY v REPUBLIC OF IRELAND 3-0 (2-0)
Comunale, Firenze

Referee: Robert Schaut (Belgium)   Attendance: 45,000

ITALY: Enrico Albertosi, Tarcisio Burgnich, Giacinto Facchetti (Cap), Mario Bertini, Roberto Rosato, Pierluigi Cera, Angelo Domenghini, Alessandro Mazzola, Roberto Boninsegna, Giancarlo De Sisti, Pierino Prati. Trainer: Ferruccio Valcareggi.

REPUBLIC OF IRELAND: Alan James Alexander Kelly, James Seamus Anthony Brennan (Cap), Anthony Brendan Byrne, John Thomas Dempsey, Patrick Dunning, Gerard Anthony Francis Conroy, Eamonn Martin Dunphy (36 Michael Lawlor), Alfred Finucane, Edward Eamonn Rogers, Daniel Joseph Givens, Raymond Christopher Patrick Treacy. Trainer: Michael Kevin Meagan.

Goals: Giancarlo De Sisti (22 pen), Roberto Boninsegna (42), Pierino Prati (84)

130. 10.05.1971   4th European Champs Qualifiers
REPUBLIC OF IRELAND v ITALY 1-2 (1-1)
Dalymount Park, Dublin
Referee: Gerhard Schulenburg (West Germany)   Att: 25,000
REPUBLIC OF IRELAND: Alan James Alexander Kelly, Anthony Brendan Byrne, Anthony Peter Dunne, Joseph Patrick Kinnear, Patrick Martin Mulligan, Eamonn Martin Dunphy, Edward Eamonn Rogers (46 Alfred Finucane), James Patrick Conway, Daniel Joseph Givens, John Michael Giles (Cap), Stephen Derek Heighway.
Trainer: Michael Kevin Meagan.
ITALY: Dino Zoff, Tarcisio Burgnich, Giacinto Facchetti (Cap), Mario Bertini, Roberto Rosato, Pierluigi Cera, Pierino Prati, Alessandro Mazzola, Roberto Boninsegna, Giancarlo De Sisti, Mario Corso.   Trainer: Ferruccio Valcareggi.
Goals: James Patrick Conway (23) /
Roberto Boninsegna (15), Pierino Prati (59)

132. 10.10.1971   4th European Champs Qualifiers
AUSTRIA v REPUBLIC OF IRELAND 6-0 (3-0)
Linzer Stadion, Linz
Referee: Karl Göppel (Switzerland)   Attendance: 15,050
AUSTRIA: Adolf Antrich, Johann Schmidradner, Gerhard Sturmberger, Johann Eigenstiller, Peter Pumm, Rudolf Horvath, Norbert Hof, Johann Ettmayer, Hans Pirkner, Thomas Parits, Kurt Jara.   Trainer: Leopold Stastny.
REPUBLIC OF IRELAND: Patrick Joseph Christopher Roche, Michael Gannon, John Herrick, Thomas McConville, Alfred Finucane (Cap), Patrick Martin Mulligan, Michael Kearin (53 Damien John Richardson), Frank Simon O'Neill, Michael Leech, Michael Paul Martin (69 Alfred Hale), Turlough O'Connor.   Trainer: William Tuohy.
Goals: Kurt Jara (12, 85), Hans Pirkner (40 pen),
Thomas Parits (45, 52, 90)

131. 30.05.1971   4th European Champs Qualifiers
REPUBLIC OF IRELAND v AUSTRIA 1-4 (0-3)
Lansdowne Road, Dublin
Referee: Henry Öberg (Norway)   Attendance: 14,674
REPUBLIC OF IRELAND: Alan James Alexander Kelly, Anthony Brendan Byrne, Anthony Peter Dunne (Cap), Eoin Kevin Joseph Colin Hand, James Christopher Dunne, Eamonn Martin Dunphy (46 Noel Campbell), Edward Eamonn Rogers, James Patrick Conway, Daniel Joseph Givens (74 James Paul Holmes), Raymond Christopher Patrick Treacy, Stephen Derek Heighway.   Trainer: Michael Kevin Meagan.
AUSTRIA: Herbert Rettensteiner, Johann Schmidradner, Gerhard Sturmberger, Johann Eigenstiller, Werner Kriess (78 Rainer Schlagbauer), August Starek, Norbert Hof, Johann Ettmayer, Josef Hickersberger, Wilhelm Kreuz, Karl Kodat.
Trainer: Leopold Stastny.
Goals: Edward Eamonn Rogers (46 pen) /
Johann Schmidradner (4 pen), Karl Kodat (11), Anthony Peter Dunne (30 own goal), August Starek (72)

133. 11.06.1972   Brazil Independence Cup
REPUBLIC OF IRELAND v IRAN 2-1 (0-1)
Santa Crux, Recife
Referee: Aurelio Angonese (Italy)   Attendance: 10,500
REPUBLIC OF IRELAND: Alan James Alexander Kelly, Joseph Patrick Kinnear, John Thomas Dempsey, Patrick Martin Mulligan (Cap), Thomas Roger Carroll, Noel Campbell, Michael Paul Martin, Edward Eamonn Rogers, Raymond Christopher Patrick Treacy, Michael Leech (78 Turlough O'Connor), Daniel Joseph Givens.   Trainer: William Tuohy.
IRAN: Nasser Hejazi, Ebrahim Ashtiyani, Jafar Ashraf Kashani, Akhbar Kargharjam, Mostafa Arab, Ali Parvin, Parviz Ghelichkani, Javad Ghurab (60 Karo Haqvardian), Hossein Kalani, Safar Iranpak (46 Mehdi Monajati), Ghulam Hussain Mazloomi.   Trainer: Mohammad Ranjbar.
Goals: Michael Leech (63), Daniel Joseph Givens (67)

134. 18.06.1972   Brazil Independence Cup
REPUBLIC OF IRELAND v ECUADOR 3-2 (1-1)
Castelo Branco, Natal
Referee: Michel Kitabdjian (France)
REPUBLIC OF IRELAND: Alan James Alexander Kelly, Joseph Patrick Kinnear, Patrick Martin Mulligan (Cap), John Thomas Dempsey, Thomas Roger Carroll, Noel Campbell, Michael Paul Martin, Edward Eamonn Rogers, Raymond Christopher Patrick Treacy (46 Turlough O'Connor), Daniel Joseph Givens, Michael Leech (46 Jeremiah Dennehy). Trainer: William Tuohy.
ECUADOR: Fernando Gilberto Maldonado, Víctor Hugo Peláez, Jefferson Donald Camacho, Rafael Enrique Guerrero, Jesús Emilio Ortiz, Miguel Angel Coronel, Jorge Washington Bolaños, Italo Eugenio Estupiñan, Raúl Patricio Peñaherrera (Héctor Morales), Félix Lasso, Marco Antonio Guime. Trainer: Ernesto Guerra & Lazo George.
Sent off: Daniel Joseph Givens
Goals: Edward Rogers (12), Michael Paul Martin (61), Turlough O'Connor (86) /
Miguel Angel Coronel (35), Félix Lasso (81)

135. 21.06.1972   Brazil Independence Cup
REPUBLIC OF IRELAND v CHILE 1-2 (0-0)
"José de Rego Maciel", Recife
Referee: Romualdo Arppi Filho (Brazil)
REPUBLIC OF IRELAND: Alan James Alexander Kelly, Joseph Patrick Kinnear, Patrick Martin Mulligan (Cap), John Thomas Dempsey, Thomas Roger Carroll (82 John Herrick), Noel Campbell, Michael Paul Martin, Edward Eamonn Rogers, Raymond Christopher Patrick Treacy, Turlough O'Connor, Jeremiah Dennehy.   Trainer: William Tuohy.
CHILE: Adolfo Nef Sanhueza, Juan Salvador Machuca Valdéz, Guillermo Azócar, Raúl Angulo, Antonio Arias Mújica, Alfonso Lara Madrid, Eduardo Peralta, Fernando Carvallo, Julio Crisosto (Fernando Espinoza), Carlos Humberto Caszely Garrido, Leonardo Véliz Díaz (Alberto Fouilloux). Trainer: Rudolf Guttendorf (West Germany).
Sent off: Turlough O'Connor
Goals: Edward Eamonn Rogers (79) /
Carlos Humberto Caszely Garrido (60), Alberto Fouilloux (68)

136. 25.06.1972   Brazil Independence Cup
PORTUGAL v REPUBLIC OF IRELAND 2-1 (2-1)
"José de Rego Maciel", Recife
Referee: Angel Norberto Coerezza (Argentina)   Att: 13,000
PORTUGAL: José Henrique de Rodrigues Marques (81 José Manuel Mourinho Félix), Artur Manuel Soares Correia, Humberto Manuel de Jesus Coelho, Messias Júlio Timula, Adolfo António da Cruz Calisto, António José da Conceiçao Oliveira "Toni", Augusto Matine, Fernando Peres da Silva, Tamagnini Manuel Gomes Baptista "Nené" (64 Jaime da Silva Graça), Artur Jorge Braga Melo Teixeira, Eusébio da Silva Ferreira (Cap).   Trainer: José Augusto Pinto de Almeida.
REPUBLIC OF IRELAND: Alan James Alexander Kelly, Joseph Patrick Kinnear, Patrick Martin Mulligan (Cap), John Thomas Dempsey, Thomas Roger Carroll, Noel Campbell, Michael Paul Martin, Edward Eamonn Rogers, Raymond Christopher Patrick Treacy (Turlough O'Connor), Daniel Joseph Givens, Michael Leech.   Trainer: William Tuohy.
Goals: Fernando Peres da Silva (35), Tamagnini Manuel Gomes Baptista "Nené" (37) / Michael Leech (38)

137. 18.10.1972   10th World Cup Qualifiers
**REPUBLIC OF IRELAND
v SOVIET UNION 1-2** (0-0)
Lansdowne Road, Dublin
Referee: Henry Öberg (Norway)   Attendance: 25,000
REPUBLIC OF IRELAND: Alan James Alexander Kelly (Cap), Joseph Patrick Kinnear, Thomas Roger Carroll, Thomas McConville, Eoin Kevin Joseph Colin Hand, Noel Campbell, Edward Eamonn Rogers (62 Michael Leech), Michael Paul Martin, Stephen Derek Heighway, Raymond Christopher Patrick Treacy, Gerard Anthony Francis Conroy. Trainer: William Tuohy.
SOVIET UNION: Vladimir Pilguy, Revaz Dzodzuashvili, Murtaz Khurtzilava (Cap), Evgeniy Lovchev, Vladimir Kaplichniy, Viktor Kolotov, Vladimir Muntyan, Vyacheslav Semënov, Vladimir Fedotov, Anatoliy Puzach, Gennadiy Evryuzhikhin.   Trainer: Aleksandr Ponomarev.
Goals: Gerard Anthony Francis Conroy (83) /
Vladimir Fedotov (55), Viktor Kolotov (65)

138. 15.11.1972   10th World Cup Qualifiers
REPUBLIC OF IRELAND v FRANCE 2-1 (1-0)
Dalymount Park, Dublin
Referee: Kaj Rasmussen (Denmark)   Attendance: 26,511
REPUBLIC OF IRELAND: Alan James Alexander Kelly, Joseph Patrick Kinnear, James Paul Holmes, Patrick Martin Mulligan, Thomas McConville, Eoin Kevin Joseph Colin Hand, Anthony Brendan Byrne (75 Noel Campbell), John Michael Giles (Cap), Gerard Anthony Francis Conroy (89 Turlough O'Connor), Raymond Christopher Patrick Treacy, Daniel Joseph Givens.   Trainer: William Tuohy.

FRANCE: Georges Carnus, José Broissart, Claude Quittet (Cap), Marius Trésor, Jean-Paul Rostagni, Jean-Noël Huck, Jean-Pierre Adams, Charly Loubet (63 Marc Molitor), Hervé Revelli, Jean-Michel Larqué, Georges Bereta.
Trainer: Georges Boulogne.

Goals: Gerard Conroy (28), Raymond Treacy (76) / Jean-Michel Larqué (66)

139. 13.05.1973   10th World Cup Qualifiers
SOVIET UNION v REPUBLIC OF IRELAND 1-0 (0-0)
Lenin, Moskva
Referee: Ove Dahlberg (Sweden)   Attendance: 65,000
SOVIET UNION: Vladimir Pilguy, Revaz Dzodzuashvili, Murtaz Khurtzilava (Cap), Evgeniy Lovchev, Vladimir Kaplichniy, Viktor Kolotov, Vladimir Muntyan (Sergey Olshanskiy), Arkadiy Andreasyan (Vladimir Fedotov), Viktor Kuznetzov, Vladimir Onishchenko, Oleg Blokhin.
Trainer: Evgeniy Goryanskiy.

REPUBLIC OF IRELAND: Alan James Alexander Kelly, Thomas Roger Carroll, Patrick Martin Mulligan, Thomas McConville, James Paul Holmes, Eoin Kevin Joseph Colin Hand, John Michael Giles (Cap) (46 Anthony Brendan Byrne), Michael Paul Martin, Raymond Christopher Patrick Treacy, Daniel Joseph Givens, Gerard Anthony Francis Conroy (46 Jeremiah Dennehy).   Trainer: William Tuohy.

Goal: Vladimir Onishchenko (58)

140. 16.05.1973
POLAND v REPUBLIC OF IRELAND 2-0 (1-0)
Olimpijski, Wrocław
Referee: Gerhard Kunze (East Germany)   Att: 35,000
POLAND: Marian Szeja, Antoni Szymanowski, Mirosław Bulzacki, Henryk Wieczorek, Adam Musiał, Zenon Kasztelan (70 Henryk Kasperczak), Lesław Ćmikiewicz, Jerzy Kraska, Bogdan Masztaler (30 Jan Banaś (75 Kazimierz Kmiecik)), Włodzimierz Lubański (Cap), Robert Gadocha.
Trainer: Kazimierz Górski.

REPUBLIC OF IRELAND: Alan James Alexander Kelly, Thomas Roger Carroll, Patrick Martin Mulligan (Cap), Thomas McConville, James Paul Holmes, Eoin Kevin Joseph Colin Hand, Michael Paul Martin, Michael Lawlor (46 Gerard Anthony Daly), Raymond Christopher Patrick Treacy, Daniel Joseph Givens, Jeremiah Dennehy (67 Turlough O'Connor).
Trainer: William Tuohy.

Goals: Włodzimierz Lubański (44, 83)

141. 19.05.1973   10th World Cup Qualifiers
FRANCE v REPUBLIC OF IRELAND 1-1 (0-0)
Parc des Princes, Paris
Referee: Nicolae Rainea (Romania)   Attendance: 40,405
FRANCE: Georges Carnus, Raymond Domenech, Claude Quittet (Cap), Marius Trésor, Jean-Paul Rostagni, Henri Michel, Jean-Pierre Adams, Louis Floch, Hervé Revelli, Jean-Michel Larqué (61 Serge Chiesa), Georges Bereta.
Trainer: Georges Boulogne.

REPUBLIC OF IRELAND: Alan James Alexander Kelly, Thomas Roger Carroll (25 John Herrick), James Paul Holmes, Patrick Martin Mulligan (Cap), Thomas McConville, Eoin Kevin Joseph Colin Hand, Michael Paul Martin, Anthony Brendan Byrne, Jeremiah Dennehy, Raymond Christopher Patrick Treacy, Daniel Joseph Givens.
Trainer: William Tuohy.

Goals: Michael Paul Martin (83) / Serge Chiesa (78)

142. 06.06.1973
NORWAY v REPUBLIC OF IRELAND 1-1 (0-1)
Ullevaal, Oslo
Referee: Martti Hirviniemi (Finland)   Attendance: 11,084
NORWAY: Geir Karlsen, Erling Meirik, Jan Birkelund, Per Pettersen, Sigbjørn Slinning, Jan Christiansen, Johannes Vold, Tor Egil Johansen, Harald Sunde, Hans Edgar Paulsen, Tom Lund.   Trainer: George Frederick Curtis (England).

REPUBLIC OF IRELAND: Alan James Alexander Kelly, Thomas Roger Carroll, Michael Paul Martin, Patrick Martin Mulligan (Cap), James Paul Holmes, Anthony Brendan Byrne (46 Damien John Richardson), Jeremiah Dennehy, Gerard Anthony Daly, Daniel Joseph Givens, Raymond Christopher Patrick Treacy (80 Eamonn Fagan), Gerard Anthony Francis Conroy.   Trainer: Sean Thomas.

Goals: Hans Edgar Paulsen (69) / Jeremiah Dennehy (17)

143. 21.10.1973
REPUBLIC OF IRELAND v POLAND 1-0 (1-0)
Dalymount Park, Dublin

Referee: Robert Matthewson (England)   Att: 25,000

REPUBLIC OF IRELAND: Peter Thomas (46 Michael Kearns), Joseph Patrick Kinnear, James Paul Holmes, Patrick Martin Mulligan (Cap), Terence John Mancini, Michael Paul Martin, Eoin Kevin Joseph Colin Hand, Anthony Brendan Byrne, Gerard Anthony Francis Conroy (10 Jeremiah Dennehy), Raymond Christopher Patrick Treacy, Daniel Joseph Givens (85 Alfred Hale).   Trainer: John Michael Giles.

POLAND: Zygmunt Kalinowski, Zbigniew Gut, Mirosław Bulzacki, Władysław Żmuda, Antoni Szymanowski, Lesław Ćmikiewicz, Kazimierz Deyna (Cap), Henryk Kasperczak, Grzegorz Lato (73 Kazimierz Kmiecik), Zdzisław Kapka (46 Jan Domarski), Robert Gadocha.   Trainer: Kazimierz Górski.

Goal: Jeremiah Dennehy (32)

144. 05.05.1974
BRAZIL v REPUBLIC OF IRELAND 2-1 (0-0)
Maracanã, Rio de Janeiro

Referee: Guillermo Velasquez Ramírez (Colombia)
Attendance: 74,696

BRAZIL: Emerson Leão, José Maria Rodrigues Alves "Zé Maria I", Luís Edmundo Pereira, Mário Perez Ulibarri "Marinho Perez", Francisco das Chagas Marinho, José Luís Carbone, Roberto Rivelino, Jair Ventura Filho "Jairzinho", João Leiva Campos Filho "Leivinha", César Augusto da Silva Lemos "César Maluco", Paulo César Lima.
Trainer: Mário Jorge Lobo Zagallo.

REPUBLIC OF IRELAND: Peter Thomas, Joseph Patrick Kinnear, James Paul Holmes (46 Anthony Peter Dunne), Patrick Martin Mulligan, Terence John Mancini, Michael Paul Martin, Eoin Kevin Joseph Colin Hand, Gerard Anthony Francis Conroy, Raymond Christopher Patrick Treacy (46 Gerard Anthony Daly), John Michael Giles (Cap), Daniel Joseph Givens.   Trainer: John Michael Giles.

Goals: João Leiva Campos Filho "Leivinha" (50), Roberto Rivelino (56) / Terence John Mancini (70)

145. 08.05.1974
URUGUAY v REPUBLIC OF IRELAND 2-0 (2-0)
Centenario, Montevideo

Referee: Ramón Ivannoe Barreto Ruiz (Uruguay)
Attendance: 37,760

URUGUAY: Gustavo Daniel Fernández, Baudilio Jorge Jáuregui, Juan Carlos Masnik, Pablo Justo Forlán, Alberto Víctor Cardaccio, Elbio Ricardo Pavoni, José César Gómez (Pedro Alvarez), Julio César Jiménez, Fernando Morena, Walter Daniel Mantegazza (Denis Alfredo Milar), Ruben Romeo Corbo.   Trainer: Roberto Porta.

REPUBLIC OF IRELAND: Michael Kearns, Joseph Patrick Kinnear, Anthony Peter Dunne, Patrick Martin Mulligan, Terence John Mancini, Michael Paul Martin, Eoin Kevin Joseph Colin Hand, Gerard Anthony Francis Conroy, James Patrick Conway, John Michael Giles (Cap), Daniel Joseph Givens (73 Gerard Anthony Daly).
Trainer: John Michael Giles.

Goals: Fernando Morena (16, 26)

146. 12.05.1974
CHILE v REPUBLIC OF IRELAND 1-2 (1-1)
Nacional, Santiago

Referee: Mario Líra González (Chile)   Attendance: 50,000

CHILE: Leopoldo Manuel Vallejos Bravo, Juan Salvador Machuca Valdéz, Rafael González Córdova, Alfonso Lara Madrid, Rolando Moisés García Jiménez, Francisco Valdés Muñoz, Guillermo Páez Cepeda, Carlos Reinoso, Carlos Humberto Caszely Garrido, Osvaldo Castro (Julio Crisosto), Guillermo Yávar (Leonardo Véliz Díaz).
Trainer: Luis Alamos Luque.

REPUBLIC OF IRELAND: Michael Kearns, Joseph Patrick Kinnear, Anthony Peter Dunne, Patrick Martin Mulligan, Terence John Mancini, Eoin Kevin Joseph Colin Hand, Michael Paul Martin, Gerard Anthony Francis Conroy, James Patrick Conway, John Michael Giles (Cap), Daniel Joseph Givens.   Trainer: John Michael Giles.

Sent off: Carlos Reinoso (60)

Goals: Francisco Valdés Muñoz (40) /
James Conway (23), Eoin Kevin Joseph Colin Hand (85)

147. 30.10.1974   5th European Champs Qualifiers
**REPUBLIC OF IRELAND
v SOVIET UNION 3-0** (2-0)
Dalymount Park, Dublin

Referee: Erik Axelryd (Sweden)   Attendance: 31,758

REPUBLIC OF IRELAND: Patrick Joseph Christopher Roche, Joseph Patrick Kinnear, Patrick Martin Mulligan, Terence John Mancini, James Paul Holmes, Michael Paul Martin, William Brady, Stephen Derek Heighway, John Michael Giles (Cap), Daniel Joseph Givens, Raymond Christopher Patrick Treacy.   Trainer: John Michael Giles.

SOVIET UNION: Vladimir Pilguy, Sergey Nikulin, Sergey Olshanskiy (Cap), Viktor Matvienko, Vladimir Kaplichniy, Evgeniy Lovchev, Vladimir Fedotov (59 Vladimir Fëdorov), Viktor Kolotov, Vladimir Onishchenko, Vladimir Veremeev, Oleg Blokhin.   Trainer: Konstantin Beskov.

Sent off: Terence John Mancini (32)

Goals: Daniel Joseph Givens (22, 30, 70)

148. 20.11.1974   5th European Champs Qualifiers
TURKEY v REPUBLIC OF IRELAND   1-1 (0-0)
Kemal Atatürk, Izmir

Referee: Marian Srodecki (Poland)   Attendance: 67,500

TURKEY: Yasin Özdenak, Alpaslan Eratlı, Ziya Şengül, İsmail Arca, Zekeriya Alp, Selçuk Yalçıntaş, Engin Verel, Mehmet Türkkan (80 Osman Arpacıoğlu), Mehmet Oğuz, Metin Kurt, Cemil Turan.   Trainer: Coşkun Özarı.

REPUBLIC OF IRELAND: Patrick Joseph Christopher Roche, Joseph Patrick Kinnear, Patrick Martin Mulligan, Eoin Kevin Joseph Colin Hand, Anthony Peter Dunne, William Brady, Michael Paul Martin, John Michael Giles (Cap), Stephen Derek Heighway, Gerard Anthony Francis Conroy (86 Jeremiah Dennehy), Daniel Joseph Givens. Trainer: John Michael Giles.

Goals: Anthony Peter Dunne (54 own goal) / Daniel Joseph Givens (60)

149. 11.03.1975
**REPUBLIC OF IRELAND
v WEST GERMANY "B"   1-0** (0-0)
Dalymount Park, Dublin

Referee: John Bartley Homewood (England)   Att: 18,000

REPUBLIC OF IRELAND: Patrick Joseph Christopher Roche, Joseph Patrick Kinnear, Eoin Kevin Joseph Colin Hand, Anthony Peter Dunne (Cap), Michael Paul Martin, Noel Campbell (65 James Patrick Conway), Gerard Anthony Daly (83 Jeremiah Dennehy), Raymond Christopher Patrick Treacy (46 Gerard Anthony Francis Conroy), William Brady, Stephen Derek Heighway, Daniel Joseph Givens. Trainer: John Michael Giles.

GERMANY: Rudi Kargus, Manfred Kaltz, Harald Konopka, Gerhard Zimmermann, Uwe Kliemann, Erich Beer, Josef Pirrung, Wolfgang Seel, Dieter Müller, Bernd Nickel, Ferdinand Keller.

Goal: James Patrick Conway (89)

150. 10.05.1975   5th European Champs Qualifiers
**REPUBLIC OF IRELAND
v SWITZERLAND   2-1** (2-0)
Lansdowne Road, Dublin

Referee: Paul Schiller (Austria)   Attendance: 48,074

REPUBLIC OF IRELAND: Patrick Joseph Christopher Roche, Joseph Patrick Kinnear, Patrick Martin Mulligan, Eoin Kevin Joseph Colin Hand, Anthony Peter Dunne, Michael Paul Martin, John Michael Giles (Cap), William Brady, Raymond Christopher Patrick Treacy, Daniel Joseph Givens, Gerard Anthony Francis Conroy.   Trainer: John Michael Giles.

SWITZERLAND: Erich Burgener, Gilbert Guyot, René Hasler, Lucio Bizzini, Max Heer, René Botteron, Jakob Kuhn, Ernst Rutschmann, Hans-Peter Schild, Daniel Jeandupeux, Kurt Müller.   Trainer: René Hüssy.

Goals: Michael Paul Martin (2), Raymond Treacy (28) / Kurt Müller (74)

151. 18.05.1975   5th European Champs Qualifiers
**SOVIET UNION
v REPUBLIC OF IRELAND   2-1** (2-0)
Central, Kiev

Referee: René Vigliani (France)   Attendance: 84,840

SOVIET UNION: Evgeniy Rudakov, Viktor Matvienko, Anatoliy Konikov, Mikhail Fomenko, Leonid Buryak, Vladimir Troshkin, Vladimir Muntyan (46 Stefan Reshko), Vladimir Onishchenko, Viktor Kolotov (Cap), Vladimir Veremeev (84 Vladimir Fëdorov), Oleg Blokhin.
Trainer: Valeriy Lobanovskiy.

REPUBLIC OF IRELAND: Patrick Joseph Christopher Roche, Joseph Patrick Kinnear, Patrick Martin Mulligan, Eoin Kevin Joseph Colin Hand, Anthony Peter Dunne, Michael Paul Martin, John Michael Giles (Cap), William Brady, Gerard Anthony Francis Conroy, Daniel Joseph Givens, Stephen Derek Heighway.   Trainer: John Michael Giles.

Goals: Oleg Blokhin (13), Viktor Kolotov (29) / Eoin Kevin Joseph Colin Hand (79)

152. 21.05.1975   5th European Champs Qualifiers
**SWITZERLAND
v REPUBLIC OF IRELAND 1-0** (0-0)
Wankdorf, Bern
Referee: Cesar da Luz Dias Correia (Portugal)   Att: 12,793
SWITZERLAND: Erich Burgener, Gilbert Guyot, Lucio Bizzini, Serge Trinchero, Pius Fischbach, Jakob Kuhn, René Hasler, René Botteron, Ernst Rutschmann (Hans-Jörg Pfister), Kurt Müller (70 Rudolf Elsener), Daniel Jeandupeux. Trainer: René Hüssy.

REPUBLIC OF IRELAND: Patrick Joseph Christopher Roche, Anthony Peter Dunne, Patrick Martin Mulligan, Eoin Kevin Joseph Colin Hand, James Paul Holmes, Michael Paul Martin, John Michael Giles (Cap) (79 Gerard Anthony Daly), William Brady, Gerard Anthony Francis Conroy, Raymond Christopher Patrick Treacy, Daniel Joseph Givens. Trainer: John Michael Giles.

Goal: Rudolf Elsener (75)

153. 29.10.1975   5th European Champs Qualifiers
REPUBLIC OF IRELAND v TURKEY 4-0 (3-0)
Dalymount Park, Dublin
Referee: Angel Franco Martínez (Spain)   Att: 25,000
REPUBLIC OF IRELAND: Patrick Joseph Christopher Roche, Anthony Peter Dunne (83 Joseph Patrick Kinnear), James Paul Holmes, Patrick Martin Mulligan, Eoin Kevin Joseph Colin Hand, Michael Paul Martin, William Brady, John Michael Giles (Cap), Raymond Christopher Patrick Treacy, Daniel Joseph Givens, Stephen Derek Heighway (46 Gerard Anthony Francis Conroy).   Trainer: John Michael Giles.

TURKEY: Yasin Özdenak (40 Rasim Kara), Sabahattin Erboğa, Fatih Terim, İsmail Arca, Alpaslan Eratlı (33 Zafer Göncüler), Kadir Özcan, Engin Verel, Necati Özçağlayan, Ali Kemal Denizci, Gökmen Özdenak, Cemil Turan. Trainer: Coşkun Özarı.

Sent off: Michael Paul Martin

Goals: Daniel Joseph Givens (27, 28, 34, 88)

154. 24.03.1976
REPUBLIC OF IRELAND v NORWAY 3-0 (2-0)
Dalymount Park, Dublin
Referee: Patrick Partridge (England)   Attendance: 22,000
REPUBLIC OF IRELAND: Michael Kearns, Anthony Patrick Grealish, Michael Paul Martin (Cap), James Paul Holmes, Raymond Christopher O'Brien, Noel Campbell, James Patrick Conway, William Brady, Daniel Joseph Givens (81 Raymond Christopher Patrick Treacy), Michael Anthony Walsh, Stephen Derek Heighway.   Trainer: John Michael Giles.

NORWAY: Tom Rüsz Jacobsen, Helge Skuseth, Svein Grøndalen, Rune Ottesen, Sigbjørn Slinning, Svein Kvia, Tor Egil Johansen, Arild Olsen (81 Arne Dokken), Stein Thunberg, Finn Roy Vådahl, Gabriel Høyland.
Trainers: Kjell Schau Andreassen & Nils Arne Eggen.

Goals: William Brady (25), James Paul Holmes (36 pen), Michael Anthony Walsh (61)

155. 26.05.1976
POLAND v REPUBLIC OF IRELAND 0-2 (0-2)
Warta, Poznań
Referee: Josef Pouček (Czechoslovakia)   Attendance: 15,000
POLAND: Jan Tomaszewski (46 Piotr Mowlik), Henryk Wawrowski, Paweł Janas, Władysław Żmuda, Wojciech Rudy, Henryk Kasperczak, Zygmunt Garłowski (46 Roman Jakóbczak), Zbigniew Boniek (46 Jan Benigier), Grzegorz Lato (Cap), Andrzej Szarmach, Kazimierz Kmiecik. Trainer: Kazimierz Górski.

REPUBLIC OF IRELAND: Michael Kearns, Anthony Patrick Grealish, Raymond Christopher O'Brien, Patrick Martin Mulligan (Cap), James Paul Holmes, Michael Paul Martin, James Patrick Conway (46 Jeremiah Dennehy), William Brady, Gerard Anthony Francis Conroy, Michael Anthony Walsh (32 Raymond Christopher Patrick Treacy), Daniel Joseph Givens. Trainer: John Michael Giles.

Goals: Daniel Joseph Givens (5, 11)

156. 08.09.1976
ENGLAND v REPUBLIC OF IRELAND 1-1 (1-0)
Wembley, London
Referee: Hugh Alexander (Scotland)   Attendance: 51,000
ENGLAND: Raymond Neal Clemence, Colin Todd, Paul Edward Madeley, Trevor John Cherry, Roy Leslie McFarland, Brian Greenhoff, Kevin Joseph Keegan (Cap), Raymond Colin Wilkins, Stuart James Pearson, Trevor David Brooking, Charles Frederick George (66 Gordon Alec Hill). Manager: Donald Revie.

REPUBLIC OF IRELAND: Michael Kearns, Patrick Martin Mulligan, James Paul Holmes, Michael Paul Martin, David Anthony O'Leary, William Brady, Gerard Anthony Daly, Gerard Anthony Francis Conroy, Stephen Derek Heighway, John Michael Giles (Cap), Daniel Joseph Givens. Trainer: John Michael Giles.

Goals: Stuart Pearson (45) / Gerard Anthony Daly (52 pen)

157. 13.10.1976
TURKEY v REPUBLIC OF IRELAND 3-3 (0-2)
19 Mayis, Ankara
Referee: Miloš Čajić (Yugoslavia)
TURKEY: Rasim Kara, Turgay Semercioğlu, Cemil Ustaoğlu, Alpaslan Eratlı, İsmail Arca, Fatih Terim, İsa Ertürk, Kemal Batmaz, Mehmet Özgül (70 Reşit Kaynak), Ali Kemal Denizci, Cemil Turan.   Trainer: Coşkun Özarı.

REPUBLIC OF IRELAND: Michael Kearns, Joseph John Wary Waters, Patrick Martin Mulligan, Michael Paul Martin, James Paul Holmes, Gerard Anthony Daly, John Michael Giles (Cap), William Brady, Gerard Anthony Francis Conroy, Francis Anthony Stapleton, Daniel Joseph Givens.
Trainer: John Michael Giles.

Goals: Cemil Turan (51, 70), İsa Ertürk (65) / Francis Anthony Stapleton (3), Gerard Anthony Daly (14), Joseph John Wary Waters (80)

158. 17.11.1976   11th World Cup Qualifiers
FRANCE v REPUBLIC OF IRELAND 2-0 (0-0)
Parc des Princes, Paris
Referee: Dušan Maksimović (Yugoslavia)   Att: 43,437
FRANCE: Dominique Baratelli, Gérard Janvion, Christian Lopez, Marius Trésor (Cap), Maxime Bossis, Dominique Bathenay, Raymond Kéruzoré, Michel Platini, Dominique Rocheteau, Bernard Lacombe (71 Olivier Rouyer), Didier Six. Trainer: Michel Hidalgo.

REPUBLIC OF IRELAND: Michael Kearns, Patrick Martin Mulligan, James Paul Holmes, Michael Paul Martin, David Anthony O'Leary, Gerard Anthony Daly, John Michael Giles (Cap), William Brady, Francis Anthony Stapleton (62 Michael Anthony Walsh), Stephen Derek Heighway, Daniel Joseph Givens.   Trainer: John Michael Giles.

Goals: Michel Platini (47), Dominique Bathenay (88)

159. 09.02.1977
REPUBLIC OF IRELAND v SPAIN 0-1 (0-1)
Lansdowne Road, Dublin
Referee: John Hunting (England)   Attendance: 22,000
REPUBLIC OF IRELAND: Michael Kearns (46 Gerald Joseph Peyton), Michael Paul Martin (Cap), David Anthony O'Leary, James Paul Holmes, Raymond Christopher O'Brien, Anthony Macken, Noel Campbell, William Brady, Daniel Joseph Givens, Francis Anthony Stapleton, Stephen Derek Heighway.   Trainer: John Michael Giles.

SPAIN: Miguel Ángel González Suárez, José Luis Capón González, Miguel Bernardo Bianquetti "Migueli", Ignacio "Iñaki" Cortabarría Arrabategui (46 Antonio Olmo Ramírez), José Antonio Camacho Alfaro, José Martínez Sánchez "Pirri" (Cap) (75 José Antonio Ramos Huete), Ángel María Villar Llona, Jesús María Satrústegui Azpiroz, Enrique Castro González "Quini" (46 Santiago Idígoras Bilbao), Juan Manuel Asensi Ripoll, José Francisco Rojo Arroitia "Chechu Rojo I".
Trainer: Ladislao Kubala.

Goal: Jesús María Satrústegui Azpiroz (10)

160. 30.03.1977   11th World Cup Qualifiers
REPUBLIC OF IRELAND v FRANCE 1-0 (0-0)
Lansdowne Road, Dublin
Referee: Erich Linemayr (Austria)   Attendance: 48,000
REPUBLIC OF IRELAND: Michael Kearns, Patrick Martin Mulligan, Michael Paul Martin, David Anthony O'Leary, James Paul Holmes, Gerard Anthony Daly, John Michael Giles (Cap), William Brady, Daniel Joseph Givens, Raymond Christopher Patrick Treacy, Stephen Derek Heighway.
Trainer: John Michael Giles.

FRANCE: André Rey, Gérard Janvion, Patrice Rio, Christian Lopez (Cap), Thierry Tusseau, Dominique Bathenay, Michel Platini, Christian Synaeghel, Olivier Rouyer, Bernard Lacombe, Dominique Rocheteau.   Trainer: Michel Hidalgo.

Goal: William Brady (11)

161. 24.04.1977
REPUBLIC OF IRELAND v POLAND 0-0
Dalymount Park, Dublin
Referee: Robert Matthewson (England)   Att: 20,000
REPUBLIC OF IRELAND: Ronald Healey, Patrick Martin Mulligan, Raymond Christopher O'Brien, Mark Thomas Lawrenson (85 Jeremiah Dennehy), James Paul Holmes, James Patrick Conway, Michael Paul Martin, Raymond Christopher Patrick Treacy, Michael Anthony Walsh, John Michael Giles (Cap), Gerard Anthony Francis Conroy.
Trainer: John Michael Giles.

POLAND: Jan Tomaszewski, Marek Dziuba, Władysław Żmuda, Henryk Wieczorek, Czesław Boguszewicz, Henryk Kasperczak, Kazimierz Deyna (Cap) (46 Zbigniew Boniek), Bogdan Masztaler, Grzegorz Lato, Andrzej Szarmach, Stanisław Terlecki.   Trainer: Jacek Gmoch.

162. 01.06.1977   11th World Cup Qualifiers
BULGARIA v REPUBLIC OF IRELAND 2-1 (1-0)
"Vasil Levski", Sofia
Referee: Nikolaos Zlatanos (Greece)   Attendance: 35,214
BULGARIA: Rumiancho Goranov, Borislav Dimitrov, Kiril Ivkov (Cap), Tsonio Vasilev, Nikolai Arabov, Todor Barzov (61 Andrei Jeliazkov), Radoslav Zdravkov (53 Atanas Aleksandrov), Krasimir Borisov, Kiril Milanov, Pavel Panov, Chavdar Tsvetkov.
Trainer: Hristo Mladenov & Ioncho Arsov.
REPUBLIC OF IRELAND: Michael Kearns, Patrick Martin Mulligan, Michael Paul Martin, David Anthony O'Leary, James Paul Holmes, William Brady, Gerard Anthony Daly (79 Noel Campbell), Francis Anthony Stapleton, John Michael Giles (Cap), Stephen Derek Heighway, Daniel Joseph Givens.
Trainer: John Michael Giles.
Sent off: Michael Paul Martin (82), Noel Campbell (82)
Goals: Pavel Panov (14), Andrei Jeliazkov (76) / Daniel Joseph Givens (46)

163. 12.10.1977   11th World Cup Qualifiers
REPUBLIC OF IRELAND v BULGARIA 0-0
Lansdowne Road, Dublin
Referee: Sergio Gonella (Italia)   Attendance: 25,000
REPUBLIC OF IRELAND: Gerald Joseph Peyton, Patrick Martin Mulligan, David Anthony O'Leary, Mark Thomas Lawrenson, James Paul Holmes, Gerard Anthony Daly, John Michael Giles (Cap), William Brady, Daniel Joseph Givens, Francis Anthony Stapleton, Stephen Derek Heighway.
Trainer: John Michael Giles.
BULGARIA: Stefan Staikov, Tsonio Vasilev (72 Nikolai Grancharov), Boris Angelov, Kiril Ivkov (Cap), Nikolai Arabov, Georgi Bonev, Angel Kolev, Vanio Kostov, Pavel Panov, Spas Djevizov, Chavdar Tsvetkov (54 Atanas Aleksandrov).
Trainer: Hristo Mladenov & Ioncho Arsov.

164. 05.04.1978
REPUBLIC OF IRELAND v TURKEY 4-2 (4-0)
Lansdowne Road, Dublin
Referee: Hugh Alexander (Scotland)   Attendance: 10,000
REPUBLIC OF IRELAND: Gerald Joseph Peyton, David Francis Langan, Noel Synnott, James Paul Holmes, Maurice Celsus Daly, Gerard Anthony Daly (67 Simon Braddish), John Michael Giles (Cap), Augustine Ashley Grimes, Paul Gerard McGee, Raymond Christopher Patrick Treacy, Gerard Joseph Ryan.   Trainer: John Michael Giles.
TURKEY: Rasim Kara (24 Şenol Güneş), Turgay Semercioğlu, Erdoğan Arica, Erol Togay, Necati Özçağlayan, Engin Verel, Volkan Yayim, Önder Mustafaoğlu, Ali Kemal Denizci, Cemil Turan, Sedat III Özden (80 Coşkun Demirkıran).
Trainer: Metin Türel.
Goals: John Michael Giles (3), Paul Gerard McGee (12), Raymond Christopher Patrick Treacy (18, 23) / Önder Mustafaoğlu (55), Cemil Turan (61)

165. 12.04.1978
POLAND v REPUBLIC OF IRELAND 3-0 (0-0)
ŁKS, Łódź
Referee: Klaus Scheurell (East Germany)   Att: 30,000
POLAND: Jan Tomaszewski, Antoni Szymanowski, Roman Wójcicki, Władysław Żmuda, Mirosław Justek (65 Rudolf Wojtowicz), Adam Nawałka (72 Włodzimierz Mazur), Kazimierz Deyna (Cap), Zbigniew Boniek, Grzegorz Lato, Włodzimierz Lubański, Andrzej Szarmach.
Trainer: Jacek Gmoch.
REPUBLIC OF IRELAND: Gerald Joseph Peyton, Eamon Gregg, Mark Thomas Lawrenson, Noel Synnott, James Paul Holmes, Simon Braddish, John Michael Giles (Cap) (79 Jerome Clarke), Augustine Ashley Grimes, Carl Mucklan, Raymond Christopher Patrick Treacy, Maurice Celsus Daly.
Trainer: John Michael Giles.
Goals: Zbigniew Boniek (52), Kazimierz Deyna (60), Włodzimierz Mazur (82)

166. 21.05.1978
NORWAY v REPUBLIC OF IRELAND 0-0
Ullevaal, Oslo
Referee: Erik Fredriksson (Sweden)   Attendance: 11,500
NORWAY: Tom Rüsz Jacobsen, Helge Karlsen, Tore Kordahl (88 Jan Birkelund), Einar Jan Aas, Trond Pedersen, Stein Thunberg, Tor Egil Johansen, Yngve Andersen (85 Tom Jacobsen), Arne Larsen Økland (60 Gabriel Høyland), Odd Iversen, Hallvar Thoresen (46 Pål Jacobsen).
Trainer: Tor Røste Fossen.
REPUBLIC OF IRELAND: Michael Kearns, David Francis Langan (46 Mark Thomas Lawrenson), David Anthony O'Leary, Patrick Martin Mulligan, James Paul Holmes, Anthony Patrick Grealish, John Michael Giles (Cap), William Brady (23 Augustine Ashley Grimes), Stephen Derek Heighway, Francis Anthony Stapleton, Daniel Joseph Givens (60 Paul Gerard McGee).   Trainer: John Michael Giles.

167. 24.05.1978   6th European Champs Qualifiers
DENMARK v REPUBLIC OF IRELAND 3-3 (1-2)

Idrætsparken, København

Referee: Jan Beck (Holland)   Attendance: 28,900

DENMARK: Birger Jensen, Johnny Hansen, Henning Munk Jensen, Per Røntved (Cap), Søren Lerby, Morten Olsen (Jan Højland), Benny Nielsen, Kristen Nygaard (Frank Arnesen), Jan Sørensen, Henning Jensen, Jørgen Kristensen.
Trainer: Kurt Børge Nielsen.

REPUBLIC OF IRELAND: Michael Kearns, Patrick Martin Mulligan, David Anthony O'Leary, Gerard Anthony Daly, James Paul Holmes (51 Eamon Gregg), Mark Thomas Lawrenson, John Michael Giles (Cap), Anthony Patrick Grealish, Francis Anthony Stapleton, Stephen Derek Heighway, Daniel Joseph Givens (46 Paul Gerard McGee).
Trainer: John Michael Giles.

Goals: Henning Jensen (31), Benny Nielsen (79 pen), Søren Lerby (80) / Francis Anthony Stapleton (11), Anthony Patrick Grealish (25), Gerard Anthony Daly (65)

168. 20.09.1978   6th European Champs Qualifiers
REPUBLIC OF IRELAND v NORTHERN IRELAND 0-0

Lansdowne Road, Dublin

Referee: Francis Rion (Belgium)   Attendance: 46,000

REPUBLIC OF IRELAND: Michael Kearns, Anthony Patrick Grealish, Mark Thomas Lawrenson, Noel Synnott, James Paul Holmes, William Brady, Gerard Anthony Daly, John Michael Giles (Cap), Paul Gerard McGee, Francis Anthony Stapleton (54 Michael Anthony Walsh), Stephen Derek Heighway (63 Daniel Joseph Givens).   Trainer: John Michael Giles.

NORTHERN IRELAND: Patrick Anthony Jennings, Patrick James Rice, Samuel Nelson, Christopher James Nicholl, Alan Hunter (72 Bryan Hamilton), James Michael Nicholl, Martin Hugh Michael O'Neill, David McCreery, Gerard Joseph Armstrong, Samuel Baxter McIlroy, Derek William Spence (69 George Terence Cochrane).
Manager: Robert Dennis Blanchflower.

169. 25.10.1978   6th European Champs Qualifiers
REPUBLIC OF IRELAND v ENGLAND 1-1 (1-1)

Lansdowne Road, Dublin

Referee: Heinz Aldinger (West Germany)   Att: 55,000

REPUBLIC OF IRELAND: Michael Kearns, Patrick Martin Mulligan (Cap), Mark Thomas Lawrenson, David Anthony O'Leary (73 Eamon Gregg), James Paul Holmes, Gerard Anthony Daly, William Brady, Anthony Patrick Grealish, Paul Gerard McGee (65 Francis Anthony Stapleton), Gerard Joseph Ryan, Daniel Joseph Givens.   Trainer: John Michael Giles.

ENGLAND: Raymond Neal Clemence, Philip George Neal, Michael Dennis Mills, Raymond Colin Wilkins, David Victor Watson (22 Philip Brian Thompson), Emlyn Walter Hughes (Cap), Kevin Joseph Keegan, Steven James Coppell, Robert Dennis Latchford, Trevor David Brooking, Peter Simon Barnes (81 Anthony Stewart Woodcock).
Manager: Ronald Greenwood.

Goals: Gerard Anthony Daly (27) / Robert Latchford (8)

170. 02.05.1979   6th European Champs Qualifiers
REPUBLIC OF IRELAND v DENMARK 2-0 (1-0)

Lansdowne Road, Dublin

Referee: Michel Vautrot (France)   Attendance: 35,000

REPUBLIC OF IRELAND: Gerald Joseph Peyton, Eamon Gregg, Michael Paul Martin, Patrick Martin Mulligan, James Paul Holmes, Gerard Anthony Daly, John Michael Giles (Cap), William Brady, Austin William Patrick Hayes (61 Michael Anthony Walsh), Francis Anthony Stapleton, Daniel Joseph Givens (72 Paul Gerard McGee).
Trainer: John Michael Giles.

DENMARK: Ole Kjær, Flemming Nielsen, Per Røntved (Cap), Lars Larsen, Søren Lerby, Flemming Lund, Morten Olsen, Frank Arnesen, Benny Nielsen (75 Henrik Agerbeck), Allan Rodenkam Simonsen, Preben Elkjær-Larsen.
Trainer: Kurt Børge Nielsen.

Goals: Gerard Anthony Daly (44), Daniel Joseph Givens (66)

171. 19.05.1979   6th European Champs Qualifiers
BULGARIA v REPUBLIC OF IRELAND 1-0 (0-0)

"Vasil Levski", Sofia

Referee: Josef Bucek (Austria)   Attendance: 25,000

BULGARIA: Iordan Filipov, Nikolai Grancharov, Kiril Ivkov (Cap), Ivan Iliev, Tsonio Vasilev, Radoslav Zdravkov, Krasimir Borisov, Pavel Panov, Voin Voinov, Andrei Jeliazkov, Chavdar Tsvetkov.   Trainer: Tsvetan Ilchev.

REPUBLIC OF IRELAND: Gerald Joseph Peyton, Eamon Gregg, David Anthony O'Leary, Michael Paul Martin, James Paul Holmes (61 Patrick Martin Mulligan), Gerard Anthony Daly, John Michael Giles (Cap), William Brady, Michael Anthony Walsh (75 Paul Gerard McGee), Daniel Joseph Givens, Stephen Derek Heighway.
Trainer: John Michael Giles.

Goal: Chavdar Tsvetkov (81)

172. 22.05.1979
REPUBLIC OF IRELAND
v WEST GERMANY 1-3 (1-1)
Lansdowne Road, Dublin
Referee: George Courtney (England)   Attendance: 25,000
REPUBLIC OF IRELAND: Gerald Joseph Peyton, Eamon Gregg, Michael Paul Martin, David Anthony O'Leary, Patrick Martin Mulligan, Anthony Patrick Grealish, John Michael Giles (Cap), William Brady, Francis Anthony Stapleton (67 Michael Anthony Walsh), Daniel Joseph Givens (16 Brendan Richard O'Callaghan), Gerard Joseph Ryan.   Trainer: John Michael Giles.

GERMANY: Josef Maier (Cap) (46 Dieter Burdenski), Manfred Kaltz, Bernhard Cullmann, Karlheinz Förster, Bernd Förster, Herbert Zimmermann (70 William Hartwig), Bernd Schuster, Hans Müller (46 Walter Kelsch), Karl-Heinz Rummenigge (70 Caspar Memering), Dieter Hoeneß, Klaus Allofs.   Trainer: Josef Derwall.

Goals: Gerard Joseph Ryan (26) / Karl-Heinz Rummenigge (29), Walter Kelsch (81), Dieter Hoeneß (90)

173. 11.09.1979
WALES v REPUBLIC OF IRELAND 2-1 (1-1)
Vetch Field, Swansea
Referee: Stevens (England)   Attendance: 6,825
WALES: William David Davies, Peter Nicholas, Joseph Patrick Jones, Leighton Phillips, George Frederick Berry, John Francis Mahoney, Terence Charles Yorath, Brian Flynn, Ian Patrick Walsh, Alan Thomas Curtis, Michael Reginald Thomas.   Manager: Michael Smith.

REPUBLIC OF IRELAND: Gerald Joseph Peyton, Eamon Gregg, David Anthony O'Leary, Michael Paul Martin, Patrick Martin Mulligan (Cap), Anthony Patrick Grealish, William Brady, Jeremiah Michael Murphy, Francis Anthony Stapleton, Brendan Richard O'Callaghan, Gerard Joseph Ryan.   Trainer: John Michael Giles.

Goals: Ian Patrick Walsh (24), Alan Thomas Curtis (53) / Joseph Patrick Jones (22 own goal)

174. 26.09.1979
CZECHOSLOVAKIA
v REPUBLIC OF IRELAND 4-1 (2-0)
Sparta, Praha
Referee: Anatoly Milchenko (Soviet Union)   Att: 10,000
CZECHOSLOVAKIA: Zdeněk Hruška, Jozef Barmoš, Rostislav Vojáček, Anton Ondruš (Cap), Koloman Gögh, Ján Kozák, František Štambachr (62 Karel Kroupa), Antonín Panenka (62 Jaroslav Pollák), Marián Masný, Zdeněk Nehoda, Miroslav Gajdůšek.   Trainer: Jozef Vengloš.

REPUBLIC OF IRELAND: Gerald Joseph Peyton, Eamon Gregg, Patrick Martin Mulligan (Cap), Pierce O'Leary, John Anthony Devine (88 John Christopher Patrick Anderson), Michael Paul Martin, Anthony Patrick Grealish, Frank O'Brien, Damien John Richardson (83 Jeffrey George Chandler), Paul Gerard McGee, Terence Christopher Donovan (46 Raymond Christopher Patrick Treacy).   Trainer: John Michael Giles.

Goals: Anton Ondruš (5), Zdeněk Nehoda (35), Karel Kroupa (72), Marián Masný (90) / Paul McGee (89)

175. 17.10.1979   6th European Champs Qualifiers
REPUBLIC OF IRELAND v BULGARIA 3-0 (1-0)
Lansdowne Road, Dublin
Referee: Heinz Einbeck (East Germany)   Att: 22,000
REPUBLIC OF IRELAND: Gerald Joseph Peyton, Patrick Martin Mulligan (Cap), David Anthony O'Leary, Pierce O'Leary, Augustine Ashley Grimes, Anthony Patrick Grealish, Michael Paul Martin, William Brady, Francis Anthony Stapleton, Paul Gerard McGee, Stephen Derek Heighway.   Trainer: John Michael Giles.

BULGARIA: Rumiancho Goranov (Cap), Tsonio Vasilev, Georgi Dimitrov, Georgi Bonev, Ivan Iliev, Vanio Kostov (46 Kostadin Kostadinov), Todor Barzov, Plamen Markov, Andrei Jeliazkov, Boicho Velichkov, Chavdar Tsvetkov.   Trainer: Dobromir Tashkov.

Goals: Michael Martin (18), Anthony Patrick Grealish (46), Francis Anthony Stapleton (83)

176. 29.10.1979
REPUBLIC OF IRELAND
v UNITED STATES 3-2 (0-1)
Lansdowne Road, Dublin
Referee: Eamonn Farrell (Republic of Ireland)   Att: 17,000
REPUBLIC OF IRELAND: Michael Kearns, Christopher William Gerard Hughton, Michael Paul Martin (Cap), Pierce O'Leary (65 John Christopher Patrick Anderson), Augustine Ashley Grimes, Jeffrey George Chandler (46 Patrick Martin Mulligan), Anthony Patrick Grealish, Jeremiah Michael Murphy, Paul Gerard McGee (46 Daniel Joseph Givens), Brendan Richard O'Callaghan, Stephen Derek Heighway.   Trainer: John Michael Giles.

UNITED STATES: Winston DuBose, Gregory Makowski, Tyrone Keough, Steve Pecher (Cap), Anthony Bellinger, Angelo di Bernardo (57 Percival Joseph van der Beck), Ringo Julio Cantillo, Boris Bandov, Louis Nanchoff, Gregory Villa, Mark Liveric (85 Njego Pesa).   Trainer: Walter Chyzowich.

Sent off: Gregory Villa

Goals: Anthony Grealish (64), Daniel Joseph Givens (66), John Christopher Patrick Anderson (68) / Angelo di Bernardo (11), Gregory Villa (63)

177. 21.11.1979   6th European Champs Qualifiers
**NORTHERN IRELAND
v REPUBLIC OF IRELAND 1-0** (0-0)
Windsor Park, Belfast

Referee: André Daina (Switzerland)   Attendance: 15,000

NORTHERN IRELAND: Patrick Anthony Jennings, James Michael Nicholl, Samuel Nelson, Christopher James Nicholl, Alan Hunter, David McCreery, Martin Hugh Michael O'Neill (66 Thomas Cassidy), Samuel Baxter McIlroy, Gerard Joseph Armstrong, Derek William Spence, Victor Moreland. Manager: Robert Dennis Blanchflower.

REPUBLIC OF IRELAND: Michael Kearns, John Anthony Devine, David Anthony O'Leary, Michael Paul Martin (Cap), Augustine Ashley Grimes, Gerard Anthony Daly (53 Joseph John Wary Waters), Pierce O'Leary, Anthony Patrick Grealish, Francis Anthony Stapleton, Paul Gerard McGee (75 Daniel Joseph Givens), Stephen Derek Heighway.
Trainer: John Michael Giles.

Goal: Gerard Joseph Armstrong (54)

178. 06.02.1980   6th European Champs Qualifiers
ENGLAND v REPUBLIC OF IRELAND 2-0 (1-0)
Wembley, London

Referee: Klaus Scheurell (East Germany)   Att: 90,299

ENGLAND: Raymond Neal Clemence, Trevor John Cherry, Kenneth Graham Sansom, Philip Brian Thompson, David Victor Watson, Bryan Robson, Kevin Joseph Keegan (Cap), Terence McDermott, David Edward Johnson (60 Steven James Coppell), Anthony Stewart Woodcock, Laurence Paul Cunningham.   Manager: Ronald Greenwood.

REPUBLIC OF IRELAND: Gerald Joseph Peyton (60 Ronald Healey), Christopher William Gerard Hughton, David Anthony O'Leary (68 Pierce O'Leary), Mark Thomas Lawrenson, Augustine Ashley Grimes, Gerard Anthony Daly, Anthony Patrick Grealish, William Brady (Cap), Frank O'Brien, Francis Anthony Stapleton, Stephen Derek Heighway.
Trainer: John Michael Giles.

Goals: Kevin Joseph Keegan (34, 74)

179. 26.03.1980   12th World Cup Qualifiers
CYPRUS v REPUBLIC OF IRELAND 2-3 (1-3)
GSP, Nicosia

Referee: Zvi Sharir (Israel)   Attendance: 10,000

CYPRUS: Fanos Stylianou, Andreas Papacostas, Fytos Neophytou, Stavros Papadopoulos, Stefanos Lysandrou, Nicos Pantziaras, Filippos Dimitriou (46 Marios Tsingis), Loizos Mavroudis, Sotiris Kaiafas, Andreas Kissonergis, Andreas Kanaris (75 Petros Theofanous).   Trainer: Costas Talianos.

REPUBLIC OF IRELAND: Gerald Joseph Peyton, Anthony Patrick Grealish, Augustine Ashley Grimes, Mark Thomas Lawrenson, David Anthony O'Leary, Gerard Anthony Daly, William Brady (Cap), Jeremiah Michael Murphy (72 Frank O'Brien), Stephen Derek Heighway (53 Gerard Joseph Ryan), Francis Anthony Stapleton, Paul Gerard McGee.
Trainer: John Michael Giles.

Goals: Nicos Pantziaras (28), Sotiris Kaiafas (73 pen) / Paul Gerard McGee (8, 37), Mark Thomas Lawrenson (23)

180. 30.04.1980
**REPUBLIC OF IRELAND
v SWITZERLAND 2-0** (2-0)
Lansdowne Road, Dublin

Referee: Clive Thomas (Wales)   Attendance: 20,000

REPUBLIC OF IRELAND: Gerald Joseph Peyton, David Francis Langan, Mark Thomas Lawrenson, Kevin Bernard Moran, Christopher William Gerard Hughton, Gerard Anthony Daly, Anthony Patrick Grealish (Cap), Gary Patrick Waddock, Paul Gerard McGee, Daniel Joseph Givens, Gerard Joseph Ryan.   Trainer: Alan Kelly.

SWITZERLAND: Karl Engel, Jörg Stohler, Heinz Hermann, Gérald Coutaz, Lucio Bizzini, Marc Schnyder (46 Roger Wehrli), Umberto Barberis, René Botteron, Claude Andrey (76 Ernie Maissen), Hans-Jörg Pfister, Claudio Sulser.
Trainer: Léo Walker.

Goals: Daniel Joseph Givens (12), Gerard Anthony Daly (41)

181. 16.05.1980
REPUBLIC OF IRELAND v ARGENTINA 0-1 (0-1)
Lansdowne Road, Dublin

Referee: George Courtney (England)   Attendance: 35,000

REPUBLIC OF IRELAND: Gerald Joseph Peyton, David Francis Langan, Pierce O'Leary, Kevin Bernard Moran, Christopher William Gerard Hughton, Anthony Patrick Grealish (Cap) (46 Raymond Christopher O'Brien), Gerard Anthony Daly, Gary Patrick Waddock (77 Gerard Joseph Ryan), Stephen Derek Heighway, Paul Gerard McGee, Daniel Joseph Givens.   Trainer: Eoin Kevin Joseph Colin Hand.

ARGENTINA: Ubaldo Matildo Fillol, Jorge Mario Olguín, Juan Ernesto Simón, Daniel Alberto Passarella (Cap), Alberto César Tarantini, Juan Alberto Barbas, Américo Rubén Gallego, Diego Armando Maradona, Santiago Santamaría, Ramón Ángel Díaz (73 Gabriel Humberto Calderón), José Daniel Valencia.   Trainer: César Luis Menotti.

Goal: José Daniel Valencia (28)

182. 10.09.1980   12th World Cup Qualifiers
REPUBLIC OF IRELAND v HOLLAND 2-1 (0-0)
Lansdowne Road, Dublin
Referee: Henning Lund-Sørensen (Denmark)   Att: 25,000
REPUBLIC OF IRELAND: Gerald Joseph Peyton, David Francis Langan, David Anthony O'Leary, Pierce O'Leary, Christopher William Gerard Hughton, Mark Thomas Lawrenson, Gerard Anthony Daly, Anthony Patrick Grealish, William Brady (Cap), Francis Anthony Stapleton, Daniel Joseph Givens.   Trainer: Eoin Kevin Joseph Colin Hand.
HOLLAND: Johannes Frederik Hiele, Hubertus Johannes Nicolaas Wijnstekers, Michael Antonius Bernardus van de Korput (46 Johannes Antonius Bernardus Metgod), Ronald Spelbos, Ernestus Wilhelmus Johannes Brandts, Dirk Hendrikus Schoenaker (63 Wilhelmus Antonius van de Kerkhof), Johannes Wilhelmus Peters (Cap), Franciscus Johannes Thijssen, Jan van Deinsen, Antoine van Mierlo, Simon Melkianus Tahamata.   Trainer: Johannes Zwartkruis.
Goals: Gerard Anthony Daly (78), Mark Lawrenson (84) / Simon Melkianus Tahamata (57)

183. 15.10.1980   12th World Cup Qualifiers
REPUBLIC OF IRELAND v BELGIUM 1-1 (1-1)
Lansdowne Road, Dublin
Referee: Norbert Rolles (Luxembourg)   Attendance: 40,000
REPUBLIC OF IRELAND: Gerald Joseph Peyton, David Francis Langan, Kevin Bernard Moran, Mark Thomas Lawrenson, Christopher William Gerard Hughton, William Brady (Cap), Gerard Anthony Daly, Anthony Patrick Grealish, Francis Anthony Stapleton, Stephen Derek Heighway, Daniel Joseph Givens (58 Paul Gerard McGee).
Trainer: Eoin Kevin Joseph Colin Hand.
BELGIUM: Jean-Marie Pfaff, Eric Gerets, Luc Millecamps (88 Michel De Wolf), Walter Meeuws, Michel Renquin, Wilfried Van Moer (84 Joseph Heyligen), Ludo Coeck, René Vandereycken, Albert Cluytens, Erwin Vandenbergh, Jan Ceulemans.   Trainer: Guy Thys.
Goals: Anthony Patrick Grealish (42) / Albert Cluytens (13)

184. 28.10.1980   12th World Cup Qualifiers
FRANCE v REPUBLIC OF IRELAND 2-0 (1-0)
Parc des Princes, Paris
Referee: Augusto Lamo Castillo (Spain)   Att: 44,800
FRANCE: Dominique Dropsy, Patrick Battiston, Léonard Specht, Christian Lopez, Maxime Bossis, Jean-François Larios, Jean Amadou Tigana, Michel Platini (Cap) (74 Jean Petit), Dominique Rocheteau, Bernard Lacombe (66 Atre Jacques "Zimako"), Didier Six.   Trainer: Michel Hidalgo.
REPUBLIC OF IRELAND: Gerald Joseph Peyton, David Francis Langan, Mark Thomas Lawrenson, Kevin Bernard Moran, Christopher William Gerard Hughton, Michael Paul Martin (78 Gerard Joseph Ryan), William Brady (Cap), Anthony Patrick Grealish, Stephen Derek Heighway, Francis Anthony Stapleton, Michael John Robinson.
Trainer: Eoin Kevin Joseph Colin Hand.
Goals: Michel Platini (11), Atre Jacques "Zimako" (77)

185. 19.11.1980   12th World Cup Qualifiers
REPUBLIC OF IRELAND v CYPRUS 6-0 (4-0)
Lansdowne Road, Dublin
Referee: Eysteinn Guðmundsson (Iceland)   Att: 25,000
REPUBLIC OF IRELAND: Gerald Joseph Peyton, David Francis Langan, Mark Thomas Lawrenson, Kevin Bernard Moran, Christopher William Gerard Hughton, Gerard Anthony Daly, William Brady (Cap), Anthony Patrick Grealish, Stephen Derek Heighway, Francis Anthony Stapleton, Michael John Robinson (74 Daniel Joseph Givens).
Trainer: Eoin Kevin Joseph Colin Hand.
CYPRUS: Andreas Constantinou II, Filippos Kalotheou, Loukis Louka, Stefanos Lysandrou, Nicos Pantziaras, Klitos Erotokritou, Fanis Theofanous, Yiannakis Yiangoudakis, Sotiris Kaiafas (46 Chrysanthos Lagos), Marios Tsingis, Andros Miamiliotis (63 Loizos Mavroudis).
Trainer: Costas Talianos.
Goals: Gerard Daly (10 pen, 24), Anthony Grealish (25), Michael John Robinson (29), Francis Anthony Stapleton (46), Christopher William Gerard Hughton (63)

186. 24.02.1981
REPUBLIC OF IRELAND v WALES 1-3 (1-2)
Tolka Park, Dublin
Referee: Peter Geoffrey Reeves (England)   Att: 15,000
REPUBLIC OF IRELAND: James Martin McDonagh, David Francis Langan, Brendan Richard O'Callaghan, James Paul Holmes, Christopher William Gerard Hughton, Anthony Patrick Grealish (Cap), Gerard Anthony Daly, Gary Patrick Waddock, Daniel Joseph Givens (46 Kevin Bernard Moran), Eamonn Gerard O'Keefe, Stephen Derek Heighway.
Trainer: Eoin Kevin Joseph Colin Hand.
WALES: William David Davies, Peter Nicholas, Kevin Ratcliffe, Paul Terence Price, Joseph Patrick Jones, Terence David John Boyle, Terence Charles Yorath, Carl Stephen Harris, Brian Flynn, Ian Patrick Walsh, Leighton James.
Manager: Harold Michael England.
Goals: Anthony Patrick Grealish (25) / Paul Terence Price (34), Terence David John Boyle (38), Terence Charles Yorath (89)

187. 25.03.1981   12th World Cup Qualifiers
BELGIUM v REPUBLIC OF IRELAND   1-0 (0-0)
Heysel, Bruxelles
Referee: Raul Joaquim Fernandes Nazarre (Portugal)
Attendance: 37,978

BELGIUM: Michel Preud'homme, Eric Gerets, Luc Millecamps, Walter Meeuws, Michel Renquin, Ludo Coeck (76 Williy Wellens), René Vandereycken, Raymond Mommens (84 Frank Vercauteren), Albert Cluytens, Erwin Vandenbergh, Jan Ceulemans.   Trainer: Guy Thys.

REPUBLIC OF IRELAND: James Martin McDonagh, David Francis Langan, Michael Paul Martin, Kevin Bernard Moran, Christopher William Gerard Hughton, Gerard Anthony Daly, Anthony Patrick Grealish, William Brady (Cap), Michael John Robinson, Francis Anthony Stapleton (71 Michael Anthony Walsh), Stephen Derek Heighway.
Trainer: Eoin Kevin Joseph Colin Hand.

Goal: Jan Ceulemans (87)

188. 29.04.1981
REPUBLIC OF IRELAND
v CZECHOSLOVAKIA   3-1 (1-0)
Lansdowne Road, Dublin

Referee: Alfred William Grey (England)   Attendance: 8,000

REPUBLIC OF IRELAND: James Martin McDonagh, David Francis Langan, David Anthony O'Leary (Cap), Kevin Bernard Moran, John Anthony Devine, Gerard Anthony Daly (63 Ronald Andrew Whelan), Michael Paul Martin, Augustine Ashley Grimes, Francis Anthony Stapleton, Michael Anthony Walsh, Kevin O'Callaghan.
Trainer: Eoin Kevin Joseph Colin Hand.

CZECHOSLOVAKIA: Stanislav Seman, František Jakubec, Libor Radimec, Luděk Macela (46 Ladislav Jurkemik), Jozef Barmoš, Ján Kozák, Jan Berger, Petr Němec (46 Přemysl Bičovský), Marián Masný, Zdeněk Nehoda (Cap), Werner Lička.   Trainer: Jozef Venglos.

Goals: Kevin Moran (18, 69), Francis Stapleton (75) / Marián Masný (55)

189. 21.05.1981
WEST GERMANY "B"
v REPUBLIC OF IRELAND   3-0 (0-0)
Weser, Bremen
Referee: Peer Frickmann (Denmark)   Attendance: 4,000

REPUBLIC OF IRELAND: James Martin McDonagh, David Francis Langan, David Anthony O'Leary, Kevin Bernard Moran, John Anthony Devine, Michael Paul Martin (77 Augustine Ashley Grimes), Gerard Anthony Daly, Anthony Patrick Grealish (Cap), Francis Anthony Stapleton, Michael John Robinson (72 Terence Christopher Donovan), Kevin O'Callaghan (57 Gerard Joseph Ryan).
Trainer: Eoin Kevin Joseph Colin Hand.

GERMANY: Norbert Nigbur (46 Walter Junghans), Karl-Heinz Geils, Meinolf Koch, Paul Steiner, Jürgen Fleer, Ulrich Bittcher, Friedhelm Funkel (71 Stefan Groß), Helmut Schröder, Karl Del'Haye, Dieter Müller (84 Martin Wiesner), Holger Willmer (64 Kurt Pinkall).

Goals: Karl Del'Haye (50), Friedhelm Funkel (62), Helmut Schröder (64)

190. 24.05.1981
POLAND v REPUBLIC OF IRELAND 3-0 (2-0)
Zawisza, Bydgoszcz

Referee: Vasile Tătar (Romania)   Attendance: 15,000

POLAND: Piotr Mowlik (65 Zdzisław Kostrzewa), Marek Dziuba (Cap) (77 Ryszard Milewski), Władysław Żmuda, Paweł Janas (46 Piotr Skrobowski), Jan Jałocha, Kazimierz Buda (46 Zdzisław Kapka), Janusz Kupcewicz, Andrzej Buncol, Andrzej Iwan, Roman Ogaza, Włodzimierz Smolarek (68 Mirosław Okoński).   Trainer: Antoni Piechniczek.

REPUBLIC OF IRELAND: Patrick Bonner, David Francis Langan, Mark Thomas Lawrenson, David Anthony O'Leary, Christopher William Gerard Hughton, Augustine Ashley Grimes (80 Gerard Anthony Daly), Kevin Bernard Moran (58 Gary Patrick Waddock), Anthony Patrick Grealish (Cap), Michael John Robinson, Francis Anthony Stapleton, Kevin O'Callaghan (62 Gerard Joseph Ryan).
Trainer: Eoin Kevin Joseph Colin Hand.

Goals: Andrzej Iwan (2), David O'Leary (38 own goal), Roman Ogaza (66)

191. 09.09.1981   12th World Cup Qualifiers
HOLLAND v REPUBLIC OF IRELAND 2-2 (1-1)
Feyenoord, Rotterdam

Referee: Vojtech Christov (Czechoslovakia)   Att: 48,000

HOLLAND: Pieter Schrijvers, Hubertus Johannes Nicolaas Wijnstekers, Rudolf Jozef Krol (Cap), Ernestus Wilhelmus Johannes Brandts, Michael Antonius Bernardus van de Korput, Franciscus Johannes Thijssen, Arnoldus Johannes Hyacinthus Mühren, John Nicolaas Rep, Geertruida Maria Geels (46 Johannes Wilhelmus Peters), Cornelis van Kooten, Tscheu La Ling (59 Reinier Lambertus van de Kerkhof).
Trainer: Cornelis Bernardus Rijvers.

REPUBLIC OF IRELAND: James Martin McDonagh, David Francis Langan, John Anthony Devine, Mark Thomas Lawrenson, David Anthony O'Leary, William Brady (Cap), Michael Paul Martin (74 Ronald Andrew Whelan), Anthony Patrick Grealish, Stephen Derek Heighway (61 Gerard Joseph Ryan), Michael John Robinson, Francis Anthony Stapleton.
Trainer: Eoin Kevin Joseph Colin Hand.

Goals: Franciscus Johannes Thijssen (11), Arnoldus Johannes Hyacinthus Mühren (64 pen) / Michael John Robinson (40), Francis Anthony Stapleton (71)

192. 14.10.1981   12th World Cup Qualifiers
REPUBLIC OF IRELAND v FRANCE 3-2 (3-1)
Lansdowne Road, Dublin

Referee: Ulf Eriksson (Sweden)   Attendance: 53,000

REPUBLIC OF IRELAND: James Martin McDonagh, David Francis Langan, David Anthony O'Leary, Kevin Bernard Moran, Christopher William Gerard Hughton, Ronald Andrew Whelan, Michael Paul Martin, Mark Thomas Lawrenson, William Brady (Cap), Francis Anthony Stapleton (87 Daniel Joseph Givens), Michael John Robinson.
Trainer: Eoin Kevin Joseph Colin Hand.

FRANCE: Jean Castaneda, Maxime Bossis, Philippe Mahut (69 François Bracci), Christian Lopez, Gérard Janvion, René Girard, Jean-François Larios, Didier Christophe, Michel Platini (Cap), Alain Couriol, Bruno Bellone (63 Didier Six).
Trainer: Michel Hidalgo.

Goals: Philippe Mahut (5 own goal), Francis Stapleton (25), Michael John Robinson (39) / Bruno Bellone (9), Michel Platini (83)

193. 28.04.1982
ALGERIA v REPUBLIC OF IRELAND 2-0 (1-0)
Olympique, Algiers

Referee: Daniel Lambert (France)   Attendance: 60,000

ALGERIA: Mahdi Cerbah, Chaabane Merzekane (46 Mustapha Kouichi), Medjadi, Mahmoud Guendouz, Nouredine Kourichi, Faouzi Mansouri, Karim Maroc, Lakhdar Belloumi (46 Ali Bencheik), Abdelmajid Bourebbou (63 Chebbal), Djamel Tlemcani (46 Rabah Madjer), Salah Assad.
Trainer: Rachid Mekhloufi (France) & Mahieddine Khalef.

REPUBLIC OF IRELAND: Patrick Bonner, John Anthony Devine, Kevin Bernard Moran (70 Eamonn Stephen Deacy), Michael Paul Martin, Augustine Ashley Grimes, Anthony Patrick Grealish (Cap), Gary Patrick Waddock (75 Gerard Joseph Ryan), Gerard Anthony Daly, Kevin O'Callaghan, Francis Anthony Stapleton, Michael John Robinson (46 Michael Anthony Walsh).
Trainer: Eoin Kevin Joseph Colin Hand.

Goals: Salah Assad (15), Rabah Madjer (64)

194. 22.05.1982
CHILE v REPUBLIC OF IRELAND 1-0 (1-0)
Nacional, Santiago

Referee: Víctor Ojeda (Chile)   Attendance: 25,000

CHILE: Mario Ignacio Osbén Méndez, Lizardo Antonio Garrido Bustamante (Mario Enrique Galindo Calixto), Elías Ricardo Figueroa Brander, Eduardo René Valenzuela Becker, Mario del Transito Soto Benavides, Vladimir David Bigorra López, Carlos Humberto Rivas Torres, Rodolfo del Rosario Dubó Segovia, Patricio Nazario Yáñez Candia, Miguel Angel Gamboa Pedemonte (Juan Carlos Letelier Pizarro), Gustavo Segundo Moscoso Huencho.   Trainer: Luis Santibáñez.

REPUBLIC OF IRELAND: James Martin McDonagh, Eamonn Stephen Deacy, Michael Paul Martin, John Christopher Patrick Anderson, Michael Thomas Walsh, William Brady, Sean Michael O'Driscoll (70 Michael Joseph Fairclough), Anthony Patrick Grealish (Cap), Gerard Anthony Daly, Michael John Robinson (75 Gerard Joseph Ryan), Kevin O'Callaghan.   Trainer: Eoin Kevin Joseph Colin Hand.

Goal: Miguel Angel Gamboa Pedemonte (1)

195. 27.05.1982
BRAZIL v REPUBLIC OF IRELAND 7-0 (1-0)
Parque do Sabiá, Uberlândia
Referee: Romualdo Arppi Filho (Brazil)   Att: 72,733
BRAZIL: Valdir de Arruda Peres (80 Paulo Sérgio de Oliveira Lima), José Leandro de Souza Ferreira "Leandro I", José Oscar Bernardi, Luiz Carlos Ferreira "Luisinho" (46 Édino Nazareth Filho "Edinho"), Leovegildo Lins Gama Júnior "Júnior I", Paulo Roberto Falcão, Sócrates Brasileiro Sampaio Vieira de Oliveira, Arthur Antunes Coimbra "Zico", Paulo Isidoro de Jesus (60 Antônio Carlos Cerezo "Toninho Cerezo"), Antônio de Oliveira Filho "Careca I" (46 Sérgio Bernardino "Serginho I"), Éder Aleixo de Assis (80 Dirceu José Guimarães "Dirceu II"). Trainer: Telê Santana da Silva.
REPUBLIC OF IRELAND: James Martin McDonagh, Eamonn Stephen Deacy, Michael Paul Martin, John Christopher Patrick Anderson, Michael Thomas Walsh, Gerard Anthony Daly, Anthony Patrick Grealish (Cap), William Brady, Sean Michael O'Driscoll, Brendan Richard O'Callaghan (70 Gerard Joseph Ryan), Kevin O'Callaghan.
Trainer: Eoin Kevin Joseph Colin Hand.
Goals: Paulo Roberto Falcão (32), Sócrates Brasileiro Sampaio Vieira de Oliveira (53), Sérgio Bernardino "Serginho I" (64), Luiz Carlos Ferreira "Luisinho" (68), Sócrates Brasileiro Sampaio Vieira de Oliveira (73), Sérgio Bernardino "Serginho I" (75), Arthur Antunes Coimbra "Zico" (78)

196. 30.05.1982
TRINIDAD & TOBAGO v REPUBLIC OF IRELAND 2-1 (1-1)
Arima, Port of Spain
Referee: Not recorded
TRINIDAD & TOBAGO: Team line-up not available.
REPUBLIC OF IRELAND: Gerald Joseph Peyton, Eamonn Stephen Deacy (Sean Michael O'Driscoll), Michael Paul Martin, John Christopher Patrick Anderson, Michael Thomas Walsh, Gerard Anthony Daly, Anthony Patrick Grealish (Cap), William Brady, John Walsh, Brendan Richard O'Callaghan (Michael Joseph Fairclough), Gerard Joseph Ryan (Kevin O'Callaghan). Trainer: Eoin Kevin Joseph Colin Hand.
Goal: William Brady (#)

197. 22.09.1982   7th European Champs Qualifiers
HOLLAND v REPUBLIC OF IRELAND 2-1 (1-0)
Feyenoord, Rotterdam
Referee: Ivan Gregr (Czechoslovakia)   Attendance: 20,500
HOLLAND: Johannes Franciscus van Breukelen, Hubertus Johannes Nicolaas Wijnstekers (Cap), Johannes Antonius Bernardus Metgod (46 Reinier Lambertus van de Kerkhof), Ronald Spelbos, Michael Antonius Bernardus van de Korput, Hubertus Jozef Margaretha Stevens, Wilhelmus Antonius van de Kerkhof, Dirk Hendrikus Schoenaker, Ruud Gullit, René van der Gijp, Gerald Mervin Vanenburg (80 Cornelis van Kooten). Trainer: Cornelis Bernardus Rijvers.
REPUBLIC OF IRELAND: James Martin McDonagh, Michael Paul Martin, Mark Thomas Lawrenson, David Anthony O'Leary, Christopher William Gerard Hughton, Anthony Patrick Grealish (Cap), Francis Anthony Stapleton, Gerard Anthony Daly (83 Michael Anthony Walsh), Anthony Galvin (73 Gary Patrick Waddock), William Brady, Michael John Robinson. Trainer: Eoin Kevin Joseph Colin Hand.
Goals: Dirk Hendrikus Schoenaker (1), Ruud Gullit (64) / Gerard Anthony Daly (79)

198. 13.10.1982   7th European Champs Qualifiers
REPUBLIC OF IRELAND v ICELAND 2-0 (1-0)
Lansdowne Road, Dublin
Referee: Paul Rion (Luxembourg)   Attendance: 23,371
REPUBLIC OF IRELAND: James Martin McDonagh, Kevin Bernard Moran, Mark Thomas Lawrenson, David Anthony O'Leary, Michael Thomas Walsh, Ronald Andrew Whelan, Anthony Patrick Grealish (Cap), Gary Patrick Waddock, William Brady (64 Kevin O'Callaghan), Michael John Robinson, Francis Anthony Stapleton.
Trainer: Eoin Kevin Joseph Colin Hand.
ICELAND: Þorsteinn Bjarnason, Viðar Halldórsson, Örn Óskarsson, Marteinn Geirsson (Cap), Sævar Jónsson, Gunnar Gíslason, Arnór Guðjohnsen, Atli Eðvaldsson, Lárus Guðmundsson, Pétur Ormslev (43 Ragnar Margeirsson), Pétur Pétursson. Trainer: Jóhannes Atlason.
Goals: Francis Stapleton (35), Anthony Patrick Grealish (73)

199. 17.11.1982   7th European Champs Qualifiers
REPUBLIC OF IRELAND v SPAIN 3-3 (1-1)
Lansdowne Road, Dublin

Referee: Jan Redelfs (West Germany)   Attendance: 35,000

REPUBLIC OF IRELAND: James Martin McDonagh, John Anthony Devine, Mark Thomas Lawrenson, Michael Paul Martin, Christopher William Gerard Hughton, Anthony Patrick Grealish (Cap) (61 Michael Anthony Walsh), William Brady, Augustine Ashley Grimes, Michael John Robinson, Francis Anthony Stapleton, Kevin O'Callaghan.
Trainer: Eoin Kevin Joseph Colin Hand.

SPAIN: Luis Miguel Arkonada Echarre (Cap), Juan José Jiménez Collar, Francisco Bonet Serrano, Antonio Maceda Francés, José Antonio Camacho Alfaro, Juan Antonio Señor Gómez, Víctor Muñoz Manrique, Rafael Gordillo Vázquez, Marcos Alonso Peña, Juan Carlos Gómez Pedraza (67 Enrique Martín Monreal Lizárraga), Carlos Alonso González "Santillana" (71 Roberto Fernández Bonillo).
Trainer: Miguel Muñoz Mozún.

Goals: Augustine Ashley Grimes (2), Francis Anthony Stapleton (64, 76) / Antonio Maceda Francés (31), Michael Martín (47 own goal), Víctor Muñoz Manrique (60)

200. 30.03.1983   7th European Champs Qualifiers
MALTA v REPUBLIC OF IRELAND 0-1 (0-0)
National, Ta'Qali

Referee: Adolf Mathias (Austria)   Attendance: 6,487

MALTA: John Bonello, Edwin Farrugia, Emanuel Farrugia, Mario Farrugia, Mario Schembri, John Holland (Cap), Silvio Demanuele, Raymond Xuereb, George Xuereb, Emanuel 'Leli' Fabri, Michael Degiorgio.   Trainer: Victor Scerri.

REPUBLIC OF IRELAND: James Martin McDonagh, John Anthony Devine, Mark Thomas Lawrenson, Michael Paul Martin (Cap), Christopher William Gerard Hughton, William Brady, Ronald Andrew Whelan, Francis Anthony Stapleton, Anthony Galvin (63 Kevin O'Callaghan), Gary Patrick Waddock, Michael John Robinson.
Trainer: Eoin Kevin Joseph Colin Hand.

Goal: Francis Anthony Stapleton (90)

201. 27.04.1983   7th European Champs Qualifiers
SPAIN v REPUBLIC OF IRELAND 2-0 (0-0)
La Romareda, Zaragoza

Referee: Valeri Butenko (Soviet Union)   Attendance: 45,000

SPAIN: Luis Miguel Arkonada Echarre (Cap), Juan José Jiménez Collar, Francisco Bonet Serrano, Antonio Maceda Francés, José Antonio Camacho Alfaro, Juan Antonio Señor Gómez, Víctor Muñoz Manrique (46 Francisco Fernández Rodríguez "Gallego"), Rafael Gordillo Vázquez, Marcos Alonso Peña, Carlos Alonso González "Santillana", Francisco José Carrasco Hidalgo (74 Hipólito Rincón Povedano).
Trainer: Miguel Muñoz Mozún.

REPUBLIC OF IRELAND: James Martin McDonagh, Mark Thomas Lawrenson, Michael Paul Martin, David Anthony O'Leary, Christopher William Gerard Hughton, Ronald Andrew Whelan (77 Gerard Anthony Daly), Anthony Patrick Grealish (Cap), Augustine Ashley Grimes (57 Kevin O'Callaghan), Gary Patrick Waddock, Michael Anthony Walsh, Francis Anthony Stapleton.
Trainer: Eoin Kevin Joseph Colin Hand.

Goals: Carlos Alonso González "Santillana" (51), Hipólito Rincón Povedano (89)

202. 21.09.1983   7th European Champs Qualifiers
ICELAND v REPUBLIC OF IRELAND 0-3 (0-2)
Laugardalsvöllur, Reykjavík

Referee: Gérard Biguet (France)   Attendance: 13,706

ICELAND: Þorsteinn Bjarnason, Viðar Halldórsson (Cap), Sigurður Lárusson, Jóhannes Eðvaldsson, Sævar Jónsson, Janus Guðlaugsson, Arnór Guðjohnsen (7 Ásgeir Elíasson), Atli Eðvaldsson, Lárus Guðmundsson, Pétur Pétursson (36 Sigurður Grétarsson), Pétur Ormslev.
Trainer: Jóhannes Atlason.

REPUBLIC OF IRELAND: James Martin McDonagh, John Anthony Devine, Mark Thomas Lawrenson, Kevin Bernard Moran, Christopher William Gerard Hughton, William Brady, Gary Patrick Waddock, Anthony Patrick Grealish (Cap), Kevin O'Callaghan, Francis Anthony Stapleton, Michael John Robinson (76 Michael Anthony Walsh).
Trainer: Eoin Kevin Joseph Colin Hand.

Goals: Gary Waddock (17), Michael John Robinson (21), Michael Anthony Walsh (82)

203. 12.10.1983   7th European Champs Qualifiers
REPUBLIC OF IRELAND v HOLLAND 2-3 (2-0)
Dalymount Park, Dublin

Referee: André Daina (Switzerland)   Attendance: 35,000

REPUBLIC OF IRELAND: James Martin McDonagh, John Anthony Devine, Mark Thomas Lawrenson, Kevin Bernard Moran, Christopher William Gerard Hughton, William Brady, Gary Patrick Waddock, Anthony Patrick Grealish (Cap) (82 Kevin Mark Sheedy), Francis Anthony Stapleton, Michael John Robinson, Kevin O'Callaghan (74 Anthony Galvin). Trainer: Eoin Kevin Joseph Colin Hand.

HOLLAND: Pieter Schrijvers, Hubertus Johannes Nicolaas Wijnstekers (Cap), Ruud Gullit, Jan Jacobus Silooy, Peter Boeve, Edo Ophof, Wilhelmus Antonius van de Kerkhof, Ronald Koeman, Adrianus Andreas van Tiggelen (46 Budde Jan Peter Maria Brocken), Gerald Mervin Vanenburg, Marcelo van Basten. Trainer: Cornelis Bernardus Rijvers.

Goals: Gary Patrick Waddock (7), William Brady (35 pen) / Ruud Gullit (51), Marcelo van Basten (65), Ruud Gullit (75)

204. 16.11.1983   7th European Champs Qualifiers
REPUBLIC OF IRELAND v MALTA 8-0 (3-0)
Dalymount Park, Dublin

Referee: Ole Amundsen (Denmark)   Attendance: 11,000

REPUBLIC OF IRELAND: Patrick Bonner, Kieran Michael O'Regan, Kevin Bernard Moran (46 James McDonagh), Mark Thomas Lawrenson (81 Gary Patrick Waddock), Christopher William Gerard Hughton, Gerard Anthony Daly, William Brady, Kevin Mark Sheedy, Michael Anthony Walsh, Francis Anthony Stapleton (Cap), Kevin O'Callaghan. Trainer: Eoin Kevin Joseph Colin Hand.

MALTA: John Bonello, Constantino Consiglio, Alex Azzopardi, Edwin Farrugia, Emanuel Farrugia, John Holland (Cap), Silvio Demanuele, Mario Farrugia (81 Emanuel 'Leli' Fabri), Noel Attard (68 George Xuereb), Carmel Busuttil, Ernest Spiteri-Gonzi.
Trainers: Victor Scerri & Guentcho Dobrev (Bulgaria).

Goals: Mark Lawrenson (24, 53), Francis Stapleton (27 pen), Kevin O'Callaghan (32), Kevin Mark Sheedy (75), William Brady (77, 84), Gerard Anthony Daly (85)

205. 04.04.1984
ISRAEL v REPUBLIC OF IRELAND 3-0 (1-0)
Bloomfield, Jaffa, Tel-Aviv

Referee: Jean-Marie Lartigot (France)   Attendance: 10,000

ISRAEL: Arie Haviv, Gabriel Lasri, Shlomo Kirat, Avi Cohen I (78 Nissim Barda), David Pizanti, Uri Malmilian (88 Nissim Cohen), Rifat Turk, Yaacov Ekhoiz, Moshe Sinai, Zahi Armeli, Eli Ohana.   Trainer: Yosef Mirmovich.

REPUBLIC OF IRELAND: Patrick Bonner, John Anthony Devine, David Anthony O'Leary, Kevin Bernard Moran, Augustine Ashley Grimes, Mark Thomas Lawrenson, Gary Patrick Waddock, Ronald Andrew Whelan (70 Anthony Galvin), William Brady, Francis Anthony Stapleton (Cap), Michael John Robinson (79 Gerard Anthony Daly). Trainer: Eoin Kevin Joseph Colin Hand.

Goals: Eli Ohana (3), Zahi Armeli (62), Moshe Sinai (65)

206. 23.05.1984
REPUBLIC OF IRELAND v POLAND 0-0
Dalymount Park, Dublin

Referee: George Courtney (England)   Attendance: 8,000

REPUBLIC OF IRELAND: James Martin McDonagh, Kieran Michael O'Regan, Michael Joseph McCarthy, David Anthony O'Leary (52 James McDonagh), Patrick Byrne II, William Brady, Anthony Patrick Grealish, Michael Anthony Walsh, Augustine Ashley Grimes, Francis Anthony Stapleton (Cap) (80 William Buckley), Gerard Joseph Ryan.
Trainer: Eoin Kevin Joseph Colin Hand.

POLAND: Józef Młynarczyk, Krzysztof Pawlak, Władysław Żmuda (Cap), Roman Wójcicki, Marek Ostrowski, Andrzej Buncol, Jerzy Wijas, Zbigniew Boniek, Waldemar Matysik, Jan Furtok (88 Mirosław Okoński), Włodzimierz Smolarek. Trainer: Antoni Piechniczek.

207. 03.06.1984   Japan Cup
REPUBLIC OF IRELAND v CHINA 1-0 (1-0)
Maryuama, Sapporo (Japan)

Referee: Not recorded   Attendance: 25,000

REPUBLIC OF IRELAND: Patrick Bonner, John Christopher Patrick Anderson, Michael Joseph McCarthy, David Anthony O'Leary, James Martin Beglin, Gerard Joseph Ryan, Anthony Patrick Grealish, Patrick Byrne II (55 Gary Patrick Howlett), Eamonn Gerard O'Keefe, Francis Anthony Stapleton (Cap), Michael Anthony Walsh.
Trainer: Eoin Kevin Joseph Colin Hand.

CHINA: Team line-up not available.

Goal: Eamonn Gerard O'Keefe (#)

208. 08.08.1984
REPUBLIC OF IRELAND v MEXICO 0-0
Dalymount Park, Dublin
Referee: Jakob Baumann (Switzerland)   Attendance: 5,000
REPUBLIC OF IRELAND: James Martin McDonagh (46 Gerald Joseph Peyton), Kieran Michael O'Regan (46 Christopher William Gerard Hughton (76 James McDonagh)), Kevin Bernard Moran, Michael Joseph McCarthy, James Martin Beglin, Patrick Byrne II (46 Gerard Anthony Daly), Anthony Patrick Grealish (Cap), Gerard Joseph Ryan, Eamonn Gerard O'Keefe, William Buckley, Anthony Galvin (46 Kevin O'Callaghan).   Trainer: Eoin Kevin Joseph Colin Hand.
MEXICO: Pablo Larios, Mario Trejo (70 Rafael Amador), Armando Manzo, Fernando Quirarte, Francisco Chávez, Javier Aguirre, Enrique López Zarza, Carlos de los Cobos, Tomás Boy, Eduardo de la Torre, Luis Flores (87 Javier Hernández). Trainer: Velibor Milutinović (Yugoslavia).

209. 12.09.1984   13th World Cup Qualifiers
REPUBLIC OF IRELAND v SOVIET UNION 1-0 (0-0)
Lansdowne Road, Dublin
Referee: Johannes Nicolaas Ignatius "Jan" Keizer (Holland) Attendance: 28,000
REPUBLIC OF IRELAND: James Martin McDonagh, John Anthony Devine, David Anthony O'Leary, Mark Thomas Lawrenson, Christopher William Gerard Hughton, Ronald Andrew Whelan, Anthony Patrick Grealish (Cap), William Brady, Michael John Robinson, Michael Anthony Walsh (82 Eamonn Gerard O'Keefe), Anthony Galvin.
Trainer: Eoin Kevin Joseph Colin Hand.
SOVIET UNION: Rinat Dasaev, Tengiz Sulakvelidze, Aleksandr Chivadze (Cap), Sergey Baltacha, Anatoliy Demyanenko, Khoren Oganesyan (67 Sergey Gotzmanov), Gennadiy Litovchenko, Vladimir Bessonov (35 Andrey Zygmantovich), Sergey Aleynikov, Sergey Rodionov, Oleg Blokhin.   Trainer: Eduard Malofeev.
Goal: Michael Anthony Walsh (64)

210. 17.10.1984   13th World Cup Qualifiers
NORWAY v REPUBLIC OF IRELAND 1-0 (1-0)
Ullevaal, Oslo
Referee: Klaus Scheurell (East Germany)   Att: 15,379
NORWAY: Erik Thorstvedt, Svein Fjælberg (33 Vidar Davidsen), Terje Kojedal, Åge Hareide, Per Edmund Mordt, Erik Solér, Kai Erik Herlovsen, Per Egil Ahlsen, Hallvar Thoresen, Arne Larsen Økland, Pål Jacobsen (89 Per Henriksen).   Trainer: Tor Røste Fossen.
REPUBLIC OF IRELAND: James Martin McDonagh, John Anthony Devine, David Anthony O'Leary, Mark Thomas Lawrenson, Christopher William Gerard Hughton, Anthony Patrick Grealish (Cap), Ronald Andrew Whelan (67 Kevin O'Callaghan), William Brady, Michael John Robinson (69 Michael Anthony Walsh), Francis Anthony Stapleton, Anthony Galvin.   Trainer: Eoin Kevin Joseph Colin Hand.
Goal: Pål Jacobsen (42)

211. 14.11.1984   13th World Cup Qualifiers
DENMARK v REPUBLIC OF IRELAND 3-0 (1-0)
Idrætsparken, København
Referee: Robert Charles Paul Würtz (France)   Att: 45,300
DENMARK: Ole Qvist, John Sivebæk, Ivan Nielsen, Morten Olsen (Cap), Søren Busk, Klaus Berggreen, Jens Jørn Bertelsen (58 Jan Mølby), Frank Arnesen, Søren Lerby, Michael Laudrup, Preben Elkjær-Larsen (64 Kenneth Brylle).
Trainer: Josef Piontek (West Germany).
REPUBLIC OF IRELAND: James Martin McDonagh, Mark Thomas Lawrenson, Michael Joseph McCarthy, David Anthony O'Leary, James Martin Beglin, Kevin Mark Sheedy, William Brady, Anthony Patrick Grealish, Anthony Galvin (46 Kevin O'Callaghan), Francis Anthony Stapleton (Cap), Michael Anthony Walsh.   Trainer: Eoin Kevin Joseph Colin Hand.
Goals: Preben Elkjær-Larsen (30, 46), Søren Lerby (55)

212. 05.02.1985
REPUBLIC OF IRELAND v ITALY 1-2 (0-2)
Dalymount Park, Dublin
Referee: Johannes Nicolaas Ignatius "Jan" Keizer (Holland) Attendance: 40,000
REPUBLIC OF IRELAND: Patrick Bonner, Christopher William Gerard Hughton, James Martin Beglin, Mark Thomas Lawrenson (10 Paul McGrath), Michael Joseph McCarthy, Kevin Mark Sheedy, William Brady, Gary Patrick Waddock, Anthony Galvin (29 Ronald Andrew Whelan), Francis Anthony Stapleton (Cap), John Frederick Byrne (77 Alan Campbell).   Trainer: Eoin Kevin Joseph Colin Hand.

ITALY: Franco Tancredi, Giuseppe Bergomi, Antonio Cabrini, Salvatore Bagni, Pietro Vierchowod, Gaetano Scirea, Bruno Conti (72 Giuseppe Dossena), Marco Tardelli (Cap), Paolo Rossi (72 Aldo Serena), Antonio Di Gennaro, Alessandro Altobelli.   Trainer: Enzo Bearzot.

Goals: Gary Patrick Waddock (53) / Paolo Rossi (5 pen), Alessandro Altobelli (18)

213. 27.02.1985
ISRAEL v REPUBLIC OF IRELAND 0-0
National, Ramat-Gan, Tel-Aviv

Referee: Pietro d'Elia (Italy)   Attendance: 3,000

ISRAEL: Arie Haviv, Shlomo Kirat, Nissim Barda, Avi Cohen I (46 Yaacov Ekhoiz), David Pizanti, Nissim Cohen (46 Baruch Maman), Rifat Turk, Moshe Sinai, Moshe Selecter, Zahi Armeli (46 Roni Rosenthal), Eli Ohana.   Trainer: Yosef Mirmovich.

REPUBLIC OF IRELAND: Patrick Bonner, Christopher William Gerard Hughton, Michael Joseph McCarthy, David Anthony O'Leary, James Martin Beglin, Ronald Andrew Whelan, Gary Patrick Waddock, Paul McGrath, Kevin Mark Sheedy, Francis Anthony Stapleton (Cap), Alan Campbell (65 John Frederick Byrne).
Trainer: Eoin Kevin Joseph Colin Hand.

214. 26.03.1985
ENGLAND v REPUBLIC OF IRELAND 2-1 (1-0)
Wembley, London

Referee: George Brian Smith (Scotland)   Att: 34,793

ENGLAND: Gary Richard Bailey, Vivian Alexander Anderson, Kenneth Graham Sansom, Trevor McGregor Steven, Mark Wright, Terence Ian Butcher, Bryan Robson (Cap) (82 Glenn Hoddle), Raymond Colin Wilkins, Mark Wayne Hateley (73 Peter Davenport), Gary Winston Lineker, Christopher Roland Waddle.   Manager: Robert Robson.

REPUBLIC OF IRELAND: Patrick Bonner, Christopher William Gerard Hughton, Mark Thomas Lawrenson, Michael Joseph McCarthy, James Martin Beglin, Ronald Andrew Whelan (70 Kevin O'Callaghan), Gary Patrick Waddock, William Brady, Paul McGrath (46 David Anthony O'Leary), Eamonn Gerard O'Keefe (80 John Frederick Byrne), Francis Anthony Stapleton (Cap).
Trainer: Eoin Kevin Joseph Colin Hand.

Goals: Trevor Steven (45), Gary Winston Lineker (76) / William Brady (88)

215. 01.05.1985   13th World Cup Qualifiers
REPUBLIC OF IRELAND v NORWAY 0-0
Lansdowne Road, Dublin

Referee: Lajos Németh (Hungary)   Attendance: 20,000

REPUBLIC OF IRELAND: Patrick Bonner, David Francis Langan (83 Paul McGrath), Mark Thomas Lawrenson, David Anthony O'Leary, James Martin Beglin, Gary Patrick Waddock, Gerard Anthony Daly, William Brady (67 Ronald Andrew Whelan), Anthony Galvin, Francis Anthony Stapleton (Cap), Michael John Robinson.
Trainer: Eoin Kevin Joseph Colin Hand.

NORWAY: Erik Thorstvedt, Svein Fjælberg, Terje Kojedal, Åge Hareide, Hans Hermann Henriksen, Kai Erik Herlovsen (57 Arne Erlandsen), Per Egil Ahlsen, Erik Solér, Arne Larsen Økland, Hallvar Thoresen. Ulf Moen (87 Pål Jacobsen).
Trainer: Tor Røste Fossen.

216. 26.05.1985
REPUBLIC OF IRELAND v SPAIN 0-0
Flower Lodge, Cork

Referee: Franz Gächter (Switzerland)   Attendance: 15,000

REPUBLIC OF IRELAND: James Martin McDonagh, David Francis Langan (81 Patrick Byrne II), David Anthony O'Leary, Michael Joseph McCarthy, Christopher William Gerard Hughton (63 Kieran Michael O'Regan), Gerard Anthony Daly, William Brady (Cap), Gary Patrick Waddock, Anthony Galvin (25 Anthony Patrick Grealish), Alan Campbell, Michael John Robinson.   Trainer: Eoin Kevin Joseph Colin Hand.

SPAIN: Andoni Zubizarreta Urreta, Gerardo Miranda Concepción, Andoni Goikoetxea Olaskoaga, Antonio Maceda Francés, José Antonio Camacho Alfaro, Víctor Muñoz Manrique, Francisco Fernández Rodríguez "Gallego" (69 Ramón María Calderé Del Rey), Marcos Alonso Peña (82 Roberto Simón Marina), Rafael Gordillo Vázquez (Cap) (75 Julio Alberto Moreno Casas), Hipólito Rincón Povedano, Carlos Alonso González "Santillana" (82 Manuel Sarabia López).   Trainer: Miguel Muñoz Mozún.

217. 02.06.1985   13th World Cup Qualifiers
**REPUBLIC OF IRELAND
v SWITZERLAND 3-0** (2-0)
Lansdowne Road, Dublin

Referee: Paolo Bergamo (Italy)   Attendance: 17,500

REPUBLIC OF IRELAND: James Martin McDonagh, David Francis Langan, David Anthony O'Leary, Michael Joseph McCarthy, James Martin Beglin, Gerard Anthony Daly (46 Ronald Andrew Whelan), Anthony Patrick Grealish (63 Paul McGrath), William Brady, Kevin Mark Sheedy, Michael John Robinson, Francis Anthony Stapleton (Cap).
Trainer: Eoin Kevin Joseph Colin Hand.

SWITZERLAND: Karl Engel (24 Erich Burgener), Roger Wehrli, Charles In-Albon, Heinz Lüdi, André Egli, Alain Geiger, Heinz Hermann, Umberto Barberis (59 Georges Brégy), Michel Decastel, Manfred Braschler, Christian Matthey.   Trainer: Paul Wolfisberg.

Goals: Francis Anthony Stapleton (7),
Anthony Patrick Grealish (33), Kevin Mark Sheedy (57)

218. 11.09.1985   13th World Cup Qualifiers
SWITZERLAND v REPUBLIC OF IRELAND 0-0
Wankdorf, Bern

Referee: Emilio Soriano Aladrén (Spain)   Att: 24,000

SWITZERLAND: Karl Engel, André Egli, Charles In-Albon, Alain Geiger, Marco Schällibaum (75 Jean-Paul Brigger), Heinz Hermann, Georges Brégy, Philippe Perret, Marcel Koller, Robert Lüthi, Christian Matthey.   Trainer: Paul Wolfisberg.

REPUBLIC OF IRELAND: James Martin McDonagh, Christopher William Gerard Hughton, Michael Joseph McCarthy, David Anthony O'Leary, James Martin Beglin, William Brady, Gerard Anthony Daly (66 Paul McGrath), Mark Thomas Lawrenson, Anthony Guy Cascarino, Francis Anthony Stapleton (Cap), Kevin Mark Sheedy (71 Kevin O'Callaghan).   Trainer: Eoin Kevin Joseph Colin Hand.

219. 16.10.1985   13th World Cup Qualifiers
**SOVIET UNION
v REPUBLIC OF IRELAND 2-0** (0-0)
Lenin, Moskva

Referee: Paolo Casarin (Italy)   Attendance: 100,000

SOVIET UNION: Rinat Dasaev (Cap), Gennadiy Morozov, Aleksandr Chivadze, Aleksandr Bubnov, Anatoliy Demyanenko, Aleksandr Zavarov (84 Vladimir Bessonov), Sergey Gotzmanov, Sergey Aleynikov, Fëdor Cherenkov, Oleg Protasov, Oleg Blokhin (55 Georgiy Kondratiev).
Trainer: Eduard Malofeev.

REPUBLIC OF IRELAND: James Martin McDonagh, Christopher William Gerard Hughton, Michael Joseph McCarthy, David Anthony O'Leary, James Martin Beglin (79 Kevin O'Callaghan), William Brady, Gary Patrick Waddock, Mark Thomas Lawrenson, Anthony Guy Cascarino, Francis Anthony Stapleton (Cap), Anthony Patrick Grealish (71 Ronald Andrew Whelan).
Trainer: Eoin Kevin Joseph Colin Hand.

Goals: Fëdor Cherenkov (61), Oleg Protasov (90)

220. 13.11.1985   13th World Cup Qualifiers
REPUBLIC OF IRELAND v DENMARK 1-4 (1-2)
Lansdowne Road, Dublin

Referee: Franz Wöhrer (Austria)   Attendance: 12,000

REPUBLIC OF IRELAND: James Martin McDonagh, Mark Thomas Lawrenson, James Martin Beglin, Kevin Bernard Moran, David Anthony O'Leary, William Brady, Paul McGrath, Anthony Patrick Grealish (30 Patrick Byrne II), Anthony Guy Cascarino, Francis Anthony Stapleton (Cap), Kevin Mark Sheedy (69 Michael John Robinson).
Trainer: Eoin Kevin Joseph Colin Hand.

DENMARK: Troels Rasmussen, John Sivebæk, Morten Olsen (Cap) (69 Frank Arnesen), Ivan Nielsen, Søren Busk, Klaus Berggreen, Jan Mølby, Søren Lerby (59 Jens Jørn Bertelsen), Jesper Olsen, Michael Laudrup, Preben Elkjær-Larsen.
Trainer: Josef Piontek (West Germany).

Goals: Francis Anthony Stapleton (6) /
Preben Elkjær-Larsen (7, 76), Michael Laudrup (49), John Sivebæk (57)

221. 26.03.1986
REPUBLIC OF IRELAND v WALES 0-1 (0-1)
Lansdowne Road, Dublin

Referee: Kenneth Johnston Hope (Scotland)   Att: 16,500

REPUBLIC OF IRELAND: Gerald Joseph Peyton, David Francis Langan, James Martin Beglin, John Christopher Patrick Anderson (50 Michael Joseph McCarthy), David Anthony O'Leary, William Brady (Cap), Paul McGrath, Raymond James Houghton, John William Aldridge, Michael John Robinson (66 Patrick Byrne II), Ronald Andrew Whelan.
Trainer: John Charlton (England).

WALES: Neville Southall (66 Anthony Joseph Norman), Robert Mark James, Kenneth Francis Jackett, Peter Nicholas, Jeremy Melvyn Charles, Joseph Patrick Jones, Stephen Robert Lowndes, David Owen Phillips, Ian James Rush, Clayton Graham Blackmore, Gordon John Davies (61 Dean Nicholas Saunders). Manager: Harold Michael England.

Goal: Ian James Rush (17)

222.   23.04.1986
REPUBLIC OF IRELAND v URUGUAY 1-1 (1-1)
Lansdowne Road, Dublin
Referee: John Martin (England)   Attendance: 14,000
REPUBLIC OF IRELAND: Patrick Bonner, David Francis Langan, Barry Murphy, Michael Joseph McCarthy, Christopher William Gerard Hughton (81 Peter Edward Eccles), Gerard Anthony Daly, Liam Francis O'Brien, Raymond James Houghton, Anthony Galvin, John William Aldridge, Francis Anthony Stapleton (Cap) (67 John Frederick Byrne). Trainer: John Charlton (England).

URUGUAY: Fernando Harry Alvez, Víctor Hugo Diogo, Cesar Javier Vega, Nelson Daniel Gutiérrez, Eliseo Rivero, Jorge Walter Barrios(Cap), Venancio Ariel Ramos, Mario Daniel Saralegui, Wilmar Rubens Cabrera, José Luis Zalazar, Rúben Walter Paz.   Trainer: Omar Borrás.

Goals: Gerard Anthony Daly (22 pen) / Michael Joseph McCarthy (23 own goal)

223.   25.05.1986   International Tournament
ICELAND v REPUBLIC OF IRELAND 1-2 (1-1)
Laugardalsvöllur, Reykjavík
Referee: Joseph Bertram Worrall (England)   Att: 4,246
ICELAND: Bjarni Sigurðsson, Gunnar Gíslason, Ágúst Már Jónsson (Guðni Bergsson), Loftur Ólafsson, Sigurður Grétarsson (Ólafur Þórðarson), Viðar Þorkelsson, Pétur Ormslev, Arnór Guðjohnsen, Halldór Áskelsson (Guðmundur Steinsson), Ragnar Margeirsson, Pétur Pétursson (Cap). Trainer: Siegfried Held (West Germany).
REPUBLIC OF IRELAND: Patrick Bonner, John Christopher Patrick Anderson, Christopher William Gerard Hughton (46 Patrick Byrne II), Kevin Bernard Moran, Michael Joseph McCarthy, Michael Francis Martin Kennedy, Paul McGrath (70 Gerard Anthony Daly), Raymond James Houghton, John William Aldridge (84 Niall John Quinn), Francis Anthony Stapleton (Cap), Anthony Galvin. Trainer: John Charlton (England).

Goals: Arnór Guðjohnsen (40) / Paul McGrath (34), Gerard Anthony Daly (84)

224.   27.05.1986   International Tournament
REPUBLIC OF IRELAND v CZECHOSLOVAKIA 1-0 (0-0)
Laugardalsvøllur, Reykjavík
Referee: Oli Olsen (Iceland)   Attendance: 1,000
REPUBLIC OF IRELAND: Gerald Joseph Peyton, Kevin Bernard Moran, Patrick Byrne II, John Christopher Patrick Anderson (46 Michael Francis Martin Kennedy), Michael Joseph McCarthy (Cap), Michael John Robinson (67 Gerard Anthony Daly), Paul McGrath, Raymond James Houghton, John William Aldridge, Niall John Quinn (54 Francis Anthony Stapleton), Anthony Galvin. Trainer: John Charlton (England).
CZECHOSLOVAKIA: Luděk Mikloško, Stanislav Levý, František Straka, Jozef Chovanec, Jan Fiala (Cap), Karel Kula, Jan Berger, Ivan Hašek, Miroslav Siva (76 Ivo Knoflíček), Milan Luhový (56 Luboš Kubík), Ladislav Vízek (80 Josef Novák II). Trainer: Josef Masopust.

Goal: Francis Anthony Stapleton (83)

225.   10.09.1986   8th European Champs Qualifiers
BELGIUM v REPUBLIC OF IRELAND 2-2 (1-1)
Heysel, Bruxelles
Referee: Ion Igna (Romania)   Attendance: 22,212
BELGIUM: Jean-Marie Pfaff, Georges Grün, Léo Albert Clijsters, Frank Richard Vander Elst, Stéphane Demol, Patrick Vervoort, Vincenzo Scifo, Jan Ceulemans, Frank Vercauteren, Philippe De Smet, Nicolaas Pieter Claesen. Trainer: Guy Thys.
REPUBLIC OF IRELAND: Patrick Bonner, David Francis Langan, Christopher William Gerard Hughton (82 James Martin Beglin), Mark Thomas Lawrenson, Kevin Bernard Moran, William Brady, Raymond James Houghton, Paul McGrath, Francis Anthony Stapleton (Cap), John William Aldridge, Anthony Galvin (80 Ronald Andrew Whelan). Trainer: John Charlton (England).

Goals: Nicolaas Pieter Claesen (14), Vincenzo Scifo (71) / Francis Anthony Stapleton (18), William Brady (90 pen)

226. 15.10.1986   8th European Champs Qualifiers
REPUBLIC OF IRELAND v SCOTLAND   0-0
Lansdowne Road, Dublin

Referee: Einar Halle (Norway)   Attendance: 48,000

REPUBLIC OF IRELAND: Patrick Bonner, David Francis Langan, James Martin Beglin, Michael Joseph McCarthy, Kevin Bernard Moran (71 Gerard Anthony Daly), William Brady, Raymond James Houghton, Paul McGrath, Francis Anthony Stapleton (Cap), John William Aldridge, Kevin Mark Sheedy.   Trainer: John Charlton (England).

SCOTLAND: James Leighton, Richard Charles Gough, Raymond Strean McDonald Stewart, David Narey, Alan David Hansen, Gordon David Strachan, Robert Sime Aitken (Cap), Paul Michael Lyons McStay, Murdo Davidson MacLeod, Graeme Marshall Sharp, Maurice Johnston.
Manager: Andrew Roxburgh.

227. 12.11.1986
POLAND v REPUBLIC OF IRELAND   1-0 (1-0)
Wojska Polskiego, Warszawa

Referee: Lajos Németh (Hungary)   Attendance: 8,000

POLAND: Jacek Kazimierski (46 Józef Wandzik), Marek Ostrowski, Paweł Król, Kazimierz Przybyś, Dariusz Wdowczyk, Andrzej Rudy (46 Marek Leśniak), Jan Karaś (Cap) (46 Dariusz Dziekanowski), Waldemar Prusik, Jan Urban, Marek Koniarek, Jan Furtok (46 Ryszard Tarasiewicz).
Trainer: Wojciech Łazarek.

REPUBLIC OF IRELAND: Patrick Bonner, David Francis Langan, Michael Joseph McCarthy, Kevin Bernard Moran, James Martin Beglin, Raymond James Houghton, Paul McGrath, William Brady, Francis Anthony Stapleton (Cap), John William Aldridge, Kevin Mark Sheedy.
Trainer: John Charlton (England).

Goal: Marek Koniarek (43)

228. 18.02.1987   8th European Champs Qualifiers
SCOTLAND v REPUBLIC OF IRELAND   0-1 (0-1)
Hampden Park, Glasgow

Referee: Henrik van Ettekoven (Holland)   Att: 45,081

SCOTLAND: James Leighton, Raymond Strean McDonald Stewart, Maurice Daniel Robert Malpas (67 Alistair Murdoch McCoist), Alan David Hansen, Richard Charles Gough, Patrick Kevin Francis Michael Nevin, Gordon David Strachan, Robert Sime Aitken (Cap), David Cooper (46 Paul Michael Lyons McStay), Brian John McClair, Maurice Johnston.
Manager: Andrew Roxburgh.

REPUBLIC OF IRELAND: Patrick Bonner, Paul McGrath, Michael Joseph McCarthy, Kevin Bernard Moran, Ronald Andrew Whelan, Raymond James Houghton, Mark Thomas Lawrenson, William Brady (60 John Frederick Byrne), Francis Anthony Stapleton (Cap), John William Aldridge, Anthony Galvin.   Trainer: John Charlton (England).

Goal: Mark Thomas Lawrenson (8)

229. 01.04.1987   8th European Champs Qualifiers
BULGARIA v REPUBLIC OF IRELAND   2-1 (1-0)
"Vasil Levski", Sofia

Referee: Carlos Alberto da Silva Valente (Portugal)
Attendance: 35,247

BULGARIA: Borislav Mihailov, Plamen Nikolov, Georgi Dimitrov (Cap), Nikolai Iliev, Krasimir Bezinski, Hristo Kolev, Nasko Sirakov, Plamen Simeonov (65 Ilia Voinov), Anio Sadkov, Lachezar Tanev, Bojidar Iskrenov (62 Petar Aleksandrov).   Trainer: Hristo Mladenov.

REPUBLIC OF IRELAND: Patrick Bonner, John Christopher Patrick Anderson, Christopher William Gerard Hughton, Kevin Bernard Moran, Michael Joseph McCarthy, Ronald Andrew Whelan, Paul McGrath, William Brady, Francis Anthony Stapleton (Cap) (85 Niall John Quinn), John William Aldridge, Anthony Galvin.
Trainer: John Charlton (England).

Goals: Anio Sadkov (41), Lachezar Tanev (81 pen) / Francis Anthony Stapleton (52)

230. 29.04.1987   8th European Champs Qualifiers
REPUBLIC OF IRELAND v BELGIUM   0-0
Lansdowne Road, Dublin

Referee: Heinz Holzmann (Austria)   Attendance: 49,000

REPUBLIC OF IRELAND: Patrick Bonner, John Christopher Patrick Anderson, Michael Joseph McCarthy, Kevin Bernard Moran, Paul McGrath, Ronald Andrew Whelan, Raymond James Houghton, William Brady (77 John Frederick Byrne), Francis Anthony Stapleton (Cap), John William Aldridge, Anthony Galvin.   Trainer: John Charlton (England).

BELGIUM: Jean-Marie Pfaff, Eric Gerets, Georges Grün, Léo Albert Clijsters, Patrick Vervoort, Frank Vercauteren, Phillipe Albert (66 Pierre Janssen), Nicolaas Pieter Claesen, Vincenzo Scifo, Philippe De Smet, Jan Ceulemans.   Trainer: Guy Thys.

231. 23.05.1987
REPUBLIC OF IRELAND v BRAZIL   1-0 (1-0)
Lansdowne Road, Dublin

Referee: George Sandoz (Switzerland)   Attendance: 30,000

REPUBLIC OF IRELAND: Patrick Bonner, John Christopher Patrick Anderson, Michael Joseph McCarthy (Cap) (63 Kenneth John Philip Petit De Mange), Kevin Bernard Moran, Ronald Andrew Whelan (60 David Francis Langan), Liam Francis O'Brien (79 Niall John Quinn), Paul McGrath, William Brady, Kevin O'Callaghan, John William Aldridge, John Frederick Byrne.   Trainer: John Charlton (England).

BRAZIL: Carlos Roberto Gallo, Josimar Higino Pereira, Geraldo Dutra Pereira "Geraldão", Ricardo Roberto Barreto da Rocha "Ricardo Rocha", Nélson Luís Kerschner "Nelsinho", William Douglas Humia Menezes, Paulo Silas do Prado Pereira, Eduardo Antônio dos Santos "Edu Manga" (64 Raí Souza Vieira de Oliveira), Luís Antônio Corrêa da Costa "Müller" (74 Sérgio Donizete Luís "João Paulo II"), Francisco Ernândi Lima da Silva "Mirandinha II" (68 Romário de Souza Faria), Valdo Cândido Filho "Valdo II".
Trainer: Carlos Alberto Silva.

Goal: William Brady (30)

232. 28.05.1987   8th European Champs Qualifiers
**LUXEMBOURG
v REPUBLIC OF IRELAND 0-2** (0-1)

Municipal, Luxembourg

Referee: Renzo Peduzzi (Switzerland)   Attendance: 4,220

LUXEMBOURG: John van Rijswijck, Laurent Schonckert, Hubert Meunier, Carlo Weis, Marcel Bossi, Jean-Paul Girres (87 Marc Thome), Guy Hellers, Jean-Pierre Barboni, Théo Malget, Robert Langers, Jeannot Reiter (70 Gérard Jeitz).
Trainer: Paul Philipp.

REPUBLIC OF IRELAND: Patrick Bonner, John Christopher Patrick Anderson (52 David Francis Langan), Michael Joseph McCarthy, Kevin Bernard Moran (46 John Frederick Byrne), Paul McGrath, Ronald Andrew Whelan, Raymond James Houghton, William Brady, Francis Anthony Stapleton (Cap), John William Aldridge, Anthony Galvin.
Trainer: John Charlton (England).

Goals: Anthony Galvin (44), Ronald Andrew Whelan (64)

233. 09.09.1987   8th European Champs Qualifiers
**REPUBLIC OF IRELAND
v LUXEMBOURG 2-1** (1-1)

Lansdowne Road, Dublin

Referee: Keith Cooper (Wales)   Attendance: 18,000

REPUBLIC OF IRELAND: Gerald Joseph Peyton, David Francis Langan, Paul McGrath, Kevin Bernard Moran, Augustine Ashley Grimes, Raymond James Houghton, Ronald Andrew Whelan, William Brady, Francis Anthony Stapleton (Cap), Anthony Galvin (56 Niall John Quinn), John Frederick Byrne. Trainer: John Charlton (England).

LUXEMBOURG: John van Rijswijck, Laurent Schonckert, Marcel Bossi, Carlo Weis, Hubert Meunier, Théo Malget, Guy Hellers, Jean-Pierre Barboni (82 Gérard Jeitz), Théo Scholten (65 Gilbert Dresch), Armin Krings, Robert Langers.
Trainer: Paul Philipp.

Goals: Francis Anthony Stapleton (31), Paul McGrath (74) / Armin Krings (29)

234. 14.10.1987   8th European Champs Qualifiers
REPUBLIC OF IRELAND v BULGARIA 2-0 (0-0)

Lansdowne Road, Dublin

Referee: Johannes Nicolaas Ignatius "Jan" Keizer (Holland)
Attendance: 22,000

REPUBLIC OF IRELAND: Patrick Bonner, Paul McGrath, Kevin Bernard Moran, Michael Joseph McCarthy, Ronald Andrew Whelan, William Brady, Mark Thomas Lawrenson, Raymond James Houghton, Francis Anthony Stapleton (Cap), John William Aldridge (77 Niall John Quinn), Anthony Galvin (77 John Frederick Byrne).
Trainer: John Charlton (England).

BULGARIA: Antonio Ananiev (56 Ilia Valov), Plamen Nikolov, Georgi Dimitrov (Cap), Nikolai Iliev, Petar Petrov, Anio Sadkov, Hristo Stoichkov, Plamen Simeonov, Nasko Sirakov, Ilia Voinov (65 Petar Aleksandrov), Bojidar Iskrenov.
Trainer: Hristo Mladenov.

Sent off: William Brady (83)

Goals: Paul McGrath (52), Kevin Bernard Moran (85)

235. 10.11.1987
REPUBLIC OF IRELAND v ISRAEL 5-0 (2-0)

Dalymount Park, Dublin

Referee: Neil Midgley (England)   Attendance: 9,500

REPUBLIC OF IRELAND: Kelham Gerard O'Hanlon, Christopher Barry Morris, Christopher William Gerard Hughton, Kevin Bernard Moran, Michael Joseph McCarthy, John Frederick Byrne, Mark Thomas Lawrenson (Cap), Raymond James Houghton (74 Liam Francis O'Brien), Niall John Quinn, David Thomas Kelly, Kevin Mark Sheedy.
Trainer: John Charlton (England).

ISRAEL: Boni Ginzburg, Avi Cohen II, Menashe Shimonov, Yehuda Amar, Eli Cohen, Uri Malmilian, Avinoam Ovadia (46 Eli Yani), Nir Klinger, Efraim Davidi, Daniel Brailovsky, Shalom Tikva (46 Moshe Eisenberg).
Trainer: Miljenko Mihić (Yugoslavia).

Goals: John Byrne (13), David Thomas Kelly (41, 56, 71 pen), Niall John Quinn (83)

236. 23.03.1988
REPUBLIC OF IRELAND v ROMANIA 2-0 (1-0)
Lansdowne Road, Dublin
Referee: John Martin (England)   Attendance: 30,000
REPUBLIC OF IRELAND: Patrick Bonner, Christopher Barry Morris, Augustine Ashley Grimes, Michael Joseph McCarthy (46 John Christopher Patrick Anderson), Kevin Bernard Moran, John Joseph Sheridan, Anthony Galvin (70 Liam Francis O'Brien), John Frederick Byrne, Francis Anthony Stapleton (Cap) (52 Niall John Quinn), David Thomas Kelly, Kevin Mark Sheedy.   Trainer: John Charlton (England).
ROMANIA: Dumitru Moraru, Mircea Popa, Mircea Rednic, Ioan Andone, Nelu Stănescu, Dorin Mateuț, Ladislau Bölöni (Cap), Marcel Coraș, Ioan Ovidiu Sabău, Claudiu Vaișcovici (46 Horațiu Victor Lasconi), Rodion Gorun Cămătaru. Trainer: Emerich Jenei.
Goals: Kevin Bernard Moran (30), David Thomas Kelly (90)

237. 27.04.1988
REPUBLIC OF IRELAND v YUGOSLAVIA 2-0 (1-0)
Lansdowne Road, Dublin
Referee: George Brian Smith (Scotland)   Att: 12,000
REPUBLIC OF IRELAND: Patrick Bonner, Christopher Barry Morris, Michael Joseph McCarthy, Kevin Bernard Moran, Christopher William Gerard Hughton (54 John Christopher Patrick Anderson), John Joseph Sheridan, Paul McGrath, Raymond James Houghton, Francis Anthony Stapleton (Cap), Mark John Kelly (89 Liam Francis O'Brien), David Thomas Kelly (79 John Frederick Byrne).
Trainer: John Charlton (England).
YUGOSLAVIA: Dragoje Leković, Branko Miljuš, Mirsad Baljić, Faruk Hadžibegić, Marko Elsner, Ljubomir Radanović, Haris Škoro, Milan Janković (88 Zvonimir Boban), Marko Mlinarić (66 Dragoljub Brnović), Mehmet Baždarević, Zlatko Vujović (Cap).   Trainer: Ivan Osim.
Goals: Michael McCarthy (24), Kevin Bernard Moran (64)

238. 22.05.1988
REPUBLIC OF IRELAND v POLAND 3-1 (3-0)
Lansdowne Road, Dublin
Referee: Francigon Roberts (Wales)   Attendance: 19,000
REPUBLIC OF IRELAND: Gerald Joseph Peyton, Christopher Barry Morris, Christopher William Gerard Hughton, Paul McGrath (53 Niall John Quinn), Kevin Bernard Moran (Cap), John Joseph Sheridan (63 Mark John Kelly), Ronald Andrew Whelan (65 John Frederick Byrne), John William Aldridge, Anthony Galvin (63 Liam Francis O'Brien), Anthony Guy Cascarino, Kevin Mark Sheedy.
Trainer: John Charlton (England).
POLAND: Józef Wandzik (46 Grzegorz Stencel), Dariusz Kubicki, Roman Wójcicki, Damian Łukasik (26 Witold Bendkowski, Wiesław Cisek, Ryszard Komornicki (46 Ryszard Tarasiewicz), Jan Urban, Waldemar Prusik (Cap), Jacek Ziober, Dariusz Dziekanowski, Roman Kosecki (46 Robert Warzycha). Trainer: Wojciech Łazarek.
Goals: Kevin Mark Sheedy (12), Anthony Guy Cascarino (31), John Joseph Sheridan (40) / Robert Warzycha (65)

239. 01.06.1988
NORWAY v REPUBLIC OF IRELAND 0-0
Ullevaal, Oslo
Referee: Kurt Sørensen (Denmark)   Attendance: 9,454
NORWAY: Erik Thorstvedt, Hugo Hansen, Erland Johnsen, Rune Bratseth, Gunnar Halle, Kjetil Osvold, Sverre Brandhaug, Ørjan Berg, Karl Petter Løken (75 Carsten Bachke), Jørn Andersen (61 Gøran Sørloth), Jan Berg.
Trainer: Tord Grip (Sweden).
REPUBLIC OF IRELAND: Patrick Bonner, Christopher Barry Morris, Michael Joseph McCarthy, Kevin Bernard Moran, Christopher William Gerard Hughton, Paul McGrath, Ronald Andrew Whelan, Raymond James Houghton, John William Aldridge, Francis Anthony Stapleton (Cap) (62 Anthony Guy Cascarino), Anthony Galvin (74 John Joseph Sheridan).   Trainer: John Charlton (England).

240. 12.06.1988   8th European Champs, 1st Round
ENGLAND v REPUBLIC OF IRELAND 0-1 (0-1)
Neckar, Stuttgart
Referee: Siegfried Kirschen (East Germany)   Att: 53,000
ENGLAND: Peter Leslie Shilton, Gary Michael Stevens, Kenneth Graham Sansom, Neil John Webb (60 Glenn Hoddle), Mark Wright, Anthony Alexander Adams, Bryan Robson (Cap), John Charles Bryan Barnes, Peter Andrew Beardsley (82 Mark Wayne Hateley), Gary Winston Lineker, Christopher Roland Waddle.   Manager: Robert Robson.
REPUBLIC OF IRELAND: Patrick Bonner, Christopher Barry Morris, Michael Joseph McCarthy, Kevin Bernard Moran, Christopher William Gerard Hughton, Raymond James Houghton, Paul McGrath, Ronald Andrew Whelan, Anthony Galvin (75 Kevin Mark Sheedy), John William Aldridge, Francis Anthony Stapleton (Cap) (62 Niall John Quinn).   Trainer: John Charlton (England).
Goal: Raymond James Houghton (6)

241. 15.06.1988   8th European Champs, 1st Round
REPUBLIC OF IRELAND
v SOVIET UNION 1-1 (1-0)
Niedersachsen, Hannover

Referee: Emilio Soriano Aladrén (Spain)   Att: 45,290

REPUBLIC OF IRELAND: Patrick Bonner, Christopher Barry Morris, Michael Joseph McCarthy, Kevin Bernard Moran, Christopher William Gerard Hughton, Raymond James Houghton, Ronald Andrew Whelan, Kevin Mark Sheedy, Anthony Galvin, John William Aldridge, Francis Anthony Stapleton (Cap) (80 Anthony Guy Cascarino). Trainer: John Charlton (England).

SOVIET UNION: Rinat Dasaev (Cap) (69 Viktor Chanov), Tengiz Sulakvelidze (46 Sergey Gotzmanov), Oleg Kuznetzov, Vagiz Khidiyatullin, Anatoliy Demyanenko, Sergey Aleynikov, Aleksandr Zavarov, Aleksey Mikhaylichenko, Vasiliy Ratz, Igor Belanov, Oleg Protasov.   Trainer: Valeriy Lobanovskiy.

Goals: Ronald Andrew Whelan (39) / Oleg Protasov (75)

242. 18.06.1988   8th European Champs, 1st Round
REPUBLIC OF IRELAND v HOLLAND 0-1 (0-0)
Park, Gelsenkirchen

Referee: Horst Brummeier (Austria)   Attendance: 70,800

REPUBLIC OF IRELAND: Patrick Bonner, Christopher Barry Morris (46 Kevin Mark Sheedy), Michael Joseph McCarthy, Kevin Bernard Moran, Christopher William Gerard Hughton, Raymond James Houghton, Paul McGrath, Ronald Andrew Whelan, Anthony Galvin, John William Aldridge, Francis Anthony Stapleton (Cap) (82 Anthony Guy Cascarino). Trainer: John Charlton (England).

HOLLAND: Johannes Franciscus van Breukelen, Hubertus Aegidius Hermanus van Aerle, Ronald Koeman, Franklin Edmundo Rijkaard, Adrianus Andreas van Tiggelen, Jan Jacobus Wouters, Arnoldus Johannes Hyacinthus Mühren (79 Johannes Jacobus Bosman), Gerald Mervin Vanenburg, Erwin Koeman (51 Willem Cornelis Nicolaas Kieft), Ruud Gullit (Cap), Marcelo van Basten.
Trainer: Marinus Henrikus Bernardus Michels.

Goal: Willem Cornelis Nicolaas Kieft (82)

243. 14.09.1988   14th World Cup Qualifiers
NORTHERN IRELAND
v REPUBLIC OF IRELAND 0-0
Windsor Park, Belfast

Referee: Michel Vautrot (France)   Attendance: 19,873

NORTHERN IRELAND: Allen Darrell McKnight, Malachy Martin Donaghy (46 Anton Gerard Patrick Rogan), Alan McDonald, John McClelland (Cap), Nigel Worthington, Stephen Alexander Penney, Daniel Joseph Wilson, Michael Andrew Martin O'Neill, Kingsley Terence Black, James Martin Quinn, Colin John Clarke.
Manager: William Laurence Bingham.

REPUBLIC OF IRELAND: Gerald Joseph Peyton, Christopher Barry Morris, Michael Joseph McCarthy, Kevin Bernard Moran (Cap), Christopher William Gerard Hughton, Raymond James Houghton, Paul McGrath, Ronald Andrew Whelan, Kevin Mark Sheedy, Anthony Guy Cascarino, John William Aldridge.   Trainer: John Charlton (England).

244. 19.10.1988
REPUBLIC OF IRELAND v TUNISIA 4-0 (3-0)
Lansdowne Road, Dublin

Referee: Alan Snoddy (Northern Ireland)   Att: 12,000

REPUBLIC OF IRELAND: Gerald Joseph Peyton, Christopher Barry Morris (46 Patrick Joseph Scully), Michael Joseph McCarthy (Cap), John Christopher Patrick Anderson, Stephen Staunton, Raymond James Houghton (46 David Thomas Kelly), Liam Francis O'Brien, Kevin Mark Sheedy, Mark John Kelly, Anthony Guy Cascarino (70 Kenneth John Philip Petit De Mange), John William Aldridge (70 Niall John Quinn).   Trainer: John Charlton (England).

TUNISIA: Mohamed Nacer Chouchane, Hachemi Ouahchi, Imed Mizouri (41 Ben Messaoud), Mohamed Mahjoubi, Noureddine Bousnina, Khaled Ben Yahia, Modher Baouab, Taoufik M'hadhebi (60 Haythem Abid), Nabil Maâloul, Morad Rannène, Yahmadi (73 Jabali).   Trainer: Mokhtar Tlili.

Goals: Anthony Cascarino (#, #), John William Aldridge (#), Kevin Mark Sheedy (#)

245. 16.11.1988   14th World Cup Qualifiers
SPAIN v REPUBLIC OF IRELAND 2-0 (0-0)
"Benito Villamarín", Sevilla

Referee: Yuriy Savchenko (Soviet Union)   Att: 50,000

SPAIN: Andoni Zubizarreta Urreta, Enrique Sánchez Flores "Quique" (84 Jesús Ángel Solana Bermejo), Manuel Jiménez Jiménez, Genar Andrinúa Cortabarría, Manuel Sanchís Hontiyuello, Alberto Górriz Echarte, José Miguel González Martín del Campo "Michel", Roberto Fernández Bonillo, Rafael Martín Vázquez, Manuel Sánchez Delgado "Manolo" (67 Ramón Vázquez García), Emilio Butragueño Santos (Cap). Trainer: Luis Suárez Miramónte.

REPUBLIC OF IRELAND: Patrick Bonner, Christopher Barry Morris, Michael Joseph McCarthy, David Anthony O'Leary, Stephen Staunton, John Joseph Sheridan (82 Liam Francis O'Brien), Kevin Bernard Moran (Cap), Raymond James Houghton, Anthony Galvin, John William Aldridge (65 Niall John Quinn), Anthony Guy Cascarino.
Trainer: John Charlton (England).

Goals: Manuel Sánchez Delgado "Manolo" (52), Emilio Butragueño Santos (66)

246. 07.02.1989
REPUBLIC OF IRELAND v FRANCE 0-0
Dalymount Park, Dublin

Referee: John Walter Lloyd (Wales)   Attendance: 22,000

REPUBLIC OF IRELAND: Patrick Bonner, Christopher Barry Morris, Michael Joseph McCarthy (Cap), Christopher William Gerard Hughton, William Brady, Paul McGrath, Ronald Andrew Whelan, Raymond James Houghton, Francis Anthony Stapleton (76 John William Aldridge), Anthony Guy Cascarino, Andrew David Townsend.
Trainer: John Charlton (England).

FRANCE: Joël Bats, Manuel Amoros (Cap), Sylvain Kastendeuch, Luc Sonor, Patrick Battiston, Frank Silvestre (74 Alain Roche), Jean-Philippe Durand, Frank Sauzée, Stéphane Paille (46 José Touré), Jean-Pierre Papin, Laurent Blanc (67 Philippe Vercruysse).   Trainer: Michel Platini.

247. 08.03.1989   14th World Cup Qualifiers
HUNGARY v REPUBLIC OF IRELAND 0-0
Népstadion, Budapest

Referee: Zoran Petrović (Yugoslavia)   Attendance: 34,000

HUNGARY: Péter Disztl, Zoltán Bognár, László Disztl, János Sass, István Kozma, Lajos Détári, Ervin Kovács, Gyula Hajszán, József Gregor (78 Imre Boda), József Kiprich, Ferenc Mészáros (46 György Bognár).   Trainer: Bertalan Bicskei.

REPUBLIC OF IRELAND: Patrick Bonner, Christopher Barry Morris, Michael Joseph McCarthy, Kevin Bernard Moran (Cap), Christopher William Gerard Hughton, Raymond James Houghton, Paul McGrath, Ronald Andrew Whelan, Kevin Mark Sheedy, John William Aldridge (80 William Brady), Anthony Guy Cascarino (80 Niall John Quinn).
Trainer: John Charlton (England).

248. 26.04.1989   14th World Cup Qualifiers
REPUBLIC OF IRELAND v SPAIN 1-0 (1-0)
Lansdowne Road, Dublin

Referee: Horst Brummeier (Austria)   Attendance: 49,600

REPUBLIC OF IRELAND: Patrick Bonner, Christopher William Gerard Hughton, Michael Joseph McCarthy (Cap), Kevin Bernard Moran, Stephen Staunton, Raymond James Houghton, Paul McGrath, Ronald Andrew Whelan, Francis Anthony Stapleton (69 Andrew David Townsend), Anthony Guy Cascarino, Kevin Mark Sheedy.
Trainer: John Charlton (England).

SPAIN: Andoni Zubizarreta Urreta, Enrique Sánchez Flores "Quique" (69 Eusebio Sacristán Mena), Manuel Jiménez Jiménez, Ricardo Jesús Serna Orozco, Alberto Górriz Echarte, Manuel Sanchís Hontiyuello, Roberto Fernández Bonillo, José Miguel González Martín del Campo "Michel", Rafael Martín Vázquez, Manuel Sánchez Delgado "Manolo", Emilio Butragueño Santos (Cap) (69 Julio Salinas Fernández).
Trainer: Luis Suárez Miramónte.

Goal: José Miguel González Martín del Campo "Michel" (16 own goal)

249. 28.05.1989   14th World Cup Qualifiers
REPUBLIC OF IRELAND v MALTA 2-0 (1-0)
Lansdowne Road, Dublin
Referee: José Rosa dos Santos (Portugal)   Att: 49,600
REPUBLIC OF IRELAND: Patrick Bonner, Christopher William Gerard Hughton, Kevin Bernard Moran (Cap), David Anthony O'Leary, Stephen Staunton, Ronald Andrew Whelan, Paul McGrath, Raymond James Houghton (69 Andrew David Townsend), Francis Anthony Stapleton (27 John William Aldridge), Anthony Guy Cascarino, Kevin Mark Sheedy. Trainer: John Charlton (England).

MALTA: David Cluett, Edwin Camilleri, Alex Azzopardi (65 David Carabott), Joseph Galea, Silvio Vella, John Buttigieg, Carmel Busuttil, Raymond Vella (Cap), Charles Scerri, Michael Degiorgio, Martin Gregory.
Trainer: Horst Heese (West Germany).

Goals: Raymond James Houghton (32), Kevin Moran (55)

250. 04.06.1989   14th World Cup Qualifiers
REPUBLIC OF IRELAND v HUNGARY 2-0 (1-0)
Lansdowne Road, Dublin
Referee: Egil Nervik (Norway)   Attendance: 50,000
REPUBLIC OF IRELAND: Patrick Bonner, Christopher William Gerard Hughton, Kevin Bernard Moran (Cap), David Anthony O'Leary, Stephen Staunton, Andrew David Townsend, Paul McGrath (79 Christopher Barry Morris), Raymond James Houghton, John William Aldridge (74 William Brady), Anthony Guy Cascarino, Kevin Mark Sheedy. Trainer: John Charlton (England).

HUNGARY: Péter Disztl, István Kozma, László Disztl, Imre Garaba, József Keller, József Fitos, Zoltán Bognár, Lajos Détári, Tibor Csehi (66 György Bognár), Ferenc Mészáros (72 István Vincze), Imre Boda.   Trainer: Bertalan Bicskei.

Goals: Paul McGrath (34), Anthony Guy Cascarino (80)

251. 06.09.1989
REPUBLIC OF IRELAND
v WEST GERMANY 1-1 (1-1)
Lansdowne Road, Dublin
Referee: Frans Van den Wijngaert (Belgium)   Att: 46,000
REPUBLIC OF IRELAND: Patrick Bonner, Christopher Barry Morris, Michael Joseph McCarthy (Cap), David Anthony O'Leary, Stephen Staunton, William Brady (35 Andrew David Townsend), Paul McGrath, Ronald Andrew Whelan, John William Aldridge (75 Anthony Guy Cascarino), Francis Anthony Stapleton (75 John Frederick Byrne), Anthony Galvin.   Trainer: John Charlton (England).

GERMANY: Bodo Illgner (46 Raimond Aumann), Klaus Augenthaler, Stefan Reuter, Guido Buchwald (46 Alois Reinhardt), Hans Pflügler, Hans Dorfner (85 Holger Fach), Pierre Littbarski (Cap), Andreas Möller, Olaf Thon, Thomas Häßler, Roland Wohlfahrt.   Trainer: Franz Beckenbauer.

Goals: Francis Anthony Stapleton (10) / Hans Dorfner (33)

252. 11.10.1989   14th World Cup Qualifiers
REPUBLIC OF IRELAND
v NORTHERN IRELAND 3-0 (1-0)
Lansdowne Road, Dublin
Referee: Pietro d'Elia (Italy)   Attendance: 45,800
REPUBLIC OF IRELAND: Patrick Bonner, Christopher Barry Morris, Michael Joseph McCarthy (Cap), Kevin Bernard Moran, Stephen Staunton (77 David Anthony O'Leary), Ronald Andrew Whelan, Andrew David Townsend, Raymond James Houghton, John William Aldridge, Anthony Guy Cascarino, Kevin Mark Sheedy.
Trainer: John Charlton (England).

NORTHERN IRELAND: George Dunlop, Gary James Fleming, Nigel Worthington, Malachy Martin Donaghy (Cap), Alan McDonald, David McCreery (72 Colin O'Neill), Daniel Joseph Wilson, Michael Andrew Martin O'Neill (80 Kevin James Wilson), Colin John Clarke, Norman Whiteside, Robert Dennison.   Manager: William Laurence Bingham.

Goals: Ronald Whelan (43), Anthony Guy Cascarino (47), Raymond James Houghton (57)

253. 15.11.1989   14th World Cup Qualifiers
MALTA v REPUBLIC OF IRELAND 0-2 (0-1)
National, Ta'Qali
Referee: Jacob Uilenberg (Holland)   Attendance: 21,942
MALTA: Reginald Cini, Silvio Vella, Alex Azzopardi (68 Hubert Suda), Joseph Galea, Charles Scerri, John Buttigieg (Cap), Carmel Busuttil, David Carabott, Michael Degiorgio, Martin Gregory, Jesmond Zerafa (68 Joseph Zarb).
Trainer: Horst Heese (West Germany).

REPUBLIC OF IRELAND: Patrick Bonner, Paul McGrath, Kevin Bernard Moran (33 Christopher Barry Morris), David Anthony O'Leary, Stephen Staunton, Raymond James Houghton, Kevin Mark Sheedy, Andrew David Townsend, Ronald Andrew Whelan (Cap), John William Aldridge, Anthony Guy Cascarino.   Trainer: John Charlton (England).

Goals: John William Aldridge (30, 68 pen)

254. 28.03.1990
REPUBLIC OF IRELAND v WALES 1-0 (0-0)
Lansdowne Road, Dublin
Referee: Allan Gunn (England)   Attendance: 41,350
REPUBLIC OF IRELAND: Patrick Bonner, Christopher Barry Morris, Michael Joseph McCarthy, Kevin Bernard Moran (75 David Anthony O'Leary), Stephen Staunton (67 Christopher William Gerard Hughton), Ronald Andrew Whelan (Cap) (46 Kevin Mark Sheedy), Andrew David Townsend, John Frederick Byrne, Bernard Joseph Slaven, Anthony Guy Cascarino, John Joseph Sheridan. Trainer: John Charlton (England).
WALES: Neville Southall, Gareth David Hall, David Owen Phillips, Peter Nicholas, Mark Aizlewood, Andrew Roger Melville, Gavin Terence Maguire, Barry Horne, Ian James Rush, Malcolm Allen, Alan Davies. Manager: Terence Charles Yorath.
Goal: Bernard Joseph Slaven (86)

255. 25.04.1990
REPUBLIC OF IRELAND v SOVIET UNION 1-0 (0-0)
Lansdowne Road, Dublin
Referee: Alfred Kleinaitis (United States)   Att: 43,990
REPUBLIC OF IRELAND: Gerald Joseph Peyton, Christopher Barry Morris (73 Christopher William Gerard Hughton), Michael Joseph McCarthy (Cap), David Anthony O'Leary (77 Kevin Bernard Moran), Stephen Staunton, Gary Patrick Waddock, Paul McGrath, Andrew David Townsend, Niall John Quinn, David Thomas Kelly, Kevin Mark Sheedy. Trainer: John Charlton (England).
SOVIET UNION: Aleksandr Uvarov, Sergey Fokin, Vagiz Khidiyatullin, Oleg Kuznetsov (Cap), Sergey Gorlukovich, Vadim Tischenko, Andrey Zygmantovich, Valeriy Broshin (76 Fëdor Cherenkov), Aleksandr Borodyuk, Vladimir Lyutyy (70 Yuriy Savichev), Igor Belanov.   Trainer: Valeriy Lobanovskiy.
Goal: Stephen Staunton (59)

256. 16.05.1990
REPUBLIC OF IRELAND v FINLAND 1-1 (0-0)
Lansdowne Road, Dublin
Referee: Roger Gifford (Wales)   Attendance: 31,556
REPUBLIC OF IRELAND: Patrick Bonner, Christopher William Gerard Hughton, Michael Joseph McCarthy, David Anthony O'Leary, Stephen Staunton (67 Christopher Barry Morris), William Brady (Cap) (27 Andrew David Townsend), Paul McGrath, Raymond James Houghton, Bernard Joseph Slaven (56 John William Aldridge), Anthony Guy Cascarino, John Frederick Byrne (63 Kevin Mark Sheedy). Trainer: John Charlton (England).
FINLAND: Olavi Huttunen, Jouko Vuorela, Ari Heikkinen, Petri Sulonen, Markku Kanerva, Hannu Jäntti (83 Jukka Turunen), Pasi Tauriainen, Petri Järvinen, Jari Litmanen (71 Vesa Tauriainen), Marko Myyry (59 Mika J. Aaltonen), Mika-Matti Paatelainen.   Trainer: Jukka Vakkila.
Goals: Kevin Mark Sheedy (85) / Vesa Tauriainen (74)

257. 27.05.1990
TURKEY v REPUBLIC OF IRELAND 0-0
Kemal Atatürk, Izmir
Referee: A. Kirkov (Soviet Union)   Attendance: 10,000
TURKEY: Engin İpekoğlu, Kemal Serdar (86 Gökhan Gedikali), Gökhan Keskin, Ogün Temizkanoğlu, Riza Çalımbay, Oğuz Çetin, Mustafa Yücedağ (67 Savaş Demiral), Ünal Karaman (73 Mehmet Özdilek), Tugay Kerimoğlu, Metin Tekin, Feyyaz Uçar (67 Hamı Mandıralı). Trainer: Josef Piontek (West Germany).
REPUBLIC OF IRELAND: Patrick Bonner, Christopher Barry Morris, Michael Joseph McCarthy (Cap), David Anthony O'Leary (67 Bernard Joseph Slaven), Stephen Staunton (51 Christopher William Gerard Hughton), Gary Patrick Waddock (51 John Frederick Byrne), Paul McGrath, Andrew David Townsend (46 John Joseph Sheridan), Kevin Mark Sheedy, Anthony Guy Cascarino, John William Aldridge. Trainer: John Charlton (England).

258. 02.06.1990
MALTA v REPUBLIC OF IRELAND 0-3 (0-1)
National, Ta'Qali
Referee: Edgar Azzopardi (Malta)   Attendance: 2,232
MALTA: Reginald Cini, Silvio Vella (63 Jesmond Delia), Kristian Laferla, Joseph Galea (83 Edwin Camilleri), Martin Gregory (74 Joseph Zarb), John Buttigieg, Jesmond Zerafa, Raymond Vella (Cap), David Carabott, Michael Degiorgio, Bernard Licari. Trainer: Horst Heese (West Germany).
REPUBLIC OF IRELAND: Gerald Joseph Peyton, Christopher William Gerard Hughton, Kevin Bernard Moran (Cap), David Anthony O'Leary, Stephen Staunton, Alan Francis McLoughlin, John Joseph Sheridan, John Frederick Byrne, Niall John Quinn, David Thomas Kelly (63 Francis Anthony Stapleton), Bernard Joseph Slaven (72 Andrew David Townsend).   Trainer: John Charlton (England).
Goals: Niall John Quinn (43), Andrew David Townsend (72), Francis Anthony Stapleton (87)

259. 11.06.1990   14th World Cup, 1st Round
ENGLAND v REPUBLIC OF IRELAND 1-1 (1-0)
Sant'Elia, Cagliari

Referee: Aron Schmidhuber (West Germany)   Att: 35,238

ENGLAND: Peter Leslie Shilton, Gary Michael Stevens, Stuart Pearce, Desmond Sinclair Walker, Terence Ian Butcher, Christopher Roland Waddle, Bryan Robson (Cap), Paul John Gascoigne, John Charles Bryan Barnes, Peter Andrew Beardsley (Stephen McMahon), Gary Winston Lineker (83 Stephen George Bull).   Manager: Robert Robson.

REPUBLIC OF IRELAND: Patrick Bonner, Christopher Barry Morris, Michael Joseph McCarthy (Cap), Kevin Bernard Moran, Stephen Staunton, Raymond James Houghton, Paul McGrath, Andrew David Townsend, Kevin Mark Sheedy, Anthony Guy Cascarino, John William Aldridge (Alan Francis McLoughlin).   Trainer: John Charlton (England).

Goals: Gary Winston Lineker (8) / Kevin Mark Sheedy (72)

260. 17.06.1990   14th World Cup, 1st Round
REPUBLIC OF IRELAND v EGYPT 0-0
La Favorita, Palermo

Referee: Marcel Van Langenhove (Belgium)   Att: 33,288

REPUBLIC OF IRELAND: Patrick Bonner, Christopher Barry Morris, Michael Joseph McCarthy (Cap), Kevin Bernard Moran, Stephen Staunton, Raymond James Houghton, Paul McGrath, Andrew David Townsend, Kevin Mark Sheedy, Anthony Guy Cascarino (84 Niall John Quinn), John William Aldridge (64 Alan Francis McLoughlin).
Trainer: John Charlton (England).

EGYPT: Ahmed Shobair, Ibrahim Hassan Hussein, Hany Guda Ramzy, Hesham Yakan Zaki, Rabie Yassin, Ahmed Abdou El-Kass (76 Gamal Abdelhamid), Ismail Awadallah Youssef, Magdi Abdelghani (Cap), Magdy Tolba (60 Taher Abouzeid Sayed), Osama Orabi, Hossam Ahmad Omar Hussein "Hossam Hassan".   Trainer: Mahmoud El-Gohary.

261. 21.06.1990   14th World Cup, 1st Round
REPUBLIC OF IRELAND v HOLLAND 1-1 (0-1)
La Favorita, Palermo

Referee: Michel Vautrot (France)   Attendance: 33,288

REPUBLIC OF IRELAND: Patrick Bonner, Christopher Barry Morris, Michael Joseph McCarthy (Cap), Kevin Bernard Moran, Stephen Staunton, Raymond James Houghton, Paul McGrath, Andrew David Townsend, Kevin Mark Sheedy (61 Ronald Andrew Whelan), Niall John Quinn, John William Aldridge (61 Anthony Guy Cascarino).
Trainer: John Charlton (England).

HOLLAND: Johannes Franciscus van Breukelen, Hubertus Aegidius Hermanus van Aerle, Franklin Edmundo Rijkaard, Ronald Koeman, Adrianus Andreas van Tiggelen, Richard Peter Witschge (59 Hendrik Fräser), Jan Jacobus Wouters, Ruud Gullit (Cap), Willem Cornelis Nicolaas Kieft (78 Johannes Maria van Loen), Johannes Paulus Gillhaus, Marcelo van Basten.   Trainer: Leo Beenhakker.

Goals: Niall John Quinn (71) / Ruud Gullit (10)

262. 25.06.1990   14th World Cup, 2nd Round
REPUBLIC OF IRELAND v ROMANIA 0-0 (AET)
Luigi Ferraris, Genova

Referee: José Ramiz Wright (Brazil)   Attendance: 31,818

REPUBLIC OF IRELAND: Patrick Bonner, Christopher Barry Morris, Michael Joseph McCarthy (Cap), Kevin Bernard Moran, Stephen Staunton (93 David Anthony O'Leary), Raymond James Houghton, Paul McGrath, Andrew David Townsend, Kevin Mark Sheedy, Niall John Quinn, John William Aldridge (21 Anthony Guy Cascarino).
Trainer: John Charlton (England).

ROMANIA: Silviu Lung (Cap), Mircea Rednic, Ioan Andone, Gheorghe Popescu, Michael Klein, Ioan Ovidiu Sabău (97 Daniel Timofte), Gheorghe Hagi, Ionuț Angelo Lupescu, Iosif Rotariu, Florin Răducioiu (64 Dănuț Lupu), Gavril Pelé Balint.
Trainer: Emerich Jenei.

Penalties: 0-1 Gheorghe Hagi, 1-1 Kevin Mark Sheedy,
1-2 Dănuț Lupu, 2-2 Raymond James Houghton,
2-3 Iosif Rotariu, 3-3 Andrew David Townsend,
3-4 Ionuț Angelo Lupescu, 4-4 Anthony Guy Cascarino,
Daniel Timofte (miss), 5-4 David Anthony O'Leary

263. 30.06.1990   14th World Cup, Quarter-Finals
ITALY v REPUBLIC OF IRELAND 1-0 (1-0)
Olimpico, Roma

Referee: Carlos Alberto da Silva Valente (Portugal)
Attendance: 73,303

ITALY: Walter Zenga, Giuseppe Bergomi (Cap), Paolo Maldini, Franco Baresi II, Riccardo Ferri II, Luigi De Agostini, Roberto Donadoni, Fernando De Napoli, Salvatore Schillaci, Giuseppe Giannini (64 Carlo Ancelotti), Roberto Baggio I (71 Aldo Serena).   Trainer: Azeglio Vicini.

REPUBLIC OF IRELAND: Patrick Bonner, Christopher Barry Morris, Michael Joseph McCarthy (Cap), Kevin Bernard Moran, Stephen Staunton, Raymond James Houghton, Paul McGrath, Andrew David Townsend, Kevin Mark Sheedy, Niall John Quinn (52 Anthony Guy Cascarino), John William Aldridge (77 John Joseph Sheridan).
Trainer: John Charlton (England).

Goal: Salvatore Schillaci (38)

264. 12.09.1990
REPUBLIC OF IRELAND v MOROCCO 1-0 (0-0)
Lansdowne Road, Dublin
Referee: Frederick McKnight (N. Ireland)   Att: 19,450
REPUBLIC OF IRELAND: Patrick Bonner, Joseph Dennis Irwin, Michael Joseph McCarthy (Cap), David Anthony O'Leary, Stephen Staunton, Ronald Andrew Whelan, Andrew David Townsend (65 John Joseph Sheridan), Raymond James Houghton, David Thomas Kelly, Niall John Quinn (59 Anthony Guy Cascarino), Mark John Kelly (70 Alan Francis McLoughlin).   Trainer: John Charlton (England).
MOROCCO: Abdelkader El Brazi, Jbilou (76 Tahar El-Khalej), Hassan Benabicha, Abderrazak Khairi, Mouhcine Bouhlal, Noureddine Jrindou Naybet, Khalid Raghib, Rachid Daoudi, Abdelmajid Bouyboud "M'Jid", Hassan Nader, Abdelssalam El Ghrissi "Laghrissi".
Trainer: Werner Olk (West Germany).
Goal: David Thomas Kelly (75)

265. 17.10.1990   9th European Champs Qualifiers
REPUBLIC OF IRELAND v TURKEY 5-0 (2-0)
Lansdowne Road, Dublin
Referee: Erik Fredriksson (Sweden)   Attendance: 46,000
REPUBLIC OF IRELAND: Patrick Bonner, Joseph Dennis Irwin, Michael Joseph McCarthy (Cap), David Anthony O'Leary, Stephen Staunton, Christopher William Gerard Hughton, Andrew David Townsend (74 Kevin Bernard Moran), Raymond James Houghton, Niall John Quinn (68 Anthony Guy Cascarino), John William Aldridge, John Joseph Sheridan.   Trainer: John Charlton (England).
TURKEY: Engin İpekoğlu, Riza Çalımbay, Tugay Kerimoğlu, Kemal Serdar, Gökhan Keskin, Ercan Koloğlu (46 Tanju Çolak), Bülent Korkmaz, Oğuz Çetin, Mehmet Özdilek, Hamı Mandıralı, Sercan Görgülü (46 Metin Tekin).
Trainer: Josef Piontek (West Germany).
Goals: John William Aldridge (11, 57, 72 pen), David Anthony O'Leary (40), Niall John Quinn (65)

266. 14.11.1990   9th European Champs Qualifiers
REPUBLIC OF IRELAND v ENGLAND 1-1 (0-1)
Lansdowne Road, Dublin
Referee: Pietro D'Elia (Italy)   Attendance: 46,000
REPUBLIC OF IRELAND: Patrick Bonner, Christopher Barry Morris, Michael Joseph McCarthy (Cap), David Anthony O'Leary, Stephen Staunton, Ronald Andrew Whelan (74 Alan Francis McLoughlin), Paul McGrath, Raymond James Houghton, Niall John Quinn (61 Anthony Guy Cascarino), John William Aldridge, Andrew David Townsend.
Trainer: John Charlton (England).
ENGLAND: Christopher Charles Eric Woods, Lee Michael Dixon, Stuart Pearce, Anthony Alexander Adams, Desmond Sinclair Walker, Mark Wright, David Andrew Platt, Gordon Sidney Cowans, Peter Andrew Beardsley, Gary Winston Lineker (Cap), Stephen McMahon.
Manager: Graham Taylor.
Goals: Anthony Cascarino (80) / David Andrew Platt (67)

267. 06.02.1991
WALES v REPUBLIC OF IRELAND 0-3 (0-1)
The Racecourse, Wrexham
Referee: Frederick McKnight (Northern Ireland)   Att: 9,168
WALES: Neville Southall, Gareth David Hall, Paul John Bodin, Mark Aizlewood, Eric Young (46 Gary Andrew Speed), Kevin Ratcliffe, Barry Horne, Peter Nicholas, Ian James Rush (51 Malcolm Allen), Dean Nicholas Saunders, Colin James Pascoe.   Manager: Terence Charles Yorath.
REPUBLIC OF IRELAND: Patrick Bonner, Joseph Dennis Irwin, Kevin Bernard Moran (Cap), Paul McGrath, Stephen Staunton, Alan Francis McLoughlin, Andrew David Townsend, John Frederick Byrne, Niall John Quinn, Bernard Joseph Slaven (68 David Thomas Kelly), Kevin Mark Sheedy.
Trainer: John Charlton (England).
Goals: Niall John Quinn (24, 66), John Frederick Byrne (86)

268. 27.03.1991   9th European Champs Qualifiers
ENGLAND v REPUBLIC OF IRELAND 1-1 (1-1)
Wembley, London
Referee: Kurt Röthlisberger (Switzerland)   Att: 77,753
ENGLAND: David Andrew Seaman, Lee Michael Dixon, Stuart Pearce, Anthony Alexander Adams (46 Lee Stuart Sharpe), Desmond Sinclair Walker, Mark Wright, Bryan Robson (Cap), David Andrew Platt, Peter Andrew Beardsley, Gary Winston Lineker (76 Ian Edward Wright), John Charles Bryan Barnes.   Manager: Graham Taylor.
REPUBLIC OF IRELAND: Patrick Bonner, Joseph Dennis Irwin, Kevin Bernard Moran (Cap), David Anthony O'Leary, Stephen Staunton, Andrew David Townsend, Paul McGrath, Raymond James Houghton, Niall John Quinn, John William Aldridge (71 Anthony Guy Cascarino), Kevin Mark Sheedy.
Trainer: John Charlton (England).
Goals: Lee Michael Dixon (9) / Niall John Quinn (27)

269. 01.05.1991   9th European Champs Qualifiers
REPUBLIC OF IRELAND v POLAND 0-0
Lansdowne Road, Dublin
Referee: John Blankenstein (Holland)   Attendance: 45,000
REPUBLIC OF IRELAND: Patrick Bonner, Joseph Dennis Irwin, Kevin Bernard Moran (Cap), David Anthony O'Leary, Stephen Staunton, Andrew David Townsend, Paul McGrath, Raymond James Houghton, Niall John Quinn (71 Anthony Guy Cascarino), John William Aldridge (68 Bernard Joseph Slaven), Kevin Mark Sheedy.
Trainer: John Charlton (England).
POLAND: Józef Wandzik, Dariusz Kubicki, Czesław Jakołcewicz, Piotr Soczyński, Dariusz Wdowczyk, Robert Warzycha, Ryszard Tarasiewicz (Cap), Piotr Czachowski, Roman Szewczyk, Jan Urban (87 Michał Gębura), Jan Furtok (89 Roman Kosecki).   Trainer: Andrzej Strejlau.

270. 22.05.1991
REPUBLIC OF IRELAND v CHILE 1-1 (0-0)
Lansdowne Road, Dublin
Referee: Daniel Roduit (Switzerland)   Attendance: 32,230
REPUBLIC OF IRELAND: Gerald Joseph Peyton, Christopher William Gerard Hughton, Kevin Bernard Moran (Cap), David Anthony O'Leary (6 Paul McGrath), Stephen Staunton, Andrew David Townsend, Roy Maurice Keane, Raymond James Houghton (64 Alan Francis McLoughlin), John Joseph Sheridan, David Thomas Kelly, Kevin Mark Sheedy (71 Anthony Guy Cascarino).
Trainer: John Charlton (England).
CHILE: Patricio Armando Toledo, Andrés Antonio Romero, Luis Abarca Aravena, Ronald Hugo Fuentes Núñez, Fabián Guevara Arredondo (15 Marcelo Miranda), Jaime Andrés Vera (63 Jorge Alejandro Contreras), Rodrígo Vicente Gómez, Nelson Rodrígo Parraguez Romero, Fabián Raphael Estay, Luis Guarda (78 Aníbal Segundo González), Hugo Eduardo Rubio.
Trainer: Arturo Salah.
Goals: David Thomas Kelly (82) / Fabián Raphael Estay (76)

271. 01.06.1991
**UNITED STATES
v REPUBLIC OF IRELAND 1-1** (0-0)
Foxboro Stadium, Foxboro
Referee: Gordon Arrowsmith (Canada)   Attendance: 51,273
UNITED STATES: Anthony Michael Meola, Jeff Agoos, Marcelo Luis Balboa, Steven Trittschuh, Bruce Savage, Janusz Michallik, Brian Quinn (86 Troy Snyder), Christopher Joel Henderson, Bruce Murray, Peter Vermes (Cap) (57 Hugo Pérez), Eric Wynalda.
Trainer: Velibor Milutinović (Yugoslavia).
REPUBLIC OF IRELAND: Patrick Bonner, Joseph Dennis Irwin (72 John Joseph Sheridan), Kevin Bernard Moran, Michael Joseph McCarthy (Cap), Stephen Staunton, Andrew David Townsend, Paul McGrath, Raymond James Houghton, Anthony Guy Cascarino, David Thomas Kelly, Kevin Mark Sheedy. Trainer: John Charlton (England).
Goals: Eric Wynalda (68) / Anthony Guy Cascarino (56)

272. 11.09.1991
HUNGARY v REPUBLIC OF IRELAND 1-2 (0-0)
Rába ETO, Győr
Referee: Periklis Vasilakis (Greece)   Attendance: 6,000
HUNGARY: Zsolt Petry, László Disztl, Péter Lipcsei, Emil Lőrincz, Tamás Mónos (74 Vendel Rugovics), István Kozma, Lajos Détári, Ervin Kovács (55 Balázs Bérczy), Tibor Csehi, Kálmán Kovács, István Vincze (65 Dénes Eszenyi).
Trainer: Kálmán Mészöly.
REPUBLIC OF IRELAND: Patrick Bonner, Joseph Dennis Irwin, Terence Michael Phelan (82 Christopher Barry Morris), Michael Joseph McCarthy (Cap), David Anthony O'Leary, John Joseph Sheridan (46 Alan Francis McLoughlin), Roy Maurice Keane, Raymond James Houghton, Niall John Quinn, David Thomas Kelly (63 John William Aldridge), Kevin Mark Sheedy.
Trainer: John Charlton (England).
Goals: Kálmán Kovács (60) /
David Thomas Kelly (61), Kevin Mark Sheedy (69)

273. 16.10.1991   9th European Champs Qualifiers
POLAND v REPUBLIC OF IRELAND 3-3 (0-1)
Lech, Poznań
Referee: Guy Goethals (Belgium)   Attendance: 20,000
POLAND: Józef Wandzik, Dariusz Kubicki (33 Andrzej Lesiak), Dariusz Wdowczyk, Piotr Soczyński, Piotr Czachowski, Roman Kosecki, Janusz Nawrocki (79 Dariusz Skrzypczak), Ryszard Tarasiewicz (Cap), Jacek Ziober, Jan Furtok, Jan Urban.   Trainer: Andrzej Strejlau.
REPUBLIC OF IRELAND: Patrick Bonner, Joseph Dennis Irwin, David Anthony O'Leary, Kevin Bernard Moran (Cap), Stephen Staunton (54 Terence Michael Phelan), Christopher Barry Morris, Andrew David Townsend, Paul McGrath, Roy Maurice Keane, Anthony Guy Cascarino, Kevin Mark Sheedy.
Trainer: John Charlton (England).
Goals: Piotr Czachowski (54), Jan Furtok (76), Jan Urban (86) / Paul McGrath (11), Andrew David Townsend (62), Anthony Guy Cascarino (68)

274. 13.11.1991 9th European Champs Qualifiers
TURKEY v REPUBLIC OF IRELAND 1-3 (1-1)
Ismet Inönü, Istanbul
Referee: Zoran Petrović (Yugoslavia) Attendance: 42,000
TURKEY: Hayrettin Demirbaş, Recep Çetin (66 Bülent Korkmaz), Turhan Sofuoğlu, Gökhan Keskin, Tugay Kerimoğlu, Ogün Temizkanoğlu, Feyyaz Uçar (46 Rıdvan Dilmen), Riza Çalımbay, Hamı Mandıralı, Oğuz Çetin, Orhan Çıkırıkçı. Trainer: Josef Piontek (Germany).
REPUBLIC OF IRELAND: Patrick Bonner, Christopher William Gerard Hughton, Terence Michael Phelan, David Anthony O'Leary, Michael Joseph McCarthy (Cap), Stephen Staunton, Paul McGrath, John Frederick Byrne, Anthony Guy Cascarino, John William Aldridge, Kevin Mark Sheedy. Trainer: John Charlton (England).
Goals: Riza Çalımbay (12 pen) /
John Frederick Byrne (7, 58), Anthony Guy Cascarino (55)

275. 19.02.1992
REPUBLIC OF IRELAND v WALES 0-1 (0-0)
Royal Dublin Society Showground, Dublin
Referee: Serge Muhmenthaler (Switzerland) Att: 15,100
REPUBLIC OF IRELAND: Patrick Bonner, Christopher Barry Morris, Joseph Dennis Irwin, David Anthony O'Leary, Liam Sean Daish, Andrew David Townsend (Cap) (46 Alan Francis McLoughlin), Terence Michael Phelan (55 John William Aldridge), John Frederick Byrne, Roy Maurice Keane, Anthony Guy Cascarino (67 Niall John Quinn), Kevin Mark Sheedy. Trainer: John Charlton (England).
WALES: Neville Southall, David Owen Phillips, Mark Rosslyn Bowen, Mark Aizlewood, Eric Young (63 Paul John Bodin), Christopher Jeremiah Symons, Barry Horne, Mark Anthony Pembridge (76 Glyn Peter Hodges), Dean Nicholas Saunders (86 Alan Bruce Neilson), Leslie Mark Hughes, Gary Andrew Speed (46 Clayton Graham Blackmore).
Manager: Terence Charles Yorath.
Goal: Mark Andrew Pembridge (72)

276. 25.03.1992
**REPUBLIC OF IRELAND
v SWITZERLAND 2-1** (1-1)
Lansdowne Road, Dublin
Referee: Raúl Dominguez (United States) Att: 23,601
REPUBLIC OF IRELAND: Patrick Bonner, Christopher Barry Morris, Terence Michael Phelan, David Anthony O'Leary (Liam Sean Daish), Paul McGrath (Cap), Roy Maurice Keane, Ronald Andrew Whelan, Edward John Paul McGoldrick (46 Liam Francis O'Brien), Thomas Coyne (80 John William Aldridge), Anthony Guy Cascarino, Stephen Staunton (55 Kevin Mark Sheedy).
Trainer: John Charlton (England).

SWITZERLAND: Martin Brunner (40 Marco Pascolo), Harald Gämperle, Christophe Ohrel (51 Régis Rothenbühler), André Egli, Peter Schepull, Thomas Bickel (66 Marcel Heldmann), Blaise Piffaretti, Alain Sutter, Alain Geiger, Stéphane Chapuisat (82 Xavier Dietlin), Kubilay Türkyilmaz.
Trainer: Roy Hodgson (England).
Goals: Thomas Coyne (28), John William Aldridge (88 pen) /
Alain Sutter (26)

277. 29.04.1992
**REPUBLIC OF IRELAND
v UNITED STATES 4-1** (0-0)
Lansdowne Road, Dublin
Referee: Michel Piraux (Belgium) Attendance: 27,000
REPUBLIC OF IRELAND: Gerald Joseph Peyton, Christopher Barry Morris, Joseph Dennis Irwin (62 Michael Joseph Milligan), David Anthony O'Leary (72 Brian Patrick Carey), Paul McGrath (Cap), Andrew David Townsend, Edward John Paul McGoldrick, Alan Francis McLoughlin, Niall John Quinn (72 Anthony Guy Cascarino), Thomas Coyne (82 John William Aldridge), Stephen Staunton.
Trainer: John Charlton (England).
UNITED STATES: Anthony Michael Meola, Desmond Armstrong, Marcelo Luis Balboa, John Joseph Doyle, Bruce Savage (73 Zak Ibsen), Fernando Clavijo, Brian Quinn (Cap), John Andrew Harkes, Hugo Pérez (70 Dominic Kinnear), Peter Vermes (83 Edward Eck), Eric Wynalda.
Trainer: Velibor Milutinović (Yugoslavia).
Goals: Andrew David Townsend (46), Joseph Irwin (52), Niall John Quinn (68), Anthony Guy Cascarino (86) /
Eric Wynalda (89)

278. 26.05.1992 15th World Cup Qualifiers
REPUBLIC OF IRELAND v ALBANIA 2-0 (0-0)
Lansdowne Road, Dublin
Referee: Jacob Uilenberg (Holland) Attendance: 29,727
REPUBLIC OF IRELAND: Patrick Bonner, Joseph Dennis Irwin, David Anthony O'Leary, Stephen Staunton, Paul McGrath (Cap), Andrew David Townsend, Roy Maurice Keane, Raymond James Houghton, Niall John Quinn, John William Aldridge (82 Thomas Coyne), Kevin Mark Sheedy (51 Michael Joseph McCarthy).
Trainer: John Charlton (England).
ALBANIA: Avenir Dani, Hysen Zmijani, Anesti Qendro (74 Artan Pali), Kastriot Peqini, Rudi Vata, Edmond Abazi, Sokol Kushta, Aleksander Vasi, Altin Rraklli, Amarildo Zela (78 Blendi Sokoli), Sulejman Demollari. Trainer: Bejkush Birçe.
Goals: John William Aldridge (61), Paul McGrath (80)

279. 30.05.1992 US Cup
UNITED STATES
v REPUBLIC OF IRELAND 3-1 (0-0)
"Robert F.Kennedy" Memorial, Washington
Referee: Mike Seifert (Canada)   Attendance: 35,696
UNITED STATES: Anthony Michael Meola (Cap), Paul David Caligiuri, Marcelo Luis Balboa, John Joseph Doyle, Thomas Dooley, Brian Quinn, John Andrew Harkes, Tabaré Ramos (79 Janusz Michallik), Bruce Murray (46 Christopher Joel Henderson (59 Fernando Clavijo)), Hugo Pérez (55 Earnest Stewart), Peter Vermes (46 Roy Wegerle).
Trainer: Velibor Milutinović (Yugoslavia).
REPUBLIC OF IRELAND: Gerald Joseph Peyton, Christopher Barry Morris (78 Joseph Dennis Irwin), Michael Joseph McCarthy, Kevin Bernard Moran, Terence Michael Phelan, Raymond James Houghton, Roy Maurice Keane (80 Alan Francis McLoughlin), Paul McGrath (Cap), Andrew David Townsend, Stephen Staunton (60 Thomas Coyne), Niall John Quinn.   Trainer: John Charlton (England).
Goals: Tabaré Ramos (54), Marcelo Luis Balboa (70), John Andrew Harkes (87) / Michael Joseph McCarthy (51)

280. 04.06.1992 US Cup
REPUBLIC OF IRELAND v ITALY 0-2 (0-1)
Foxboro Stadium, Foxboro
Referee: Jack D'Aquila (USA)   Attendance: 34,797
REPUBLIC OF IRELAND: Patrick Bonner, Joseph Dennis Irwin (63 Gerald Joseph Peyton), Michael Joseph McCarthy (Cap) (46 Alan Francis McLoughlin), David Anthony O'Leary, Stephen Staunton, Edward John Paul McGoldrick (80 Terence Michael Phelan), Andrew David Townsend, Paul McGrath, Raymond James Houghton, Niall John Quinn (72 Thomas Coyne), John William Aldridge (78 David Thomas Kelly).
Trainer: John Charlton (England).
ITALY: Walter Zenga, Paolo Maldini, Amedeo Carboni (51 Moreno Mannini), Luca Danilo Fusi (46 Giorgio Venturin), Alessandro Costacurta, Franco Baresi II (Cap) (77 Riccardo Ferri II), Alessandro Bianchi (73 Attilio Lombardo), Roberto Galia, Pier Luigi Casiraghi, Roberto Mancini (81 Gianluca Vialli), Giuseppe Signori.   Trainer: Arrigo Sacchi.
Sent off: Patrick Bonner (63)
Goals: Giuseppe Signori (17), Aless. Costacurta (67 pen)

281. 07.06.1992 US Cup
REPUBLIC OF IRELAND v PORTUGAL 2-0 (1-0)
Foxboro Stadium, Foxboro
Referee: Helder Dias (United States)   Attendance: 41,227
REPUBLIC OF IRELAND: Gerald Joseph Peyton, Christopher Barry Morris, Michael Joseph McCarthy (Cap), David Anthony O'Leary, Stephen Staunton, Raymond James Houghton, Alan Francis McLoughlin, Paul McGrath, Terence Michael Phelan (89 Edward John Paul McGoldrick), David Thomas Kelly (58 Thomas Coyne), Niall John Quinn (87 John William Aldridge).   Trainer: John Charlton (England).
PORTUGAL: Vítor Manuel Martins Baía, João Domingos Silva Pinto (Cap), Samuel António Silva Tavares Quina, Fernando Manuel Silva Couto, José Martins Leal (71 Jaime Fernandes Magalhães), Luis Filipe Madeira Caeiro "Figo" (46 Domingos José Paciência Oliveira), Vítor Manuel da Costa Araújo "Paneira" (46 Filipe Manuel Esteves Ramos), José Orlando Vinha Rocha Semedo (46 Paulo Jorge Ferreira de Sousa), Rui Filipe Tavares Bastos, Jorge António Pinto Couto (46 João Manuel Vieira Pinto), Jorge Paulo Cadete Santos Reis.
Trainer: Carlos Manuel Brito Leal Queiroz.
Goals: Stephen Staunton (39), Thomas Coyne (89)

282. 09.09.1992 15th World Cup Qualifiers
REPUBLIC OF IRELAND v LATVIA 4-0 (1-0)
Lansdowne Road, Dublin
Referee: Anders Frisk (Sweden)   Attendance: 32,000
REPUBLIC OF IRELAND: Patrick Bonner, Joseph Dennis Irwin, Alan Nigel Kernaghan, Paul McGrath, Stephen Staunton, Andrew David Townsend (Cap), Roy Maurice Keane, Ronald Andrew Whelan, Niall John Quinn (61 Thomas Coyne), John William Aldridge, Kevin Mark Sheedy (76 Terence Michael Phelan).   Trainer: John Charlton (England).
LATVIA: Konstantins Igošins, Vitālijs Astafjevs, Oļegs Aleksejenko, Rolands Bulders, Einars Gnedojs, Jurijs Popkovs (64 Aleksejs Semjonovs), Dzintars Sprogis, Romans Abzinovs (36 Romans Sidorovs), Aleksandrs Jelisejevs, Ainars Linards, Aleksandrs Glazovs.   Trainer: Jānis Gilis.
Goals: Kevin Sheedy (30), John Aldridge (59, 82 pen, 86)

283. 14.10.1992   15th World Cup Qualifiers
DENMARK v REPUBLIC OF IRELAND 0-0
Parken, København
Referee: Ryszard Wójcik (Poland)   Attendance: 40,100
DENMARK: Peter Schmeichel, John Sivebæk, Torben Piechnik, Lars Olsen (Cap), Jan Heintze, Marc Rieper, John Jensen, Kim Vilfort, Flemming Povlsen (76 Bent Christensen), Henrik Larsen, Brian Laudrup.
Trainer: Richard Møller Nielsen.
REPUBLIC OF IRELAND: Patrick Bonner, Joseph Dennis Irwin, Terence Michael Phelan, Kevin Bernard Moran, Alan Nigel Kernaghan, Roy Maurice Keane, Andrew David Townsend (Cap), Raymond James Houghton, Niall John Quinn, John William Aldridge (72 David Thomas Kelly), Edward John Paul McGoldrick.
Trainer: John Charlton (England).

284. 18.11.1992   15th World Cup Qualifiers
SPAIN v REPUBLIC OF IRELAND 0-0
"Ramón Sánchez Pizjuán", Sevilla
Referee: Alphonse Constantin (Belgium)   Att: 52,000
SPAIN: Andoni Zubizarreta Urreta, Albert Ferrer Llopis, Roberto Solozábal Villanueva, Juan Manuel López Martínez, Jon Andoni Goikoetxea Lasa, José Miguel González Martín del Campo "Michel", Guillermo Amor Martínez, Fernando Ruiz Hierro (III), Rafael Martín Vázquez, Julio Salinas Fernández (52 José María Bakero Eskudero), Emilio Butragueño Santos (Cap) (61 Aítor Beguiristán Mújika).
Trainer: Javier Clemente Lazaro.
REPUBLIC OF IRELAND: Patrick Bonner, Joseph Dennis Irwin, Terence Michael Phelan, Paul McGrath, Kevin Bernard Moran, Roy Maurice Keane, Andrew David Townsend (Cap), Raymond James Houghton, Niall John Quinn, John William Aldridge, Stephen Staunton.
Trainer: John Charlton (England).
Sent off: Juan Manuel López Martínez (57)

285. 17.02.1993
REPUBLIC OF IRELAND v WALES 2-1 (0-1)
Tolka Park, Dublin
Referee: Bo Karlsson (Sweden)   Attendance: 9,500
REPUBLIC OF IRELAND: Patrick Bonner (46 Alan Thomas Kelly), Christopher Barry Morris, Edward John Paul McGoldrick, Brian Patrick Carey, David Anthony O'Leary (Cap) (7 Ronald Andrew Whelan (46 Kevin Mark Sheedy)), Roy Maurice Keane, Liam Francis O'Brien, John Frederick Byrne, Anthony Guy Cascarino (82 Bernard Joseph Slaven), David Thomas Kelly (69 Thomas Coyne), Alan Francis McLoughlin.   Trainer: John Charlton (England).
WALES: Neville Southall (83 Anthony Mark Roberts), David Owen Phillips, Paul John Bodin, Mark Aizlewood, Eric Young (46 Christopher Coleman), Christopher Jeremiah Symons, Barry Horne, David Geraint Williams (73 Malcolm Allen), Leslie Mark Hughes, Mark Anthony Pembridge, Gary Andrew Speed.   Manager: Terence Charles Yorath.
Goals: Kevin Mark Sheedy (75), Thomas Coyne (81) / Leslie Mark Hughes (18)

286. 31.03.1993   15th World Cup Qualifiers
**REPUBLIC OF IRELAND
v NORTHERN IRELAND 3-0** (3-0)
Lansdowne Road, Dublin
Referee: Kurt Röthlisberger (Switzerland)   Att: 33,000
REPUBLIC OF IRELAND: Patrick Bonner, Joseph Dennis Irwin, Terence Michael Phelan, Kevin Bernard Moran, Paul McGrath, Roy Maurice Keane, Andrew David Townsend (Cap), Raymond James Houghton, Niall John Quinn (84 Edward John Paul McGoldrick), Thomas Coyne (78 Anthony Guy Cascarino), Stephen Staunton.
Trainer: John Charlton (England).
NORTHERN IRELAND: Thomas James Wright, Malachy Martin Donaghy, Nigel Worthington, Gerald Paul Taggart, Alan McDonald, Stephen Joseph Morrow, James Magilton (50 James Martin Quinn), Michael Andrew Martin O'Neill (60 Kingsley Terence Black), Iain Dowie, Philip Gray, Michael Eamonn Hughes.   Manager: William Laurence Bingham.
Goals: Andrew David Townsend (20), Niall John Quinn (22), Stephen Staunton (28)

287. 28.04.1993   15th World Cup Qualifiers
REPUBLIC OF IRELAND v DENMARK 1-1 (0-1)
Lansdowne Road, Dublin
Referee: Rémy Harrel (France)   Attendance: 33,000

REPUBLIC OF IRELAND: Patrick Bonner, Joseph Dennis Irwin, Edward John Paul McGoldrick, Paul McGrath, Alan Nigel Kernaghan, Raymond James Houghton, Andrew David Townsend (Cap), Roy Maurice Keane, Stephen Staunton, John William Aldridge (63 Anthony Guy Cascarino), Niall John Quinn.   Trainer: John Charlton (England).

DENMARK: Peter Schmeichel, Marc Rieper, Lars Olsen (Cap), Jakob Kjeldbjerg, Brian Steen Nielsen, John Jensen, Kim Vilfort, Jacob Friis-Hansen, Brian Laudrup, Frank Pingel (61 Bjørn Kristensen), Lars Elstrup.
Trainer: Richard Møller Nielsen.

Goals: Niall John Quinn (75) / Kim Vilfort (28)

288. 26.05.1993   15th World Cup Qualifiers
ALBANIA v REPUBLIC OF IRELAND 1-2 (1-1)
Qemal Stafa, Tiranë
Referee: Walter Cinciripini (Italy)   Attendance: 10,000

ALBANIA: Perlat Musta, Hysen Zmijani (60 Indrit Fortuzi), Ilir Shulku, Shyqry Shala, Rudi Vata, Artur Lekbello, Kastriot Peqini, Arben Milori, Sulejman Demollari, Sokol Kushta, Altin Rraklli (84 Kliton Bozgo).   Trainer: Bejkush Birçe.

REPUBLIC OF IRELAND: Patrick Bonner, Joseph Dennis Irwin, Terence Michael Phelan, Kevin Bernard Moran, Alan Nigel Kernaghan, Raymond James Houghton, Roy Maurice Keane, Andrew David Townsend (Cap), Stephen Staunton, John William Aldridge (74 Anthony Guy Cascarino), Niall John Quinn.   Trainer: John Charlton (England).

Goals: Sokol Kushta (8) /
Stephen Staunton (15), Anthony Guy Cascarino (78)

289. 09.06.1993   15th World Cup Qualifiers
LATVIA v REPUBLIC OF IRELAND 0-2 (0-2)
Daugava, Riga
Referee: Dick Jol (Holland)   Attendance: 5,200

LATVIA: Oļegs Karavajevs, Gatis Erglis, Jurijs Ševļakovs, Valerijs Ivanovs, Einars Gnedojs, Jurijs Popkovs, Aleksejs Šarando (55 Jevgenijs Gorjačilovs), Vitālijs Astafjevs, Rolands Bulders, Ainars Linards, Vladimirs Babičevs (46 Aleksandrs Jelisejevs).   Trainer: Jānis Gilis.

REPUBLIC OF IRELAND: Patrick Bonner, Joseph Dennis Irwin, Terence Michael Phelan, Paul McGrath, Alan Nigel Kernaghan, Raymond James Houghton, Roy Maurice Keane, Andrew David Townsend (Cap), Stephen Staunton, John William Aldridge (80 John Joseph Sheridan), Niall John Quinn (74 Anthony Guy Cascarino).
Trainer: John Charlton (England).

Goals: John William Aldridge (15), Paul McGrath (43)

290. 16.06.1993   15th World Cup Qualifiers
LITHUANIA v REPUBLIC OF IRELAND 0-1 (0-1)
Žalgiris, Vilnius
Referee: Roger Philippi (Luxembourg)   Attendance: 6,000

LITHUANIA: Voldemaras Martinkenas, Tomas Žiukas, Virginijus Baltušnikas, Romas Mažeikis, Vladimiras Buzmakovas, Aurelijus Skarbalius (46 Ričardas Zdančius), Stasys Baranauskas (Cap), Valdas Urbonas (67 Tomas Ramelis), Irmantas Stumbrys, Igoris Kirilovas, Vaidotas Šlekys. Trainer: Algimantas Liubinskas.

REPUBLIC OF IRELAND: Patrick Bonner, Joseph Dennis Irwin, Terence Michael Phelan, Paul McGrath, Alan Nigel Kernaghan, Raymond James Houghton, Roy Maurice Keane, Andrew David Townsend (Cap), Stephen Staunton, John William Aldridge (76 Ronald Andrew Whelan), Niall John Quinn.   Trainer: John Charlton (England).

Goal: Stephen Staunton (38)

291. 08.09.1993   15th World Cup Qualifiers
REPUBLIC OF IRELAND v LITHUANIA 2-0 (2-0)
Lansdowne Road, Dublin
Referee: Rune Pedersen (Norway)   Attendance: 48,000
REPUBLIC OF IRELAND: Patrick Bonner, Joseph Dennis Irwin, Terence Michael Phelan, Kevin Bernard Moran, Alan Nigel Kernaghan, Raymond James Houghton, Roy Maurice Keane, Andrew David Townsend (Cap) (69 Ronald Andrew Whelan), Stephen Staunton, Niall John Quinn (74 Anthony Guy Cascarino), John William Aldridge.
Trainer: John Charlton (England).
LITHUANIA: Gintaras Staučė, Tomas Žiukas, Virginijus Baltušnikas, Gyrius Kalvaitis, Andrijus Tereškinas, Vytautas Apanavičius, Stasys Baranauskas (Cap), Aurelijus Skarbalius (83 Andrius Štaliūnas), Irmantas Stumbrys, Igoris Kirilovas (68 Darius Maciulevičius), Vaidotas Šlekys.
Trainer: Algimantas Liubinskas.
Goals: John William Aldridge (4), Alan Nigel Kernaghan (25)

292. 13.10.1993   15th World Cup Qualifiers
REPUBLIC OF IRELAND v SPAIN 1-3 (0-3)
Lansdowne Road, Dublin
Referee: Fabio Baldas (Italy)   Attendance: 33,000
REPUBLIC OF IRELAND: Patrick Bonner, Joseph Dennis Irwin, Terence Michael Phelan, Kevin Bernard Moran (Cap) (23 John Joseph Sheridan), Alan Nigel Kernaghan, Ronald Andrew Whelan, Roy Maurice Keane, Paul McGrath, Raymond James Houghton, Stephen Staunton (46 Anthony Guy Cascarino), Niall John Quinn.
Trainer: John Charlton (England).
SPAIN: Andoni Zubizarreta Urreta (Cap), Albert Ferrer Llopis, Salvador González Marco "Voro", Francisco José Camarasa Castellar, Fernando Giner Gil, Miguel Ángel Nadal Homar, Jon Andoni Goikoetxea Lasa, Fernando Ruiz Hierro (III), José Luis Pérez Caminero (30 José María Bakero Eskudero), Luis Enrique Martínez García, Julio Salinas Fernández (68 Josep Guardiola Sala).
Trainer: Javier Clemente Lazaro.
Goals: John Joseph Sheridan (72) /
José Luis Pérez Caminero (11), Julio Fernández (15, 26)

293. 17.11.1993   15th World Cup Qualifiers
**NORTHERN IRELAND
v REPUBLIC OF IRELAND 1-1** (0-0)
Windsor Park, Belfast
Referee: Ahmet Çakar (Turkey)   Attendance: 10,500
NORTHERN IRELAND: Thomas James Wright, Gary James Fleming, Alan McDonald, Gerald Paul Taggart, Nigel Worthington, Malachy Martin Donaghy, Kevin James Wilson (83 Kingsley Terence Black), James Magilton, Michael Eamonn Hughes, Philip Gray (71 Iain Dowie), James Martin Quinn.   Manager: William Laurence Bingham.
REPUBLIC OF IRELAND: Patrick Bonner, Joseph Dennis Irwin, Terence Michael Phelan, Alan Nigel Kernaghan, Paul McGrath, Raymond James Houghton (70 Alan Francis McLoughlin), Roy Maurice Keane, Andrew David Townsend (Cap), Edward John Paul McGoldrick, Niall John Quinn, John William Aldridge (80 Anthony Guy Cascarino).
Trainer: John Charlton (England).
Goals: James Quinn (73) / Alan Francis McLoughlin (76)

294. 23.03.1994
REPUBLIC OF IRELAND v RUSSIA 0-0
Lansdowne Road, Dublin
Referee: Christer Fallström (Sweden)   Attendance: 34,550
REPUBLIC OF IRELAND: Patrick Bonner (46 Alan Thomas Kelly), Garry Kelly, Edward John Paul McGoldrick, Brian Patrick Carey, Philip Andrew Babb, Jason Wynn McAteer, Liam Francis O'Brien, Ronald Andrew Whelan (Cap), Alan Francis McLoughlin, David Thomas Kelly (50 Thomas Coyne), Anthony Guy Cascarino.   Trainer: John Charlton (England).
RUSSIA: Dmitriy Kharin, Sergey Gorlukovich, Rashid Rakhimov, Yuriy Kovtun, Omari Tetradze, Dmitriy Popov, Dmitriy Kuznetsov, Igor Korneyev (60 Andrey Chernyshov), Dmitriy Radchenko (88 Aleksey Kosolapov), Aleksandr Borodyuk (Cap), Oleg Salenko.   Trainer: Pavel Sadyrin.

295. 20.04.1994
HOLLAND v REPUBLIC OF IRELAND 0-1 (0-0)

Willem II, Tilburg

Referee: Hartmut Strampe (Germany) Attendance: 14,000

HOLLAND: Eduard Franciscus de Goey, Stanislaus Henricus Christina Valckx, Ronald Koeman (Cap) (46 Johannes Hildebrand de Wolf), Franciscus de Boer, Franklin Edmundo Rijkaard, Wilhelmus Maria Jonk (46 Aron Mohammed Winter), Edgar Steven Davids, Marc Overmars, Dennis Nicolaas Maria Bergkamp (46 Gaston Taument), Bryan Eduard Steven Roy, Ronaldus de Boer. Trainer: Dirk Nicolaas Advocaat.

REPUBLIC OF IRELAND: Patrick Bonner, Garry Kelly, Terence Michael Phelan (83 Alan Francis McLoughlin), Kevin Bernard Moran, Philip Andrew Babb, Ronald Andrew Whelan, Andrew David Townsend (Cap), Edward John Paul McGoldrick (70 Jason Wynn McAteer), Thomas Coyne (83 Owen Columba Coyle), John Joseph Sheridan, Stephen Staunton. Trainer: John Charlton (England).

Goal: Thomas Coyne (57)

296. 24.05.1994
REPUBLIC OF IRELAND v BOLIVIA 1-0 (0-0)

Lansdowne Road, Dublin

Referee: Alan Howells (Wales) Attendance: 32,500

REPUBLIC OF IRELAND: Patrick Bonner, Joseph Dennis Irwin (46 Garry Kelly), Terence Michael Phelan, Kevin Bernard Moran (46 Alan Nigel Kernaghan), Philip Andrew Babb, Raymond James Houghton (60 Jason Wynn McAteer), Roy Maurice Keane, Andrew David Townsend (Cap), John Joseph Sheridan, Stephen Staunton, Thomas Coyne (83 Anthony Guy Cascarino). Trainer: John Charlton (England).

BOL: Carlos Leonel Trucco, Gustavo Domingo Quinteros, Modesto Soruco (87 Juan Manuel Peña Montaño), Miguel Ángel Rimba, Marco Antonio Sandy, José Milton Melgar, Luis Héctor Cristaldo, Mario Daniel Pinedo (55 Carlos Fernando Borja), Julio César Baldivieso, Juan Mauricio Ramos, Álvaro Guillermo Peña (46 Ramiro Castillo Salinas). Trainer: Xabier Azkargorta (Spain).

Goal: John Joseph Sheridan (85)

297. 29.05.1994
GERMANY v REPUBLIC OF IRELAND 0-2 (0-1)

Niedersachsen, Hannover

Referee: José Manuel García-Aranda Encinar (Spain) Attendance: 50,000

GERMANY: Bodo Illgner, Lothar Herbert Matthäus (Cap), Guido Buchwald (36 Thomas Berthold), Jürgen Kohler (46 Thomas Häßler), Thomas Strunz, Mario Basler, Matthias Sammer, Martin Wagner, Andreas Möller (46 Stefan Effenberg), Jürgen Klinsmann, Karlheinz Riedle (68 Rudolf Völler). Trainer: Hans-Hubert Vogts.

REPUBLIC OF IRELAND: Alan Thomas Kelly, Joseph Dennis Irwin (46 Garry Kelly), Paul McGrath, Terence Michael Phelan, Philip Andrew Babb, Jason Wynn McAteer (87 Raymond James Houghton), Roy Maurice Keane, Andrew David Townsend (Cap), John Joseph Sheridan (46 Ronald Andrew Whelan), Stephen Staunton, Anthony Guy Cascarino (69 Thomas Coyne). Trainer: John Charlton (England).

Goals: Anthony Guy Cascarino (31), Garry Kelly (69)

298. 05.06.1994
REPUBLIC OF IRELAND v CZECH REPUBLIC 1-3 (1-1)

Lansdowne Road, Dublin

Referee: Leif Sundell (Sweden) Attendance: 43,465

REPUBLIC OF IRELAND: Patrick Bonner, Garry Kelly, Terence Michael Phelan, Paul McGrath (77 Philip Andrew Babb), Alan Nigel Kernaghan, Edward John Paul McGoldrick (53 Roy Maurice Keane), Andrew David Townsend (Cap), John Joseph Sheridan, John William Aldridge (53 Jason Wynn McAteer), Stephen Staunton, Anthony Guy Cascarino (65 Thomas Coyne). Trainer: John Charlton (England).

CZECH REPUBLIC: Petr Kouba, Tomáš Řepka, Luboš Kubík (Cap), Martin Kotůlek, Jan Suchopárek, Karel Poborský, Jiří Němec (88 Pavel Nedvěd), Martin Frýdek (89 Petr Samec), Jiří Novotný, Daniel Šmejkal, Pavel Kuka. Trainer: Dušan Uhrin.

Goal: Andrew David Townsend (43) / Pavel Kuka (25 pen, 54), Jan Suchopárek (81)

299. 18.06.1994 15th World Cup, 1st Round
ITALY v REPUBLIC OF IRELAND 0-1 (0-1)
Giants, New York (East Rutherford)
Referee: Mario van der Ende (Holland)   Attendance: 73,511
ITALY: Gianluca Pagliuca, Mauro Tassotti, Paolo Maldini, Demetrio Albertini, Alessandro Costacurta, Franco Baresi II (Cap), Roberto Donadoni, Dino Baggio, Giuseppe Signori (84 Nicola Berti), Roberto Baggio I, Alberigo Evani (46 Daniele Massaro). Trainer: Arrigo Sacchi.
REPUBLIC OF IRELAND: Patrick Bonner, Joseph Dennis Irwin, Philip Andrew Babb, Paul McGrath, Terence Michael Phelan, Raymond James Houghton (67 Jason Wynn McAteer), Roy Maurice Keane, John Joseph Sheridan, Andrew David Townsend (Cap), Stephen Staunton, Thomas Coyne (89 John William Aldridge). Trainer: John Charlton (England).
Goal: Raymond James Houghton (12)

301. 28.06.1994 15th World Cup, 1st Round
REPUBLIC OF IRELAND v NORWAY 0-0
Giants, New York (East Rutherford)
Referee: José Cadena Torres (Colombia)   Att: 76,332
REPUBLIC OF IRELAND: Patrick Bonner, Garry Kelly, Philip Andrew Babb, Paul McGrath, Stephen Staunton, Jason Wynn McAteer, Raymond James Houghton, Roy Maurice Keane, Andrew David Townsend (Cap) (74 Ronald Andrew Whelan), John Joseph Sheridan, John William Aldridge (64 David Thomas Kelly). Trainer: John Charlton (England).
NORWAY: Erik Thorstvedt, Gunnar Halle (33 Jahn Ivar Jakobsen), Rune Bratseth, Erland Johnsen, Stig Inge Bjørnebye, Jostein Flo, Erik Mykland, Øyvind Leonhardsen (68 Lars Bohinen), Henning Berg, Kjetil Rekdal, Gøran Sørloth. Trainer: Egil Roger Olsen.

300. 24.06.1994 15th World Cup, 1st Round
MEXICO v REPUBLIC OF IRELAND 2-1 (1-0)
Citrus Bowl, Orlando
Referee: Kurt Röthlisberger (Switzerland)   Att: 61,219
MEXICO: Jorge Campos, Jorge Rodríguez (79 Raúl Gutiérrez), Claudio Suárez, Juan de Dios Ramírez Perales, Joaquín del Olmo, Ignacio Ambríz (Cap), Marcelino Bernal, Alberto García Aspe, Luis García Postigo, Carlos Manuel Hermosillo (79 Luis Miguel Salvador), Luis Roberto Alves. Trainer: Miguel Mejía Barón.
REPUBLIC OF IRELAND: Patrick Bonner, Joseph Dennis Irwin, Philip Andrew Babb, Paul McGrath, Terence Michael Phelan, Raymond James Houghton, Andrew David Townsend (Cap), Roy Maurice Keane, John Joseph Sheridan, Stephen Staunton (65 Jason Wynn McAteer), Thomas Coyne (66 John William Aldridge). Trainer: John Charlton (England).
Goals: Luis García Postigo (43, 65) / John Aldridge (84)

302. 04.07.1994 15th World Cup, 2nd Round
HOLLAND v REPUBLIC OF IRELAND 2-0 (2-0)
Citrus Bowl, Orlando
Referee: Peter Mikkelsen (Denmark)   Attendance: 61,355
HOLLAND: Eduard Franciscus de Goey, Aron Mohammed Winter, Stanislaus Henricus Christina Valckx, Ronald Koeman (Cap), Franciscus de Boer, Franklin Edmundo Rijkaard, Wilhelmus Maria Jonk, Robert Witschge (78 Arthur Johannes Numan), Marc Overmars, Dennis Nicolaas Maria Bergkamp, Peter van Vossen (69 Bryan Eduard Steven Roy). Trainer: Dirk Nicolaas Advocaat.
REPUBLIC OF IRELAND: Patrick Bonner, Garry Kelly, Philip Andrew Babb, Paul McGrath, Terence Michael Phelan, Raymond James Houghton, Roy Maurice Keane, John Joseph Sheridan, Andrew David Townsend (Cap), Stephen Staunton (62 Jason Wynn McAteer), Thomas Coyne (73 Anthony Guy Cascarino). Trainer: John Charlton (England).
Goals: Dennis Nicolaas Maria Bergkamp (11), Wilhelmus Maria Jonk (41)

303. 07.09.1994   10th European Champs Qualifiers
LATVIA v REPUBLIC OF IRELAND 0-3 (0-2)
Daugava, Riga
Referee: Anders Frisk (Sweden)   Attendance: 2,300
LATVIA: Oļegs Karavajevs, Igors Troickis, Vitālijs Astafjevs, Mihails Zemļinskis, JurijsŠevļakovs, Valentīns Lobaņovs, Aleksejs Šarando, Vadims Mikuckis (64 Aleksandrs Jelisejevs), Vladimirs Babičevs, Jevgenijs Milevskis (46 Igors V. Stepanovs), Rolands Bulders.   Trainer: Jānis Gilis.
REPUBLIC OF IRELAND: Alan Thomas Kelly, Garry Kelly, Joseph Dennis Irwin, Paul McGrath, Philip Andrew Babb, Stephen Staunton, Jason Wynn McAteer (82 Edward John Paul McGoldrick), Andrew David Townsend (Cap), John William Aldridge, Niall John Quinn (71 Anthony Guy Cascarino), John Joseph Sheridan.   Trainer: John Charlton (England).
Goals: John Aldridge (16, 75 pen), John Joseph Sheridan (29).

304. 12.10.1994   10th European Champs Qualifiers
**REPUBLIC OF IRELAND
v LIECHTENSTEIN 4-0** (3-0)
Lansdowne Road, Dublin
Referee: Bragi Bergmann (Iceland)   Attendance: 32,980
REPUBLIC OF IRELAND: Patrick Bonner (Cap), Garry Kelly, Joseph Dennis Irwin (46 Alan Francis McLoughlin), Alan Nigel Kernaghan, Philip Andrew Babb, Stephen Staunton, Jason Wynn McAteer, Edward John Paul McGoldrick, Thomas Coyne, Niall John Quinn, John Joseph Sheridan.   Trainer: John Charlton (England).
LIECHTENSTEIN: Martin Heeb, Patrik Hefti, Jürg Ritter, Wolfgang Ospelt, Roland Moser, Daniel Telser, Thomas Hanselmann, Harry Zech, Mario Frick, Modestus Haas (78 Peter Klaunzer), Armin Heidegger (72 Christian Matt).   Trainer: Dietrich Weise (Germany).
Goals: Thomas Coyne (2, 4), Niall John Quinn (30, 82).

305. 16.11.1994   10th European Champs Qualifiers
**NORTHERN IRELAND
v REPUBLIC OF IRELAND 0-4** (0-3)
Windsor Park, Belfast
Referee: Serge Muhmenthaler (Switzerland)   Att: 10,336
NORTHERN IRELAND: Paul Victor Kee, Gary James Fleming, Nigel Worthington, Gerald Paul Taggart, Stephen Joseph Morrow, Michael Andrew Martin O'Neill (46 Darren James Patterson), Keith Robert Gillespie (62 Kevin James Wilson), James Magilton, Iain Dowie, Philip Gray, Michael Eamonn Hughes.   Manager: Bryan Hamilton.
REPUBLIC OF IRELAND: Alan Thomas Kelly, Garry Kelly, Joseph Dennis Irwin, Philip Andrew Babb, Paul McGrath, Stephen Staunton, Roy Maurice Keane (46 Jason Wynn McAteer), Andrew David Townsend (Cap), John Joseph Sheridan, Niall John Quinn, John William Aldridge (80 Thomas Coyne).   Trainer: John Charlton (England).
Goals: John William Aldridge (6), Roy Maurice Keane (11), John Joseph Sheridan (38), Andrew David Townsend (54)

306. 15.02.1995
REPUBLIC OF IRELAND v ENGLAND 1-0 (1-0)
Lansdowne Road, Dublin
Referee: Dick Jol (Holland)   Attendance: 46,000
REPUBLIC OF IRELAND: Alan Thomas Kelly, Terence Michael Phelan, Joseph Dennis Irwin, Paul McGrath, Alan Nigel Kernaghan, Stephen Staunton, Edward John Paul McGoldrick, Andrew David Townsend (Cap), John Joseph Sheridan, Niall John Quinn, David Thomas Kelly.   Trainer: John Charlton (England).
ENGLAND: David Andrew Seaman, Warren Dean Barton, Anthony Alexander Adams, Gary Andrew Pallister, Graeme Pierre Le Saux, Darren Robert Anderton, David Andrew Platt (Cap), Paul Emerson Ince, Matthew Paul Le Tissier, Peter Andrew Beardsley, Alan Shearer.   Manager: Terence Frederick Venables.
Goal: David Thomas Kelly (23)

The match was abandoned after 27 minutes due to crowd trouble.

307. 29.03.1995   10th European Champs Qualifiers
**REPUBLIC OF IRELAND
v NORTHERN IRELAND 1-1** (0-0)
Lansdowne Road, Dublin
Referee: Mario van der Ende (Holland)   Attendance: 32,200
REPUBLIC OF IRELAND: Alan Thomas Kelly, Garry Kelly, Joseph Dennis Irwin, Philip Andrew Babb, Paul McGrath, Stephen Staunton, Roy Maurice Keane, Andrew David Townsend (Cap), David Thomas Kelly (74 Jason Wynn McAteer), Niall John Quinn (82 Anthony Guy Cascarino), John Joseph Sheridan.   Trainer: John Charlton (England).
NORTHERN IRELAND: Allan William Fettis, Darren James Patterson, Nigel Worthington, Gerald Paul Taggart, Alan McDonald, Stephen Joseph Morrow, Keith Robert Gillespie, James Magilton, Iain Dowie, Colin Frederick Hill, Michael Eamonn Hughes.   Manager: Bryan Hamilton.
Goals: Niall John Quinn (47) / Iain Dowie (72)

308. 26.04.1995   10th European Champs Qualifiers
REPUBLIC OF IRELAND v PORTUGAL 1-0 (1-0)
Lansdowne Road, Dublin
Referee: Angelo Amendolia (Italy)   Attendance: 33,000
REPUBLIC OF IRELAND: Alan Thomas Kelly, Garry Kelly, Joseph Dennis Irwin, Philip Andrew Babb, Paul McGrath, Stephen Staunton, Raymond James Houghton (84 Jeffrey Jude Kenna), Andrew David Townsend (Cap), John William Aldridge (84 Anthony Guy Cascarino), Niall John Quinn, John Joseph Sheridan.   Trainer: John Charlton (England).
PORTUGAL: Vítor Manuel Martins Baía, João Domingos Silva Pinto (Cap), Jorge Paulo Costa Almeida, Hélder Marino Rodrigues Cristóvão (64 António José dos Santos Folha), Fernando Manuel Silva Couto, Paulo Manuel Carvalho de Sousa, Luis Filipe Madeira Caeiro "Figo" (76 Pedro Alexandre Santos Barbosa), João Manuel Vieira Pinto, Domingos José Paciência Oliveira, Rui Manuel César Costa, João Paulo Maio Santos "Paulinho Santos".
Trainer: António Luís Alves Ribeiro Oliveira.
Goal: Vítor Manuel Martins Baía (45 own goal)

309. 03.06.1995   10th European Champs Qualifiers
LIECHTENSTEIN v REPUBLIC OF IRELAND 0-0
Sportpark, Eschen/Mauren
Referee: Charles Agius (Malta)   Attendance: 4,500
LIECHTENSTEIN: Martin Heeb, Thomas Hanselmann, Jürgen Ospelt (32 Jürgen Zech), Wolfgang Ospelt (64 Patrick Marxer), Daniel Hasler, Daniel Telser, Jürg Ritter, Roland Hilti, Mario Frick, Harry Zech, Alex Burgmaier.
Trainer: Dietrich Weise (Germany).
REPUBLIC OF IRELAND: Alan Thomas Kelly, Garry Kelly, Joseph Dennis Irwin, Philip Andrew Babb, Paul McGrath, Stephen Staunton, Ronald Andrew Whelan (Cap), Jason Wynn McAteer (73 Jeffrey Jude Kenna), John William Aldridge, Niall John Quinn (60 Anthony Guy Cascarino), John Joseph Sheridan.   Trainer: John Charlton (England).

310. 11.06.1995   10th European Champs Qualifiers
REPUBLIC OF IRELAND v AUSTRIA 1-3 (0-0)
Lansdowne Road, Dublin
Referee: Dr. Markus Merk (Germany)   Attendance: 33,000
REPUBLIC OF IRELAND: Alan Thomas Kelly, Garry Kelly, Paul McGrath, Philip Andrew Babb, Joseph Dennis Irwin, John Joseph Sheridan, Stephen Staunton (46 Jeffrey Jude Kenna), Raymond James Houghton, Ronald Andrew Whelan (Cap), Thomas Coyne, Niall John Quinn (56 Anthony Guy Cascarino).   Trainer: John Charlton (England).
AUSTRIA: Michael Konsel, Anton Pfeffer, Peter Schöttel, Christian Fürstaller, Stefan Marasek, Dietmar Kühbauer, Dieter Ramusch (72 Andreas Ogris), Johann Kogler, Christian Prosenik, Heimo Pfeifenberger (82 Adolf Hütter), Anton Polster.   Trainer: Herbert Prohaska.
Goals: Raymond James Houghton (67) / Anton Polster (70, 80), Andreas Ogris (74)

311. 06.09.1995   10th European Champs Qualifiers
AUSTRIA v REPUBLIC OF IRELAND 3-1 (1-0)
"Ernst Happel", Wien
Referee: Ahmet Çakar (Turkey)   Attendance: 24,000
AUSTRIA: Michael Konsel, Markus Schopp, Peter Schöttel, Anton Pfeffer, Christian Fürstaller, Stefan Marasek, Heimo Pfeifenberger, Dietmar Kühbauer, Andreas Herzog, Peter Stöger, Anton Polster (79 Harald Cerny).
Trainer: Herbert Prohaska.
REPUBLIC OF IRELAND: Alan Thomas Kelly, Garry Kelly, Joseph Dennis Irwin, Alan Nigel Kernaghan, Paul McGrath, Roy Maurice Keane, Andrew David Townsend (Cap), Raymond James Houghton (67 Anthony Guy Cascarino), Niall John Quinn, John Joseph Sheridan, Mark Kennedy.   Trainer: John Charlton (England).
Goals: Peter Stöger (3, 64, 77) / Paul McGrath (74)

312. 11.10.1995 10th European Champs Qualifiers
REPUBLIC OF IRELAND v LATVIA 2-1 (0-0)
Lansdowne Road, Dublin

Referee: Juan Antonio Fernández Marín (Spain)
Attendance: 33,000

REPUBLIC OF IRELAND: Alan Thomas Kelly, Garry Kelly, Terence Michael Phelan, Philip Andrew Babb, Paul McGrath, Stephen Staunton, Jeffrey Jude Kenna, Andrew David Townsend (Cap), Jason Wynn McAteer, Niall John Quinn, John William Aldridge (79 David Thomas Kelly (84 Mark Kennedy)). Trainer: John Charlton (England).

LATVIA: Oļegs Karavajevs, Igors Troickis, Vitālijs Astafjevs, Mihails Zemļinskis, Jurijs Ševļakovs, Igors N. Stepanovs, Valerijs Ivanovs, Armands Zeiberliņš, Vīts Rimkus, Vladimirs Babičevs (73 Aleksandrs Jelisejevs), Artūrs Zakreševskis. Trainer: Jānis Gilis.

Goals: John William Aldridge (61 pen, 64) / Vīts Rimkus (78)

313. 15.11.1995 10th European Champs Qualifiers
(Play-Offs)
PORTUGAL v REPUBLIC OF IRELAND 3-0 (0-0)
da Luz, Lisboa

Referee: Piero Ceccarini (Italy)   Attendance: 80,000

PORTUGAL: Vítor Manuel Martins Baía (Cap) (85 Adelino Augusto Graça Barbosa Barros "Neno"), Carlos Alberto Oliveira "Secretário", Hélder Marino Rodrigues Cristóvão, Oceano Andrade da Cruz, Fernando Manuel Silva Couto, Paulo Manuel Carvalho de Sousa, Luis Filipe Madeira Caeiro "Figo", João Manuel Vieira Pinto (68 Jorge Paulo Cadete Santos Reis), Domingos José Paciência Oliveira (72 António José dos Santos Folha), Rui Manuel César Costa, João Paulo Maio Santos "Paulinho Santos".
Trainer: António Luís Alves Ribeiro Oliveira.

REPUBLIC OF IRELAND: Alan Thomas Kelly, Garry Kelly, Joseph Dennis Irwin, Philip Andrew Babb, Paul McGrath, Stephen Staunton (Cap) (78 Alan Nigel Kernaghan), Jason Wynn McAteer, Mark Kennedy (75 Anthony Guy Cascarino), Jeffrey Jude Kenna, Niall John Quinn, John William Aldridge. Trainer: John Charlton (England).

Goals: Rui Manuel César Costa (59), Hélder Marino Rodrigues Cristóvão (74), Jorge Paulo Cadete Santos Reis (89)

314. 13.12.1995 10th European Champs Qualifiers
(Play-Offs)
HOLLAND v REPUBLIC OF IRELAND 2-0 (1-0)
Anfield Road, Liverpool

Referee: Vadim Zhuk (Belarus)   Attendance: 40,050

HOLLAND: Edwin van der Sar, Michael John Reiziger, Dirk Franciscus Blind (Cap), Clarence Clyde Seedorf, Winston Lloyd Bogarde, Ronaldus de Boer, Marc Overmars, Edgar Steven Davids, Patrick Steven Kluivert, Dennis Nicolaas Maria Bergkamp (57 Johan de Kock), Glenn Helder (80 Aron Mohammed Winter). Trainer: Guus Hiddink.

REPUBLIC OF IRELAND: Alan Thomas Kelly, Garry Kelly, Joseph Dennis Irwin, Philip Andrew Babb, Paul McGrath, Jeffrey Jude Kenna, Andrew David Townsend (Cap) (50 Jason Wynn McAteer), Terence Michael Phelan, John William Aldridge (72 Alan Nigel Kernaghan), Anthony Guy Cascarino, John Joseph Sheridan. Trainer: John Charlton (England).

Goals: Patrick Steven Kluivert (29, 88)

315. 27.03.1996
REPUBLIC OF IRELAND v RUSSIA 0-2 (0-1)
Lansdowne Road, Dublin

Referee: Hugo Luyten (Holland)   Attendance: 41,600

REPUBLIC OF IRELAND: Seamus John Given, Terence Michael Phelan, Stephen Staunton, Alan Nigel Kernaghan, Paul McGrath, Roy Maurice Keane, Andrew David Townsend (Cap) (46 Jeffrey Jude Kenna), Jason Wynn McAteer, Niall John Quinn (86 Thomas Coyne), John William Aldridge (63 Anthony Guy Cascarino), Mark Kennedy.
Trainer: Michael Joseph McCarthy.

RUSSIA: Stanislav Cherchesov, Vladislav Radimov (46 Omari Tetradze), Yuriy Nikiforov, Viktor Onopko (Cap), Yuriy Kovtun, Andrey Kanchelskis, Valeriy Karpin, Aleksandr Mostovoi, Ilya Tsymbalar (46 Dmitriy Radchenko), Sergey Kiryakov (66 Igor Simutenkov), Igor Kolyvanov (70 Igor Shalimov). Trainer: Oleg Romantsev.

Sent off: Roy Maurice Keane (88)

Goals: Aleksandr Mostovoi (34), Igor Kolyvanov (53)

316. 24.04.1996
CZECH REPUBLIC v REPUBLIC OF IRELAND 2-0 (0-0)
Strahov, Praha

Referee: Hartmut Strampe (Germany)   Attendance: 6,118

CZECH REPUBLIC: Petr Kouba, Miroslav Kadlec (46 Luboš Kubík), Michal Horňák (73 Karel Rada), Tomáš Řepka, Radoslav Látal (59 Pavel Nedvěd), Václav Němeček (Cap) (46 Radek Bejbl), Patrik Berger, Martin Frýdek, Pavel Hapal, Radek Drulák, Pavel Kuka (78 Milan Kerbr). Trainer: Dušan Uhrin.

REPUBLIC OF IRELAND: Seamus John Given, Joseph Dennis Irwin (46 Curtis Fleming), Jeffrey Jude Kenna, Kenneth Edward Cunningham, Philip Andrew Babb (77 Liam Sean Daish), Paul McGrath, Raymond James Houghton, Mark Kennedy, Andrew David Townsend (Cap), Alan Moore, Niall John Quinn.   Trainer: Michael Joseph McCarthy.

Goals: Martin Frýdek (61), Pavel Kuka (68).

317. 29.05.1996
REPUBLIC OF IRELAND v PORTUGAL 0-1 (0-0)
Lansdowne Road, Dublin

Referee: Claude Detrouche (Switzerland)   Att: 26,576

REPUBLIC OF IRELAND: Seamus John Given, Curtis Fleming, Terence Michael Phelan, Alan Nigel Kernaghan (88 Gary Patrick Breen), Kenneth Edward Cunningham, Jeffrey Jude Kenna, Andrew David Townsend (Cap), Alan Francis McLoughlin, David James Connolly (63 Keith Padre Gerard O'Neill), Anthony Guy Cascarino (75 Niall John Quinn), Gareth Farrelly (60 David Thomas Patrick Savage). Trainer: Michael Joseph McCarthy.

PORTUGAL: Vítor Manuel Martins Baía (Cap), Hélder Marino Rodrigues Cristóvão, João Paulo Maio Santos "Paulinho Santos", Fernando Manuel Silva Couto, Dimas Manuel Marques Teixeira, Oceano Andrade da Cruz (68 Hugo Cardoso Porfírio), Vítor Manuel da Costa Araújo "Paneira" (46 Ricardo Manuel Silva Sá Pinto), José Fernando Gomes Tavares, João Manuel Vieira Pinto, António José dos Santos Folha, Jorge Paulo Cadete Santos Reis (73 Carlos Alberto Oliveira "Secretário").   Trainer: António Luís Alves Ribeiro Oliveira.

Goal: António José dos Santos Folha (90).

318. 02.06.1996
REPUBLIC OF IRELAND v CROATIA 2-2 (1-2)
Lansdowne Road, Dublin

Referee: Philippe Leduc (France)   Attendance: 29,100

REPUBLIC OF IRELAND: Seamus John Given, Gary Patrick Breen (74 Anthony Guy Cascarino), Liam Sean Daish, Jeffrey Jude Kenna (64 Alan Nigel Kernaghan), Kenneth Edward Cunningham (90 Curtis Fleming), Alan Francis McLoughlin (71 David Thomas Patrick Savage), Mark Kennedy, Liam Francis O'Brien, Terence Michael Phelan (46 Ian Patrick Harte), Niall John Quinn (Cap), Keith Padre Gerard O'Neill (46 Alan Moore).   Trainer: Michael Joseph McCarthy.

CROATIA: Marijan Mrmić (46 Dražen Ladić), Mario Stanić (78 Zvonimir Soldo), Robert Jarni, Igor Štimac, Nikola Jerkan, Slaven Bilić, Aljoša Asanović, Alen Bokšić, Davor Šuker, Zvonimir Boban, Goran Vlaović (71 Nikola Jurčević). Trainer: Miroslav Blažević.

Goals: Keith Padre Gerard O'Neill (24), Niall Quinn (87) / Davor Šuker (14), Zvonimir Boban (46).

319. 04.06.1996
HOLLAND v REPUBLIC OF IRELAND 3-1 (1-1)
Feyenoord, Rotterdam

Referee: Finn Lambek (Denmark)   Attendance: 22,000

HOLLAND: Edwin van der Sar, Michael John Reiziger, Dirk Franciscus Blind (Cap) (46 Johan de Kock), Winston Lloyd Bogarde, Ronaldus de Boer (46 Aron Mohammed Winter), Richard Peter Witschge, Clarence Clyde Seedorf, Dennis Nicolaas Maria Bergkamp, Edgar Steven Davids, Johannes Jordi Cruijff (75 Phillip John William Cocu), Peter Hoekstra (27 Gaston Taument).   Trainer: Guus Hiddink.

REPUBLIC OF IRELAND: Seamus John Given, Gary Patrick Breen, Alan Nigel Kernaghan (Cap), Jeffrey Jude Kenna (78 Curtis Fleming), Ian Patrick Harte, Liam Francis O'Brien (70 Kenneth Edward Cunningham), Alan Francis McLoughlin, Terence Michael Phelan, Alan Moore (46 Mark Kennedy), David James Connolly (64 Niall John Quinn), Anthony Guy Cascarino (46 Keith Padre Gerard O'Neill). Trainer: Michael Joseph McCarthy.

Goals: Dennis Bergkamp (27), Clarence Clyde Seedorf (77), Phillip John William Cocu (88) / Gary Patrick Breen (13).

320. 09.06.1996   US Cup
**UNITED STATES
v REPUBLIC OF IRELAND 2-1** (0-0)
Foxboro Stadium, Foxboro

Referee: Peter Prendergast (Jamaica)   Attendance: 25,332

UNITED STATES: Bradley Howard Friedel, Mike Burns, Marcelo Luis Balboa, Thomas Dooley, Panayotis Alexi Lalas, Jeff Agoos, John Andrew Harkes, Claudio Reyna (77 Jovan Kirovski), Tabaré Ramos (77 Roy Lassiter), Cobi Ngai Jones, Eric Wynalda (88 Paul David Caligiuri).
Trainer: Steve Sampson.

REPUBLIC OF IRELAND: Seamus John Given, Gary Patrick Breen, Alan Nigel Kernaghan (Cap), Kenneth Edward Cunningham, Jeffrey Jude Kenna (40 Curtis Fleming), Liam Francis O'Brien (87 David Thomas Patrick Savage), Gareth Farrelly (61 Mark Kennedy), Alan Francis McLoughlin, Terence Michael Phelan, Niall John Quinn (87 Keith Padre Gerard O'Neill), David James Connolly.
Trainer: Michael Joseph McCarthy.

Goals: Tabaré Ramos (58), Claudio Reyna (76) / David James Connolly (57)

321. 12.06.1996   US Cup
MEXICO v REPUBLIC OF IRELAND 2-2 (1-1)
Giants, New York (East Rutherford)

Referee: Raúl Dominguez (United States)   Att: 21,322

MEXICO: Oswaldo Sánchez, Germán Villa, Claudio Suárez, Duilio Davino, Joaquín del Olmo, Raúl Rodrigo Lara, Manuel Sol, Rafael García Torres (53 Cuahtémoc Blanco), Juan Francisco Palencia (46 José Manuel Abundis), Enrique Alfaro, Luis García Postigo.
Trainer: Velibor Milutinović (Yugoslavia).

REPUBLIC OF IRELAND: Patrick Bonner (Cap), Curtis Fleming, Gary Patrick Breen, Liam Sean Daish, Ian Patrick Harte, Mark Kennedy (72 Terence Michael Phelan), David Thomas Patrick Savage, Alan Francis McLoughlin, Alan Moore, Keith Padre Gerard O'Neill, David James Connolly.
Trainer: Michael Joseph McCarthy.

Sent off: Liam Sean Daish

Goals: Luis García Postigo (40, 70 pen) / David James Connolly (44), Duilio Davino (49 own goal)

322. 15.06.1996   US Cup
REPUBLIC OF IRELAND v BOLIVIA 3-0 (3-0)
Giants, New York (East Rutherford)

Referee: Esfandiar Baharmast (United States)   Att: 14,624

REPUBLIC OF IRELAND: Seamus John Given (85 Patrick Bonner), Kenneth Edward Cunningham, Alan Nigel Kernaghan (Cap) (35 Gary Patrick Breen), Ian Patrick Harte, Curtis Fleming, David Thomas Patrick Savage, Liam Francis O'Brien (46 Alan Francis McLoughlin), Gareth Farrelly (65 Mark Kennedy), Terence Michael Phelan, Keith Padre Gerard O'Neill, Alan Moore.   Trainer: Michael Joseph McCarthy.

BOL: Mauricio Ronald Soria Portillo, Juan Manuel Peña Montaño, Óscar Carmelo Sánchez, Miguel Ángel Rimba, Ramiro Castillo Salinas, Julio César Baldivieso, Marco Antonio Etcheverry, Juan Mauricio Ramos (41 Luis Héctor Cristaldo), Freddy Cossío, Marco Antonio Sandy, Jaime Moreno Morales (46 Milton Coimbra Suizer).
Trainer: Dušan Drašković (Yugoslavia).

Goals: Keith Padre Gerard O'Neill (12, 33), Ian Harte (45)

323. 31.08.1996   16th World Cup Qualifiers
**LIECHTENSTEIN
v REPUBLIC OF IRELAND 0-5** (0-4)
Sportpark, Eschen/Mauren

Referee: Sergei Shmolik (Belarus)   Attendance: 3,900

LIECHTENSTEIN: Martin Heeb, Thomas Hanselmann (82 Daniel Telser, Martin Stocklasa, Roland Hilti, Daniel Hasler, Patrik Hefti, Alexander Quaderer, Harry Zech (65 Herbert Bicker), Harry Schädler, Mario Frick, Franz Schädler (78 Peter Klaunzer).   Trainer: Dietrich Weise (Germany).

REPUBLIC OF IRELAND: Seamus John Given, Joseph Dennis Irwin, Ian Patrick Harte, Jeffrey Jude Kenna, Gary Patrick Breen, Stephen Staunton, Andrew David Townsend (Cap) (83 Anthony Guy Cascarino), Raymond James Houghton, Niall John Quinn, Alan Francis McLoughlin, Keith Padre Gerard O'Neill (73 Alan Moore).
Trainer: Michael Joseph McCarthy.

Goals: Andrew Townsend (5), Keith O'Neill (7), Niall John Quinn (11, 61), Ian Patrick Harte (19)

324. 09.10.1996   16th World Cup Qualifiers
REPUBLIC OF IRELAND v MACEDONIA 3-0 (1-0)
Lansdowne Road, Dublin
Referee: Knud Erik Fisker (Denmark)   Attendance: 31,671
REPUBLIC OF IRELAND: Alan Thomas Kelly, Joseph Dennis Irwin, Jeffrey Jude Kenna, Gary Patrick Breen, Ian Patrick Harte (86 Alan Moore), Stephen Staunton, Alan Francis McLoughlin (88 Liam Francis O'Brien), Andrew David Townsend (Cap), Jason Wynn McAteer, Anthony Guy Cascarino, Keith Padre Gerard O'Neill (82 John William Aldridge).   Trainer: Michael Joseph McCarthy.
MACEDONIA: Dančo Čelevski, Zoran Jovanovski, Husein Beganović (74 Artim Šakiri), Igor Saša Nikolovski, Goce Sedloski, Risto Milosavov, Vlatko Gošev, Toni Mičevski, Sašo Miloševski (61 Srdjan Zaharievski), Sašo Ćirić, Gjorgji Hristov.   Trainer: Gjoko Hadžievski.
Goals: Jason McAteer (8), Anthony Guy Cascarino (47, 70)

325. 10.11.1996   16th World Cup Qualifiers
REPUBLIC OF IRELAND v ICELAND 0-0
Lansdowne Road, Dublin
Referee: Stefan Ormandjiev (Bulgaria)   Attendance: 33,069
REPUBLIC OF IRELAND: Alan Thomas Kelly, Joseph Dennis Irwin (63 Ian Patrick Harte), Philip Andrew Babb, Jeffrey Jude Kenna (63 Kenneth Edward Cunningham), Gary Patrick Breen, Roy Maurice Keane, Alan Francis McLoughlin, Andrew David Townsend (Cap), Jason Wynn McAteer, Anthony Guy Cascarino, David Thomas Kelly (78 Alan Moore).   Trainer: Michael Joseph McCarthy.
ICELAND: Birkir Kristinsson, Hlynur Birgisson, Ólafur Adolfsson, Lárus Orri Sigurðsson, Siðurdur Jónsson (Cap), Rúnar Kristinsson (71 Arnar Grétarsson), Heimir Guðjónsson (81 Ólafur Þórðarson), Eyjólfur Sverrisson, Ágúst Gylfason, Helgi Sigurðsson, Þórður Guðjónsson.   Trainer: Logi Ólafsson.

326. 11.02.1997
WALES v REPUBLIC OF IRELAND 0-0
Ninian Park, Cardiff
Referee: William S.G. Young (Scotland)   Attendance: 7,000
WALES: Mark Geoffrey Crossley, Karl Ready, Gary Andrew Speed, Christopher Jeremiah Symons, Mark Anthony Pembridge, Andrew Legg, Vincent Peter Jones (73 Ceri Morgan Hughes), Barry Horne, John Robert Campbell Robinson (62 Mark Rosslyn Bowen), John Hartson (69 Gareth Keith Taylor), Leslie Mark Hughes (88 Robert William Savage).   Manager: Robert Anthony Gould.
REPUBLIC OF IRELAND: Keith Graham Branagan, Terence Michael Phelan, Kenneth Edward Cunningham, Paul McGrath, Jason Wynn McAteer, Stephen Staunton, Alan Francis McLoughlin (52 Garry Kelly), Ian Patrick Harte, Roy Maurice Keane (75 David Thomas Kelly), Anthony Guy Cascarino, Jonathan Goodman.   Trainer: Michael McCarthy.

327. 02.04.1997   16th World Cup Qualifiers
MACEDONIA v REPUBLIC OF IRELAND 3-2 (2-1)
Gradski, Skopje
Referee: Alfredo Trentalange (Italy)   Attendance: 8,000
MACEDONIA: Dančo Čelevski, Ljupčo Markovski, Igor Saša Nikolovski, Goce Sedloski, Risto Milosavov, Vlatko Gošev, Artim Šakiri, Mitko Stojkovski, Dževdat Šainovski (82 Ilčo Georgioski), Gjorgji Hristov (78 Husein Beganović), Dejvi Glavevski (87 Vančo Mičevski).   Trainer: Gjoko Hadžievski.
REPUBLIC OF IRELAND: Alan Thomas Kelly, Joseph Dennis Irwin, Gary Patrick Breen, Stephen Staunton, Alan Francis McLoughlin, Andrew David Townsend (Cap), Jason Wynn McAteer, Roy Maurice Keane, Terence Michael Phelan (56 Ian Patrick Harte), Anthony Guy Cascarino (46 Keith Padre Gerard O'Neill (76 David Thomas Kelly)), Jonathan Goodman.   Trainer: Michael Joseph McCarthy.
Sent off: Mitko Stojkovski (90), Jason Wynn McAteer (90)
Goals: Mitko Stojkovski (28 pen, 44 pen), Gjorgji Hristov (59) / Alan Francis McLoughlin (8), David Thomas Kelly (78)

328. 30.04.1997   16th World Cup Qualifiers
ROMANIA v REPUBLIC OF IRELAND 1-0 (1-0)
Steaua, București
Referee: Mario van der Ende (Holland)   Attendance: 21,500
ROMANIA: Bogdan Stelea, Dan Petrescu, Daniel Claudiu Prodan, Anton Doboş, Tibor Selymes, Iulian Sebastian Filipescu, Gheorghe Popescu (71 Iosif Rotariu), Gheorghe Hagi (Cap) (86 Gheorghe Craioveanu), Dorinel Ionel Munteanu, Adrian Bucurel Ilie (83 Gabriel Popescu), Viorel Dinu Moldovan.   Trainer: Anghel Iordănescu.
REPUBLIC OF IRELAND: Alan Thomas Kelly, Joseph Dennis Irwin (46 Jeffrey Jude Kenna), Ian Patrick Harte, Kenneth Edward Cunningham, Stephen Staunton, Raymond James Houghton, Andrew David Townsend (Cap), Roy Maurice Keane, Garry Kelly, Mark Kennedy (82 Jonathan Goodman), David James Connolly (82 Anthony Guy Cascarino).   Trainer: Michael Joseph McCarthy.
Goal: Adrian Bucurel Ilie (33)

329. 21.05.1997   16th World Cup Qualifiers
REPUBLIC OF IRELAND
v LIECHTENSTEIN 5-0 (3-0)
Lansdowne Road, Dublin
Referee: Andrei Butenko (Russia)   Attendance: 33,200
REPUBLIC OF IRELAND: Seamus John Given, Ian Patrick Harte, Kenneth Edward Cunningham, Stephen Staunton, Jeffrey Jude Kenna, Raymond James Houghton (53 Anthony Guy Cascarino), Andrew David Townsend (Cap), Roy Maurice Keane, Garry Kelly, Mark Kennedy (65 Curtis Fleming), David James Connolly (78 Jonathan Goodman).
Trainer: Michael Joseph McCarthy.
LIECHTENSTEIN: Martin Heeb, Christoph Frick, Patrik Hefti, Thomas Hanselmann (78 Ralf Ackermann), Martin Stocklasa, Daniel Hasler, Daniel Telser (57 Thomas Verling), Mario Frick (46 Jürgen Ospelt), Franz Schädler, Peter Klaunzer, Daniel Frick.   Trainer: Alfred Riedl (Austria).
Goals: David James Connolly (29, 34, 40), Anthony Guy Cascarino (60, 77).

330. 20.08.1997   16th World Cup Qualifiers
REPUBLIC OF IRELAND v LITHUANIA 0-0
Lansdowne Road, Dublin
Referee: Jorge Emanuel Monteiro Coroado (Portugal)   Attendance: 48,000
REPUBLIC OF IRELAND: Seamus John Given, Jeffrey Jude Kenna, Kenneth Edward Cunningham, Ian Patrick Harte, Stephen Staunton, Roy Maurice Keane, Andrew David Townsend (Cap) (84 David Thomas Kelly), Raymond James Houghton, Niall John Quinn (60 Anthony Guy Cascarino), David James Connolly, Mark Kennedy (74 Alan Francis McLoughlin).   Trainer: Michael Joseph McCarthy.
LITHUANIA: Gintaras Staučė (Cap), Tomas Žiukas, Tomas Kančelskis, Andrijus Tereškinas, Raimundas Vainoras, Andrius Skerla, Raimondas Žutautas, Sakalas Mikalajūnas, Aidas Preikšaitis (46 Dainius Suliauskas), Edgaras Jankauskas (58 Orestas Buitkus (80 Arūnas Šuika)), Arminas Narbekovas.
Trainer: Benjaminas Zelkevičius.

331. 06.09.1997   16th World Cup Qualifiers
ICELAND v REPUBLIC OF IRELAND 2-4 (1-1)
Laugardalsvöllur, Reykjavík
Referee: Ante Kulušić (Croatia)   Attendance: 3,981
REPUBLIC OF IRELAND: Seamus John Given, Jeffrey Jude Kenna (63 Jason Wynn McAteer), Kenneth Edward Cunningham, Ian Patrick Harte, Stephen Staunton, Roy Maurice Keane, Andrew David Townsend (Cap) (87 Anthony Guy Cascarino), Alan Francis McLoughlin, Garry Kelly, Kevin Daniel Kilbane (46 Mark Kennedy), David James Connolly.
Trainer: Michael Joseph McCarthy.
ICELAND: Kristján Finnbogason, Lárus Orri Sigurðsson, Guðni Bergsson (Cap), Eyjólfur Sverrisson, Hermann Hreiðarsson, Rúnar Kristinsson, Brynjar Björn Gunnarsson (85 Bjarni Eggerts Guðjónsson), Þórður Guðjónsson, Siðurdur Jónsson, Einar Þór Daníelsson (69 Tryggvi Guðmundsson), Helgi Sigurðsson (66 Ríkharður Daðason).
Trainer: Guðjón Þórdarson.
Goals: Brynjar Björn Gunnarsson (45), Helgi Sigurðsson (47) / David James Connolly (13), Roy Maurice Keane (54, 64), Mark Kennedy (79)

332. 10.09.1997   16th World Cup Qualifiers
LITHUANIA v REPUBLIC OF IRELAND 1-2 (0-1)
Žalgiris, Vilnius
Referee: Georgios Bikas (Greece)   Attendance: 8,000
LITHUANIA: Gintaras Staučė (Cap), Tomas Žiukas, Tomas Kančelskis, Andrijus Tereškinas (77 Vaidotas Šlekys), Raimundas Vainoras, Andrius Skerla, Raimondas Žutautas, Valdas Ivanauskas, Sakalas Mikalajūnas (46 Rimantas Žvingilas), Aidas Preikšaitis (46 Edgaras Jankauskas), Arminas Narbekovas.   Trainer: Benjaminas Zelkevičius.
REPUBLIC OF IRELAND: Seamus John Given, Joseph Dennis Irwin, Kenneth Edward Cunningham, Ian Patrick Harte, Stephen Staunton (Cap), Garry Kelly, Roy Maurice Keane, Alan Francis McLoughlin, Jason Wynn McAteer (84 Philip Andrew Babb), Anthony Guy Cascarino, David James Connolly (90 Gary Patrick Breen).
Trainer: Michael Joseph McCarthy.
Goals: Tomas Žiukas (51) / Anthony Guy Cascarino (17, 72)

333. 11.10.1997   16th World Cup Qualifiers
REPUBLIC OF IRELAND v ROMANIA 1-1 (0-0)
Lansdowne Road, Dublin
Referee: Nikolai Levnikov (Russia)   Attendance: 49,000
REPUBLIC OF IRELAND: Alan Thomas Kelly, Jeffrey Jude Kenna, Philip Andrew Babb, Gary Patrick Breen, Terence Michael Phelan (89 Curtis Fleming), Raymond James Houghton (Cap), Alan Francis McLoughlin (60 David Thomas Kelly), Jason Wynn McAteer, Lee Kevin Carsley, Mark Kennedy, Anthony Guy Cascarino (85 Michael James Evans). Trainer: Michael Joseph McCarthy.

ROMANIA: Bogdan Stelea, Dan Petrescu, Anton Doboș, Liviu Ciobotariu, Tibor Selymes, Constantin Gâlcă, Gheorghe Popescu, Gheorghe Hagi (Cap) (84 Ilie Dumitrescu), Dorinel Ionel Munteanu, Adrian Bucurel Ilie (76 Marius Lăcătuș), Viorel Dinu Moldovan (62 Iulian Sebastian Filipescu). Trainer: Anghel Iordănescu.

Goals: Anthony Guy Cascarino (83) / Gheorghe Hagi (53)

335. 15.11.1997   16th World Cup Qualifiers (Play-Offs)
BELGIUM v REPUBLIC OF IRELAND 2-1 (1-0)
"Roi Baudouin", Bruxelles
Referee: Günter Benkö (Austria)   Attendance: 31,455
BELGIUM: Filip De Wilde, Eric Deflandre, Goran Vidovic (64 Vital Borkelmans), Glen De Boeck, Mike Verstraeten, Frank Richard Vander Elst, Danny Boffin, Gert Claessens (75 Philippe Léonard), Gert Verheyen, Luc Nilis (88 Michaël Goossens), Luis Airton Oliveira Barosso. Trainer: Georges Leekens.

REPUBLIC OF IRELAND: Seamus John Given, Jeffrey Jude Kenna, Kenneth Edward Cunningham, Ian Patrick Harte, Stephen Staunton, Andrew David Townsend (Cap) (86 David Thomas Kelly), Lee Kevin Carsley, Mark Kennedy (74 David James Connolly), Garry Kelly, Alan Francis McLoughlin (49 Raymond James Houghton), Anthony Guy Cascarino. Trainer: Michael Joseph McCarthy.

Goals: Luis Airton Oliveira Barosso (25), Luc Nilis (70) / Raymond James Houghton (59)

334. 29.10.1997   16th World Cup Qualifiers (Play-Offs)
REPUBLIC OF IRELAND v BELGIUM 1-1 (1-1)
Lansdowne Road, Dublin
Referee: László Vágner (Hungary)   Attendance: 32,305
REPUBLIC OF IRELAND: Seamus John Given, Joseph Dennis Irwin, Kenneth Edward Cunningham, Ian Patrick Harte, Garry Kelly, Stephen Staunton, Andrew David Townsend (Cap) (75 Lee Kevin Carsley), Raymond James Houghton, Mark Kennedy (33 Jeffrey Jude Kenna), Anthony Guy Cascarino, David James Connolly (82 Thomas Coyne). Trainer: Michael Joseph McCarthy.

BELGIUM: Filip De Wilde, Régis Genaux, Eric Van Meir, Goran Vidovic, Mike Verstraeten, Frank Richard Vander Elst, Danny Boffin, Marc Wilmots, Nico Van Kerckhoven, Luc Nilis (88 Gilles De Bilde), Michaël Goossens (88 Gert Verheyen). Trainer: Georges Leekens.

Goals: Joseph Dennis Irwin (8) / Luc Nilis (30)

336. 25.03.1998
CZECH REPUBLIC v REPUBLIC OF IRELAND 2-1 (0-1)
Andruv, Olomouc
Referee: Attila Juhos (Hungary)   Attendance: 14,694
CZECH REPUBLIC: Tomáš Poštulka, Radoslav Látal (84 Tomáš Votava), Luboš Kozel, Jiří Novotný, Karel Rada, Martin Čížek (71 Edvard Lasota), Jiří Němec (Cap), Karel Poborský, Radek Bejbl, Pavel Kuka (60 Vratislav Lokvenc), Vladimír Šmicer (89 Milan Fukal).   Trainer: Jozef Chovanec.

REPUBLIC OF IRELAND: Seamus John Given, Jeffrey Jude Kenna, Kenneth Edward Cunningham (Cap), Gary Patrick Breen, Alan Maybury (46 Robert David Keane), Garry Kelly, Lee Kevin Carsley (84 Graham Anthony Kavanagh), Mark Anthony Kinsella, Gareth Farrelly (60 Alan Francis McLoughlin), David James Connolly (60 Kevin Daniel Kilbane), Damien Anthony Duff (72 Rory John Delap). Trainer: Michael Joseph McCarthy.

Goals: Vladimír Šmicer (49), Edvard Lasota (76) / Gary Patrick Breen (9)

337. 22.04.1998
REPUBLIC OF IRELAND v ARGENTINA 0-2 (0-2)
Lansdowne Road, Dublin

Referee: Stuart Dougal (Scotland)   Attendance: 38,500

REPUBLIC OF IRELAND: Seamus John Given (46 Alan Thomas Kelly), Jeffrey Jude Kenna (77 Rory John Delap), Gary Patrick Breen, Ian Patrick Harte (46 Philip Andrew Babb), Stephen Staunton, Garry Kelly, Kevin Daniel Kilbane (46 Joseph Dennis Irwin), Lee Kevin Carsley, Mark Anthony Kinsella, Niall John Quinn (Cap), Robert David Keane. Trainer: Michael Joseph McCarthy.

ARGENTINA: Germán Adrián Ramón Burgos, Nelson David Vivas, Roberto Fabián Ayala, Roberto Néstor Sensini, Matías Jesús Almeyda, Sergio Ángel Berti (63 Héctor Mauricio Pineda), Ariel Arnaldo Ortega, Diego Pablo Simeone (Cap), Juan Sebastián Verón, Gabriel Omar Batistuta, Claudio Javier López (84 Marcelo Alejandro Delgado). Trainer: Daniel Alberto Passarella.

Goals: Gabriel Batistuta (26), Ariel Arnaldo Ortega (40)

338. 23.05.1998
REPUBLIC OF IRELAND v MEXICO 0-0
Lansdowne Road, Dublin

Referee: John Ashman (Wales)   Attendance: 28,500

REPUBLIC OF IRELAND: Seamus John Given, Curtis Fleming, Gary Patrick Breen, Ian Patrick Harte, Philip Andrew Babb, Garry Kelly (Cap), Lee Kevin Carsley, Gareth Farrelly, David James Connolly (73 Mark Kennedy), Robert David Keane, Damien Anthony Duff (73 Rory John Delap). Trainer: Michael Joseph McCarthy.

MEXICO: Jorge Campos, Pavel Pardo, Duilio Davino, Claudio Suárez, Joél Sánchez, Braulio Luna, Jaime Ordiales (46 Juan Francisco Palencia), Jesús Ramón Ramírez (60 Ricardo Peláez), Alberto García Aspe, Luis Hernández (83 Paulo César Chávez), Cuauhtémoc Blanco.   Trainer: Manuel Lapuente.

339. 05.09.1998   11th European Champs Qualifiers
REPUBLIC OF IRELAND v CROATIA 2-0 (2-0)
Lansdowne Road, Dublin

Referee: Vítor Manuel Melo Pereira (Portugal)   Att: 34,000

REPUBLIC OF IRELAND: Seamus John Given, Joseph Dennis Irwin, Kenneth Edward Cunningham, Philip Andrew Babb, Stephen Staunton, Jason Wynn McAteer, Mark Anthony Kinsella, Roy Maurice Keane (Cap), Keith Padre Gerard O'Neill (5 Anthony Guy Cascarino), Robert David Keane (61 Lee Kevin Carsley), Damien Anthony Duff (46 Jeffrey Jude Kenna).   Trainer: Michael Joseph McCarthy.

CROATIA: Dražen Ladić, Dario Šimić, Robert Jarni, Igor Štimac, Zvonimir Soldo (78 Mario Tokić), Igor Tudor (63 Petar Krpan), Aljoša Asanović, Krunoslav Jurčić, Mario Stanic, Zvonimir Boban, Silvio Marić (46 Igor Pamić). Trainer: Miroslav Blažević.

Sent off: Mario Stanic (70), Krunoslav Jurčić (71)

Goals: Joseph Dennis Irwin (2 pen), Roy Maurice Keane (15)

340. 14.10.1998   11th European Champs Qualifiers
REPUBLIC OF IRELAND v MALTA 5-0 (2-0)
Lansdowne Road, Dublin

Referee: Roy Helge Olsen (Norway)   Attendance: 34,500

REPUBLIC OF IRELAND: Seamus John Given, Gary Patrick Breen, Jeffrey Jude Kenna, Kenneth Edward Cunningham, Stephen Staunton, Jason Wynn McAteer (84 Lee Kevin Carsley), Mark Anthony Kinsella, Roy Maurice Keane (Cap), Niall John Quinn (74 Anthony Guy Cascarino), Robert David Keane (83 Mark Kennedy), Damien Anthony Duff. Trainer: Michael Joseph McCarthy.

MALTA: Reginald Cini, Darren Debono, John Buttigieg, Michael Spiteri, David Carabott, Joseph Brincat (Cap), Antoine Zahra (70 Ivan Zammit), Paul Sixsmith (77 David Camilleri), Jeffrey Chetcuti, Noel Turner, Hubert Suda (65 Gilbert Agius). Trainer: Josif Ilić (Yugoslavia).

Goals: Robert David Keane (16, 18), Roy Maurice Keane (54), Niall John Quinn (63), Gary Patrick Breen (82)

341. 18.11.1998   11th European Champs Qualifiers
**YUGOSLAVIA
v REPUBLIC OF IRELAND 1-0** (0-0)
Crvena zvezda, Beograd
Referee: Karl Erik Nilsson (Sweden)   Attendance: 28,250
YUGOSLAVIA: Ivica Kralj, Jovan Stanković, Goran Đorović, Slaviša Jokanović, Miroslav Đukić, Dejan Stanković, Vladimir Jugović (84 Nenad Grozdić), Predrag Mijatović, Savo Milošević (78 Ljubinko Drulović), Dragan Stojković (Cap) (46 Darko Kovačević), Siniša Mihajlović.   Trainer: Milan Živadinović.

REPUBLIC OF IRELAND: Seamus John Given, Joseph Dennis Irwin, Kenneth Edward Cunningham, Gary Patrick Breen, Stephen Staunton, Jason Wynn McAteer (82 Keith Padre Gerard O'Neill), Alan Francis McLoughlin (73 David James Connolly), Mark Anthony Kinsella, Damien Anthony Duff, Roy Maurice Keane (Cap), Niall John Quinn (73 Anthony Guy Cascarino).   Trainer: Michael Joseph McCarthy.

Goal: Predrag Mijatović (63)

342. 10.02.1999
REPUBLIC OF IRELAND v PARAGUAY 2-0 (1-0)
Lansdowne Road, Dublin
Referee: Gylfi Þór Orrason (Iceland)   Attendance: 27,600
REPUBLIC OF IRELAND: Seamus John Given (68 Alan Thomas Kelly), Joseph Dennis Irwin, Kenneth Edward Cunningham, Gary Patrick Breen, Ian Patrick Harte (73 Philip Andrew Babb), Jason Wynn McAteer (83 Alan Francis McLoughlin), Mark Anthony Kinsella (68 Lee Kevin Carsley), Roy Maurice Keane (Cap), Damien Anthony Duff, Robert David Keane (68 David James Connolly), Niall John Quinn (70 Anthony Guy Cascarino).
Trainer: Michael Joseph McCarthy.

PARAGUAY: Ricardo Javier Tavarelli Paiva, Jorge Valdéz, Ignacio Rolón, Juan Ramón Ortíz, Denis Ramón Caniza, Miguel Ángel Acosta, Edgar Aguilera, Carlos Humberto Paredes Monges, Mauro Antonio Caballero (71 Edilberto Brítez), Juan Carlos Franco (80 Cristián Esquivel), Raúl Basilio Román Garay (58 Juan Esteban Peralta).
Trainer: Ever Hugo Almeida Almada.

Goals: Joseph Dennis Irwin (38 pen), David Connolly (73)

343. 28.04.1999
REPUBLIC OF IRELAND v SWEDEN 2-0 (0-0)
Lansdowne Road, Dublin
Referee: Pascal Garibian (France)   Attendance: 29,300
REPUBLIC OF IRELAND: Seamus John Given, Stephen Carr, Kenneth Edward Cunningham, Gary Patrick Breen (46 Philip Andrew Babb), Stephen Staunton (Cap), Jason Wynn McAteer (46 Graham Anthony Kavanagh), Mark Anthony Kinsella (46 Kevin Daniel Kilbane), Alan Francis McLoughlin, Mark Kennedy (79 Damien Anthony Duff), David James Connolly (71 Anthony Guy Cascarino), Niall John Quinn (80 Robert David Keane).   Trainer: Michael Joseph McCarthy.

SWEDEN: Magnus Kihlstedt, Pontus Kåmark, Patrik Jonas Andersson, Joachim Björklund (46 Andreas Jakobsson), Teddy Lucic, Stefan Schwarz, Håkan Mild (46 Niclas Alexandersson), Daniel Andersson, Jesper Blomqvist, Henrik Larsson, Jörgen Pettersson (80 Mattias Jonson).   Trainer: Tommy Söderberg.

Goals: Graham Anthony Kavanagh (75), Mark Kennedy (76)

344. 29.05.1999
**REPUBLIC OF IRELAND
v NORTHERN IRELAND 0-1** (0-0)
Lansdowne Road, Dublin
Referee: Ceri Richards (Wales)   Attendance: 12,100
REPUBLIC OF IRELAND: Seamus John Given, Stephen Carr, Kenneth Edward Cunningham (Cap), Philip Andrew Babb, Alan Maybury, Mark Anthony Kinsella (80 Graham Anthony Kavanagh), Lee Kevin Carsley (46 Alan Francis McLoughlin), Damien Anthony Duff (56 Keith Padre Gerard O'Neill), Mark Kennedy, Robert David Keane (56 David James Connolly), Niall John Quinn (72 Anthony Guy Cascarino).
Trainer: Michael Joseph McCarthy.

NORTHERN IRELAND: Maik Stefan Taylor (46 Roy Eric Carroll), Aaron William Hughes, Darren James Patterson, Barry Victor Hunter, Mark Stuart Williams, Keith Rowland (74 Damien Michael Johnson), Neil Francis Lennon (79 Daniel Joseph Griffin), Jonathan David McCarthy, Iain Dowie (46 Adrian Coote), Stephen James Quinn, Stephen Robinson.
Manager: Lawrie McMenemy.

Goal: Daniel Joseph Griffin (85)

345. 09.06.1999   11th European Champs Qualifiers
REPUBLIC OF IRELAND v MACEDONIA 1-0 (0-0)
Lansdowne Road, Dublin

Referee: Urs Meier (Switzerland)   Attendance: 28,108

REPUBLIC OF IRELAND: Alan Thomas Kelly, Stephen Carr, Joseph Dennis Irwin, Kenneth Edward Cunningham, Gary Patrick Breen, Damien Anthony Duff (63 Kevin Daniel Kilbane), Mark Kennedy, Mark Anthony Kinsella, Niall John Quinn (Cap) (81 David James Connolly), Robert David Keane (68 Anthony Guy Cascarino), Lee Kevin Carsley.   Trainer: Michael Joseph McCarthy.

MACEDONIA: Petar Miloševski, Goran Stavrevski, Boban Babunski, Milan Stojanovski, Igor Saša Nikolovski, Vančo Trajčov (46 Nedžmedin Memedi), Toni Mičevski, Viktor Trenevski (77 Gjorgji Hristov), Dževdat Šainovski (70 Goce Sedloski), Artim Šakiri, Sašo Ćirić.   Trainer: Gjoko Hadžievski.

Goal: Niall John Quinn (67)

346. 01.09.1999   11th European Champs Qualifiers
**REPUBLIC OF IRELAND
v YUGOSLAVIA 2-1** (0-0)
Lansdowne Road, Dublin

Referee: Pierluigi Collina (Italy)   Attendance: 31,400

REPUBLIC OF IRELAND: Alan Thomas Kelly, Joseph Dennis Irwin (66 Stephen Carr), Gary Patrick Breen, Kenneth Edward Cunningham, Stephen Staunton, Roy Maurice Keane (Cap) (69 Lee Kevin Carsley), Kevin Daniel Kilbane, Mark Anthony Kinsella, Niall John Quinn (78 Anthony Guy Cascarino), Robert David Keane, Mark Kennedy.   Trainer: Michael Joseph McCarthy.

YUGOSLAVIA: Aleksandar Kocić, Slobodan Komljenović, Dražen Bolić, Dejan Govedarica, Miroslav Đukić, Dejan Stanković, Albert Nađ (76 Darko Kovačević), Predrag Mijatović, Savo Milošević, Dejan Savićević (56 Ljubinko Drulović), Siniša Mihajlović (69 Niša Saveljić).   Trainer: Vujadin Boškov.

Goals: Robert David Keane (53), Mark Kennedy (69) / Dejan Stanković (59)

347. 04.09.1999   11th European Champs Qualifiers
CROATIA v REPUBLIC OF IRELAND 1-0 (0-0)
Maksimir, Zagreb

Referee: Manuel Diaz Vega (Spain)   Attendance: 30,000

CROATIA: Dražen Ladić, Dario Šimić, Zvonimir Soldo, Igor Štimac, Slaven Bilić (46 Tomislav Rukavina), Aljoša Asanović, Mario Stanić (84 Josip Šimić), Milan Rapaić, Robert Kovač, Robert Jarni, Davor Šuker.   Trainer: Miroslav Blažević.

REPUBLIC OF IRELAND: Alan Thomas Kelly, Stephen Carr, Gary Patrick Breen, Kenneth Edward Cunningham, Stephen Staunton (Cap), Lee Kevin Carsley, Garry Kelly (73 Ian Patrick Harte), Mark Anthony Kinsella, Anthony Guy Cascarino (83 Niall John Quinn), Alan Francis McLoughlin, Damien Anthony Duff (57 Kevin Daniel Kilbane).   Trainer: Michael Joseph McCarthy.

Goal: Davor Šuker (90)

348. 08.09.1999   11th European Champs Qualifiers
MALTA v REPUBLIC OF IRELAND 2-3 (0-2)
National, Ta'Qali

Referee: Sorin Corpodean (Romania)   Attendance: 8,122

MALTA: Ernest Barry, Brian Said, Jeffrey Chetcuti (23 Richard Buhagiar), David Carabott, Darren Debono, John Buttigieg (29 Silvio Vella), Carmel Busuttil (Cap), Nicholas Saliba, Chucks Nwoko, David Camilleri, Gilbert Agius (67 Daniel Theuma).   Trainer: Josif Ilić (Yugoslavia).

REPUBLIC OF IRELAND: Alan Thomas Kelly, Stephen Carr, Gary Patrick Breen (75 Ian Patrick Harte), Kenneth Edward Cunningham, Stephen Staunton (Cap), Lee Kevin Carsley, Kevin Daniel Kilbane (56 Damien Anthony Duff), Mark Anthony Kinsella, Niall John Quinn, Robert David Keane, Mark Kennedy (55 Alan Francis McLoughlin).   Trainer: Michael Joseph McCarthy.

Goals: Brian Said (62), David Carabott (68 pen) / Robert David Keane (13), Gary Patrick Breen (21), Stephen Staunton (73)

349. 09.10.1999 11th European Champs Qualifiers
MACEDONIA v REPUBLIC OF IRELAND 1-1 (0-1)
Gradski, Skopje
Referee: Juan António Fernandez Marín (Spain)
Attendance: 14,000
MACEDONIA: Antonio Filevski, Goran Stavrevski, Zoran Jovanovski (77 Nedžmedin Memedi), Goce Sedloski, Boban Babunski, Marjan Gerasimovski, Milan Stojanovski (56 Ardžent Beciri), Toni Savevski, Dževdat Šainovski, Gjorgji Hristov, Goran Stanić (70 Srdjan Zaharievski). Trainer: Dragan Kanatlarovski.
REPUBLIC OF IRELAND: Alan Thomas Kelly, Joseph Dennis Irwin, Gary Patrick Breen, Kenneth Edward Cunningham, Stephen Staunton, Alan Francis McLoughlin, Garry Kelly, Mark Anthony Kinsella, Niall John Quinn (78 Anthony Guy Cascarino), Robert David Keane (66 Keith Padre Gerard O'Neill), Mark Kennedy (85 Matthew Rhys Holland). Trainer: Michael Joseph McCarthy.
Goals: Goran Stavrevski (90) / Niall John Quinn (18)

350. 13.11.1999 11th European Champs Qualifiers (Play-Offs)
REPUBLIC OF IRELAND v TURKEY 1-1 (0-0)
Lansdowne Road, Dublin
Referee: Anders Frisk (Sweden) Attendance: 33,610
REPUBLIC OF IRELAND: Alan Thomas Kelly (61 Dean Lawrence Kiely), Stephen Carr, Joseph Dennis Irwin, Gary Patrick Breen, Kenneth Edward Cunningham, Roy Maurice Keane (Cap), Rory John Delap (53 Damien Anthony Duff), Lee Kevin Carsley, Kevin Daniel Kilbane, Anthony Guy Cascarino (75 David James Connolly), Robert David Keane. Trainer: Michael Joseph McCarthy.
TURKEY: Rüştü Reçber, Ali Eren Beşerler, Ogün Temizkanoğlu, Alpay Özalan, Tayfur Havutçu, Abdullah Ercan, Tayfun Korkut, Ümit Davala (46 Arif Erdem), Sergen Yalçin (85 Mert Korkmaz), Hakan Ünsal (67 Tugay Kerimoğlu), Hakan Şükür. Trainer: Mustafa Denizli.
Goals: Robert David Keane (79) / Tayfur Havutçu (83 pen)

351. 17.11.1999 11th European Champs Qualifiers (Play-Offs)
TURKEY v REPUBLIC OF IRELAND 0-0
Atatürk, Bursa
Referee: Gilles Veissière (France) Attendance: 19,900
TURKEY: Rüştü Reçber (38 Engin İpekoğlu), Ali Eren Beşerler, Ogün Temizkanoğlu, Tayfur Havutçu, Alpay Özalan, Arif Erdem (84 Ümit Davala), Abdullah Ercan, Okan Buruk, Sergen Yalçin, Tayfun Korkut (46 Fatih Akyel), Hakan Şükür. Trainer: Mustafa Denizli.
REPUBLIC OF IRELAND: Dean Lawrence Kiely, Stephen Carr (4 Jeffrey Jude Kenna (81 Anthony Guy Cascarino)), Joseph Dennis Irwin, Gary Patrick Breen, Kenneth Edward Cunningham, Roy Maurice Keane (Cap), Rory John Delap, Mark Anthony Kinsella, Niall John Quinn, David James Connolly (78 Damien Anthony Duff), Kevin Daniel Kilbane. Trainer: Michael Joseph McCarthy.

352. 23.02.2000
REPUBLIC OF IRELAND v CZECH REPUBLIC 3-2 (2-2)
Lansdowne Road, Dublin
Referee: Bruno Coué (France) Attendance: 30,543
REPUBLIC OF IRELAND: Alan Thomas Kelly, Garry Kelly, Kenneth Edward Cunningham, Ian Patrick Harte, Paul John Butler (46 Philip Andrew Babb), Mark Kennedy (46 Jason Wynn McAteer), Roy Maurice Keane (Cap), Mark Anthony Kinsella, Kevin Daniel Kilbane (83 Stephen Staunton), Niall John Quinn, Robert David Keane (90 David James Connolly). Trainer: Michael Joseph McCarthy.
CZECH REPUBLIC: Ladislav Maier, Tomáš Řepka (46 Jan Suchopárek), Karel Rada, Petr Gabriel, Karel Poborský, Radek Bejbl, Pavel Nedvěd (82 Tomáš Rosický), Jiří Němec (Cap) (62 Radoslav Látal), Patrik Berger (72 Pavel Horváth), Jan Koller (69 Pavel Kuka), Vladimír Šmicer (57 René Wagner). Trainer: Jozef Chovanec.
Goals: Karel Rada (16 own goal), Ian Patrick Harte (43), Robert David Keane (87) / Jan Koller (4, 35)

353. 26.04.2000
REPUBLIC OF IRELAND v GREECE 0-1 (0-1)
Lansdowne Road, Dublin
Referee: Hugh Dallas (Scotland)   Attendance: 23,157
REPUBLIC OF IRELAND: Seamus John Given (46 Dean Lawrence Kiely), Richard Patrick Dunne, Kenneth Edward Cunningham, Gary Patrick Breen, Stephen Staunton, Barry Quinn (33 Rory John Delap), Mark Anthony Kinsella, Kevin Daniel Kilbane, Stephen John Finnan (71 Gary Michael Thomas Doherty), Robert David Keane, David James Connolly (54 Alan Joseph Mahon).
Trainer: Michael Joseph McCarthy.

GREECE: Antónis Nikopolídis, Giórgos Amanatídis, Nikolaos Dabizas, Marínos Ouzounidis (Cap), Ilías Poursanidis, Stélios Venetídis, Angelos Basinás (75 Giánnis Góumas), Nikolaos Liberópoulos (89 Dimítris Nalitzis), Vasílis Tsiártas (58 Thomás Kyparissis), Vasílis Lákis (65 Andréas Vasílis Zikos), Giórgos Hrístos Georgiádis (88 Andréas Niniadis).
Trainer: Vasílis Danííl.

Goal: Vasílis Lákis (16)

355. 04.06.2000   US Cup
REPUBLIC OF IRELAND v MEXICO 2-2 (0-1)
Soldier's Field, Chicago
Referee: Kevin Scott (United States)   Attendance: 36,469
REPUBLIC OF IRELAND: Dean Lawrence Kiely, Stephen Carr, Gary Patrick Breen, Richard Patrick Dunne (82 Philip Andrew Babb), Terence Michael Phelan, Mark Kennedy, Matthew Rhys Holland, Jason Wynn McAteer, Barry Quinn (41 Kevin Daniel Kilbane), Niall John Quinn, Robert David Keane (46 Dominic Joseph Foley).
Trainer: Michael Joseph McCarthy.

MEXICO: Sergio Bernal, Joaquin Beltrán, Christian Ramírez (69 Gilberto Jiménez), Raúl Alpizar, Israel López, Gerardo Torrado, Luis Ernesto Pérez Gómez, Antonio Sancho (81 Gerardo Galindo), Horacio Sánchez Hierro, Luis Ignacio González, Daniel Osorno.   Trainer: Hugo Sánchez Márquez.

Goals: Richard Dunne (60), Dominic Joseph Foley (71) / Daniel Osorno (38), Horacio Sánchez Hierro (54)

354. 30.05.2000
REPUBLIC OF IRELAND v SCOTLAND 1-2 (1-2)
Lansdowne Road, Dublin
Referee: Vítor Manuel Melo Pereira (Portugal)   Att: 30,200
REPUBLIC OF IRELAND: Alan Thomas Kelly, Stephen Carr, Gary Patrick Breen (77 Richard Patrick Dunne), Kevin Daniel Kilbane, Philip Andrew Babb, Mark Kennedy (61 Damien Anthony Duff), Jason Wynn McAteer, Stephen John Finnan, Stephen McPhail (61 Terence Michael Phelan), Niall John Quinn (77 Dominic Joseph Foley), Robert David Keane.
Trainer: Michael Joseph McCarthy.

SCOTLAND: Neil Sullivan, Christian Edward Dailly, Gary Andrew Naysmith (Iain Durrant), Brian O'Neil, Matthew Stephen Elliott, Craig William Burley, Barry Ferguson (84 Colin Cameron), Paul Lambert (Cap) (75 Allan Johnston), Neil McCann (90 Steven Pressley), Donald Hutchison, William Dodds (46 Kevin William Gallacher).
Manager: Craig Brown.

Goals: Mark Kennedy (2) / Donald Hutchison (15), Barry Ferguson (27)

356. 06.06.2000   US Cup
UNITED STATES v REPUBLIC OF IRELAND 1-1 (0-1)
Foxboro Stadium, Foxboro
Referee: Benito Archundia Téllez (Mexico)   Att: 16,319
UNITED STATES: Bradley Howard Friedel, Frank Daniel Hejduk, Gregg Berhalter, Charles J. Brown, Gregory Vanney, John Patrick O'Brien (58 Claudio Reyna), Jovan Kirovski, Benjamin Robert Olsen (75 Anthony Sanneh), Steve Ralston (46 Earnest Stewart), Jason Kreis (65 Cobi Ngai Jones), Ante Razov (88 Brian John McBride).   Trainer: Bruce Arena.

REPUBLIC OF IRELAND: Alan Thomas Kelly, Stephen Carr, Gary Patrick Breen, Philip Andrew Babb, Terence Michael Phelan, Kevin Daniel Kilbane, Matthew Rhys Holland, Stephen McPhail (37 Jason Wynn McAteer), Gareth Farrelly (72 Mark Kennedy), Gary Michael Thomas Doherty (72 Niall John Quinn), Dominic Joseph Foley (88 Barry Quinn).
Trainer: Michael Joseph McCarthy.

Goals: Ante Razov (68) / Dominic Joseph Foley (31)

357. 11.06.2000   US Cup
**REPUBLIC OF IRELAND
v SOUTH AFRICA 2-1** (1-1)
Giants, New York (East Rutherford)
Referee: Rodrigo Badilla Sequeira (Costa Rica)   Att: 45,008
REPUBLIC OF IRELAND: Seamus John Given, Stephen Carr, Gary Patrick Breen, Philip Andrew Babb, Terence Michael Phelan, Matthew Rhys Holland, Jason Wynn McAteer (44 Mark Kennedy), Alan Joseph Mahon (42 Kevin Daniel Kilbane), Stephen McPhail (85 Barry Quinn), Niall John Quinn (76 Gary Michael Thomas Doherty), Dominic Joseph Foley (46 Robert David Keane).
Trainer: Michael Joseph McCarthy.
SOUTH AFRICA: Andre Arendse, Cyril Nzama, Andrew Rabutla, Quinton Fortune (76 Arthur Zwane), Helman Mhkalele (76 Thabo Mngomeni), Dumisi Ngobe (46 Patrick Mayo), Aaron Mokoena, Jacob Lekgetho, Delron Buckley (46 Godfrey Sapula), Benedict McCarthy (46 Dillon Sheppard), Shaun Bartlett.   Trainer: Trott Moloto.
Goals: Stephen McPhail (43), Niall John Quinn (69) / Benedict McCarthy (14)

358. 02.09.2000   17th World Cup Qualifiers
HOLLAND v REPUBLIC OF IRELAND 2-2 (0-1)
ArenA, Amsterdam
Referee: Luboš Michel (Slovakia)   Attendance: 45,000
HOLLAND: Edwin van der Sar, Michael John Reiziger (46 Clarence Clyde Seedorf), Hubertus Gerard Konterman (65 Jeffrey Dennis Talan), Franciscus de Boer (Cap), Giovanni Christiaan van Bronckhorst, Paul Bosvelt, Richard Peter Witschge (61 Arnold Bruggink), Ronaldus de Boer, Phillip John William Cocu, Wilfred Bouma, Patrick Steven Kluivert.
Trainer: Aloysius Paulus Maria van Gaal.
REPUBLIC OF IRELAND: Alan Thomas Kelly, Stephen Carr, Gary Patrick Breen, Richard Patrick Dunne, Ian Patrick Harte, Jason Wynn McAteer (75 Garry Kelly), Roy Maurice Keane (Cap), Mark Anthony Kinsella, Kevin Daniel Kilbane (80 Stephen Staunton), Niall John Quinn (62 David James Connolly), Robert David Keane.
Trainer: Michael Joseph McCarthy.
Goals: Jeffrey Dennis Talan (71), Giovanni Christiaan van Bronckhorst (84) / Robert Keane (21), Jason McAteer (65)

359. 07.10.2000   17th World Cup Qualifiers
PORTUGAL v REPUBLIC OF IRELAND 1-1 (0-0)
da Luz, Lisboa
Referee: Atanas Uzunov (Bulgaria)   Attendance: 65,000
PORTUGAL: Joaquim Manuel Sampaio Silva "Quim", Roberto Luís Gaspar Deus Severo "Beto", Jorge Paulo Costa Almeida, Fernando Manuel Silva Couto (Cap), Dimas Manuel Marques Teixeira (88 Nuno Fernando Gonçalves Rocha "Capucho"), José Luís da Cruz Vidigal, Rui Manuel César Costa, Sérgio Paulo Marceneiro Conceição, Luis Filipe Madeira Caeiro "Figo", Ricardo Manuel Silva Sá Pinto (77 "Simão" Pedro Fonseca Sabrosa), João Manuel Vieira Pinto (77 Pedro Miguel Carreiro Resendes "Pauleta").
Trainer: António Luís Alves Ribeiro Oliveira.
REPUBLIC OF IRELAND: Alan Thomas Kelly, Stephen Carr, Gary Patrick Breen, Richard Patrick Dunne, Ian Patrick Harte, Jason Wynn McAteer (69 Damien Anthony Duff), Roy Maurice Keane (Cap), Mark Anthony Kinsella, Kevin Daniel Kilbane, Niall John Quinn (46 Matthew Rhys Holland), Robert David Keane (83 Stephen John Finnan).
Trainer: Michael Joseph McCarthy.
Goals: Sérgio Paulo Marceneiro Conceição (58) / Matthew Rhys Holland (72)

360. 11.10.2000   17th World Cup Qualifiers
REPUBLIC OF IRELAND v ESTONIA 2-0 (1-0)
Lansdowne Road, Dublin
Referee: Terje Hauge (Norway)   Attendance: 34,962
REPUBLIC OF IRELAND: Alan Thomas Kelly, Stephen Carr, Gary Patrick Breen, Richard Patrick Dunne, Ian Patrick Harte, Jason Wynn McAteer (46 Damien Anthony Duff), Roy Maurice Keane (Cap), Mark Anthony Kinsella, Kevin Daniel Kilbane (88 Stephen John Finnan), Niall John Quinn, Robert David Keane (88 Dominic Joseph Foley).
Trainer: Michael Joseph McCarthy.
ESTONIA: Mart Poom, Teet Allas, Marek Lemsalu, Andrei Stepanov, Erko Saviauk, Aivar Anniste, Martin Reim, Sergei Terehhov, Kristen Viikmäe (68 Kert Haavistu), Andres Oper, Indrek Zelinski (68 Dmitri Ustritski).
Trainer: Tarmo Rüütli.
Goals: Mark Kinsella (25), Richard Patrick Dunne (51)

361. 15.11.2000
REPUBLIC OF IRELAND v FINLAND 3-0 (1-0)
Lansdowne Road, Dublin
Referee: Paul Durkin (England)   Attendance: 22,368
REPUBLIC OF IRELAND: Seamus John Given, Garry Kelly (46 Jason Wynn McAteer), Gary Patrick Breen, Richard Patrick Dunne, Ian Patrick Harte (46 Stephen Staunton), Mark Anthony Kinsella, Kevin Daniel Kilbane, Matthew Rhys Holland, Stephen John Finnan, Robert David Keane (90 David James Connolly), Dominic Joseph Foley (46 Lee Kevin Carsley).   Trainer: Michael Joseph McCarthy.

FINLAND: Jussi Jääskeläinen, Kaj Wilhelm Nylund, Janne Saarinen, Petri Pasanen (78 Mika Nurmela), Hannu Tihinen, Teemu Tainio (66 Toni Kuivasto), Jonatan Johansson (46 Tommi Grönlund), Aki Riihilahti, Jari Litmanen (Cap), Mikael Forssell (46 Shefki Kuqi), Joonas Kolkka (86 Mika Kottila).   Trainer: Antti Muurinen.

Goals: Stephen John Finnan (14), Kevin Daniel Kilbane (85), Stephen Staunton (90)

362. 24.03.2001   17th World Cup Qualifiers
CYPRUS v REPUBLIC OF IRELAND 0-4 (0-2)
GSP, Nicosia
Referee: Frank De Bleeckere (Belgium)   Attendance: 13,000
CYPRUS: Nicos Panayiotou, Petros Konnafis, Vasos Melanarkitis (55 Filippos Filippou), Ioakim Ioakim, Marios Charalambous, Panicos Pounas (43 Costas Malekkos), Georgios Theodotou, Milenko Spoljaric, Yiannakis Okkas (75 Marios Agathocleous), Marios Christodoulou, Michalis Constantinou.   Trainer: Stavros Papadopoulos.

REPUBLIC OF IRELAND: Seamus John Given, Garry Kelly, Ian Patrick Harte, Kenneth Edward Cunningham, Gary Patrick Breen, Roy Maurice Keane (Cap), Jason Wynn McAteer (77 Matthew Rhys Holland), Mark Anthony Kinsella, David James Connolly, Robert David Keane (87 Gary Michael Thomas Doherty), Kevin Daniel Kilbane (81 Damien Anthony Duff).   Trainer: Michael Joseph McCarthy.

Goals: Roy Maurice Keane (32, 88), Ian Harte (42 pen), Garry Kelly (80)

363. 28.03.2001   17th World Cup Qualifiers
ANDORRA v REPUBLIC OF IRELAND 0-3 (0-1)
Mini-Estadi, Barcelona (Spain)
Referee: Ihor Ishchenko (Ukraine)   Attendance: 5,000
ANDORRA: Alfonso Sánchez, Roberto Jonás Alonso Martínez (90 Francisco Xavier Soria Gómez), José Manuel García Luena "Txema", Ildefons Lima Sola, Agusti Pol Pérez, Óscar Sonejee Masand, Emiliano González Arquez (81 Jordi Escura Aixas), Justo Ruíz González, Jesús Julián Lucendo Heredia, Antonio Lima Sola, Julián Sánchez Soto (87 Manuel Jiménez Soria).   Trainer: David Rodrigo (Spain).

REPUBLIC OF IRELAND: Seamus John Given, Garry Kelly, Ian Patrick Harte, Kenneth Edward Cunningham, Gary Patrick Breen, Roy Maurice Keane (Cap), Damien Anthony Duff, Matthew Rhys Holland, David James Connolly (26 Gary Michael Thomas Doherty), Robert David Keane, Kevin Daniel Kilbane (85 Stephen John Finnan).   Trainer: Michael Joseph McCarthy.

Goals: Ian Patrick Harte (33 pen), Kevin Daniel Kilbane (76), Matthew Rhys Holland (80)

364. 25.04.2001   17th World Cup Qualifiers
REPUBLIC OF IRELAND v ANDORRA 3-1 (2-1)
Lansdowne Road, Dublin
Referee: Kristinn Jakobsson (Iceland)   Attendance: 35,000
REPUBLIC OF IRELAND: Seamus John Given, Garry Kelly, Ian Patrick Harte, Richard Patrick Dunne, Gary Patrick Breen (85 Stephen Staunton), Matthew Rhys Holland, Mark Kennedy (68 Stephen Carr), Mark Anthony Kinsella (79 Stephen John Finnan), Gary Michael Thomas Doherty, David James Connolly, Kevin Daniel Kilbane.
Trainer: Michael Joseph McCarthy.

ANDORRA: Alfonso Sánchez, Roberto Jonás Alonso Martínez, José Manuel García Luena "Txema", Ildefons Lima Sola, Jordi Escura Aixas, Óscar Sonejee Masand, Emiliano González Arquez (87 Francisco Xavier Soria Gómez), Justo Ruíz González, Antonio Lima Sola, Manuel Jiménez Soria (81 Marc Pujol Pons), Julián Sánchez Soto (90 Juli Fernández Ariza).   Trainer: David Rodrigo (Spain).

Goals: Kevin Kilbane (34), Mark Anthony Kinsella (36), Gary Patrick Breen (76) / Ildefons Lima Sola (31)

365. 02.06.2001   17th World Cup Qualifiers
REPUBLIC OF IRELAND v PORTUGAL 1-1 (0-0)
Lansdowne Road, Dublin
Referee: Knud-Erik Fisker (Denmark)   Attendance: 35,000
REPUBLIC OF IRELAND: Seamus John Given, Stephen Carr, Ian Patrick Harte, Richard Patrick Dunne, Stephen Staunton, Roy Maurice Keane (Cap), Garry Kelly, Mark Anthony Kinsella (80 Gary Michael Thomas Doherty), Niall John Quinn (75 Matthew Rhys Holland), Robert David Keane (61 Damien Anthony Duff), Kevin Daniel Kilbane. Trainer: Michael Joseph McCarthy.
PORTUGAL: Ricardo Alexandre Martins Soares Pereira, Roberto Luís Gaspar Deus Severo "Beto", Carlos Manuel Oliveira Magalhães "Litos" (88 Luís Boa Morte Pereira), Jorge Paulo Costa Almeida, Rui Jorge de Sousa Dias Macedo de Oliveira (74 João Manuel Vieira Pinto), Nuno Miguel Frechaut Barreto, Armando Gonçalves Teixeira "Petit", Rui Manuel César Costa, Pedro Alexandre Santos Barbosa (71 Nuno Fernando Gonçalves Rocha "Capucho"), Luis Filipe Madeira Caeiro "Figo" (Cap), Pedro Miguel Carreiro Resendes "Pauleta". Trainer: António Luís Alves Ribeiro Oliveira.
Goals: Roy Maurice Keane (68) /
Luis Filipe Madeira Caeiro "Figo" (78)

366. 06.06.2001   17th World Cup Qualifiers
ESTONIA v REPUBLIC OF IRELAND 0-2 (0-2)
Lilleküla, Tallinn
Referee: Marian Mircea Salomir (Romania)   Att: 9,300
REPUBLIC OF IRELAND: Seamus John Given, Stephen Carr, Ian Patrick Harte, Richard Patrick Dunne, Stephen Staunton (Cap), Matthew Rhys Holland, Garry Kelly, Mark Anthony Kinsella, Niall John Quinn (36 Gary Michael Thomas Doherty), Damien Anthony Duff (89 Andrew James O'Brien), Kevin Daniel Kilbane.   Trainer: Michael Joseph McCarthy.
ESTONIA: Martin Kaalma, Erkko Saviauk, Andrei Stepanov, Raio Piiroja, Urmas Rooba (71 Teet Allas), Martin Reim, Kert Haavistu (52 Sergei Terehhov), Jevgeni Novikov (74 Dmitri Ustritski), Indrek Zelinski, Marko Kristal, Andres Oper. Trainer: Arnoldus Dick Pijpers (Holland).
Goals: Richard Dunne (8), Matthew Rhys Holland (39)

367. 15.08.2001
REPUBLIC OF IRELAND v CROATIA 2-2 (1-0)
Lansdowne Road, Dublin
Referee: Andreas Schluchter (Switzerland)   Att: 27,000
REPUBLIC OF IRELAND: Seamus John Given (46 Alan Thomas Kelly), Garry Kelly (84 John Francis O'Shea), Richard Patrick Dunne (46 Andrew James O'Brien), Stephen Staunton, Ian Patrick Harte (60 Stephen McPhail), Steven John Reid (46 Stephen John Finnan), Roy Maurice Keane (46 Jason Wynn McAteer), Lee Kevin Carsley, Mark Kennedy (46 Kevin Daniel Kilbane), Damien Anthony Duff (52 Clinton Hubert Morrison), Robert David Keane (52 David James Connolly). Trainer: Michael Joseph McCarthy.
CROATIA: Stipe Pletikosa, Dario Šimić (73 Stjepan Tomas), Igor Tudor, Robert Jarni (62 Danijel Šarić), Zvonimir Soldo (73 Robert Prosinečki), Robert Kovač, Mario Stanić (46 Igor Bišćan), Milan Rapaić (46 Boris Živković), Niko Kovač (82 Nenad Bjelica), Boško Balaban (46 Davor Vugrinec), Alen Bokšić (73 Davor Šuker).   Trainer: Mirko Jozić.
Goals: Damien Duff (20), Clinton Hubert Morrison (77) /
Davor Vugrinec (80), Davor Šuker (90 pen)

368. 01.09.2001   17th World Cup Qualifiers
REPUBLIC OF IRELAND v HOLLAND 1-0 (0-0)
Lansdowne Road, Dublin
Referee: Hellmut Krug (Germany)   Attendance: 35,400
REPUBLIC OF IRELAND: Seamus John Given, Garry Kelly, Ian Patrick Harte (87 Niall John Quinn), Richard Patrick Dunne, Stephen Staunton, Roy Maurice Keane (Cap), Jason Wynn McAteer (90 Andrew James O'Brien), Matthew Rhys Holland, Damien Anthony Duff, Robert David Keane (60 Stephen John Finnan), Kevin Daniel Kilbane. Trainer: Michael Joseph McCarthy.
HOLLAND: Edwin van der Sar, Mario Melchiot, Jacob Stam, Kevin Hofland, Arthur Johannes Numan (63 Petrus Ferdinandus van Hooijdonk), Mark Peter Gertruda Andreas van Bommel, Boudewijn Zenden (55 Jerrel Floyd Hasselbaink), Phillip Cocu (Cap), Rutgerus Johannes Martinus van Nistelrooy, Patrick Steven Kluivert, Marc Overmars (71 Giovanni Christiaan van Bronckhorst). Trainer: Aloysius Paulus Maria van Gaal.
Sent off: Garry Kelly (58)
Goal: Jason Wynn McAteer (68)

369. 06.10.2001   17th World Cup Qualifiers
REPUBLIC OF IRELAND v CYPRUS 4-0 (2-0)
Lansdowne Road, Dublin
Referee: Juan Ansuategui Roca (Spain)   Attendance: 35,000
REPUBLIC OF IRELAND: Seamus John Given, Stephen John Finnan, Ian Patrick Harte, Gary Patrick Breen, Stephen Staunton, Roy Maurice Keane, Mark Kennedy (63 Lee Kevin Carsley), Matthew Rhys Holland, Niall John Quinn (68 Clinton Hubert Morrison), David James Connolly, Kevin Daniel Kilbane (83 Stephen McPhail).
Trainer: Michael Joseph McCarthy.

CYPRUS: Nicos Panayiotou, Petros Konnafis (68 Loukas Louka), Christos Kotsonis, Dimitris Daskalakis, Nicos K. Nicolaou, Vasos Melanarkitis, Georgios Theodoutou, Marinos Satsias, Yiannakis Okkas (82 Marios Themistocleous), Marios Christodoulou, Yiasoumakis Yiasoumi (87 Lefteris Kontolefteros). Trainer: Christos Charalambous.

Goals: Ian Patrick Harte (3), Niall John Quinn (11), David James Connolly (63), Roy Maurice Keane (67)

370. 10.11.2001   17th World Cup Qualifiers
(Play-Offs)
REPUBLIC OF IRELAND v IRAN 2-0 (1-0)
Lansdowne Road, Dublin
Referee: Antonio Pereira Da Silva (Brazil)   Att: 36,538
REPUBLIC OF IRELAND: Seamus John Given, Stephen John Finnan, Ian Patrick Harte, Gary Patrick Breen, Stephen Staunton (75 Kenneth Edward Cunningham), Roy Maurice Keane (Cap), Jason Wynn McAteer (84 Garry Kelly), Matthew Rhys Holland, Niall John Quinn, Robert David Keane, Kevin Daniel Kilbane. Trainer: Michael Joseph McCarthy.

IRAN: Ebrahim Mirzapour, Rahman Rezaei, Mohammad Peyravani, Yahya Golmohammadi, Mehdi Mahdavikia, Hamed Kavianpour, Mehrdad Minavand, Karim Bagheri, Mohammad Ali Karimi Pashaki, Ali Reza Vahedi Nikbaht (46 Mojahed Khaziravi), Ali Daei. Trainer: Miroslav Blažević (Croatia).

Goals: Ian Patrick Harte (43 pen), Robert David Keane (49)

371. 15.11.2001   17th World Cup Qualifiers
(Play-Offs)
IRAN v REPUBLIC OF IRELAND 1-0 (0-0)
Azadi, Teheran
Referee: William Mattus Vega (Costa Rica)   Att: 95,000
IRAN: Ebrahim Mirzapour, Rahman Rezaei, Mohammad Peyravani, Yahya Golmohammadi, Ali Reza Vahedi Nikbaht, Hamed Kavianpour, Mehrdad Minavand, Mehdi Mahdavikia, Karim Bagheri, Mohammad Ali Karimi Pashaki, Ali Daei.
Trainer: Miroslav Blažević (Croatia).

REPUBLIC OF IRELAND: Seamus John Given, Stephen John Finnan, Ian Patrick Harte, Gary Patrick Breen, Stephen Staunton (Cap), Mark Anthony Kinsella, Jason Wynn McAteer, Matthew Rhys Holland, Robert David Keane (76 Clinton Hubert Morrison), David James Connolly, Kevin Daniel Kilbane (82 Garry Kelly).
Trainer: Michael Joseph McCarthy.

Goal: Yahya Golmohammadi (90)

372. 13.02.2002
REPUBLIC OF IRELAND v RUSSIA 2-0 (2-0)
Lansdowne Road, Dublin
Referee: Dermott Gallagher (England)   Attendance: 44,000
REPUBLIC OF IRELAND: Seamus John Given (46 Dean Lawrence Kiely), Stephen John Finnan (72 Stephen Staunton), Andrew James O'Brien (46 Richard Patrick Dunne), Kenneth Edward Cunningham (46 Gary Patrick Breen), Ian Patrick Harte (72 Jason Wynn McAteer (90 Niall John Quinn)), Steven John Reid (46 Gary Kelly), Colin Healy (46 Lee Kevin Carsley), Roy Maurice Keane (Cap) (86 Matthew Rhys Holland), Kevin Daniel Kilbane (46 Mark Kennedy), Robert David Keane (72 Richard Thomas Sadlier), Damien Anthony Duff (46 Clinton Hubert Morrison). Trainer: Michael Joseph McCarthy.

RUSSIA: Ruslan Nigmatullin, Dmitriy Khlestov (90 Vyacheslav Dayev), Viktor Onopko (Cap), Yuriy Nikiforov (68 Igor Chugainov), Yuriy Kovtun, Dmitriy Khokhlov (53 Marat Izmailov), Aleksandr Mostovoi, Yegor Titov, Valeriy Karpin, Dmitriy Alenichev (71 Sergey Semak), Vladimir Beschastnykh. Trainer: Oleg Romantsev.

Goals: Steven John Reid (3), Robert David Keane (20)

373. 27.03.2002
REPUBLIC OF IRELAND v DENMARK 3-0 (1-0)
Lansdowne Road, Dublin
Referee: Brian Lawlor (Wales)   Attendance: 42,000
REPUBLIC OF IRELAND: Dean Lawrence Kiely (46 Nicholas Vincent Colgan), Garry Kelly, Kenneth Edward Cunningham, Stephen Staunton (Cap), Ian Patrick Harte, Jason Wynn McAteer (66 Steven John Reid), Matthew Rhys Holland, Mark Anthony Kinsella (64 Colin Healy), Damien Anthony Duff (84 Richard Patrick Dunne), Robert David Keane (77 David James Connolly), Clinton Hubert Morrison. Trainer: Michael Joseph McCarthy.
DENMARK: Thomas Sørensen (46 Peter Kjær), Thomas Rytter, Martin Laursen, René Henriksen, Jan Heintze (Cap) (81 Niclas Jensen), Christian Bager Poulsen, Brian Steen Nielsen, Jesper Grønkjær, Allan Nielsen (46 Peter Madsen), Dennis Rommedahl (69 Peter Løvenkrands), Ebbe Sand. Trainer: Morten Olsen.
Goals: Ian Patrick Harte (19), Robert David Keane (54), Clinton Hubert Morrison (90)

374. 17.04.2002
REPUBLIC OF IRELAND v UNITED STATES 2-1 (1-1)
Lansdowne Road, Dublin
Referee: Philippe Leuba (Switzerland)   Attendance: 39,000
REPUBLIC OF IRELAND: Seamus John Given, Stephen John Finnan (46 Garry Kelly), Ian Patrick Harte (46 Stephen Staunton), Andrew James O'Brien (46 Kenneth Edward Cunningham), Gary Patrick Breen (72 Gary Michael Thomas Doherty), Colin Healy, Rory John Delap, Mark Anthony Kinsella (46 Matthew Rhys Holland), Kevin Daniel Kilbane (46 Steven John Reid), Damien Anthony Duff (46 David James Connolly), Robert David Keane (83 Clinton Hubert Morrison). Trainer: Michael Joseph McCarthy.
UNITED STATES: Bradley Howard Friedel (46 Kasey Keller), Jeff Agoos, George Edward Pope, Gregg Berhalter (46 Gregory Vanney), Anthony Sanneh, Christopher Armas, John Patrick O'Brien (46 Edward Lewis), Earnest Stewart (46 Landon Timothy Donovan), Claudio Reyna (72 Frank Daniel Hejduk), Brian John McBride (46 Joseph-Max Moore), Clint Mathis (64 Joshua David Wolff).   Trainer: Bruce Arena.
Goals: Mark Anthony Kinsella (7), Gary Doherty (83) / George Edward Pope (34)

375. 16.05.2002
REPUBLIC OF IRELAND v NIGERIA 1-2 (0-1)
Lansdowne Road, Dublin
Referee: Antonia Almeida Costa (Portugal)   Att: 42,652
REPUBLIC OF IRELAND: Seamus John Given, Stephen Staunton, Ian Patrick Harte, Stephen John Finnan, Kenneth Edward Cunningham, Jason Wynn McAteer (46 Steven John Reid), Matthew Rhys Holland, Kevin Daniel Kilbane (61 Garry Kelly), Damien Anthony Duff (60 David James Connolly), Robert David Keane (60 Clinton Hubert Morrison), Roy Maurice Keane (Cap) (64 Mark Anthony Kinsella). Trainer: Michael Joseph McCarthy.
NIGERIA: Ike Shorunmu, Efetobore Sodje, Taribo West, Isaac Okoronkwo, Albert Joseph Yobo, Augustine Azuka Okocha (66 Wilson Oruma), Nwankwo Kanu, Julius Aghahowa, Pius Ikedia, Femi Opabunmi, Bartholomew Ogbeche. Trainer: Adegboye Onigbinde.
Goals: Steven John Reid (68) / Julius Aghahowa (13), Efetobore Sodje (46)

376. 01.06.2002   17th World Cup, 1st Round
REPUBLIC OF IRELAND v CAMEROON 1-1 (0-1)
Niigata Stadium, Niigata (Japan)
Referee: Toru Kamikawa (Japan)   Attendance: 33,679
REPUBLIC OF IRELAND: Seamus John Given, Ian Patrick Harte (77 Steven John Reid), Stephen Staunton (Cap), Jason Wynn McAteer (46 Stephen John Finnan), Matthew Rhys Holland, Damien Anthony Duff, Robert David Keane, Kevin Daniel Kilbane, Mark Anthony Kinsella, Gary Patrick Breen, Garry Kelly.   Trainer: Michael Joseph McCarthy.
CAMEROON: Alioum Boukar, Bill Mbiayi Tchato, Pierre Womé Nlend, Rigobert Song Bahanag (Cap), Raymond Kalla Nkongo, Geremi Fotso Sorele Njitap, Samuel EtO'o Fils, Patrick Henri Mboma Dem (69 Hervé Patrick Suffo Kengene), Bisan Lauren Etamé-Mayer, Marc-Vivien Foé, René Salomon Olembe.   Trainer: Winfried Schäfer (Germany).
Goals: Matthew Rhys Holland (52) / Patrick Henri Mboma Dem (39)

377. 05.06.2002   17th World Cup, 1st Round
REPUBLIC OF IRELAND v GERMANY 1-1 (0-1)
Kashima Soccer Stadium, Ibaraki
Referee: Kim Milton Nielsen (Denmark)   Att: 35,900
REPUBLIC OF IRELAND: Seamus John Given, Stephen John Finnan, Ian Patrick Harte (73 Steven John Reid), Stephen Staunton (Cap) (87 Kenneth Edward Cunningham), Matthew Rhys Holland, Damien Anthony Duff, Robert David Keane, Kevin Daniel Kilbane, Mark Anthony Kinsella, Gary Patrick Breen, Garry Kelly (73 Niall John Quinn).
Trainer: Michael Joseph McCarthy.
GERMANY: Oliver Kahn (Cap), Thomas Linke, Carsten Ramelow, Christoph Metzelder, Torsten Frings, Dietmar Hamann, Christian Ziege, Bernd Schneider (90 Jens Jeremies), Michael Ballack, Miroslav Klose (85 Marco Bode), Carsten Jancker (75 Oliver Bierhoff).   Trainer: Rudolf Völler.
Goals: Robert David Keane (90) / Miroslav Klose (19)

378. 11.06.2002   17th World Cup, 1st Round
**REPUBLIC OF IRELAND
v SAUDI ARABIA 3-0** (1-0)
International, Yokohama (Japan)
Referee: Falla Ndoye (Senegal)   Attendance: 65,320
REPUBLIC OF IRELAND: Seamus John Given, Stephen John Finnan, Ian Patrick Harte (46 Niall John Quinn), Stephen Staunton (Cap), Matthew Rhys Holland, Damien Anthony Duff, Robert David Keane, Kevin Daniel Kilbane, Mark Anthony Kinsella (89 Lee Kevin Carsley), Gary Patrick Breen, Garry Kelly (80 Jason Wynn McAteer).
Trainer: Michael Joseph McCarthy.
SAUDI ARABIA: Mohammed Al Deayea, Mohammed Al Jahani (79 Ahmed Dukhi Al Dosari), Redha Tukar Fallatah, Abdullah Sulaiman Zubromawi (68 Abdullah Gaman Al Dosari), Fawzi Al Shehri, Ibrahim Sowed Al Shahrani, Hussein Abdul Ghani Sulimani, Abdulaziz Al Khathran (67 Mohammad Al Shlhoub), Khamis Al Owairan Al Dossari, Nawaf Al Temyat, Al Hassan Al Yami.
Trainer: Nasser Al Johar.
Goals: Robert David Keane (7), Gary Patrick Breen (61), Damien Anthony Duff (87)

379. 16.06.2002   17th World Cup, 2nd Round
**SPAIN
v REPUBLIC OF IRELAND 1-1** (1-0, 1-1) (AET)
Suwon World Cup Stadium, Suwon (South Korea)
Referee: Anders Frisk (Sweden)   Attendance: 38,926
SPAIN: Iker Casillas Fernández, Carles Puyol Soforcada, Fernando Ruiz Hierro (III) (Cap), Iván Helguera Bujía, Juan Francisco García García "Juanfran", Rubén Baraja Vegas, Juan Carlos Valerón Santana, Francisco Javier De Pedro Falque (66 Gaizka Mendieta Zabala), Raúl González Blanco (79 Albert Luque Martos), Fernando Morientes Sánchez (72 David Albelda Aliqués), Luis Enrique Martínez García.
Trainer: José Antonio Camacho.
REPUBLIC OF IRELAND: Seamus John Given, Stephen John Finnan, Ian Patrick Harte (82 David James Connolly), Stephen Staunton (Cap) (50 Kenneth Edward Cunningham), Matthew Rhys Holland, Damien Anthony Duff, Robert David Keane, Kevin Daniel Kilbane, Mark Anthony Kinsella, Gary Patrick Breen, Garry Kelly (55 Niall John Quinn).
Trainer: Michael Joseph McCarthy.
Goals: Fernando Morientes Sánchez (8) / Robert David Keane (90 pen)
Penalties: Robert Keane (0-1), Fernando Ruiz Hierro (1-1), Matthew Rhys Holland (miss), Rubén Baraja Vegas (1-2), David James Connolly (saved), Juan Francisco García García "Juanfran" (miss), Kevin Daniel Kilbane (saved), Juan Carlos Valerón Santana (miss), Stephen John Finnan (2-2), Gaizka Mendieta Zabala (3-2)

380. 21.08.2002
FINLAND v REPUBLIC OF IRELAND 0-3 (0-1)
Olympiastadion, Helsinki
Referee: Rune Pedersen (Norway)   Attendance: 12,225
FINLAND: Jussi Jääskeläinen, Petri Pasanen, Hannu Tihinen, Sami Hyypiä (46 Toni Kuivasto), Janne Saarinen, Mika Nurmela (69 Peter Kopteff), Teemu Tainio (80 Janne Hietanen), Jari Ilola (59 Aki Riihilahti), Joonas Kolkka (78 Mika Kottila), Jari Litmanen (Cap), Jonatan Johansson (59 Shefki Kuqi).   Trainer: Antti Muurinen.
REPUBLIC OF IRELAND: Dean Lawrence Kiely (76 Seamus John Given), Garry Kelly, Ian Patrick Harte (Cap) (76 Graham Barrett), Kenneth Edward Cunningham (46 Gary Michael Thomas Doherty), Gary Patrick Breen, Lee Kevin Carsley (87 Matthew Rhys Holland), Jason Wynn McAteer (46 Colin Healy), Mark Anthony Kinsella (46 Stephen McPhail), Damien Anthony Duff (46 Rory John Delap), Robert David Keane (83 James Goodwin), Thomas Butler (46 Kevin Daniel Kilbane).
Trainer: Michael Joseph McCarthy.
Goals: Robert David Keane (12), Colin Healy (74), Graham Barrett (83)

381. 07.09.2002   12th European Champs Qualifiers
RUSSIA v REPUBLIC OF IRELAND   4-2 (2-0)
Lokomotiv, Moskva
Referee: Claude Colombo (France)   Attendance: 26,000
RUSSIA: Sergey Ovchinnikov, Gennadiy Nizhegorodov, Sergey Ignashevich, Yevgeniy Aldonin, Sergey Semak (Cap) (75 Dmitriy Khokhlov), Igor Yanovskiy, Viktor Onopko, Rolan Gusev (29 Andrey Solomatin), Andrey Karyaka, Dmitriy Loskov, Vladimir Beschastnykh (46 Aleksandr Kerzhakov). Trainer: Valeriy Gazzayev.
REPUBLIC OF IRELAND: Seamus John Given, Stephen John Finnan, Ian Patrick Harte (Cap), Kenneth Edward Cunningham, Gary Patrick Breen, Matthew Rhys Holland, Jason Wynn McAteer (65 Gary Michael Thomas Doherty), Mark Anthony Kinsella, Damien Anthony Duff (17 Clinton Hubert Morrison), Robert David Keane, Kevin Daniel Kilbane (86 Philip Andrew Babb). Trainer: Michael Joseph McCarthy.
Goals: Andrey Karyaka (20), Vladimir Beschastnykh (25), Aleksandr Kerzhakov (71), Philip Babb (88 own goal) / Gary Doherty (69), Clinton Hubert Morrison (76)

382. 16.10.2002   12th European Champs Qualifiers
**REPUBLIC OF IRELAND
v SWITZERLAND   1-2** (0-1)
Lansdowne Road, Dublin
Referee: Rune Pedersen (Norway)   Attendance: 35,000
REPUBLIC OF IRELAND: Seamus John Given, Garry Kelly, Ian Patrick Harte (86 Gary Michael Thomas Doherty), Kenneth Edward Cunningham, Gary Patrick Breen, Matthew Rhys Holland, Colin Healy, Mark Anthony Kinsella, Damien Anthony Duff (83 Thomas Butler), Robert David Keane, Kevin Daniel Kilbane (62 Clinton Hubert Morrison). Trainer: Michael Joseph McCarthy.
SWITZERLAND: Jörg Stiel, Bernt Haas, Patrick Müller, Murat Yakin, Ludovic Magnin, Johann Vogel, Ricardo Cabanas, Raphaël Wicky (85 Mario Cantaluppi), Hakan Yakin (85 Fabio Celestini), Alexander Frei (71 Léonard Thurre), Stéphane Chapuisat.   Trainer: Jakob Kühn.
Goals: Ludovic Magnin (78 own goal) / Hakan Yakin (45), Fabio Celestini (87)

383. 20.11.2002
GREECE v REPUBLIC OF IRELAND   0-0
"Apóstolos Nikolaïdis", Athína
Referee: Alfredo Trentalange (Italy)   Attendance: 2,100
GREECE: Antónis Nikopolídis (46 Dionísis Hiotis), Giórgos Seitarídis (46 Hrístos Patsatzoglou), Panagiótis Fyssas (46 Stélios Venetídis), Nikolaos Dabizas (46 Giánnis Góumas), Sotírios Kyrgiakos, Angelos Basinás (60 Théodoros Zagorakis), Stylianos Giannakópoulos (46 Giórgos Hrístos Georgiádis), Giórgos Karagoúnis (60 Panteleimon Kafés), Angelos Haristéas, Vasílis Tsiártas (46 Giánnis Amanatídis), Thémistoklis Nikolaïdis (46 Dimítris Papadópulos). Trainer: Otto Rehhagel (Germany).
REPUBLIC OF IRELAND: Seamus John Given, Stephen John Finnan, John Francis O'Shea, Kenneth Edward Cunningham (Cap), Richard Patrick Dunne, Colin Healy, Lee Kevin Carsley, Matthew Rhys Holland, Stephen McPhail, Gary Michael Thomas Doherty, Glen Michael Crowe (87 Rory John Delap).   Trainer: Daniel Joseph Givens.

384. 12.02.2003
SCOTLAND v REPUBLIC OF IRELAND   0-2 (0-2)
Hampden Park, Glasgow
Referee: Eric Braamhaar (Holland)   Attendance: 33,337
SCOTLAND: Neil Sullivan (46 Paul Gallacher), Stephen Caldwell, Russell Anderson, Christian Edward Dailly, Graham Alexander, Paul Lambert (Cap) (46 Scot Gemmill), Barry Ferguson (65 Colin Cameron), Gary Andrew Naysmith, Neil McCann (65 James Smith), Steven Crawford (65 Steven Thompson), Donald Hutchison (46 Paul John Devlin). Manager: Hans-Hubert Vogts (Germany).
REPUBLIC OF IRELAND: Dean Lawrence Kiely (82 Nicholas Vincent Colgan), Stephen Carr, John Francis O'Shea (81 Richard Patrick Dunne), Gary Patrick Breen (90 Andrew James O'Brien), Ian Patrick Harte, Steven John Reid (78 Colin Healy), Matthew Rhys Holland, Mark Anthony Kinsella (78 Lee Kevin Carsley), Kevin Daniel Kilbane, Clinton Hubert Morrison, Gary Michael Thomas Doherty (73 David James Connolly).   Trainer: Brian Kerr.
Goals: Kevin Kilbane (7), Clinton Hubert Morrison (16)

385. 29.03.2003   12th European Champs Qualifiers
GEORGIA v REPUBLIC OF IRELAND 1-2 (0-1)

Lokomotiv, Tbilisi

Referee: Kyros Vassaras (Greece)   Attendance: 15,000

GEORGIA: Giorgi Lomaia, Otar Khizaneishvili, Giorgi Shashiashvili, Aleksandre Amisulashvili, Levan Kobiashvili, Levan Tskitishvili, Giorgi Nemsadze (Cap), Gocha Jamarauli, Temur Ketsbaia (46 Giorgi Demetradze), Giorgi Kinkladze (72 Givi Didava), Aleksandre Iashvili.
Trainer: Aleksandre Chivadze.

REPUBLIC OF IRELAND: Seamus John Given, Stephen Carr, Kenneth Edward Cunningham, Gary Patrick Breen, John Francis O'Shea, Matthew Rhys Holland, Damien Anthony Duff, Mark Anthony Kinsella, Gary Michael Thomas Doherty, Lee Kevin Carsley, Kevin Daniel Kilbane.   Trainer: Brian Kerr.

Goals: Levan Kobiashvili (62) / Damien Anthony Duff (18), Gary Michael Thomas Doherty (84)

386. 02.04.2003   12th European Champs Qualifiers
ALBANIA v REPUBLIC OF IRELAND 0-0

Qemal Stafa, Tiranë

Referee: Stefano Farina (Italy)   Attendance: 20,000

ALBANIA: Fotaq Strakosha, Elvin Beqiri, Geri Çipi, Ardian Aliaj, Altin Lala, Besnik Hasi, Klodian Duro, Ervin Skela (85 Alban Bushi), Edvin Murati (66 Arjan Bellai), Igli Tare, Altin Rraklli (69 Florian Myrtaj).
Trainer: Hans-Peter Briegel (Germany).

REPUBLIC OF IRELAND: Seamus John Given, Stephen Carr, John Francis O'Shea, Matthew Rhys Holland, Mark Anthony Kinsella, Gary Patrick Breen, Kenneth Edward Cunningham, Lee Kevin Carsley, Damien Anthony Duff, Kevin Daniel Kilbane, Robert David Keane (66 Gary Michael Thomas Doherty).   Trainer: Brian Kerr.

387. 30.04.2003
REPUBLIC OF IRELAND v NORWAY 1-0 (1-0)

Lansdowne Road, Dublin

Referee: Michael McCurry (Scotland)   Attendance: 32,643

REPUBLIC OF IRELAND: Seamus John Given (60 Nicholas Vincent Colgan), Stephen Carr, Ian Patrick Harte (60 Stephen John Finnan), Gary Patrick Breen, Richard Patrick Dunne, Matthew Rhys Holland, Damien Anthony Duff (73 Alan Lee), Mark Anthony Kinsella (65 Lee Kevin Carsley), David James Connolly (73 Colin Healy), Robert David Keane (90 Glen Michael Crowe), Kevin Daniel Kilbane (86 Alan Quinn).   Trainer: Brian Kerr.

NORWAY: Frode Olsen (46 Erik Holtan), Christer Basma (56 Alexander Aas), Brede Paulsen Hangeland, Ronny Johnsen (46 Torjus Hansén), André Bergdølmo, John Alieu Carew, Tommy Svindal Larsen, Trond Andersen (90 Frode Johnsen), Øyvind Leonhardsen, Steffen Iversen (65 Petter Rudi), Sigurd Rushfeldt (46 Tore André Flo).   Trainer: Nils Johan Semb.

Goal: Damien Anthony Duff (17)

388. 07.06.2003   12th European Champs Qualifiers
REPUBLIC OF IRELAND v ALBANIA 2-1 (1-1)

Lansdowne Road, Dublin

Referee: Tomasz Mikulski (Poland)   Attendance: 33,000

REPUBLIC OF IRELAND: Seamus John Given, Stephen Carr, John Francis O'Shea, Gary Patrick Breen, Kenneth Edward Cunningham, Matthew Rhys Holland, Damien Anthony Duff, Mark Anthony Kinsella (55 Lee Kevin Carsley), David James Connolly (65 Gary Michael Thomas Doherty), Robert David Keane, Kevin Daniel Kilbane (76 Steven John Reid).   Trainer: Brian Kerr.

ALBANIA: Fotaq Strakosha (79 Arian Beqaj), Elvin Beqiri, Geri Çipi, Klodian Duro, Besnik Hasi, Edvin Murati (58 Arjan Bellai), Altin Lala, Ervin Skela, Ardian Aliaj, Altin Rraklli (85 Florian Myrtaj), Igli Tare.
Trainer: Hans-Peter Briegel (Germany).

Goals: Robert David Keane (6), Ardian Aliaj (90 own goal) / Ervin Skela (8)

389. 11.06.2003   12th European Champs Qualifiers
REPUBLIC OF IRELAND v GEORGIA 2-0 (1-0)

Lansdowne Road, Dublin

Referee: Eduardo Iturralde González (Spain)   Att: 36,000

REPUBLIC OF IRELAND: Seamus John Given, Stephen Carr, John Francis O'Shea, Gary Patrick Breen, Kenneth Edward Cunningham, Matthew Rhys Holland, Lee Kevin Carsley, Colin Healy (86 Mark Anthony Kinsella), Gary Michael Thomas Doherty (89 Alan Lee), Robert David Keane, Kevin Daniel Kilbane.   Trainer: Brian Kerr.

GEORGIA: Giorgi Lomaia, Otar Khizaneishvili, Zurab Khizanishvili, Kakhaber Kaladze (Cap), Aleksandre Amisulashvili, Givi Didava (77 Rati Aleksidze), Aleksandre Rekhviashvili, Vladimir Burduli, Malkhaz Asatiani, Giorgi Demetradze (61 Vitali Daraselia), Shota Arveladze.
Trainer: Ivan Šušak (Croatia).

Goals: Gary Doherty (43), Robert David Keane (59)

390. 19.08.2003
REPUBLIC OF IRELAND v AUSTRALIA 2-1 (0-0)
Lansdowne Road, Dublin
Referee: Karel Vidlák (Czech Republic)   Attendance: 37,200
REPUBLIC OF IRELAND: Nicholas Vincent Colgan, Stephen Carr (57 Ian Patrick Harte), Kenneth Edward Cunningham (83 Richard Patrick Dunne), Gary Patrick Breen (46 Andrew James O'Brien), John Francis O'Shea, Stephen John Finnan (66 Kevin Daniel Kilbane), Matthew Rhys Holland (19 Colin Healy), Mark Anthony Kinsella, Damien Anthony Duff (79 Alan Quinn), Gary Michael Thomas Doherty (57 Clinton Hubert Morrison), Robert David Keane (46 David James Connolly).   Trainer: Brian Kerr.
AUSTRALIA: Mark Schwarzer, Lucas Neill, Hayden Foxe, Tony Popovic, Stan Lazaridis, Brett Emerton, Paul Okon (67 Vince Grella), Marco Bresciano, Danny Tiatto (69 Tony Vidmar), Mark Viduka (77 John Aloisi), Scott Chipperfield. Trainer: Frank Farina.
Goals: John O'Shea (74), Clinton Hubert Morrison (80) / Mark Viduka (84)

392. 09.09.2003
REPUBLIC OF IRELAND v TURKEY 2-2 (1-0)
Lansdowne Road, Dublin
Referee: Jan Wegereef (Holland)   Attendance: 27,200
REPUBLIC OF IRELAND: Nicholas Vincent Colgan (75 Joseph Murphy), Stephen John Finnan, Andrew James O'Brien (75 Richard Patrick Dunne), Gary Patrick Breen (88 Clinton Hubert Morrison), Ian Patrick Harte (89 Stephen Carr), Colin Healy (88 Stephen McPhail), Mark Anthony Kinsella, Kevin Daniel Kilbane, Damien Anthony Duff (46 Steven John Reid), David James Connolly, Gary Michael Thomas Doherty.   Trainer: Brian Kerr.
TURKEY: Rüştü Reçber (60 Ömer Çatkıç (87 Zafer Özgültekin)), Emre Belözoğlu (60 Gökdenız Karadenız), Bülent Korkmaz (87 Ümit Davala), Fatih Akyel, Alpay Özalan (46 Deniz Barış), Ergün Penbe, Tugay Kerimoğlu (74 Ahmet Yıldırım), Hakan Şükür (87 Tümer Metin), Tuncay Şanlı (74 Okan Yılmaz), Tayfun Korkut (46 Okan Buruk), Hasan Gökhan Şaş (46 İbrahim Üzülmez).   Trainer: Şenol Güneş.
Goals: David Connolly (35), Richard Patrick Dunne (90) / Hakan Şükür (52), Okan Yılmaz (87)

391. 06.09.2003   12th European Champs Qualifiers
REPUBLIC OF IRELAND v RUSSIA 1-1 (1-1)
Lansdowne Road, Dublin
Referee: Luboš Michel (Slovakia)   Attendance: 36,000
REPUBLIC OF IRELAND: Seamus John Given, Stephen Carr, John Francis O'Shea (26 Ian Patrick Harte), Kenneth Edward Cunningham, Gary Patrick Breen, Matthew Rhys Holland, Lee Kevin Carsley (46 Steven John Reid), Colin Healy, Damien Anthony Duff, Clinton Hubert Morrison (73 Gary Michael Thomas Doherty), Kevin Daniel Kilbane. Trainer: Brian Kerr.
RUSSIA: Sergey Ovchinnikov, Dmitriy Sennikov, Vadim Yevseyev, Aleksey Smertin, Dmitriy Alenichev (39 Yevgeniy Aldonin), Sergey Ignashevich, Viktor Onopko (Cap), Rolan Gusev, Dmitriy Bulykin, Aleksandr Mostovoi, Valeriy Yesipov (34 Aleksandr Kerzhakov).   Trainer: Georgiy Yartsev.
Goals: Damien Anthony Duff (35) / Sergey Ignashevich (42)

393. 11.10.2003   12th European Champs Qualifiers
SWITZERLAND v REPUBLIC OF IRELAND 2-0 (1-0)
St.Jakob Park, Basel
Referee: Anders Frisk (Sweden)   Attendance: 31,006
SWITZERLAND: Jörg Stiel, Bernt Haas, Christoph Spycher, Patrick Müller, Murat Yakin, Johann Vogel, Benjamin Huggel, Raphaël Wicky, Hakan Yakin (55 Fabio Celestini), Alexander Frei (90 Stéphane Henchoz), Stéphane Chapuisat (68 Marco Streller).   Trainer: Jakob Kühn.
REPUBLIC OF IRELAND: Seamus John Given, Stephen Carr, Ian Patrick Harte, John Francis O'Shea, Gary Patrick Breen, Matthew Rhys Holland (74 Mark Anthony Kinsella), Damien Anthony Duff, Colin Healy, David James Connolly (58 Clinton Hubert Morrison), Robert David Keane, Kevin Daniel Kilbane (74 Stephen John Finnan).   Trainer: Brian Kerr.
Goals: Hakan Yakin (6), Alexander Frei (60)

394. 18.11.2003
REPUBLIC OF IRELAND v CANADA 3-0 (1-0)
Lansdowne Road, Dublin
Referee: Mark Whitby (Wales)   Attendance: 23,253
REPUBLIC OF IRELAND: Seamus John Given (82 Nicholas Vincent Colgan), Stephen Carr (46 Ian Patrick Harte), Kenneth Edward Cunningham, Richard Patrick Dunne, John Francis O'Shea (88 John Thompson), Steven John Reid (62 Rory John Delap), Graham Anthony Kavanagh (11 Matthew Rhys Holland), Andrew Matthew Reid (73 Stephen McPhail), Damien Anthony Duff (88 Kevin Daniel Kilbane), Robert David Keane, Gary Michael Thomas Doherty (46 Clinton Hubert Morrison).   Trainer: Brian Kerr.

CANADA: Lars Hirschfeld, Jason Bent, Richard Corey Hastings (87 Paul Fenwick), Marc Bircham (78 Martin Nash), Jason deVos (Cap) (81 Mark Rogers), Kevin McKenna, Paul Stalteri, Daniel Imhof, Tomasz Radzinski, Paolo Pasquale Peschisolido (74 Patrice Bernier), Ante Jazic.
Trainer: Colin Fyfe Miller.

Goals: Damien Anthony Duff (23), Robert Keane (60, 84)

395. 18.02.2004
REPUBLIC OF IRELAND v BRAZIL 0-0
Lansdowne Road, Dublin
Referee: Anders Frisk (Sweden)   Attendance: 44,000
REPUBLIC OF IRELAND: Seamus John Given, Stephen Carr, Kenneth Edward Cunningham (Cap), Andrew James O'Brien, John Francis O'Shea, Matthew Rhys Holland, Graham Anthony Kavanagh, Kevin Daniel Kilbane, Andrew Matthew Reid (65 Jason Wynn McAteer), Clinton Hubert Morrison, Robert David Keane.   Trainer: Brian Kerr.

BRAZIL: Nélson de Jesus Silva "Dida", Marcos Evangelista de Moraes "Cafu" (Cap), Lucimar da Silva Ferreira "Lúcio", José Vítor Roque Júnior, Roberto Carlos da Silva, José Kléberson Pereira (46 Júlio César Clement Baptista), Ricardo Izecson dos Santos Leite "Kaká", Gilberto Aparecido da Silva (14 Edmílson José Gomes de Moraes), José Roberto da Silva Júnior "Zé Roberto", Ronaldo de Assis Moreira "Ronaldinho", Ronaldo Luís Nazário de Lima.
Trainer: Carlos Alberto Gomes Parreira.

396. 31.03.2004
REPUBLIC OF IRELAND v CZECH REPUBLIC 2-1 (0-0)
Lansdowne Road, Dublin
Referee: Knud Erik Fisker (Denmark)   Attendance: 42,000
REPUBLIC OF IRELAND: Seamus John Given (82 Patrick Kenny), Alan Maybury, Ian Patrick Harte, Kenneth Edward Cunningham (Cap), Gary Michael Thomas Doherty (70 William Peter Miller, Matthew Rhys Holland, Damien Anthony Duff (76 Mark Anthony Kinsella), Andrew Matthew Reid (66 Rory John Delap), Clinton Hubert Morrison (76 Alan Lee), Robert David Keane, Kevin Daniel Kilbane.
Trainer: Brian Kerr.

CZECH REPUBLIC: Petr Čech (46 Martin Vaniak), Martin Jiránek (69 Jaroslav Plašil), Tomáš Ujfaluši, René Bolf (58 David Rozehnal), Marek Jankulovski, Libor Sionko (46 Marek Heinz), Tomáš Galásek, Pavel Nedvěd (Cap) (46 Jiří Štajner), Roman Týce, Jan Koller (46 Vratislav Lokvenc), Milan Baroš (84 Petr Voříšek).   Trainer: Karel Brückner.

Goals: Ian Patrick Harte (52), Robert David Keane (90) / Milan Baroš (81)

397. 28.04.2004
POLAND v REPUBLIC OF IRELAND 0-0
Zawisza, Bydgoszcz
Referee: Serhiy Shebek (Ukraine)   Attendance: 15,500
POLAND: Jerzy Dudek (59 Artur Boruc), Michał Żewłakow (84 Paweł Kaczorowski), Arkadiusz Głowacki (46 Tomasz Hajto), Tomasz Rząsa, Maciej Żurawski, Tomasz Kłos (81 Bartosz Bosacki), Mariusz Lewandowski, Mirosław Szymkowiak (85 Arkadiusz Radomski), Sebastian Mila (66 Euzebiusz Smolarek), Jacek Krzynówek (46 Kamil Kosowski), Emmanuel Olisadebe (46 Andrzej Niedzielan).
Trainer: Paweł Janas.

REPUBLIC OF IRELAND: Seamus John Given (71 Nicholas Vincent Colgan), John Francis O'Shea, Kenneth Edward Cunningham (Cap), Gary Michael Thomas Doherty (81 Andrew James O'Brien), Ian Patrick Harte (65 Alan Maybury), Steven John Reid, Mark Anthony Kinsella, William Peter Miller, Andrew Matthew Reid (81 Jonathan Douglas), Clinton Hubert Morrison (90 Jason Byrne), Alan Lee (65 Graham Barrett).   Trainer: Brian Kerr.

398. 27.05.2004
REPUBLIC OF IRELAND v ROMANIA 1-0 (0-0)
Lansdowne Road, Dublin
Referee: Jiří Jaroslav (Czech Republic)   Attendance: 44,000
REPUBLIC OF IRELAND: Seamus John Given, Stephen John Finnan, Andrew James O'Brien, Kenneth Edward Cunningham (Cap), Alan Maybury, William Peter Miller, Roy Maurice Keane, Matthew Rhys Holland, Andrew Matthew Reid (78 Martin Rowlands), Clinton Hubert Morrison, Robert David Keane.   Trainer: Brian Kerr.
ROMANIA: Bogdan Ionuț Lobonț (46 Bogdan Stelea), Mirel Matei Rădoi (82 Marius Marcel Constantin), Adrian Mihai Iencsi (90 Cosmin Bărcăuan), Sorin Ghionea, Cristian Ioan Dancia (78 Petre Marin), Florentin Dumitru, Florin Costin Șoavă (88 Ovidiu Petre), Mihăiță Păunel Pleșan (60 Marian Aliuță), Constantin Nicolae Dică (78 Dan Alexa), Ioan Viorel Ganea (Cap) (86 Daniel George Niculae, Ionel Daniel Dănciulescu (60 Adrian Constantin Neaga).
Trainer: Anghel Iordănescu.
Goal: Matthew Rhys Holland (85)

399. 29.05.2004   Unity Cup
REPUBLIC OF IRELAND v NIGERIA 0-3 (0-1)
The Walley, London
Referee: Andrew D'Urso (England)   Attendance: 7,500
REPUBLIC OF IRELAND: Nicholas Vincent Colgan, Stephen John Finnan, Kenneth Edward Cunningham (Cap), Gary Michael Thomas Doherty, Alan Maybury (46 Clive Clarke), William Peter Miller (46 Martin Rowlands), Matthew Rhys Holland (66 Jonathan Douglas), Mark Anthony Kinsella, Stephen McPhail, Robert David Keane (83 Graham Barrett), Alan Lee.   Trainer: Brian Kerr.
NIGERIA: Sunday Rotimi, George Abbey (90 Yakubu Adamu), Seyi Olajengbesi, Joseph Enakarhire, Garba Lawal, John Utaka, Seyi Olofinjana (86 Paul Obiefule), Christian Obodo, Ifeanyi Ekwueme, Obafemi Martins (85 Enoch Showumni), Bartholomew Ogbeche (72 Rabiu Baita).
Trainer: Christian Chukwu.
Goals: Bartholomew Ogbeche (36, 69), Obafemi Martins (50)

400. 02.06.2004   Unity Cup
REPUBLIC OF IRELAND v JAMAICA 1-0 (1-0)
The Walley, London
Referee: Robert Styles (England)   Attendance: 6,000
REPUBLIC OF IRELAND: Patrick Kenny, Alan Maybury, John Francis O'Shea (46 Clive Clarke), Gary Michael Thomas Doherty, Andrew James O'Brien, Mark Anthony Kinsella (Cap), Graham Barrett, Alan Quinn (83 Matthew Rhys Holland) Alan Lee (83 Aiden McGeady), Andrew Matthew Reid (76 Martin Rowlands), Clinton Hubert Morrison.
Trainer: Brian Kerr.
JAMAICA: Donovan Ricketts, Gerald Neil, Damion Stewart, Ian Goodison, Garfield Reid, Fabian Davis, Cornel Chin Sue (66 Richard Langley), Micah Hyde, Marlon King (85 Craig Dobson), Deon Burton (83 Narada Bernard), Kevin Lisbie (61 Jermaine Johnson).   Trainer: Carl Brown.
Goal: Graham Barrett (26)

401. 05.06.2004
HOLLAND v REPUBLIC OF IRELAND 0-1 (0-1)
ArenA, Amsterdam
Referee: Mike Dean (England)   Attendance: 42,000
HOLLAND: Edwin van der Sar, Michael John Reiziger (46 John Gijsbert Alan Heitinga), Jacob Stam, Wilfred Bouma (84 Petrus Ferdinandus van Hooijdonk), Giovanni Christiaan van Bronckhorst, Wesley Sneijder (46 Clarence Clyde Seedorf, 63 Paul Bosvelt), Phillip Cocu (Cap), Rafael Ferdinand van der Vaart, Edgar Steven Davids (66 Arjen Robben), Patrick Steven Kluivert (46 Andy van der Meyde), Rutgerus Johannes Martinus van Nistelrooy (66 Rodolfus Antonius Makaay).
Trainer: Dirk Nicolaas Advocaat.
REPUBLIC OF IRELAND: Seamus John Given, Stephen John Finnan, Kenneth Edward Cunningham (Cap), Andrew James O'Brien, Alan Maybury, Graham Barrett, Matthew Rhys Holland, Alan Quinn, Andrew Matthew Reid (88 Michael Doyle), Clinton Hubert Morrison (83 Alan Lee), Robert David Keane.   Trainer: Brian Kerr.
Goal: Robert David Keane (45)

402. 18.08.2004
REPUBLIC OF IRELAND v BULGARIA 1-1 (1-0)
Lansdowne Road, Dublin

Referee: Ian Brines (Scotland)   Attendance: 31,887

REPUBLIC OF IRELAND: Seamus John Given (71 Patrick Kenny), Stephen John Finnan (71 Alan Quinn), Gary Michael Thomas Doherty (46 Gary Patrick Breen), Kenneth Edward Cunningham (Cap), John Francis O'Shea, William Peter Miller (52 Stephen Carr), Roy Maurice Keane (63 Graham Anthony Kavanagh), Kevin Daniel Kilbane, Andrew Matthew Reid, Damien Anthony Duff, Clinton Hubert Morrison (63 Jonathan Paul Macken).   Trainer: Brian Kerr.

BULGARIA: Zdravko Zdravkov (46 Dimitar Ivankov), Radostin Kishishev, Rosen Kirilov, Georgi Markov, Ilian Stoianov (64 Elin Topuzakov), Valeri Bojinov, Chavdar Yankov (76 Martin Kamburov), Stilian Petrov, Marian Hristov (46 Hristo Yanev), Zdravko Lazarov (56 Vladimir Manchev), Dimitar Berbatov (46 Emil Gargorov).
Trainer: Hristo Stoichkov.

Goals: Andrew Matthew Reid (15) / Valeri Bojinov (71)

403. 04.09.2004   18th World Cup Qualifiers
REPUBLIC OF IRELAND v CYPRUS 3-0 (2-0)
Lansdowne Road, Dublin

Referee: Levan Paniashvili (Georgia)   Attendance: 35,900

REPUBLIC OF IRELAND: Seamus John Given, Stephen Carr (70 Stephen John Finnan), John Francis O'Shea (83 Alan Maybury), Kenneth Edward Cunningham (Cap), Andrew James O'Brien, Andrew Matthew Reid, Graham Anthony Kavanagh, Kevin Daniel Kilbane, Damien Anthony Duff, Clinton Hubert Morrison (81 Alan Lee), Robert David Keane.
Trainer: Brian Kerr.

CYPRUS: Nicos Panayiotou, Georgios Theodotou, Loizos Kakoyiannis, Stelios Okkarides, Lambros Lambrou, Marinos Satsias, Constantinos Makrides, Michalis Constantinou, Constantinos Charalambides (70 Chrysostomos Michael), Yiannakis Okkas (78 Assimakis Krassas), Elias Charalambous (65 Marios Elia).
Trainer: Momčilo Vukotić (Serbia & Montenegro).

Goals: Clinton Morrison (33), Andrew Matthew Reid (38), Robert David Keane (55 pen)

404. 08.09.2004   18th World Cup Qualifiers
SWITZERLAND v REPUBLIC OF IRELAND 1-1 (1-1)
St.Jakob-Park, Basel

Referee: Kyros Vassaras (Greece)   Attendance: 28,000

SWITZERLAND: Pascal Zuberbühler, Bernt Haas, Murat Yakin, Patrick Müller, Ludovic Magnin, Ricardo Cabanas, Johann Vogel, Tranquillo Barnetta, Hakan Yakin, Johan Vonlanthen (73 Johann Lonfat), Alexandre Rey.
Trainer: Jakob Kühn.

REPUBLIC OF IRELAND: Seamus John Given, Stephen Carr, Andrew James O'Brien, Kenneth Edward Cunningham (Cap), Stephen John Finnan, Andrew Matthew Reid (73 Graham Anthony Kavanagh), Roy Maurice Keane, Kevin Daniel Kilbane, Damien Anthony Duff, Robert David Keane, Clinton Hubert Morrison (84 Gary Michael Thomas Doherty).
Trainer: Brian Kerr.

Goals: Hakan Yakin (17) / Clinton Hubert Morrison (9)

405. 09.10.2004   18th World Cup Qualifiers
FRANCE v REPUBLIC OF IRELAND 0-0
Stade de France, Saint-Denis, Paris

Referee: Arturo Daudén Ibañez (Spain)   Attendance: 78,863

REPUBLIC OF IRELAND: Seamus John Given, Stephen Carr, Andrew James O'Brien, Kenneth Edward Cunningham (Cap), Stephen John Finnan, John Francis O'Shea, Roy Maurice Keane, Damien Anthony Duff, Kevin Daniel Kilbane, Robert David Keane, Clinton Hubert Morrison (41 Andrew Matthew Reid).   Trainer: Brian Kerr.

FRANCE: Fabien Barthez (Cap), William Éric Gallas, Gaël Givet, Sébastien Squillaci, Mikaël Silvestre, Olivier Dacourt (63 Alou Diarra), Rio Antonio Mavuba, Robert Pires, Sylvain Wiltord, Thierry Henry, Djibril Cissé (81 Sidney Govou).
Trainer: Raymond Domenech.

406. 13.10.2004   18th World Cup Qualifiers
REPUBLIC OF IRELAND v FAROE ISLANDS 2-0 (2-0)
Lansdowne Road, Dublin

Referee: Romans Lajuks (Latvia)   Attendance: 36,000

REPUBLIC OF IRELAND: Seamus John Given, Stephen Carr, Kenneth Edward Cunningham (Cap), Andrew James O'Brien, John Francis O'Shea (56 William Peter Miller), Stephen John Finnan, Roy Maurice Keane, Kevin Daniel Kilbane, Andrew Matthew Reid (76 Gary Michael Thomas Doherty), Robert David Keane, Damien Anthony Duff.
Trainer: Brian Kerr.

FAROE ISLANDS: Jákup Mikkelsen, Súni Olsen, Óli Johannesen (Cap), Pól Thorsteinsson, Jón Rói Jacobsen, Rógvi Jacobsen (57 Heðin á Lakjuni), Fróði Benjaminsen, Julian Schantz Johnsson, Jákup á Borg (85 Atli Danielsen), John Petersen, Jónhard Frederiksberg (82 Andrew av Fløtum).
Trainer: Henrik Larsen (Denmark).

Goals: Robert David Keane (14 pen, 32)

407. 16.11.2004
REPUBLIC OF IRELAND v CROATIA 1-0 (1-0)
Lansdowne Road, Dublin
Referee: Gylfi Þór Orrason (Iceland)   Attendance: 33,000
REPUBLIC OF IRELAND: Patrick Kenny (77 Seamus John Given), Stephen John Finnan, Gary Patrick Breen (53 Kenneth Edward Cunningham), Richard Patrick Dunne, John Francis O'Shea, William Peter Miller, Graham Anthony Kavanagh, Kevin Daniel Kilbane (Cap) (80 Alan Quinn), Damien Anthony Duff, Stephen Elliott (85 Graham Barrett), Robert David Keane (90 Aiden McGeady).   Trainer: Brian Kerr.
CROATIA: Tomislav Butina, Darijo Srna, Igor Tudor (46 Boško Balaban), Robert Kovač, Josip Šimunić (73 Mato Neretljak), Jurica Vranješ (64 Ivan Leko), Niko Kovač, Stjepan Tomas (65 Mario Tokić), Niko Kranjčar, Marko Babić (59 Danijel Pranjić), Ivan Klasnić (59 Eduardo Alves da Silva). Trainer: Zlatko Kranjčar.
Goal: Robert David Keane (24)

409. 26.03.2005   18th World Cup Qualifiers
ISRAEL v REPUBLIC OF IRELAND 1-1 (0-1)
National, Ramat-Gan, Tel-Aviv
Referee: Valentin Ivanov (Russia)   Attendance: 32,150
ISRAEL: David Awat, Omri Affek (65 Avi Nimni), Shimon Gershon, Tal Ben Haim, Arik Benado (Cap), Adoram Keissy, Walid Badir, Idan Tal (65 Pini Balili), Yossi Benayoun, Yaniv Katan, Omer Golan (74 Abbas Souan).
Trainer: Avraham Grant.
REPUBLIC OF IRELAND: Seamus John Given, Stephen Carr, Kenneth Edward Cunningham (Cap), Andrew James O'Brien, John Francis O'Shea, Stephen John Finnan, Roy Maurice Keane, Kevin Daniel Kilbane, Damien Anthony Duff, Clinton Hubert Morrison (85 Matthew Rhys Holland), Robert David Keane.   Trainer: Brian Kerr.
Goals: Abbas Souan (90) / Clinton Hubert Morrison (4)

408. 09.02.2005
REPUBLIC OF IRELAND v PORTUGAL 1-0 (1-0)
Lansdowne Road, Dublin
Referee: Matthew Messias (England)   Attendance: 44,100
REPUBLIC OF IRELAND: Seamus John Given, Stephen John Finnan, Kenneth Edward Cunningham (60 Richard Patrick Dunne), Andrew James O'Brien, John Francis O'Shea, Matthew Rhys Holland, Kevin Daniel Kilbane (46 Graham Anthony Kavanagh), Damien Anthony Duff (68 William Peter Miller), Andrew Matthew Reid, Clinton Hubert Morrison, Robert David Keane (82 Aiden McGeady).
Trainer: Brian Kerr.
PORTUGAL: Ricardo Alexandre Martins Soares Pereira, Paulo Renato Rebocho Ferreira (46 Hugo Miguel Ferreira Viana), Jorge Manuel Almeida Gomes de Andrade, Marco António Simões Caneira, Rogério Pedro Campinho Marques Matias, Armando Gonçalves Teixeira "Petit", Tiago Cardoso Mendes (46 Fernando José da Silva Freitas Meira), Cristiano Ronaldo Santos Aveiro (68 Manuel Henrique Tavares Fernandes), Anderson Luís de Souza "Deco" (46 Ricardo Miguel Moreira da Costa), "Simão" Pedro Fonseca Sabrosa (60 Luís Boa Morte Pereira), Pedro Miguel Carreiro Resendes "Pauleta" (Cap) (46 Nuno Miguel Soares Pereira Ribeiro "Nuno Gomes").   Trainer: Luiz Felipe Scolari (Brazil).
Goal: Andrew James O'Brien (21)

410. 29.03.2005
REPUBLIC OF IRELAND v CHINA 1-0 (0-0)
Lansdowne Road, Dublin
Referee: Richard Casha (Malta)   Attendance: 35,222
REPUBLIC OF IRELAND: Patrick Kenny, Alan Maybury, Kenneth Edward Cunningham (46 Andrew James O'Brien), Richard Patrick Dunne, John Francis O'Shea, Andrew Matthew Reid, Graham Anthony Kavanagh, Kevin Daniel Kilbane (66 Roy Maurice Keane), Damien Anthony Duff (46 William Peter Miller), Stephen Elliott (73 Gary Michael Thomas Doherty), Robert David Keane (62 Clinton Hubert Morrison).   Trainer: Brian Kerr.
CHINA: Li Leilei, Li Weifeng (Cap), Wei Xin (46 Wang Liang), Zhang Yonghai (75 Zhang Yaokun), Ji Mingyi, Sun Xiang, Hu Zhaojun (86 Zheng Bin), Chen Yongqiang (38 Li Yan), Shao Jiayi (64 Du Wei), Zhao Junzhe, Li Yi (46 Shi Jun). Trainer: Zhu Guanghu.
Goal: Clinton Hubert Morrison (83)

411. 04.06.2005   18th World Cup Qualifiers
REPUBLIC OF IRELAND v ISRAEL 2-2 (2-2)
Lansdowne Road, Dublin

Referee: Kyros Vassaras (Greece)   Attendance: 36,000

REPUBLIC OF IRELAND: Seamus John Given, Kenneth Edward Cunningham (Cap), John Francis O'Shea, Andrew James O'Brien, Ian Patrick Harte, Andrew Matthew Reid (64 Gary Michael Thomas Doherty), Kevin Daniel Kilbane, Damien Anthony Duff, Matthew Rhys Holland, Clinton Hubert Morrison, Robert David Keane (27 Graham Anthony Kavanagh).   Trainer: Brian Kerr.

ISRAEL: David Awat, Rahamin Saban, Shimon Gershon, Avi Yehiel, Arik Benado, Adoram Keissy, Idan Tal, Avi Nimni (Cap) (78 Omer Golan), Yossi Benayoun, Yaniv Katan (66 Pini Balili), Abbas Souan.   Trainer: Avraham Grant.

Sent off: Andrew James O'Brien (83)

Goals: Ian Patrick Harte (4), Robert David Keane (11) / Avi Yehiel (39), Avi Nimni (45)

412. 08.06.2005   18th World Cup Qualifiers
**FAROE ISLANDS
v REPUBLIC OF IRELAND 0-2** (0-0)
Tórsvøllur, Tórshavn

Referee: Anton Guenov (Bulgaria)   Attendance: 5,180

FAROE ISLANDS: Jákup Mikkelsen, Johan Byrial Hansen, Óli Johannesen (Cap), Atli Danielsen, Súni Olsen, Rógvi Jacobsen, Julian Schantz Johnsson, Heðin á Lakjuni, Fróði Benjaminsen (76 Jákup á Borg), Claus Bech Jørgensen (76 Tór-Ingar Akselsen), Andrew av Fløtum (59 Christian Høgni Jacobsen).   Trainer: Henrik Larsen (Denmark).

REPUBLIC OF IRELAND: Seamus John Given, Stephen Carr, Kenneth Edward Cunningham (Cap), John Francis O'Shea, Ian Patrick Harte, Andrew Matthew Reid, Roy Maurice Keane, Kevin Daniel Kilbane, Damien Anthony Duff, Stephen Elliott, Clinton Hubert Morrison (78 Gary Michael Thomas Doherty).   Trainer: Brian Kerr.

Goals: Ian Patrick Harte (51 pen), Kevin Daniel Kilbane (58)

413. 17.08.2005
REPUBLIC OF IRELAND v ITALY 1-2 (1-2)
Lansdowne Road, Dublin

Referee: Paulo Manuel Gomes Costa (Portugal)   Att: 44,000

REPUBLIC OF IRELAND: Seamus John Given, Stephen John Finnan (57 Stephen Carr), Richard Patrick Dunne (46 Andrew James O'Brien), Kenneth Edward Cunningham (Cap), John Francis O'Shea (78 William Peter Miller), Matthew Rhys Holland (39 Ian Patrick Harte), Andrew Matthew Reid (73 Stephen Elliott), Steven John Reid, Kevin Daniel Kilbane, Clinton Hubert Morrison, Damien Anthony Duff.   Trainer: Brian Kerr.

ITALY: Flavio Roma, Cristian Zaccardo, Fabio Cannavaro (Cap) (64 Andrea Barzagli), Alessandro Nesta (46 Marco Materazzi), Gianluca Zambrotta, Gennaro Gattuso, Andrea Pirlo (77 Simone Barone), Daniele De Rossi (46 Aimo Stefano Diana), Christian Vieri, Alberto Gilardino (46 Vincenzo Iaquinta), Alessandro Del Piero (46 Fabio Grosso).   Trainer: Marcello Lippi.

Goals: Andrew Matthew Reid (32) / Andrea Pirlo (10), Alberto Gilardino (31)

414. 07.09.2005   18th World Cup Qualifiers
REPUBLIC OF IRELAND v FRANCE 0-1 (0-0)
Lansdowne Road, Dublin

Referee: Herbert Fandel (Germany)   Attendance: 36,000

REPUBLIC OF IRELAND: Seamus John Given, Stephen Carr, Kenneth Edward Cunningham (Cap), Richard Patrick Dunne, John Francis O'Shea, Roy Maurice Keane, Andrew Matthew Reid, Kevin Daniel Kilbane (80 Ian Patrick Harte), Clinton Hubert Morrison (80 Gary Michael Thomas Doherty), Robert David Keane, Damien Anthony Duff.   Trainer: Brian Kerr.

FRANCE: Grégory Coupet, Willy Sagnol (90 Gaël Givet), Lilian Thuram, Jean-Alain Boumsong, William Éric Gallas, Patrick Vieira, Claude Makélélé, Zinedine Zidane (Cap) (69 Florent Malouda), Vikash Dhorasoo, Sylvain Wiltord, Thierry Henry (76 Djibril Cissé).   Trainer: Raymond Domenech.

Goal: Thierry Henry (68)

415. 08.10.2005   18th World Cup Qualifiers
CYPRUS v REPUBLIC OF IRELAND 0-1 (0-1)
GSP, Nicosia
Referee: Viktor Kassai (Hungary)   Attendance: 13,546
CYPRUS: Nicos Panayiotou, Marios Elia (73 Christos Marangos), Lambros Lambrou, Loukas Louka, Constantinos Makrides, Chrysostomos Michael (30 Assimakis Krassas), Constantinos Charalambides, Alexandros Garpozis, Efstathios Panayotis Aloneftis, Yiannakis Okkas (Cap) (68 Yiasoumakis Yiasoumi), Michalis Constantinou.
Trainer: Angelos Anastasiadis (Greece).
REPUBLIC OF IRELAND: Seamus John Given, Stephen Carr, Richard Patrick Dunne, Kenneth Edward Cunningham (Cap), John Francis O'Shea, Stephen John Finnan (46 Matthew Rhys Holland), Graham Anthony Kavanagh, Kevin Daniel Kilbane, Damien Anthony Duff (61 Steven John Reid), Stephen Elliott, Robert David Keane (88 David James Connolly).   Trainer: Brian Kerr.
Goal: Stephen Elliott (6)

417. 01.03.2006
REPUBLIC OF IRELAND v SWEDEN 3-0 (1-0)
Lansdowne Road, Dublin
Referee: Damien Ledentu (France)   Attendance: 44,109
REPUBLIC OF IRELAND: Seamus John Given (49 Wayne Henderson), Joseph O'Brien (60 William Peter Miller), Andrew James O'Brien, Richard Patrick Dunne, Ian Patrick Harte (60 Kevin Daniel Kilbane), Stephen Elliott (49 Stephen James Ireland), Steven John Reid, John Francis O'Shea (49 Graham Anthony Kavanagh), Damien Anthony Duff, Robert David Keane (Cap), Kevin Edward Doyle (68 Clinton Hubert Morrison). Trainer: Stephen Staunton.
SWEDEN: Andreas Isaksson, Alexander Östlund (74 Christoffer Andersson), Olof Mellberg (Cap), Petter Hansson, Erik Edman, Tobias Linderoth (70 Daniel Andersson), Johan Elmander (61 Mattias Jonson), Kim Källström (61 Anders Svensson), Christian Wilhelmsson, Zlatan Ibrahimovic (38 Markus Rosenberg), Henrik Larsson (80 Marcus Allbäck).
Trainer: Lars Lagerbäck.
Goals: Damien Anthony Duff (36), Robert David Keane (48), William Peter Miller (71)

416. 12.10.2005   18th World Cup Qualifiers
REPUBLIC OF IRELAND v SWITZERLAND 0-0
Lansdowne Road, Dublin
Referee: Dr. Markus Merk (Germany)   Attendance: 35,944
REPUBLIC OF IRELAND: Seamus John Given, Stephen Carr, Richard Patrick Dunne, Kenneth Edward Cunningham (Cap), Ian Patrick Harte, Andrew Matthew Reid (80 Steven John Reid), John Francis O'Shea, Matthew Rhys Holland, Kevin Daniel Kilbane, Clinton Hubert Morrison (87 Gary Michael Thomas Doherty), Robert David Keane (68 Stephen Elliott).   Trainer: Brian Kerr.
SWITZERLAND: Pascal Zuberbühler, Philipp Degen, Philippe Senderos, Patrick Müller, Ludovic Magnin, Tranquillo Barnetta (88 Daniel Gygax), Johann Vogel, Ricardo Cabanas, Raphaël Wicky, Alexander Frei, Johan Vonlanthen (53 Marco Streller).   Trainer: Jakob Kühn.

418. 24.05.2006
REPUBLIC OF IRELAND v CHILE 0-1 (0-0)
Lansdowne Road, Dublin
Referee: Martin Ingvarsson (Sweden)   Attendance: 36,171
REPUBLIC OF IRELAND: Seamus John Given (54 Wayne Henderson), Stephen Michael Kelly (85 Andrew Matthew Reid), Gary Patrick Breen (54 Ian Patrick Harte), Richard Patrick Dunne, Kevin Daniel Kilbane, Steven John Reid, William Peter Miller (54 Graham Anthony Kavanagh), John Francis O'Shea (54 Aiden McGeady), Damien Anthony Duff, Kevin Edward Doyle (72 Jason Byrne), Robert David Keane. Trainer: Stephen Staunton.
CHILE: Claudio Andrés Bravo Muñoz, Gonzalo Alejandro Jara Reyes, Jorge Francisco Vargas Palacios, Pablo Andrés Contreras Fica, Rafael Olarra Guerrero, Manuel Rolando Iturra Urrutia, Jorge Acuña, Luis Antonio Jiménez Garcés, Mark Dennis González Hoffman (90 Mauricio Zenteno Morales), Humberto Andrés Suazo Pontivo (79 Patricio Sebastián Galaz Sepulveda), Reinaldo Patricio Navia Amador (75 Alexis Alejandro Sánchez Sánchez).
Trainer: Nelson Acosta López.
Goal: Manuel Rolando Iturra Urrutia (48)

419. 16.08.2006
REPUBLIC OF IRELAND v HOLLAND 0-4 (0-2)
Lansdowne Road, Dublin
Referee: Tom Henning Øvrebø (Norway)   Att: 42,400
REPUBLIC OF IRELAND: Patrick Kenny, Stephen Carr (46 Alan O'Brien), Andrew James O'Brien, John Francis O'Shea, Stephen John Finnan (64 Stephen Michael Kelly), Aiden McGeady, Steven John Reid (Cap) (46 William Peter Miller), Graham Anthony Kavanagh (46 Jonathan Douglas), Stephen Elliott, Kevin Daniel Kilbane, Clinton Hubert Morrison (46 Kevin Edward Doyle).   Trainer: Stephen Staunton.

HOLLAND: Edwin van der Sar (Cap), John Gijsbert Alan Heitinga, André Antonius Maria Ooijer (77 Kew Jaliens), Joris Mathijsen, Tim de Cler (61 Urby Emanuelson), Denny Domingoes Landzaat (46 Nigel de Jong), Stijn Schaars (83 Theodorus Janssen), Rafael Ferdinand van der Vaart, Robin van Persie, Klaas Jan Huntelaar, Arjen Robben (46 Dirk Kuijt). Trainer: Marcelo van Basten.

Goals: Klaas Jan Huntelaar (25), Arjen Robben (41), Klaas Jan Huntelaar (53), Robin van Persie (70)

421. 07.10.2006   13th European Champs Qualifiers
CYPRUS v REPUBLIC OF IRELAND 5-2 (2-2)
Neo GSP, Lefkosía
Referee: Lucílio Cardoso Cortez Batista (Portugal)
Attendance: 12,000
CYPRUS: Michalis Morphis, Georgios Theodotou, Lambros Lambrou, Loukas Louka, Alexandros Garpozis (77 Elias Charalambous), Constantinos Makrides, Marinos Satsias, Chrysostomos Michael (46 Constantinos Charalambides), Efstathios Panayotis Aloneftis, Yiannakis Okkas (Cap) (86 Yiasoumakis Yiasoumi), Michalis Constantinou. Trainer: Angelos Anastasiadis (Greece).

REPUBLIC OF IRELAND: Patrick Kenny, Stephen John Finnan, Andrew James O'Brien (71 Alan Lee), Richard Patrick Dunne, John Francis O'Shea, Aiden McGeady (80 Alan O'Brien), Stephen James Ireland (83 Jonathan Douglas), Kevin Daniel Kilbane, Damien Anthony Duff, Clinton Hubert Morrison, Robert David Keane (Cap).
Trainer: Stephen Staunton.

Sent off: Richard Patrick Dunne (78)

Goals: Michalis Constantinou (10, 51 pen), Alexandros Garpozis (16), Constantinos Charalambides (60, 75) / Stephen James Ireland (8), Richard Patrick Dunne (43)

420. 02.09.2006   13th European Champs Qualifiers
GERMANY v REPUBLIC OF IRELAND 1-0 (0-0)
Gottlieb-Daimler, Stuttgart
Referee: Luis Medina Cantalejo (Spain)   Attendance: 53,198
GERMANY: Jens Lehmann, Phillip Lahm, Arne Friedrich, Manuel Friedrich, Marcell Jansen, Bernd Schneider (84 Tim Borowski), Torsten Frings, Michael Ballack (Cap), Bastian Schweinsteiger, Miroslav Klose, Lukas Podolski (76 Olivier Neuville).   Trainer: Joachim Löw.

REPUBLIC OF IRELAND: Seamus John Given, Stephen Carr, Andrew James O'Brien, Richard Patrick Dunne, Stephen John Finnan, Steven John Reid, John Francis O'Shea, Kevin Daniel Kilbane (83 Alan O'Brien), Robert David Keane (Cap), Damien Anthony Duff (77 Aiden McGeady), Kevin Edward Doyle (79 Stephen Elliott).   Trainer: Stephen Staunton.

Goal: Lukas Podolski (57)

422. 11.10.2006   13th European Champs Qualifiers
REPUBLIC OF IRELAND
v CZECH REPUBLIC 1-1 (0-0)
Lansdowne Road, Dublin
Referee: Bertrand Layec (France)   Attendance: 36,000
REPUBLIC OF IRELAND: Wayne Henderson, Stephen John Finnan, John Francis O'Shea, Stephen Michael Kelly, Lee Kevin Carsley, Jonathan Douglas, Kevin Daniel Kilbane (79 Alan O'Brien), Damien Anthony Duff, Andrew Matthew Reid (71 Alan Quinn), Paul David McShane, Robert David Keane (Cap). Trainer: Stephen Staunton.

CZECH REPUBLIC: Petr Čech, Tomáš Ujfaluši, Martin Jiránek, David Rozehnal, Marek Jankulovski, Radoslav Kováč, Jaroslav Plašil (85 Zdeněk Grygera), Tomáš Rosický (Cap), Jan Polák, Jan Koller, Milan Baroš (83 David Jarolím). Trainer: Karel Brückner.

Goals: Kevin Daniel Kilbane (62) / Jan Koller (64)

423. 15.11.2006 13th European Champs Qualifiers
REPUBLIC OF IRELAND
v SAN MARINO 5-0 (3-0)
Lansdowne Road, Dublin
Referee: Lassin Isaksen (Faroe Islands)   Attendance: 34,018
REPUBLIC OF IRELAND: Seamus John Given, John Francis O'Shea, Richard Patrick Dunne, Stephen John Finnan, Lee Kevin Carsley (50 Jonathan Douglas), Andrew Matthew Reid, Kevin Daniel Kilbane (79 Alan Lee), Damien Anthony Duff, Paul David McShane, Robert David Keane (Cap), Kevin Edward Doyle (63 Aiden McGeady).
Trainer: Stephen Staunton.
SAN MARINO: Federico Valentini, Carlo Valentini, Nicola Albani, Davide Simoncini (81 Giovanni Bonini), Simone Bacciocchi, Damiano Vannucci (72 Federico Crescentini), Matteo Andreini, Matteo Bugli, Manuel Marani, Paolo Mariotti (59 Michele Marani), Andy Selva (Cap).
Trainer: Gian Paolo Mazza.
Goals: Andrew Matthew Reid (7), Kevin Edward Doyle (24), Robert David Keane (31, 58 pen, 85)

424. 07.02.2007 13th European Champs Qualifiers
SAN MARINO
v REPUBLIC OF IRELAND 1-2 (0-0)
Olimpico, Serravalle
Referee: Peter Rasmussen (Denamrk)   Attendance: 3,294
SAN MARINO: Aldo Simoncini, Carlo Valentini, Nicola Albani, Davide Simoncini, Marco Domeniconi (88 Matteo Bugli), Alex Gasperoni (66 Matteo Andreini), Michele Marani, Giovanni Bonini (76 Damiano Vannucci), Riccardo Muccioli, Manuel Marani, Andy Selva (Cap).
Trainer: Gian Paolo Mazza.
REPUBLIC OF IRELAND: Wayne Henderson, Stephen John Finnan, Richard Patrick Dunne, John Francis O'Shea (46 Paul David McShane), Ian Patrick Harte (74 Stephen Patrick Hunt), Damien Anthony Duff, Lee Kevin Carsley, Stephen James Ireland, Kevin Daniel Kilbane, Robert David Keane (Cap), Shane Patrick Long (81 Anthony Stokes).
Trainer: Stephen Staunton.
Goals: Manuel Marani (86) /
Kevin Daniel Kilbane (49), Stephen James Ireland (90+5)

425. 24.03.2007 13th European Champs Qualifiers
REPUBLIC OF IRELAND v WALES 1-0 (1-0)
Croke Park, Dublin
Referee: Terje Hauge (Norway)   Attendance: 67,000
REPUBLIC OF IRELAND: Seamus John Given, Stephen John Finnan, Richard Patrick Dunne, John Francis O'Shea, Lee Kevin Carsley, Kevin Daniel Kilbane, Jonathan Douglas (80 Stephen Patrick Hunt), Damien Anthony Duff, Stephen James Ireland (59 Kevin Edward Doyle), Paul David McShane, Robert David Keane (Cap) (89 Aiden McGeady).
Trainer: Stephen Staunton.
WALES: Daniel Coyne, Samuel Ricketts, Gareth Frank Bale (74 Daniel Lewis Collins), James Collins, Steven Evans, Lewin John Nyatanga, Joseph Christopher Ledley (46 Carl Neil Fletcher), Carl Phillip Robinson (90+1 Jermaine Maurice Easter), Simon Davies, Ryan Joseph Giggs (Cap), Craig Douglas Bellamy.   Manager: John Benjamin Toshack.
Goal: Stephen James Ireland (39)

426. 28.03.2007 13th European Champs Qualifiers
REPUBLIC OF IRELAND v SLOVAKIA 1-0 (1-0)
Croke Park, Dublin
Referee: Yuriy Baskakov (Russia)   Attendance: 71,297
REPUBLIC OF IRELAND: Seamus John Given, Stephen John Finnan, Richard Patrick Dunne, John Francis O'Shea, Lee Kevin Carsley, Kevin Daniel Kilbane, Kevin Edward Doyle (74 Shane Patrick Long), Damien Anthony Duff, Stephen James Ireland (70 Stephen Patrick Hunt), Paul David McShane, Aiden McGeady (87 Alan Quinn).
Trainer: Stephen Staunton.
SLOVAKIA: Kamil Čontofalský, Peter Šinglár (79 Stanislav Šesták), Igor Žofčák, Martin Škrteľ, Maroš Klimpl, Vratislav Greško, Marek Sapara (72 Filip Hološko), Balázs Borbély, Dušan Švento (87 Ľubomír Michalík), Róbert Vittek, Martin Jakubko.   Trainer: Jan Kocián.
Goal: Kevin Edward Doyle (13)

427. 23.05.2007
REPUBLIC OF IRELAND v ECUADOR 1-1 (1-1)
Giants, New York (East Rutherford)
Referee: Not recorded   Attendance: 20,823
REPUBLIC OF IRELAND: Colin Doyle, Stephen Michael Kelly, Alexander Stephen Bruce, Alan Bennett, Stephen O'Halloran (73 Joseph O'Cearuill), Andrew Declan Keogh (69 Joseph Gamble), Darren Potter, Kevin Daniel Kilbane (Cap) (79 Stephen Gleeson), Stephen Patrick Hunt (69 Anthony Stokes), Daryl Murphy (85 Joseph Lapira), Kevin Edward Doyle (60 Shane Patrick Long).   Trainer: Stephen Staunton.

ECUADOR: Marcelo Ramón Elizaga Ferrero, Jairo Eliécer Montaño, Carlos Ernesto Castro, Jairo Rolando Campos León, Óscar Bagüí, Mario David Quiroz Villón (66 Franklin Agustín Salas Narváez), Patricio Javier Urrutia Espinoza, Luis Andrés Caicedo De la Cruz, Walter Orlando Ayoví Corozo, Christian Rogelio Benítez Betancourt, Jaime Iván Kaviedes Llorenty (81 Pablo David Palacios Herreria).
Trainer: Luis Fernando Suárez.

Goals: Kevin Edward Doyle (44) /
Christian Rogelio Benítez Betancourt (13)

429. 22.08.2007
DENMARK v REPUBLIC OF IRELAND 0-4 (0-2)
NRGi Park, Århus
Referee: Thomas Einweller (Austria)   Attendance: 17,331
DENMARK: Jesper Christiansen, Kasper Bøgelund (46 William Kvist Jørgensen), Michael Gravgaard (46 Martin Laursen), Daniel Agger, Niclas Jensen (46 Jan Kristiansen), Rasmus Würtz (68 Peter Løvenkrands), Daniel Jensen (46 Thomas Kahlenberg), Nicklas Bendtner, Jon Dahl Tomasson (Cap) (59 Morten Nordstrand), Dennis Rommedahl, Jesper Grønkjær.   Trainer: Morten Olsen.

REPUBLIC OF IRELAND: Wayne Henderson, Stephen Carr, Stephen John Finnan (62 Kevin Daniel Kilbane), John Francis O'Shea, Richard Patrick Dunne, Aiden McGeady, Darren Potter (66 Stephen Michael Kelly), Andrew Matthew Reid (46 Darron Thomas Daniel Gibson), Stephen Patrick Hunt (46 Andrew Declan Keogh), Kevin Edward Doyle (46 Shane Patrick Long), Robert David Keane (56 Daryl Murphy).
Trainer: Stephen Staunton.

Goals: Robert Keane (29, 40), Shane Patrick Long (54, 66)

428. 26.05.2007
REPUBLIC OF IRELAND v BOLIVIA 1-1 (1-1)
Gillette, Foxboro (United States)
Referee: Not recorded   Attendance: Not recorded
REPUBLIC OF IRELAND: Nicholas Vincent Colgan (46 Wayne Henderson), Joseph O'Cearuill, Alan Bennett, Peter Murphy (46 Stephen O'Halloran), Stephen Michael Kelly, Joseph Gamble (46 Daryl Murphy), Kevin Daniel Kilbane (Cap) (66 Stephen Patrick Hunt), Darren Potter, Alan O'Brien (77 Stephen Gleeson), Anthony Stokes, Shane Patrick Long (54 Kevin Edward Doyle).   Trainer: Stephen Staunton.

BOL: Hugo Suárez Vaca, Miguel Ángel Hoyos Guzmán, Juan Manuel Peña Montaño, Lorgio Álvarez Roca, Ronald Lázaro García Justiniano (61 Sacha Silvestro Lima Saucedo), Gualberto Mojica Olmos, Leonel Alfredo Reyes Saravia (82 Limbert Pizarro Vaca), Joselito Vaca Velasco (74 Gonzalo Germán Galindo Sánchez), Limberg Méndez Rocha, Jaime Moreno Morales (46 Diego Aroldo Cabrera Flores), Juan Carlos Arce Justiniano (69 Gustavo Pinedo).
Trainer: Erwin Sánchez Frerking.

Goals: Shane Long (12) / Miguel Ángel Hoyos Guzmán (14)

430. 08.09.2007   13th European Champs Qualifiers
SLOVAKIA v REPUBLIC OF IRELAND 2-2 (1-1)
Tehelné pole, Bratislava
Referee: Stefano Farina (Italy)   Attendance: 12,360
SLOVAKIA: Štefan Senecký, Matej Krajčík, Maroš Klimpl, Ján Ďurica, Marek Čech, Stanislav Šesták (65 Branislav Obžera), Marek Sapara (71 Filip Šebo), Vratislav Greško, Marek Hamšík, Marek Mintál, Filip Hološko.   Trainer: Jan Kocián.

REPUBLIC OF IRELAND: Seamus John Given, John Francis O'Shea, Paul David McShane, Richard Patrick Dunne, Stephen Michael Kelly, Lee Kevin Carsley, Aiden McGeady (61 Darron Thomas Daniel Gibson), Stephen James Ireland (76 Jonathan Douglas), Kevin Daniel Kilbane, Kevin Edward Doyle (89 Daryl Murphy), Robert David Keane.
Trainer: Stephen Staunton.

Goals: Maroš Klimpl (37), Marek Čech (90) /
Stephen James Ireland (7), Kevin Edward Doyle (57)

431. 12.09.2007   13th European Champs Qualifiers
**CZECH REPUBLIC
v REPUBLIC OF IRELAND 1-0** (1-0)
AXA (AC Sparta Stadium), Praha

Referee: Kyros Vassaras (Greece)   Attendance: 16,648

CZECH REPUBLIC: Petr Čech, Tomáš Ujfaluši, Radoslav Kováč, David Rozehnal, Marek Jankulovski, Libor Sionko (74 Stanislav Vlček), Tomáš Galásek (46 Tomáš Sivok), Tomáš Rosický (Cap), Jan Polák, Jaroslav Plašil, Milan Baroš (89 David Jarolím).   Trainer: Karel Brückner.

REPUBLIC OF IRELAND: Seamus John Given, John Francis O'Shea (38 Stephen Patrick Hunt, Paul David McShane, Richard Patrick Dunne, Stephen Michael Kelly, Aiden McGeady (62 Shane Patrick Long), Lee Kevin Carsley (82 Andrew Declan Keogh), Andrew Matthew Reid, Kevin Daniel Kilbane, Kevin Edward Doyle, Robert David Keane. Trainer: Stephen Staunton.

Sent off: Patrick Hunt (61)

Goal: Marek Jankulovski (15)

432. 13.10.2007   13th European Champs Qualifiers
REPUBLIC OF IRELAND v GERMANY 0-0
Croke Park, Dublin

Referee: Martin Hansson (Sweden)   Attendance: 67,495

REPUBLIC OF IRELAND: Seamus John Given, Stephen John Finnan, Joseph O'Brien, Richard Patrick Dunne, Stephen Michael Kelly, Andrew Declan Keogh (80 Aiden McGeady), Lee Kevin Carsley, Andrew Matthew Reid, Kevin Daniel Kilbane (90+2 Daryl Murphy), Kevin Edward Doyle (70 Shane Patrick Long), Robert David Keane. Trainer: Stephen Staunton.

GERMANY: Jens Lehmann, Arne Friedrich, Per Mertesacker, Christoph Metzelder, Marcell Jansen, Clemens Fritz, Torsten Frings, Bastian Schweinsteiger (18 Simon Rolfes), Piotr Trochowski (90 Gonzalo Castro), Mario Gomez (64 Lukas Podolski), Kevin Dennis Kurányi.   Trainer: Joachim Löw.

433. 17.10.2007   13th European Champs Qualifiers
REPUBLIC OF IRELAND v CYPRUS 1-1 (0-0)
Croke Park, Dublin

Referee: Mikko Vuorela (Finland)   Attendance: 45,500

REPUBLIC OF IRELAND: Seamus John Given, John Francis O'Shea, Stephen John Finnan, Paul David McShane, Joseph O'Brien (46 William Peter Miller), Kevin Daniel Kilbane, Andrew Matthew Reid, Andrew Declan Keogh (63 Aiden McGeady), Kevin Edward Doyle, Stephen Patrick Hunt (74 Daryl Murphy), Robert David Keane (Cap).
Trainer: Stephen Staunton.

CYPRUS: Antonis Georgallides, Stelios Okkarides, Marinos Satsias (69 Christos Marangos), Paraskevas Christou, Constantinos Charalambides, Marios Elia, Alexandros Garpozis, Constantinos Makrides (86 Christos Theofilou), Marios Nicolaou, Yiasoumakis Yiasoumi (73 Chrysostomos Michael), Yiannakis Okkas.
Trainer: Angelos Anastasiadis (Greece).

Sent off: Marios Elia (90)

Goals: Stephen John Finnan (90+3) / Stelios Okkarides (80)

434. 17.11.2007   13th European Champs Qualifiers
WALES v REPUBLIC OF IRELAND 2-2 (1-1)
Millennium, Cardiff

Referee: Oleh Oriekhov (Ukraine)   Attendance: 24,619

WALES: Wayne Robert Hennessey, Neal James Eardley (81 David Rhys George Best Cotterill), Daniel Leon Gabbidon, James Collins, Christopher Ross Gunter, Joseph Christopher Ledley, Jason Koumas, Carl Phillip Robinson (37 David Alexander Edwards), Carl Neil Fletcher, Simon Davies (Cap), Freddy Eastwood (59 Jermaine Maurice Easter).
Manager: John Benjamin Toshack.

REPUBLIC OF IRELAND: Seamus John Given, Stephen John Finnan, Paul David McShane, John Francis O'Shea, Kevin Daniel Kilbane, Aiden McGeady, Lee Kevin Carsley, William Peter Miller (59 Stephen Patrick Hunt), Andrew Matthew Reid (87 Darren Potter), Kevin Edward Doyle, Robert David Keane (Cap).   Trainer: Daniel Joseph Givens.

Goals: Jason Koumas (23, 89 pen) /
Robert David Keane (31), Kevin Edward Doyle (60)

435. 06.02.2008
REPUBLIC OF IRELAND v BRAZIL 0-1 (0-0)
Croke Park, Dublin
Referee: René Rogalla (Switzerland)   Attendance: 30,000

REPUBLIC OF IRELAND: Seamus John Given, Stephen Michael Kelly, Richard Patrick Dunne, John Francis O'Shea, Kevin Daniel Kilbane, Aiden McGeady, William Peter Miller (46 Darren Potter), Lee Kevin Carsley, Damien Anthony Duff, Kevin Edward Doyle (72 Stephen Patrick Hunt), Robert David Keane (Cap).   Trainer: Daniel Joseph Givens.

BRAZIL: Júlio César Soares de Espíndola, Leonardo da Silva Moura, Anderson Luís da Silva "Luisão", Alex Rodrigo Dias da Costa "Alex Costa", Richarlyson Barbosa Felisbino, Gilberto Aparecido da Silva, Josué Anunciado de Oliveira (83 Lucas Pezzini Leiva "Lucas II"), Diego Ribas da Cunha (78 Ânderson Luís de Abreu Oliveira "Ânderson II"), Robson de Souza "Robinho", Luís Fabiano Clemente (84 Rafael Augusto Sóbis), Júlio César Clement Baptista.
Trainer: Carlos Caetano Bledorn Verri "Dunga".

Goal: Robson de Souza "Robinho" (67)

436. 24.05.2008
REPUBLIC OF IRELAND v SERBIA 1-1 (0-0)
Croke Park, Dublin
Referee: Simon Evans (Wales)   Attendance: 42,500

REPUBLIC OF IRELAND: Dean Lawrence Kiely, Stephen Michael Kelly, Paul David McShane, Richard Patrick Dunne, Damien Delaney, Damien Anthony Duff, Glenn Whelan, William Peter Miller, Stephen Patrick Hunt (80 Andrew Declan Keogh), Kevin Edward Doyle (86 Shane Patrick Long), Robert David Keane (Cap) (69 Daryl Murphy).
Trainer: Giovanni Trapattoni.

SERBIA: Vladimir Stojković, Antonio Rukavina, Branislav Ivanović, Slobodan Rajković, Ivica Dragutinović, Milan Smiljanić (90 Nenad Kovačević), Zdravko Kuzmanović, Boško Janković, Stefan Babović (80 Marjan Marković), Saša Ilić (86 Gojko Kačar), Danko Lazović (69 Marko Pantelić).
Trainer: Miroslav Đukić.

Goals: Andrew Declan Keogh (90) / Marko Pantelić (75)

437. 29.05.2008
REPUBLIC OF IRELAND v COLOMBIA 1-0 (1-0)
Craven Cottage, London (England)
Referee: Mark Clattenburg (England)   Attendance: 18,612

REPUBLIC OF IRELAND: Dean Lawrence Kiely, John Francis O'Shea, Paul David McShane, Richard Patrick Dunne, Damien Delaney, Glenn Whelan, William Peter Miller, Aiden McGeady, Andrew Declan Keogh (90 Wesley Hoolahan), Kevin Edward Doyle (85 Daryl Murphy), Robert David Keane (Cap).
Trainer: Giovanni Trapattoni.

COLOMBIA: Róbinson Zapata Montaño, Cristián Eduardo Zapata Valencia, Rubén Darío Bustos Torres (46 Gerardo Vallejo), Luis Amaranto Perea Mosquera (66 Walter Moreno), Elvis González (70 Pablo Armero), Freddy Alejandro Guarín Vásquez, Carlos Alberto Sánchez Moreno, Juan Carlos Escobar (63 Elkin Soto Jaramillo), Macnelly Torres (73 Giovanni Hernández), Édixon Perea Valencia, Radamel Falcao García Zárate (65 Roberto Polo).   Trainer: Jorge Luis Pinto.

Goal: Robert David Keane (3)

438. 20.08.2008
NORWAY v REPUBLIC OF IRELAND 1-1 (0-1)
Ullevaal, Oslo
Referee: Mark Whitby (Wales)   Attendance: 16,037

NORWAY: Rune Almenning Jarstein, Tom Høgli, Tore Reginiussen, Brede Paulsen Hangeland, John Arne Riise, Fredrik Strømstad (43 Kristofer Hæstad), Martin Andresen, Daniel Fredheim Holm (46 Morten Gamst Pedersen), Fredrik Winsnes, Mohammed Abdellaoue (80 Christian Grindheim), Thorsten Helstad (57 Erik Nevland).   Trainer: Åge Hareide.

REPUBLIC OF IRELAND: Seamus John Given (46 Dean Lawrence Kiely), Stephen John Finnan (69 Stephen Michael Kelly), John Francis O'Shea, Richard Patrick Dunne, Kevin Daniel Kilbane, Aiden McGeady (69 Stephen Patrick Hunt), Steven John Reid, Glenn Whelan, Damien Anthony Duff, Robert David Keane (Cap), Kevin Edward Doyle (64 Daryl Murphy).   Trainer: Giovanni Trapattoni.

Goals: Tore Reginiussen (60) / Robert David Keane (44)

439. 06.09.2008   19th World Cup Qualifiers
GEORGIA v REPUBLIC OF IRELAND 1-2 (0-1)
Stadion am Bruchweg, Mainz (Germany)
Referee: Zsolt Szabó (Hungary)   Attendance: 4,500
GEORGIA: Giorgi Loria, Ucha Lobjanidze, Zurab Khizanishvili (83 Malkhaz Asatiani), Kakhaber Kaladze (Cap), Giorgi Shashiashvili, Zurab Menteshashvili, Levan Kenia, David Odikadze, Levan Kobiashvili, Aleksandre Iashvili (77 Levan Mchedlidze), Rati Aleksidze (61 David Siradze). Trainer: Héctor Raúl Cúper (Argentina).
REPUBLIC OF IRELAND: Seamus John Given, Stephen John Finnan (80 Paul David McShane), John Francis O'Shea, Richard Patrick Dunne, Kevin Daniel Kilbane, Aiden McGeady (86 Andrew Declan Keogh), Steven John Reid, Glenn Whelan, Stephen Patrick Hunt, Robert David Keane (Cap), Kevin Edward Doyle (77 William Peter Miller). Trainer: Giovanni Trapattoni.
Goals: Levan Kenia (90+2) / Kevin Edward Doyle (13), Glenn Whelan (70).

441. 15.10.2008   19th World Cup Qualifiers
REPUBLIC OF IRELAND v CYPRUS 1-0 (1-0)
Croke Park, Dublin
Referee: Alexandru Dan Tudor (Romania)   Att: 55,833
REPUBLIC OF IRELAND: Seamus John Given, John Francis O'Shea, Richard Patrick Dunne, Paul David McShane, Kevin Daniel Kilbane, Darron Thomas Daniel Gibson, Glenn Whelan, Aiden McGeady, Damien Anthony Duff, Robert David Keane (Cap), Kevin Edward Doyle (90+2 Caleb Colman Folan). Trainer: Giovanni Trapattoni.
CYPRUS: Antonis Georgallides, Elias Charalambous, Marios Elia, Lambros Lambrou (46 Andreas Papathanasiou), Demetris Christofi, Andreas Constantinou, Alexandros Garpozis, Christos Marangos (52 Georgios Panayi), Constantinos Makrides, Yiannakis Okkas (Cap), Michalis Constantinou (79 Yiasoumakis Yiasoumi). Trainer: Angelos Anastasiadis (Greece).
Goal: Robert David Keane (5).

440. 10.09.2008   19th World Cup Qualifiers
MONTENEGRO v REPUBLIC OF IRELAND 0-0
Gradski, Podgorica
Referee: Sten Kaldma (Estonia)   Attendance: 12,000
MONTENEGRO: Vukasin Poleksić, Elsad Zverotić, Savo Pavićević, Milan Jovanović, Radoslav Batak, Jovan Tanasijević, Vladimir Božović (54 Simon Vukčević), Milorad Peković, Nikola Drinčić, Stevan Jovetić, Mirko Vučinić (Cap). Trainer: Zoran Filipović.
REPUBLIC OF IRELAND: Seamus John Given, Stephen John Finnan, John Francis O'Shea, Richard Patrick Dunne, Kevin Daniel Kilbane, Aiden McGeady, Steven John Reid, Glenn Whelan, Stephen Patrick Hunt, Robert David Keane (Cap), Kevin Edward Doyle.   Trainer: Giovanni Trapattoni.

442. 19.11.2008
REPUBLIC OF IRELAND v POLAND 2-3 (0-1)
Croke Park, Dublin
Referee: Kristinn Jakobson (Iceland)   Attendance: 61,000
REPUBLIC OF IRELAND: Seamus John Given, Paul David McShane (61 Alexander Stephen Bruce), John Francis O'Shea, Richard Patrick Dunne, Kevin Daniel Kilbane, Andrew Declan Keogh (61 Stephen Patrick Hunt), Darron Thomas Daniel Gibson (73 Keith Joseph Andrews), Glenn Whelan, Damien Anthony Duff (66 Shane Patrick Long), Kevin Edward Doyle (60 Noel Hunt), Caleb Colman Folan. Trainer: Giovanni Trapattoni.
POLAND: Łukasz Fabiański, Marcin Wasilewski, Jakub Wawrzyniak, Dariusz Dudka, Bartosz Bosacki, Jacek Krzynówek (81 Tomasz Jodłowiec), Jakub Błaszczykowski (46 Roger Guerreiro), Łukasz Garguła, Mariusz Lewandowski, Rafał Boguski (Sławomir Peszko), Paweł Brożek (46 Robert Lewandowski).   Trainer: Leo Beenhakker (Holland).
Goals: Stephen Hunt (88 pen), Keith Joseph Andrews (90) / Mariusz Lewandowski (3), Roger Guerreiro (47), Robert Lewandowski (89).

443. 11.02.2009   19th World Cup Qualifier
REPUBLIC OF IRELAND v GEORGIA 2-1 (0-1)
Croke Park, Dublin

Referee: Jouni Hyytiä (Finland)   Attendance: 45,000

REPUBLIC OF IRELAND: Shay Given, John O'Shea, Stephen Kelly, Richard Dunne, Damien Duff (80 Stephen Hunt), Keith Andrews, Glenn Whelan, Kevin Kilbane, Robbie Keane, Kevin Doyle, Aiden McGeady.   Manager: Giovanni Trapattoni

GEORGIA: Georgi Lomaia, Ucha Lobjanidze, Dato Kvirkvelia, Zurab Khizanishvili, Kakha Kaladze, David Siradze (77 Rati Aleksidze), Zurab Menteshashvili (70 Levan Khmaladze), Levan Kobiashvili, Luka Razmadze, Aleksandr Iashvili, Beka Gotsiridze (68 Giorgi Merebashvili).   Manager: Héctor Raúl Cúper

Goals: Robbie Keane (73 pen, 78) / Aleksandr Iashvili (1)

444. 28.03.2009   19th World Cup Qualifier
REPUBLIC OF IRELAND v BULGARIA 1-1 (1-0)
Croke Park, Dublin

Referee: Ivan Bebek (Croatia)   Attendance: 60,002

REPUBLIC OF IRELAND: Shay Given, Paul McShane, Richard Dunne, John O'Shea, Kevin Kilbane, Stephen Hunt, Keith Andrews, Glenn Whelan, Aiden McGeady (90 Andy Keogh), Robbie Keane, Kevin Doyle.   Manager: Giovanni Trapattoni

BULGARIA: Dimitar Ivankov, Zhivko Milanov (24 Radostin Kishishev), Igor Tomasic, Stanislav Manolev, Ilian Stoyanov, Stilian Petrov, Dimityr Telkiyski, Ivelin Popov (46 Velizar Dimitrov), Blagoy Georgiev (66 Dimitar Makriev), Stanislav Angelov, Dimitar Rangelov.   Manager: Stanimir Stoilov

Goals: Richard Dunne (1) / Kevin Kilbane (74 og)

445. 01.04.2009   19th World Cup Qualifier
ITALY v REPUBLIC OF IRELAND 1-1 (1-0)
San Nicola, Bari

Referee: Wolfgang Stark (Germany)   Attendance: 48,000

ITALY: Gianluigi Buffon, Gianluca Zambrotta, Fabio Grosso, Giorgio Chiellini, Fabio Cannavaro, Andrea Pirlo (44 Angelo Palombo), Simone Pepe (55 Andrea Dossena), Daniele De Rossi, Matteo Brighi, Giampaolo Pazzini, Vincente Iaquinta (89 Fabio Quagliarella).   Manager: Marcello Lippi

REPUBLIC OF IRELAND: Shay Given, John O'Shea, Paul McShane, Richard Dunne, Glenn Whelan, Kevin Kilbane, Stephen Hunt, Keith Andrews (54 Darron Gibson), Andy Keogh (22 Caleb Folan), Robbie Keane, Kevin Doyle (63 Noel Hunt).   Manager: Giovanni Trapattoni

Sent off: Giampaolo Pazzini (4)

Goals: Vincenzo Iaquinta (9) / Robbie Keane (89)

446. 29.05.2009
REPUBLIC OF IRELAND v NIGERIA 1-1 (1-1)
Craven Cottage, London

Referee: William Collum (Scotland)   Attendance: 11,263

REPUBLIC OF IRELAND: Shay Given (46 Keiren Westwood), Kevin Foley (72 Paul McShane), Eddie Nolan, Richard Dunne, Sean St Ledger, Liam Miller, Liam Lawrence (81 Stephen Hunt), Damien Duff (46 Aiden McGeady), Keith Andrews (58 Glenn Whelan), Robbie Keane (46 Shane Long), Leon Best.   Manager: Giovanni Trapattoni

NIGERIA: Austin Ejide, Sam Sodje (78 Obinna Nwaneri), Mohamed Yusuf, Ayodele Adeleye, Olubayo Adefemi, Seyi Olofinjana, Kalu Uche, Sone Aluko (61 Peter Odemwingie), Joseph Akpala (61 Victor Obinna), John Utaka, Michael Eneramo.   Manager: Shaibu Amodu

Goals: Robbie Keane (38) / Michael Eneramo (30)

447. 06.06.2009   19th World Cup Qualifier
BULGARIA v REPUBLIC OF IRELAND 1-1 (1-1)
Vasil Levski, Sofia

Referee: Claus Bo Larsen (Denmark)   Attendance: 38,000

BULGARIA: Dimitar Ivankov, Igor Tomasic, Ilian Stoyanov, Zhivko Milanov, Radostin Kishishev, Dimityr Telkiyski (81 Velizar Dimitrov), Stilian Petrov, Martin Petrov (61 Blagoy Georgiev), Stanislav Angelov, Valeri Bojinov (59 Dimitar Makriev), Dimitar Berbatov.   Manager: Stanimir Stoilov

REPUBLIC OF IRELAND: Shay Given, Sean St Ledger, John O'Shea (82 Stephen Kelly), Richard Dunne, Glenn Whelan, Kevin Kilbane, Stephen Hunt (71 Aiden McGeady), Damien Duff, Keith Andrews, Robbie Keane (74 Leon Best), Caleb Folan.   Manager: Giovanni Trapattoni

Goals: Dimityr Telkiyski (29) / Richard Dunne (24)

448. 12.08.2009
REPUBLIC OF IRELAND v AUSTRIA 0-3 (0-2)
Thomond Park, Limerick

Referee: Alfonso Pérez Burrull (Spain)   Attendance: 19,000

REPUBLIC OF IRELAND: Shay Given (68 Keiren Westwood), John O'Shea, Sean St Ledger, Richard Dunne, Glenn Whelan, Kevin Kilbane (63 Eddie Nolan), Darron Gibson (62 Keith Andrews), Damien Duff (46 Stephen Hunt), Aiden McGeady (81 Shane Long), Robbie Keane, Kevin Doyle (46 Caleb Folan).   Manager: Giovanni Trapattoni

AUSTRALIA: Mark Schwarzer, Rhys Williams, Luke Wilkshire, Jade North (72 Matthew Spiranovic), Patrick Kisnorbo (46 Adrian Madaschi), Harry Kewell, Mile Jedinak (89 James Holland), David Carney, Tim Cahill (46 Nikita Rukavytsya), Mark Bresciano (78 Nick Carle), Scott McDonald (46 Brett Holman).   Manager: Pim Verbeek

Goals: Tim Cahill (38, 44), David Carney (90)

449.　05.09.2009　19th World Cup Qualifier
CYPRUS v REPUBLIC OF IRELAND 1-2 (1-1)
Neo GSP, Nicosia
Referee: Thomas Einwaller (Austria)　Attendance: 5,191
CYPRUS: Sofronis Avgousti, Marios Elia, Paraskevas Christou, Costas Charalambides, Marinos Satsias (90 Dimitris Christofi), Mários Nikolaou, Chrysis Michael (71 Nektarios Alexandrou), Elias Charalambous, Yiannis Okkas (90 Christos Marangos), Efstathios Aloneftis, Andreas Avraam. Manager: Angelos Anastasiadis
REPUBLIC OF IRELAND: Shay Given, Sean St Ledger, John O'Shea, Richard Dunne, Glenn Whelan, Kevin Kilbane, Stephen Hunt (67 Aiden McGeady), Damien Duff, Keith Andrews, Robbie Keane, Kevin Doyle (75 Caleb Folan). Manager: Giovanni Trapattoni
Goals: Marios Elia (30) / Kevin Doyle (5), Robbie Keane (83)

450.　08.09.2009
REPUBLIC OF IRELAND v SOUTH AFRICA 1-0 (1-0)
Thomond Park, Limerick
Referee: Craig Alexander Thomson (Scotland)　Att: 14,572
REPUBLIC OF IRELAND: Keiren Westwood, Darren O'Dea, Sean St Ledger, Stephen Kelly (62 Paul McShane), Eddie Nolan, Liam Lawrence, Darron Gibson, Keith Andrews, Kevin Doyle (59 Leon Best), Caleb Folan, Andy Keogh (78 Damien Duff).　Manager: Giovanni Trapattoni
SOUTH AFRICA: Rowen Fernández, Benson Mhlongo, Tsepo Masilela (78 Lucas Thwala), Morgan Gould, Siboniso Gaxa, Aaron Mokoena, Kagisho Dikgacoi (81 Clifford Ngobeni), Elrio van Heerden (59 Mabhuti Khenyeza), Steven Pienaar, Katlego Mphela (74 Richard Henyekane), Bernard Parker (63 Siphiwe Tshabalala).
Manager: Natalino Joel Santana
Goal: Liam Lawrence (37)

451.　10.10.2009　19th World Cup Qualifier
REPUBLIC OF IRELAND v ITALY 2-2 (1-1)
Croke Park, Dublin
Referee: Terje Hauge (Norway)　Attendance: 70,640
REPUBLIC OF IRELAND: Shay Given, Sean St Ledger, John O'Shea, Richard Dunne, Glenn Whelan (70 Martin Rowlands), Liam Lawrence, Kevin Kilbane, Keith Andrews, Aiden McGeady (78 Stephen Hunt), Robbie Keane, Kevin Doyle (66 Leon Best).　Manager: Giovanni Trapattoni

ITALY: Gianluigi Buffon, Gianluca Zambrotta, Nicola Legrottaglie, Fabio Grosso (76 Salvatore Bocchetti), Giorgio Chiellini, Andrea Pirlo, Angelo Palombo (89 Simone Pepe), Daniele De Rossi, Mauro Camoranesi, Vincente Iaquinta, Antonio Di Natale (76 Alberto Gilardino).
Manager: Marcello Lippi
Goals: Glen Whelan (8), Sean St Ledger (87) / Mauro Camoranesi (26), Alberto Gilardino (90)

452.　14.10.2009　19th World Cup Qualifier
REPUBLIC OF IRELAND v MONTENEGRO 0-0
Croke Park, Dublin
Referee: Vladimir Hrinák (Slovakia)　Attendance: 50,212
REPUBLIC OF IRELAND: Shay Given, Sean St Ledger, Paul McShane, Richard Dunne, Damien Duff, Martin Rowlands (40 John O'Shea), Liam Miller, Kevin Kilbane, Stephen Hunt (88 Andy Keogh), Robbie Keane, Noel Hunt (68 Leon Best). Manager: Giovanni Trapattoni
MONTENEGRO: Vukasin Poleksic, Marko Basa, Elsad Zverotic, Radoslav Batak (31 Miodrag Dzudovic), Milan Jovanovic, Simon Vukcevic, Milorad Pekovic, Mitar Novakovic, Nikola Drincic, Branko Boskovic (81 Mladen Kascelan), Andrija Delibasic (69 Dejan Damjanovic).
Manager: Zoran Filipovic

453.　14.11.2009　19th World Cup Qualifier Play-offs
REPUBLIC OF IRELAND v FRANCE 0-1 (0-0)
Croke Park, Dublin
Referee: Dr.Felix Brych (Germany)　Attendance: 74,103
REPUBLIC OF IRELAND: Shay Given, John O'Shea, Sean St Ledger, Richard Dunne, Glenn Whelan, Liam Lawrence (80 Stephen Hunt), Kevin Kilbane, Damien Duff (76 Aiden McGeady), Keith Andrews, Robbie Keane, Kevin Doyle (71 Leon Best).　Manager: Giovanni Trapattoni
FRANCE: Hugo Lloris, William Gallas, Éric Abidal, Bacary Sagna, Patrice Evra, Yoann Gourcuff, Lassana Diarra, Alou Diarra, André-Pierre Gignac (90+1 Florent Malouda), Nicolas Anelka, Thierry Henry.　Manager: Raymond Domenech
Goal: Nicolas Anelka (72)

454. 18.11.2009   19th World Cup Qualifier Play-offs
FRANCE v REPUBLIC OF IRELAND 1-1 (0-1, 0-1) (AET)
Stade de France, Paris-St.Denis
Referee: Martin Wittberg (Sweden)   Attendance: 79,145
FRANCE: Hugo Lloris, William Gallas, Julien Escudé (9 Sébastien Squillaci), Patrice Evra, Bacary Sagna, Lassana Diarra, Alou Diarra, Yoann Gourcuff (88 Florent Malouda), André-Pierre Gignac (57 Sidney Govou), Nicolas Anelka, Thierry Henry.   Manager: Raymond Domenech
REPUBLIC OF IRELAND: Shay Given, John O'Shea (67 Paul McShane), Richard Dunne, Sean St Ledger, Kevin Kilbane, Damien Duff, Keith Andrews, Glenn Whelan (63 Darron Gibson), Liam Lawrence (107 Aiden McGeady), Robbie Keane, Kevin Doyle.   Manager: Giovanni Trapattoni
Goals: William Gallas (102) / Robbie Keane (32)

455. 02.03.2010
REPUBLIC OF IRELAND v BRAZIL 0-2 (0-1)
Emirates Stadium, London (England)
Referee: Mike Dean (England)   Attendance: 40,082
REPUBLIC OF IRELAND: Shay Given, Paul McShane, Stephen Kelly, Sean St Ledger, Glenn Whelan (57 Darron Gibson), Liam Lawrence (69 James McCarthy), Kevin Kilbane, Damien Duff (57 Aiden McGeady), Keith Andrews, Robbie Keane, Kevin Doyle (77 Leon Best).   Manager: Giovanni Trapattoni
BRAZIL: JÚLIO CÉSAR Soares Espíndola, MAICON Douglas Sisenando (84 CARLOS EDUARDO Marques), Lucimar da Silva Ferreira "Lúcio" (82 Anderson Luís da Silva "Luisão"), JUAN Silveira dos Santos, RAMIRES Santos do Nascimento (64 Daniel "Dani" ALVES da Silva), MICHEL Fernandes BASTOS, GILBERTO Aparecido da SILVA, FELIPE MELO de Carvalho, Ricardo Izecson dos Santos Leite "Kaká", Robson de Souza "Robinho" (77 NILMAR Honorato da Silva), ADRIANO Leite Ribeiro (64 Edinaldo Batista Líbanio "Grafite").   Manager: Carlos Caetano Bledorn Verri "Dunga"
Goals: K. Andrews (44 og), Robson de Souza "Robinho" (76)

456. 25.05.2010
REPUBLIC OF IRELAND v PARAGUAY 2-1 (2-0)
RDS Stadium, Dublin
Referee: Jérôme Laperrière (Switzerland)   Att: 16,722
REPUBLIC OF IRELAND: Keirin Westwood, John O'Shea, Paul McShane, Stephen Kelly, Sean St Ledger, Glenn Whelan (68 Paul Green), Liam Lawrence (82 Kevin Foley), Damien Duff (76 Keith Fahey), Keith Andrews, Robbie Keane (63 Cillian Sheridan), Kevin Doyle (87 Shane Long).   Manager: Giovanni Trapattoni
PARAGUAY: ALDO Antonio BOBADILLA Ávalos, ANTOLÍN ALCÁRAZ Viveros, CLAUDIO Marcelo MOREL Rodríguez (65 AURELIANO TORRES Román), PAULO César DA SILVA Barrios, DENIS Ramón CANIZA Acuña, ENRIQUE Daniel VERA Torres (66 CARLOS BONET Cáceres), JONATHAN SANTANA Ghere (82 SERGIO Daniel AQUINO), CRISTIAN Miguel RIVEROS Núñez (66 NÉSTOR Ezequiel ORTIGOZA), ROQUE Luis SANTA CRUZ Cantero (78 OSVALDO David MARTÍNEZ Arce), LUCAS Ramón BARRIOS Cáceres, RODOLFO Vicente GAMARRA Varela.
Manager: GERARDO Daniel MARTINO Capiglioni
Goals: Kevin Doyle (7), Liam Lawrence (39) / LUCAS Ramón BARRIOS Cáceres (57)

457. 28.05.2010
REPUBLIC OF IRELAND v ALGERIA 3-0 (1-0)
RDS Stadium, Dublin
Referee: Eric Braamhaar (Netherlands)   Attendance: 16,888
REPUBLIC OF IRELAND: Keirin Westwood (86 Joe Murphy), John O'Shea (36 Darren O'Dea), Stephen Kelly, Sean St Ledger, Glenn Whelan (75 Keith Andrews), Liam Lawrence (87 Shane Long), Paul Green, Damien Duff (65 Keith Fahey), Robbie Keane, Greg Cunningham, Kevin Doyle (72 Cillian Sheridan).   Manager: Giovanni Trapattoni
ALGERIA: Fawzi Chaouchi (68 Raïs M'Bolhi), Habib Bellaïd, Nadir Belhadj (67 Ryad Boudebouz), Rafik Halliche, Yazid Mansouri (67 Foued Kadir), Karim Ziani, Djamel Mesbah, Medhi Lacen, Adlène Guédioura, Abdelkader Ghezzal (77 Djamel Abdoun), Rafik Djebbour (58 Rafik Saïfi).   Manager: Rabah Saâdane
Goals: Paul Green (31), Robbie Keane (51, 86 pen)

458. 11.08.2010
REPUBLIC OF IRELAND v ARGENTINA 0-1 (0-1)
Aviva Stadium, Dublin
Referee: Peter Rasmussen (Denmark)   Attendance: 45,200
REPUBLIC OF IRELAND: Shay Given, John O'Shea, Paul McShane, Richard Dunne, Kevin Kilbane (57 Greg Cunningham), Paul Green, Keith Fahey (77 Keith Treacy), Damien Duff, Keith Andrews (67 Darron Gibson), Cillian Sheridan (57 Andy Keogh), Robbie Keane.   Manager: Giovanni Trapattoni
ARGENTINA: SERGIO Germán ROMERO, NICOLÁS Andrés BURDISSO (46 DIEGO Alberto MILITO), WALTER Adrián SAMUEL (83 FABRICIO COLOCCINI), GABRIEL Iván HEINZE (72 EMILIANO Adrián INSÚA), MARTÍN Gastón DEMICHELIS, FERNANDO Rubén GAGO, ÉVER Maximiliano David BANEGA, JAVIER Alejandro MASCHERANO, ÁNGEL Fabián DI MARÍA (75 JONÁS Manuel GUTIÉRREZ), LIONEL Andrés MESSI Cuccitini (58 EZEQUIEL Iván LAVEZZI), GONZALO Gerardo HIGUAÍN (46 PABLO Javier ZABALETA Girod).
Manager: SERGIO Daniel BATISTA
Goal: ÁNGEL Fabián DI MARÍA (20)

459.　03.09.2010　14th European Champs Qualifier
ARMENIA v REPUBLIC OF IRELAND　0-1　(0-0)
Hanrapetakan, Yerevan
Referee: Zsolt Szabó (Hungary)　Attendance: 8,600
ARMENIA: Roman Berezovskiy, Artak Yedigaryan (71 Hovjannes Hambardzumyan), Robert Arzumanyan, Ararat Arakelyan, Artur Yedigaryan (68 Davit Manoyan), Sargis Hovsepyan, Levon Pachajyan, Karlen Mktrchyan, Henrikh Mkhitaryan, Edgar Malakyan (79 Edgar Manucharyan), Yura Movsisyan.　Manager: Vardan Minasyan
REPUBLIC OF IRELAND: Shay Given, John O'Shea, Sean St Ledger, Richard Dunne, Glenn Whelan, Liam Lawrence, Kevin Kilbane, Paul Green, Aiden McGeady (69 Keith Fahey), Robbie Keane (85 Andy Keogh), Kevin Doyle.
Manager: Giovanni Trapattoni
Goal: Keith Fahey (76)

460.　07.09.2010　14th European Champs Qualifier
REPUBLIC OF IRELAND v ANDORRA　3-1　(2-1)
Aviva Stadium, Dublin
Referee: Leontios Trattou (Cyprus)　Attendance: 40,283
REPUBLIC OF IRELAND: Shay Given, John O'Shea (75 Stephen Kelly), Sean St Ledger, Richard Dunne, Glenn Whelan (61 Darron Gibson), Liam Lawrence, Kevin Kilbane, Paul Green, Aiden McGeady, Robbie Keane, Kevin Doyle (82 Andy Keogh).　Manager: Giovanni Trapattoni
ANDORRA: JOSEP Antonio GÓMES Moreira, CRISTIÁN MARTÍNEZ Alego, JORDI ESCURA Aixas, MARC BERNAUS Cano, ILDEFONS LIMA Solà, MÁRCIO VIEIRA de Vasconcelos, MARC PUJOL Pons (86 ÓSCAR Masand SONEJEE), Josep Manel "Jose" AYALA Díaz (71 Xavier "Xavi" ANDORRÀ Julià), FERNANDO José SILVA García, Sergio "Sergi" MORENO Marín (59 Manolo "Manel" JIMÉNEZ Soria), SEBASTIÁN GÓMEZ Pérez.
Manager: Jesús Luis "Koldo" Álvarez de Eulate Güergue
Goals: Kevin Kilbane (14), Kevin Doyle (41), Robbie Keane (54) / CRISTIÁN MARTÍNEZ Alego (45)

461.　08.10.2010　14th European Champs Qualifier
REPUBLIC OF IRELAND v RUSSIA　2-3　(0-2)
Aviva Stadium, Dublin
Referee: Kevin Blom (Netherlands)　Attendance: 50,411
REPUBLIC OF IRELAND: Shay Given, John O'Shea, Sean St Ledger, Richard Dunne, Glenn Whelan (66 Darron Gibson), Liam Lawrence (61 Shane Long), Kevin Kilbane, Paul Green, Aiden McGeady, Robbie Keane, Kevin Doyle (71 Keith Fahey).
Manager: Giovanni Trapattoni

RUSSIA: Igor Akinfeev, Sergey Ignashevich, Vasiliy Berezutskiy, Aleksandr Anyukov, Konstantin Zyryanov (68 Igor Semshov), Yuriy Zhirkov, Roman Shirokov, Alan Dzagoev (84 Aleksey Berezutskiy), Aleksandr Kerzhakov (80 Pavel Pogrebnyak), Igor Denisov, Andrey Arshavin.
Manager: Dick Advocaat
Goals: Robbie Keane (72 pen), Shane Long (78) / Aleksandr Kerzhakov (10), Alan Dzagoev (28), Roman Shirokov (51)

462.　12.10.2010　14th European Champs Qualifier
SLOVAKIA v REPUBLIC OF IRELAND　1-1　(1-1)
Stadión pod Dubnom, Zilina
Referee: Alberto Undiano Mallenco (Spain)　Att: 10,892
SLOVAKIA: Ján Mucha, Tomáš Hubocan, Ján Durica, Radoslav Zabavník, Kornel Saláta, Juraj Kucka, Miroslav Karhan, Marek Hamšík, Vladimír Weiss (70 Filip Holosko), Stanislav Sesták (70 Miroslav Stoch), Erik Jendrisek (84 Tomáš Oravec).　Manager: Vladimír Weiss
REPUBLIC OF IRELAND: Shay Given, John O'Shea, Richard Dunne, Sean St Ledger, Kevin Kilbane, Paul Green (41 Darron Gibson), Keith Fahey (71 Andy Keogh), Glenn Whelan, Aiden McGeady, Shane Long, Robbie Keane.
Manager: Giovanni Trapattoni
Goals: Ján Durica (36) / Sean St Ledger (16)

Robbie Keane missed a penalty kick (45+2).

463.　17.11.2010
REPUBLIC OF IRELAND v NORWAY　1-2　(1-1)
Aviva Stadium, Dublin
Referee: Kristinn Jakobsson (Iceland)　Attendance: 25,000
REPUBLIC OF IRELAND: Shay Given, John O'Shea, Darren O'Dea (67 Kevin Foley), Stephen Kelly, Glenn Whelan, Liam Lawrence (46 Jon Walters), Keith Fahey, Damien Duff (74 Stephen Hunt), Shane Long, Greg Cunningham, Kevin Doyle (46 Aiden McGeady).　Manager: Giovanni Trapattoni
NORWAY: Jon Knudsen (46 Espen Pettersen), Kjetil Wæhler, John Arne Riise, Tom Høgli, Brede Hangeland, Petter Moen (78 Kristofer Hæstad), Erik Huseklepp (90 Morten Moldskred), Henning Hauger, Morten Pedersen, Christian Grindheim (55 Ruben Jenssen), Thorstein Helstad (46 Bjørn Helge Riise).　Manager: Egil Olsen
Goals: Shane Long (5 pen) /
Morten Pedersen (34), Erik Huseklepp (86)

464. 08.02.2011   Nations Cup
REPUBLIC OF IRELAND v WALES 3-0 (0-0)
Aviva Stadium, Dublin
Referee: Mark Courtney (Northern Ireland)   Att: 19,783
REPUBLIC OF IRELAND: Shay Given, John O'Shea (85 Darren O'Dea), Séamus Coleman (58 Keith Fahey), Ciaran Clark, Sean St Ledger, Richard Dunne, Glenn Whelan (76 Paul Green), Darron Gibson (81 Marc Wilson), Damien Duff (71 Andy Keogh), Jon Walters, Kevin Doyle (46 Shane Long). Manager: Giovanni Trapattoni
WALES: Wayne Hennessey, Sam Ricketts (83 Lewin Nyatanga), Neal Eardley (46 Chris Gunter), Andrew Crofts, James Collins, Danny Collins, David Vaughan (61 Joe Ledley), Andy King, Robert Earnshaw (80 Jermaine Easter), Simon Church, Hal Robson-Kanu (68 Freddy Eastwood). Manager: Gary Speed
Goals: Darron Gibson (60), Damien Duff (66), Keith Fahey (82)

465. 26.03.2011   14th European Champs Qualifier
REPUBLIC OF IRELAND v MACEDONIA 2-1 (2-1)
Aviva Stadium, Dublin
Referee: István Vad (Hungary)   Attendance: 33,200
REPUBLIC OF IRELAND: Keiren Westwood, Darren O'Dea, Kevin Foley, Richard Dunne, Glenn Whelan, Kevin Kilbane, Darron Gibson (77 Keith Fahey), Damien Duff, Aiden McGeady, Robbie Keane (87 James McCarthy), Kevin Doyle (20 Shane Long).   Manager: Giovanni Trapattoni
MACEDONIA: Edin Nuredinoski, Nikolce Noveski, Boban Grncharov, Vance Shikov, Darko Tasevski (61 Mario Djurovski), Velice Sumulikoski, Goran Popov, Muhamed Demiri (84 Slavco Georgijevski), Ivan Trichkovski, Goran Pandev, Ilco Naumoski (67 Stevica Ristic). Manager: Mirsad Jonuz
Goals: Aiden McGeady (2), Robbie Keane (21) / Ivan Trichkovski (45)

466. 29.03.2011
REPUBLIC OF IRELAND v URUGUAY 2-3 (1-3)
Aviva Stadium, Dublin
Referee: Said Ennjimi (France)   Attendance: 20,200
REPUBLIC OF IRELAND: Keiren Westwood, Ciaran Clark (75 Damien Delaney), Darren O'Dea, Stephen Kelly, Kevin Foley, James McCarthy (67 Keith Treacy), Liam Lawrence (78 Aiden McGeady), Paul Green, Keith Fahey (66 Darron Gibson), Shane Long, Andy Keogh (85 Anthony Stokes).   Manager: Giovanni Trapattoni
URUGUAY: Nestor FERNANDO MUSLERA, DIEGO Alfredo LUGANO Moreno, José MARTÍN CÁCERES Silva, Victorio Maximiliano "Maxi" PEREIRA Páez, DIEGO Roberto GODÍN Leal, DIEGO Fernando PÉREZ Aguado (90 ANDRÉS SCOTTI Ponce de León), EGIDIO Raúl ARÉVALO Ríos (64 WALTER Alejandro GARGANO Guevara), ÁLVARO Daniel PEREIRA Barragán, DIEGO Martín FORLÁN Corazo, ABEL Mathías HERNÁNDEZ (84 SEBASTIÁN EGUREN Ledesma), EDINSON Roberto Gómez CAVANI.
Manager: ÓSCAR Washington TABÁREZ Sclavo
Goals: Shane Long (15), Keith Fahey (48 pen) / DIEGO Alfredo LUGANO Moreno (12), EDINSON Roberto Gómez CAVANI (22), ABEL Mathías HERNÁNDEZ (40)

467. 24.05.2011   Nations Cup
REPUBLIC OF IRELAND v NORTHERN IRELAND 5-0 (3-0)
Aviva Stadium, Dublin
Referee: Craig Thomson (Scotland)   Attendance: 12,083
REPUBLIC OF IRELAND: Shay Given (72 David Forde), Keith Treacy, Paul McShane, Stephen Kelly, Séamus Coleman (55 Liam Lawrence), Kevin Foley (70 Stephen Hunt), Stephen Ward, Damien Delaney, Keith Andrews, Robbie Keane (62 Andy Keogh), Simon Cox.   Manager: Giovanni Trapattoni
NORTHERN IRELAND: Alan Blayney, Adam Thompson, Gareth McAuley, Lee Hodson, Craig Cathcart, Josh McQuoid (46 Oliver Norwood), Johnny Gorman (55 Colin Coates), Sammy Clingan, Steven Davis (76 Robert Garrett), Warren Feeney (72 Liam Boyce), Josh Carson (73 Niall McGinn). Manager: Nigel Worthington
Goals: Stephen Ward (24), Robbie Keane (37, 54 pen), Craig Cathcart (44 og), Simon Cox (80)

468. 29.05.2011   Nations Cup
REPUBLIC OF IRELAND v SCOTLAND 1-0 (1-0)
Aviva Stadium, Dublin
Referee: Mark Whitby (Wales)   Attendance: 17,694
REPUBLIC OF IRELAND: Shay Given, Darren O'Dea (66 Kevin Foley), Paul McShane, Stephen Kelly, Stephen Ward, Keith Fahey, Keith Andrews, Liam Lawrence (62 Séamus Coleman), Stephen Hunt, Robbie Keane (83 Keith Treacy), Simon Cox.   Manager: Giovanni Trapattoni
SCOTLAND: Allan McGregor, Christophe Berra, Phil Bardsley, Steven Whittaker, Grant Hanley, Charlie Adam (63 Barry Bannan), Barry Robson (75 Chris Maguire), Steven Naismith, Scott Brown, Kenny Miller, James Forrest (85 Ross McCormack).   Manager: Craig Levein
Goal: Robbie Keane (23)

469. 04.06.2011   14th European Champs Qualifier
MACEDONIA v REPUBLIC OF IRELAND 0-2 (0-2)
Filip II. Makedonski, Skopje
Referee: Florian Meyer (Germany)   Attendance: 29,500
MACEDONIA: Martin Bogatinov, Nikolce Noveski, Boban Grncharov, Vance Shikov, Velice Sumulikoski, Goran Popov, Filip Despotovski (57 Mario Djurovski), Muhamed Demiri (72 Dusan Savic), Ivan Trichkovski, Goran Pandev, Ilco Naumoski (10 Ferhan Hasani).   Manager: Mirsad Jonuz
REPUBLIC OF IRELAND: Shay Given, John O'Shea, Darren O'Dea, Stephen Kelly, Glenn Whelan, Kevin Kilbane, Stephen Hunt, Keith Andrews, Aiden McGeady, Robbie Keane, Simon Cox (64 Shane Long).   Manager: Giovanni Trapattoni
Goals: Robbie Keane (8, 37)

Ivan Trichkovski missed a penalty kick in the 41st minute.

470. 07.06.2011
REPUBLIC OF IRELAND v ITALY 2-0 (1-0)
Stade Sclessin, Liége (Belgium)
Referee: Serge Gumienney (Belgium)   Attendance: 20,000
REPUBLIC OF IRELAND: David Forde, Darren O'Dea (83 Stephen Kelly), Paul McShane, Kevin Foley (60 Glenn Whelan), Séamus Coleman, Stephen Ward (90+3 Damien Delaney), Sean St Ledger, Stephen Hunt, Keith Andrews, Shane Long (60 Simon Cox), Andy Keogh (75 Keith Treacy).   Manager: Giovanni Trapattoni
ITALY: Emiliano Viviano, Alessandro Gamberini, Domenico Criscito (66 Federico Balzaretti), Mattia Cassani, Giorgio Chiellini, Riccardo Montolivo, Antonio Nocerino (59 Sebastian Giovinco), Claudio Marchisio, Andrea Pirlo (46 Angelo Palombo), Giuseppe Rossi (46 Alessandro Matri), Giampaolo Pazzini (58 Alberto Gilardino).   Manager: Cesare Prandelli
Goals: Keith Andrew (36), Simon Cox (89)

471. 10.08.2011
REPUBLIC OF IRELAND v CROATIA 0-0
Aviva Stadium, Dublin
Referee: Ton Hagen (Norway)   Attendance: 20,000
REPUBLIC OF IRELAND: Shay Given (64 Keiren Westwood), Stephen Kelly, Stephen Ward, Sean St Ledger, Richard Dunne, Glenn Whelan (74 Darren O'Dea), Stephen Hunt (64 Andy Keogh), Darron Gibson, Damien Duff (83 Keith Treacy), Shane Long (83 Simon Cox), Robbie Keane.   Manager: Giovanni Trapattoni
CROATIA: Stipe Pletikosa, Ivan Strinic, Josip Simunic, Dejan Lovren, Vedran Corluka (73 Sime Vrsaljko), Niko Kranjcar (65 Ivo Ilicevic), Ognjen Vukojevic (86 Tomislav Dujmovic), Darijo Srna, Luka Modric, Mario Mandzukic (73 Nikola Kalinic), EDUARDO Alves da Silva (46 Ivica Olic).   Manager: Slaven Bilic

472. 02.09.2011   14th European Champs Qualifier
REPUBLIC OF IRELAND v SLOVAKIA 0-0
Aviva Stadium, Dublin
Referee: PEDRO PROENÇA Oliveira Alves Garcia (Portugal)   Attendance: 44,761
REPUBLIC OF IRELAND: Shay Given, Stephen Ward, John O'Shea, Sean St Ledger, Richard Dunne, Glenn Whelan, Damien Duff, Keith Andrews, Aiden McGeady (84 Stephen Hunt), Robbie Keane, Kevin Doyle (64 Simon Cox).   Manager: Giovanni Trapattoni
SLOVAKIA: Ján Mucha, Martin Skrtel, Peter Pekarík, Ján Durica, Marek Cech, Vladimír Weiss (85 Erik Jendrisek), Juraj Kucka (76 Karim Guédé), Miroslav Karhan, Marek Hamsík, Miroslav Stoch, Filip Holosko (88 Róbert Vittek).   Manager: Vladimir Weiss

473. 06.09.2011   14th European Champs Qualifier
RUSSIA v REPUBLIC OF IRELAND 0-0
Luzhniki, Moskva
Referee: Dr. Felix Brych (Germany)   Attendance: 48,717
RUSSIA: Vyacheslav Malafeev, Sergey Ignashevich, Vasiliy Berezutskiy, Aleksey Berezutskiy, Aleksandr Anyukov, Igor Semshov, Konstantin Zyryanov, Yuriy Zhirkov (76 Diniyar Bilyaletdinov), Roman Shirokov, Aleksandr Kerzhakov (54 Roman Pavlyuchenko), Andrey Arshavin.   Manager: Dick Advocaat
REPUBLIC OF IRELAND: Shay Given, Stephen Ward, Darren O'Dea, Stephen Kelly, Richard Dunne, Glenn Whelan, Damien Duff (67 Stephen Hunt), Keith Andrews, Aiden McGeady, Robbie Keane, Kevin Doyle (59 Simon Cox).   Manager: Giovanni Trapattoni

474. 07.10.2011   14th European Champs Qualifier
ANDORRA v REPUBLIC OF IRELAND 0-2 (0-2)
Estadi Comunal, Andorra la Vella
Referee: Libor Kovarik (Czech Republic)   Attendance: 860
ANDORRA: JOSEP Antonio GÓMES Moreira, CRISTIÁN MARTÍNEZ Alego, EMILI Josep GARCÍA Miramontes, MARC BERNAUS Cano, ILDEFONS LIMA Solà (80 ÓSCAR Masand SONEJEE), ALEXANDRE Ruben MARTÍNEZ Gutiérrez (78 IVÁN LORENZO Roncero), MÁRCIO VIEIRA de Vasconcelos, MARC PUJOL Pons (59 Carlos Eduardo "Edu" PEPPE Britos), Josep Manel "Jose" AYALA Díaz, FERNANDO José SILVA García, Sergio "Sergi" MORENO Marín.   Manager: Jesús Luis "Koldo" Álvarez de Eulate Güergue
REPUBLIC OF IRELAND: Shay Given, Stephen Ward, John O'Shea, Darren O'Dea, Sean St Ledger, Glenn Whelan (65 Keith Fahey), Damien Duff (75 Stephen Hunt), Keith Andrews, Aiden McGeady, Robbie Keane, Kevin Doyle (71 Shane Long).   Manager: Giovanni Trapattoni
Goals: Kevin Doyle (8), Aiden McGeady (20)

475.   11.10.2011   14th European Champs Qualifier
REPUBLIC OF IRELAND v ARMENIA 2-1 (1-0)
Aviva Stadium, Dublin
Referee: Eduardo Iturralde González (Spain)   Att: 45,200
REPUBLIC OF IRELAND: Shay Given, John O'Shea, Stephen Kelly, Sean St Ledger, Richard Dunne, Glenn Whelan (76 Keith Fahey), Damien Duff, Keith Andrews, Aiden McGeady (67 Stephen Hunt), Simon Cox (80 Jon Walters), Kevin Doyle.   Manager: Giovanni Trapattoni
ARMENIA: Roman Berezovskiy, Sargis Hovsepyan, Karlen Mktrchyan, Henrikh Mkhitaryan, Edgar Malakyan (28 Arsen Petrosyan goalkeeper), Valeri Aleksanyan, Hrayr Mkoyan, Levon Hayrapetyan, Gevorg Ghazaryan (63 Artur Sarkisov), Marcos Pizzelli (53 Edgar Manucharyan), Yura Movsisyan. Manager: Vardan Minasyan
Sent off: Roman Berezovskiy (26), Kevin Doyle (81)
Goals: Valeri Aleksanyan (43 og), Richard Dunne (60) / Henrikh Mkhitaryan (62)

476.   11.11.2011   14th European Championships Qualification Play-offs
ESTONIA v REPUBLIC OF IRELAND 0-4 (0-1)
A. Le Coq Arena, Tallinn
Referee: Viktor Kassai (Hungary)   Attendance: 9,692
ESTONIA: Sergei Pareiko, Dmitriy Kruglov, Enar Jääger, Andrei Stepanov, Raio Piiroja, Ragnar Klavan, Aleksandr Dmitrijev, Martin Vunk (61 Joel Lindpere), Konstantin Vassiljev, Tarmo Kink (67 Ats Purje), Jarmo Ahjupera (55 Vladimir Voskoboinikov).   Manager: Tarmo Rüütli
REPUBLIC OF IRELAND: Shay Given, Stephen Ward, Stephen Kelly, Sean St Ledger, Richard Dunne, Damien Duff (73 Stephen Hunt), Keith Andrews, Glenn Whelan (78 Keith Fahey), Jon Walters (83 Simon Cox), Aiden McGeady, Robbie Keane.   Manager: Giovanni Trapattoni
Sent off: Andrei Stepanov (34), Raio Piiroja (76)
Goals: Keith Andrews (13), Jon Walters (67), Robbie Keane (71, 88 pen)

477.   15.11.2011   14th European Championships Qualification Play-offs
REPUBLIC OF IRELAND v ESTONIA 1-1 (1-0)
Aviva Stadium, Dublin
Referee: Björn Kuipers (Netherlands)   Attendance: 51,151
REPUBLIC OF IRELAND: Shay Given, Stephen Ward, John O'Shea, Sean St Ledger, Richard Dunne, Stephen Hunt (59 Aiden McGeady), Damien Duff (79 Keith Fahey), Keith Andrews, Glenn Whelan, Robbie Keane (67 Simon Cox), Kevin Doyle.   Manager: Giovanni Trapattoni
ESTONIA: Pavel Londak, Taavi Rähn, Dmitriy Kruglov (18 Sander Puri), Enar Jääger, Ragnar Klavan, Joel Lindpere (54 Tarmo Kink), Martin Vunk, Konstantin Vassiljev, Taijo Teniste, Kaimar Saag, Vladimir Voskoboinikov (73 Ats Purje). Manager: Tarmo Rüütli
Goals: Stephen Ward (32) / Konstantin Vassiljev (57)

478.   29.02.2012
REPUBLIC OF IRELAND v CZECH REPUBLIC 1-1 (0-0)
Aviva Stadium, Dublin
Referee: Manuel JORGE Neves Moreira de SOUSA (Portugal)
Attendance: 37,741
REPUBLIC OF IRELAND: Shay Given, Stephen Ward, John O'Shea, Darren O'Dea, Sean St Ledger, Glenn Whelan (63 Stephen Hunt), Aiden McGeady (79 James McClean), Damien Duff (63 Paul Green), Keith Andrews, Shane Long (71 Simon Cox), Robbie Keane (71 Jon Walters).
Manager: Giovanni Trapattoni
CZECH REPUBLIC: Petr Cech, Theodor Gebre Selassie (67 Václav Pilar), David Limbersky, Michal Kadlec, Tomás Sivok, Jaroslav Plasil, Milan Petrzela (67 Frantisek Rajtoral), Petr Jirácek (46 Tomás Hübschman), Jirí Stajner (59 Daniel Kolár), Jan Rezek (87 Tomás Pekhart), Milan Baros (59 David Lafata).
Manager: Michal Bílek
Goals: Simon Cox (86) / Milan Baros (50)

479.   26.05.2012
REPUBLIC OF IRELAND v BOSNIA-HERZEGOVINA 1-0 (0-0)
Aviva Stadium, Dublin
Referee: Nikolaj Hänni (Switzerland)   Attendance: 37,100
REPUBLIC OF IRELAND: Keiren Westwood, Stephen Ward, Darren O'Dea, Paul McShane (78 Stephen Kelly), Richard Dunne (69 Sean St Ledger), Glenn Whelan (46 Keith Andrews), Darron Gibson, Damien Duff (46 Aiden McGeady), James McClean, Robbie Keane (63 Shane Long), Kevin Doyle (62 Jon Walters).   Manager: Giovanni Trapattoni
BOSNIA-HERZEGOVINA: Asmir Begovic, Boris Pandza, Sanel Jahic, Mensur Mujdza (56 Adnan Zahirovic), Elvir Rahimic (46 Miroslav Stevanovic), Miralem Pjanic, Zvjezdan Misimovic (82 Mehmed Alispahic), Haris Medunjanin (46 Damir Vrancic), Senad Lulic, Vedad Ibisevic (70 Stojan Vranjes), Edin Dzeko.   Manager: Safet Susic
Goal: Shane Long (77)

480.   04.06.2012
HUNGARY v REPUBLIC OF IRELAND   0-0
Puskás Ferenc Stadion, Budapest
Referee: Kenn Hansen (Denmark)   Attendance: 17,000
HUNGARY: Ádám Bogdán, Zsolt Korcsmár, József Varga, Péter Szakály (65 Imre Szabics), Norbert Mészáros, Vladimir Koman, Péter Halmosi (70 Tamás Kádár), Ádám Pintér (46 Vilmos Vanczák), Ádám Szalai (78 Krisztián Németh), Adám Gyurcsó (86 Tamas Koltai), Balász Dzsudzsák.   Manager: Sándor Egervári

REPUBLIC OF IRELAND: Shay Given (46 Keiren Westwood), Stephen Ward, John O'Shea, Sean St Ledger, Richard Dunne, Glenn Whelan (85 Paul Green), Aiden McGeady, Damien Duff (63 Stephen Hunt), Keith Andrews (65 Darron Gibson), Robbie Keane (62 Simon Cox), Kevin Doyle (46 Jon Walters).   Manager: Giovanni Trapattoni

481.   10.06.2012   14th European Champs Group C
REPUBLIC OF IRELAND v CROATIA   1-3 (1-2)
INEA stadion, Poznan (Poland)
Referee: Björn Kuipers (Netherlands)   Attendance: 39,550
REPUBLIC OF IRELAND: Shay Given, Sean St Ledger, Stephen Ward, John O'Shea, Richard Dunne, Glenn Whelan, Aiden McGeady (54 Simon Cox), Keith Andrews, Damien Duff, Kevin Doyle (54 Jon Walters), Robbie Keane (74 Shane Long).   Manager: Giovanni Trapattoni
CROATIA: Stipe Pletikosa, Ivan Strinic, Vedran Corluka, Darijo Srna, Gordon Schildenfeld, Ivan Rakitic (90+2 Tomislav Dujmovic), Ognjen Vukojevic, Luka Modric, Ivan Perisic (89 EDUARDO Alves da Silva), Nikica Jelavic (72 Niko Kranjcar), Mario Mandzukic.   Manager: Slaven Bilic
Goals: Sean St Ledger (19) /
Mario Mandzukic (3, 48), Nikica Jelavic (43)

482.   14.06.2012   14th European Champs Group C
SPAIN v REPUBLIC OF IRELAND   4-0 (1-0)
PGE Arena Gdansk, Gdansk
Referee: PEDRO PROENÇA Oliveira Alves Garcia (Portugal)   Attendance: 39,150
SPAIN: IKER CASILLAS Fernández, Gerard PIQUÉ i Bernabéu, SERGIO RAMOS García, Álvaro ARBELOA Coca, JORDI ALBA Ramos, Andrés INIESTA Luján (78 Santiago "Santi" CAZORLA González), "Xavi" Xavier Hernández i Creus, Xabier "Xabi" ALONSO Olano (65 Javier "Javi" MARTÍNEZ Aginaga), Sergio BUSQUETS Burgos, DAVID Jiménez SILVA, FERNANDO José TORRES Sanz (73 Francesc "CESC" FÀBREGAS Soler).
Manager: Vicente DEL BOSQUE González

REPUBLIC OF IRELAND: Shay Given, Sean St Ledger, Stephen Ward, John O'Shea, Richard Dunne, Glenn Whelan (80 Paul Green), Aiden McGeady, Keith Andrews, Damien Duff (76 James McClean), Robbie Keane, Simon Cox (46 Jon Walters).   Manager: Giovanni Trapattoni
Goals: FERNANDO José TORRES Sanz (4, 70), DAVID Jiménez SILVA (49), Francesc "CESC" FÀBREGAS Soler (82)

483.   18.06.2012   14th European Champs Group C
ITALY v REPUBLIC OF IRELAND   2-0 (1-0)
INEA stadion, Poznan (Poland)
Referee: Cüneyt Çakir (Turkey)   Attendance: 38,794
ITALY: Gianluigi Buffon, Giorgio Chiellini (57 Leonardo Bonucci), Federico Balzaretti, Andrea Barzagli, Thiago Motta, Ignazio Abate, Claudio Marchisio, Daniele De Rossi, Andrea Pirlo, Antonio Cassano (63 Alessandro Diamanti), Antonio Di Natale (74 Mario Balotelli).   Manager: Cesare Prandelli
REPUBLIC OF IRELAND: Shay Given, Sean St Ledger, Stephen Ward, John O'Shea, Richard Dunne, Glenn Whelan, Aiden McGeady (65 Shane Long), Keith Andrews, Damien Duff, Kevin Doyle (76 Jon Walters), Robbie Keane (86 Simon Cox).   Manager: Giovanni Trapattoni
Sent off: Keith Andrews (89)
Goals: Antonio Cassano (35), Mario Balotelli (90)

484.   15.08.2012
SERBIA v REPUBLIC OF IRELAND   0-0
Stadion Rajko Mitic, Beograd
Referee: Alexandru Tudor (Romania)   Attendance: 7,800
SERBIA: Vladimir Stojkovic, Aleksandar Kolarov, Branislav Ivanovic, Milan Bisevac (46 Nikola Maksimovic), Dusan Tadic (63 Filip Djuricic), Matija Nastasic, Zdravko Kuzmanovic (82 Dusan Basta), Aleksandar Ignjovski, Zoran Tosic (82 Nemanja Tomic), Srdan Mijailovic (64 Milos Ninkovic), Dejan Lekic (46 Lazar Markovic).   Manager: Sinisa Mihajlovic
REPUBLIC OF IRELAND: Keiren Westwood, Stephen Kelly, John O'Shea, Darren O'Dea, Paul McShane, Aiden McGeady (79 Séamus Coleman), James McCarthy, Glenn Whelan (60 Paul Green), James McClean (69 Andy Keogh), Simon Cox, Jon Walters (79 Joey O'Brien).   Manager: Giovanni Trapattoni

485. 07.09.2012 20th World Cup Qualifier
**KAZAKHSTAN
v REPUBLIC OF IRELAND 1-2** (1-0)

Astana Arena, Astana

Referee: Marius Avram (Romania) Attendance: 12,384

KAZAKHSTAN: Andrey Sidelnikov, Mukhtar Mukhtarov, Aleksandr Kislitsyn, Aleksandr Kirov, Mikhail Rozhkov, Kayrat Nurdauletov, Ulan Konysbaev (85 Sergey Gridin), Heinrich Schmidtgal, Anatoliy Bogdanov, Sergey Ostapenko, Tanat Nuserbaev (69 Bauyrzhan Dzholchiev). Manager: Miroslav Beránek

REPUBLIC OF IRELAND: Keiren Westwood, Darren O'Dea, Stephen Ward, John O'Shea, Sean St Ledger, Aiden McGeady, James McCarthy, Glenn Whelan, Robbie Keane, Simon Cox (58 Kevin Doyle), Jon Walters (71 Shane Long). Manager: Giovanni Trapattoni

Goals: Kayrat Nurdauletov (37) / Robbie Keane (88 pen), Kevin Doyle (90)

486. 11.09.2012
REPUBLIC OF IRELAND v OMAN 4-1 (3-0)

Craven Cottage, London

Referee: Andre Marriner (England) Attendance: 6,420

REPUBLIC OF IRELAND: David Forde (46 Darren Randolph), Marc Wilson (46 Alex Pearce), Stephen Kelly, Séamus Coleman, Sean St Ledger, David Meyler, James McCarthy (65 Simon Cox), Robbie Brady (70 Aiden McGeady), Shane Long (73 Joey O'Brien), Andy Keogh, Kevin Doyle (61 James McClean). Manager: Giovanni Trapattoni

OMAN: ALI Abdullah Harib AL HABSI, SAAD Suhail Juma AL MUKHAINI, HASSAN Yousuf Mudhafar AL GHEILANI, MOHAMED Abdullah Mubarak Ramadhan AL SHEIBA Al Balushi (78 ABDUL SALAM Amur Juma AL MUKHAINI), AHMED Kano Mubarak Obaid AL MAHAJIRI (77 ALI Hilal Saud AL JABRI), RAED IBRAHIM SALEH Heikal Al Mukhaini (69 HUSSEIN Ali Farah AL HADHRI), MOHAMMED Saleh Ali AL MUSALAMI, Juma Darwish JUMA AL MASHARI, Eid Mohammed EID AL FARSI, ABDUL AZIZ Humaid Mubarak AL MUQBALI (69 FAWZI BASHEER Rajab Bait Doorbeen), EMAD Ali Sulaiman AL HOSANI. Manager: Paul Le Guen

Goals: Shane Long (7), Robbie Brady (23), Kevin Doyle (36), Alex Pearce (85) / Eid Al Farsi (72)

487. 12.10.2012 20th World Cup Qualifier
REPUBLIC OF IRELAND v GERMANY 1-6 (0-2)

Aviva Stadium, Dublin

Referee: Nicola Rizzoli (Italy) Attendance: 49,850

REPUBLIC OF IRELAND: Keiren Westwood, Stephen Ward, John O'Shea, Darren O'Dea, Séamus Coleman, Aiden McGeady (69 Andy Keogh), James McCarthy, Keith Fahey (52 Shane Long), Keith Andrews, Jon Walters, Simon Cox (84 Robbie Brady). Manager: Giovanni Trapattoni

GERMANY: Manuel Neuer, Marcel Schmelzer, Per Mertesacker, Jérôme Boateng, Holger Badstuber, Bastian Schweinsteiger, Marco Reus (66 Lukas Podolski), Mesut Özil, Sami Khedira (46 Toni Kroos), Thomas Müller, Miroslav Klose (72 André Schürrle). Manager: Joachim Löw

Goals: Andy Keogh (90+2) / Marco Reus (32, 40), Mesut Özil (55 pen), Miroslav Klose (58), Toni Kroos (61, 83)

488. 16.10.2012 20th World Cup Qualifier
**FAROE ISLANDS
v REPUBLIC OF IRELAND 1-4** (0-0)

Tórvøllur, Tórshavn

Referee: Lorenc Jemini (Albania) Attendance: 4,300

FAROE ISLANDS: Gunnar Nielsen, Jónas Næs, Pól Justinussen, Rógvi Baldvinsson, Odmar Færø (60 Erling Jacobsen), Daniel Udsen (60 Arnbjørn Hansen), Christian Holst, Hallur Hansson, Jóan Edmundsson (78 Hjalgrím Elttør), Fródi Benjaminsen, Símun Samuelsen. Manager: Lars Olsen

REPUBLIC OF IRELAND: Keiren Westwood, Marc Wilson, John O'Shea, Darren O'Dea, Séamus Coleman, Aiden McGeady, James McCarthy, Keith Andrews (90 David Meyler), Robbie Brady (46 Simon Cox), Jon Walters, Robbie Keane (80 Shane Long). Manager: Giovanni Trapattoni

Goals: Arnbjørn Hansen (69) / Marc Wilson (46), Jon Walters (53), Pól Justinussen (73 og), Darren O'Dea (88)

489.   14.11.2012
REPUBLIC OF IRELAND v GREECE   0-1 (0-1)
Aviva Stadium, Dublin
Referee: Eitan Shmeulevitch (Israel)   Attendance: 16,256
REPUBLIC OF IRELAND: David Forde, Séamus Coleman, Ciaran Clark, Stephen Ward, John O'Shea, Glenn Whelan (34 Keith Andrews), James McCarthy (70 David Meyler), Robbie Brady (46 Wes Hoolahan), Simon Cox (61 Andy Keogh), James McClean, Shane Long (46 Kevin Doyle).
Manager: Giovanni Trapattoni
GREECE: Orestis Karnezis, José Lloyd Holebas (46 Stefanos Athanasiadis), Kostas Stafylidis (82 Nikos Spyropoulos), Vasilios Torosidis (61 Ioannis Maniatis), Kyriakos Papadopoulos, Sokratis Papastathopoulos, Alexandros Tziolis, Sotiris Ninis (60 Loukas Vyntra), Panagiotis Tachtsidis, Kostas Mitroglou (46 Kostas Fortounis), Georgios Samaras (46 Dimitrios Salpingidis).
Manager: FERNANDO Manuel Fernandes da Costa SANTOS
Goal: José Lloyd Holebas (29)

490.   06.02.2013
REPUBLIC OF IRELAND v POLAND   2-0 (1-0)
Aviva Stadium, Dublin
Referee: Sebastien Delferière (Belgium)   Att: 43,112
REPUBLIC OF IRELAND: David Forde, Ciaran Clark (84 Richard Keogh), John O'Shea, Paul McShane, Greg Cunningham, Glenn Whelan (46 Paul Green), James McCarthy (71 Jeff Hendrick), Robbie Brady (71 Jon Walters), Conor Sammon, James McClean (81 Simon Cox), Shane Long (62 Wes Hoolahan).   Manager: Giovanni Trapattoni
POLAND: Artur Boruc (46 Wojciech Szczesny), Damien Perquis, Sebastian Boenisch (46 Kamil Grosicki), Jakub Wawrzyniak, Grzegorz Krychowiak, Kamil Glik, Ludovic Obraniak (60 Arkadiusz Milik), Daniel Lukasik (77 Adrian Mierzejewski), Jakub Blaszczykowski, Szymon Pawlowski (46 Marcin Wasilewski), Robert Lewandowski.
Manager: Waldemar Fornalik
Goals: Ciaran Clark (35), Wes Hoolahan (76)

491.   22.03.2013   20th World Cup Qualifier
SWEDEN v REPUBLIC OF IRELAND   0-0
Friends Arena, Solna
Referee: Alberto Undiano Mallenco (Spain)   Att: 49,436
SWEDEN: Andreas Isaksson, Behrang Safari, Jonas Olsson, Mikael Lustig (46 Mikael Antonsson), Andreas Granqvist, Alexander Kacaniklic, Tobias Hysén (73 Ola Toivonen), Sebastian Larsson (87 Jimmy Durmaz), Kim Källström, Rasmus Elm, Zlatan Ibrahimovic.   Manager: Erik Hamrén

REPUBLIC OF IRELAND: David Forde, Marc Wilson, John O'Shea, Séamus Coleman, Ciaran Clark, James McCarthy, Paul Green, Jon Walters, James McClean (83 Andy Keogh), Shane Long (87 Conor Sammon), Robbie Keane (76 Wes Hoolahan).   Manager: Giovanni Trapattoni

492.   26.03.2013   20th World Cup Qualifier
REPUBLIC OF IRELAND v AUSTRIA   2-2 (2-1)
Aviva Stadium, Dublin
Referee: Marijo Strahonja (Croatia)   Attendance: 36,100
REPUBLIC OF IRELAND: David Forde, Marc Wilson, John O'Shea, Séamus Coleman, Ciaran Clark (72 Sean St Ledger), Glen Whelan, James McCarthy, Jon Walters, Conor Sammon, James McClean, Shane Long (83 Paul Green).
Manager: Giovanni Trapattoni
AUSTRIA: Heinz Lindner, György Garics, Christian Fuchs, Aleksandar Dragovic, Emanuel Pogatetz, David Alaba, Veli Kavlak (69 Andreas Weimann), Zlatko Junuzovic (27 Julian Baumgartlinger), Martin Harnik, Marko Arnautovic, Philipp Hosiner (62 Marc Janko).   Manager: Marcel Koller
Goals: Jon Walters (25 pen, 45+1) / Martin Harnik (11), David Alaba (90+2)

493.   29.05.2013
ENGLAND v REPUBLIC OF IRELAND   1-1 (1-1)
Wembley, London
Referee: William Collum (Scotland)   Attendance: 80,126
ENGLAND: Joe Hart (46 Ben Foster), Gary Cahill, Glen Johnson (46 Phil Jones), Phil Jagielka, Ashley Cole (53 Leighton Baines), Michael Carrick, Frank Lampard, Theo Walcott, Daniel Sturridge (33 Jermain Defoe), Wayne Rooney, Alex Oxlade-Chamberlain (87 James Milner).
Manager: Roy Hodgson
REPUBLIC OF IRELAND: David Forde, Séamus Coleman, John O'Shea, Stephen Kelly, Sean St Ledger, Glenn Whelan (73 Jeff Hendrick), Aiden McGeady (68 James McClean), James McCarthy, Jon Walters (81 Conor Sammon), Shane Long, Robbie Keane (65 Simon Cox).
Manager: Giovanni Trapattoni
Goals: Frank Lampard (23) / Shane Long (13)

494. 02.06.2013
REPUBLIC OF IRELAND v GEORGIA 4-0 (1-0)
Aviva Stadium, Dublin
Referee: Sebastian Coltescu (Romania)   Attendance: 20,100
REPUBLIC OF IRELAND: Keiren Westwood, Marc Wilson (65 Richard Dunne), Paul McShane, Richard Keogh, Damien Delaney, James McCarthy (72 Conor Sammon), Wes Hoolahan (76 Stephen Quinn), James McClean (65 Aiden McGeady), Shane Long (72 Jeff Hendrick), Andy Keogh (46 Robbie Keane), Simon Cox.   Manager: Giovanni Trapattoni
GEORGIA: Giorgi Loria, Ucha Lobzhanidze (46 David Targamadze), Dato Kvirkvelia (69 Giorgi Popkhadze), Zurab Khizanishvili, Guram Kashia, Akaki Khubutia, Aleksandr Kobakhidze (90 Tornike Gorgiashvili), Jaba Kankava, Murtaz Daushvili (54 Irakli Dzaria), Jano Ananidze (22 Omar Migineishvili goalkeeper), Nikoloz Gelashvili (61 Irakli Maisuradze).   Manager: Temur Ketsbaia
Sent off: Giorgi Loria (20)
Goals: Richard Keogh (42), Simon Cox (48), Robbie Keane (77, 88)

496. 12.06.2013
SPAIN v REPUBLIC OF IRELAND 2-0 (0-0)
Yankee Stadium, New York (USA)
Referee: Jair Marrufo (USA)   Attendance: 39.368
SPAIN: VÍCTOR VALDÉS Arribas (59 IKER CASILLAS Fernández), Álvaro ARBELOA Coca, SERGIO RAMOS García, Gerard PIQUÉ i Bernabéu, JORDI ALBA Ramos, "Xavi" Xavier Hernández i Creus (69 Juan Manuel MATA García), Andrés INIESTA Luján (59 Francesc "CESC" FÀBREGAS Soler), DAVID Jiménez SILVA (46 JESÚS NAVAS González), Sergio BUSQUETS Burgos, PEDRO Eliezer Rodríguez Ledesma (80 Santiago "Santi" CAZORLA González), DAVID VILLA Sánchez (59 Roberto SOLDADO Rillo).
Manager: Vicente DEL BOSQUE González
REPUBLIC OF IRELAND: David Forde (74 Darren Randolph), Darren O'Dea, Paul McShane, Stephen Kelly (90 Damien Delaney), Séamus Coleman, Sean St Ledger, James McCarthy (84 David Meyler), Jeff Hendrick (46 Stephen Quinn), Conor Sammon, Andy Keogh (74 James McClean), Robbie Keane (57 Simon Cox).
Manager: Giovanni Trapattoni
Goals: Roberto SOLDADO Rillo (69), Juan Manuel MATA García (88)

495. 07.06.2013   20th World Cup Qualifier
REPUBLIC OF IRELAND v FAROE ISLANDS 3-0 (1-0)
Aviva Stadium, Dublin
Referee: Mattias Gestranius (Finland)   Attendance: 30,805
REPUBLIC OF IRELAND: David Forde, Marc Wilson (81 Stephen Kelly), John O'Shea, Séamus Coleman, Sean St Ledger, Glen Whelan, Aiden McGeady (77 James McClean), Wes Hoolahan, Jon Walters (73 Conor Sammon), Robbie Keane, Simon Cox.   Manager: Giovanni Trapattoni
FAROE ISLANDS: Gunnar Nielsen, Heini Vatnsdal, Pól Justinussen, Ári Jónsson, Atli Gregersen, Rógvi Baldvinsson, Súni Olsen, Christian Holst (84 Hans Pauli Samuelsen), Páll Klettskard (65 Jóan Edmundsson), Símun Samuelsen, Jónhard Frederiksberg.   Manager: Lars Olsen
Goals: Robbie Keane (5, 55, 81)

497. 14.08.2013
WALES v REPUBLIC OF IRELAND 0-0
Cardiff City Stadium, Cardiff
Referee: Pavel Královec (Czech Republic)   Att: 20,000
WALES: Glyn Oliver "Boaz" Myhill, Ashley Williams, Sam Ricketts, Chris Gunter, Ben Davies, Joe Ledley (59 Andy King), Jack Collison (81 Craig Davies), Joe Allen (86 Andrew Crofts), Jonathan Williams, Craig Bellamy (59 Sam Vokes), Hal Robson-Kanu (74 Neil Taylor).   Manager: Chris Coleman
REPUBLIC OF IRELAND: Keiren Westwood, Marc Wilson, John O'Shea (60 Darren O'Dea), Séamus Coleman, Ciaran Clark, Glenn Whelan (60 Paul Green), James McCarthy, Wes Hoolahan (69 Paddy Madden), Robbie Brady (46 James McClean), Jon Walters (84 Conor Sammon), Shane Long (74 Andy Keogh).   Manager: Giovanni Trapattoni

498. 06.09.2013   20th World Cup Qualifier
REPUBLIC OF IRELAND v SWEDEN 1-2 (1-1)
Aviva Stadium, Dublin
Referee: Damir Skomina (Slovenia)   Attendance: 49,500
REPUBLIC OF IRELAND: David Forde, Marc Wilson, John O'Shea, Séamus Coleman, Richard Dunne, Glenn Whelan, James McCarthy, Jon Walters (68 Simon Cox), James McClean (74 Anthony Pilkington), Shane Long, Robbie Keane. Manager: Giovanni Trapattoni
SWEDEN: Andreas Isaksson, Per Nilsson, Martin Olsson, Mikael Lustig (64 Adam Johansson), Mikael Antonsson, Alexander Kacaniklic, Anders Svensson (68 Pontus Wernbloom), Sebastian Larsson, Albin Ekdal, Zlatan Ibrahimovic, Johan Elmander (90=2 Jonas Olsson). Manager: Erik Hamrén
Goals: Robbie Keane (22) / Johan Elmander (33), Anders Svensson (57)

499. 10.09.2013   20th World Cup Qualifier
AUSTRIA v REPUBLIC OF IRELAND 1-0 (0-0)
Ernst-Happel-Stadion, Wien
Referee: OLEGARIO Manuel Bartolo Faustino BENQUERENÇA (Portugal)   Attendance: 48,500
AUSTRIA: Robert Almer, Sebastian Prödl, György Garics, Christian Fuchs, Aleksandar Dragovic, Veli Kavlak (45+1 Christoph Leitgeb), David Alaba, Martin Marnik, Guido Burgstaller (60 Marko Arnautovic), Julian Baumgartlinger, Andreas Weimann (73 Marc Janko). Manager: Marcel Koller
REPUBLIC OF IRELAND: David Forde, Marc Wilson, John O'Shea (49 Ciaran Clark), Séamus Coleman, Richard Dunne, Anthony Pilkington (73 James McClean), James McCarthy, Paul Green, Jon Walters, Shane Long (81 Conor Sammon), Robbie Keane. Manager: Giovanni Trapattoni
Goal: David Alaba (84)

500. 11.10.2013   20th World Cup Qualifier
GERMANY v REPUBLIC OF IRELAND 3-0 (1-0)
RheinEnergieStadion, Köln
Referee: Serge Gumienny (Belgium)   Attendance: 46,237
GERMANY: Manuel Neuer, Per Mertesacker, Philipp Lahm, Marcell Jansen, Jérôme Boateng, Bastian Schweinsteiger, Mesut Özil, Toni Kroos, Sami Khedira (82 Max Kruse), André Schürrle (86 Mario Götze), Thomas Müller (88 Sidney Sam). Manager: Joachim Löw
REPUBLIC OF IRELAND: David Forde, Marc Wilson, Stephen Kelly, Séamus Coleman, Ciaran Clark, Damien Delaney, Glenn Whelan, James McCarthy, Darron Gibson, Anthony Stokes, Kevin Doyle. Manager: Noel King
Goals: Sami Khedira (12), André Schürrle (58), Mesut Özil (90+1)

501. 15.10.2013   20th World Cup Qualifier
REPUBLIC OF IRELAND v KAZAKHSTAN 3-1 (2-1)
Aviva Stadium, Dublin
Referee: Vadims Direktorenko (Latvia)   Attendance: 21,700
REPUBLIC OF IRELAND: David Forde, Séamus Coleman, Marc Wilson, John O'Shea, Richard Dunne, Andy Reid (75 Aiden McGeady), James McCarthy, Darron Gibson (37 Glenn Whelan), Anthony Stokes (87 Wes Hoolahan), Robbie Keane, Kevin Doyle. Manager: Noel King
KAZAKHSTAN: Andrey Sidelnikov, Konstantin Engel, Aleksandr Kislitsyn (32 Andrey Finonchenko), Viktor Dmitrenko, Mark Gorman, Maksat Bayzhanov, Andrey Karpovich (84 Pavel Shabalin), Dmitriy Shomko, Valeriy Korobkin, Aleksey Shchetkin (61 Igor Yurin), Sergey Khizhnichenko. Manager: Miroslav Beránek
Goals: Robbie Keane (17 pen), John O'Shea (26), Dmitriy Shomko (78 og) / Dmitriy Shomko (13)

502. 15.11.2013
REPUBLIC OF IRELAND v LATVIA 3-0 (1-0)
Aviva Stadium, Dublin
Referee: Andreas Ekberg (Sweden)   Attendance: 37,100
REPUBLIC OF IRELAND: Keiren Westwood, Stephen Ward, John O'Shea, Séamus Coleman, Marc Wilson, Aiden McGeady (72 Andy Reid), James McCarthy (81 Kevin Doyle), Wes Hoolahan (73 Shane Long), Glenn Whelan (81 Paul Green), James McClean (80 Anthony Stokes), Robbie Keane (73 Jon Walters). Manager: Martin O'Neill
LATVIA: Andris Vanins, Renārs Rode, Vitālijs Maksimenko, Kaspars Gorkss, Nauris Bulvitis, Vladislavs Gabovs, Artis Lazdins, Juris Laizāns (72 Alans Sinelnikovs), Ritvars Rugins (27 Aleksandrs Fertovs), Māris Verpakovskis (46 Eduards Visnakovs), Valērijs Sabala (62 Daniils Turkovs). Manager: Marian Pahars
Goals: Robbie Keane (22), Aiden McGeady (68), Shane Long (80)

503. 19.11.2013
POLAND v REPUBLIC OF IRELAND 0-0
INEA Stadion, Poznan
Referee: Richard Trutz (Slovakia)   Attendance: 31,094
POLAND: Wojciech Szczesny, Adam Marciniak, Marcin Kowalczyk, Piotr Celeban, Lukasz Szukala, Michal Pazdan, Waldemar Sobota (81 Tomasz Brzyski), Krzysztof Maczynski (60 Tomasz Jodlowiec), Jakub Blaszczykowski (89 Marcin Robak), Piotr Cwielong (81 Pawel Olkowski), Robert Lewandowski (60 Lukasz Teodorczyk). Manager: Adam Nawalka

REPUBLIC OF IRELAND: David Forde, Stephen Kelly, Marc Wilson (76 Glenn Whelan), Stephen Ward, Sean St Ledger (32 John O'Shea), Aiden McGeady (63 James McClean), James McCarthy (63 Alex Pearce), Paul Green, Shane Long (73 Wes Hoolahan), Jon Walters, Anthony Stokes (68 Kevin Doyle). Manager: Martin O'Neill

504.   05.03.2014
REPUBLIC OF IRELAND v SERBIA   1-2 (1-0)
Aviva Stadium, Dublin
Referee: Viktor Kassai (Hungary)   Attendance: 37,243
REPUBLIC OF IRELAND: David Forde, Marc Wilson, Stephen Ward (64 Ciaran Clark), Shane Long (72 Jon Walters), Richard Keogh, Séamus Coleman, Glenn Whelan (80 Stephen Quinn), Aiden McGeady (73 Daryl Murphy), James McCarthy (61 David Meyler), Wes Hoolahan (61 Anthony Pilkington), James McClean.   Manager: Martin O'Neill

SERBIA: Vladimir Stojkovic, Antonio Rukavina (89 Nemanja Gudelj), Aleksandar Kolarov, Branislav Ivanovic, Milan Bisevac, Dusan Basta (59 Zoran Tosic), Dusan Tadic (80 Adem Ljajic), Nemanja Matic, Lazar Markovic (75 Miralem Sulejmani), Ljubomir Fejsa, Filip Djordjevic (86 Stefan Scepovic).   Manager: Ljublinko Drulovic

Goals: Sean Long (8) /
James McCarthy (48 og), Filip Djordjevic (60)

505.   25.05.2014
REPUBLIC OF IRELAND v TURKEY   1-2 (0-1)
Aviva Stadium, Dublin
Referee: Ruddy Buquet (France)   Attendance: 15,000
REPUBLIC OF IRELAND: Rob Elliot, Marc Wilson, Stephen Ward, John O'Shea, Shane Long (66 Daryl Murphy), Damien Delaney (65 David Meyler), Séamus Coleman, Glenn Whelan (82 Stephen Quinn), Aiden McGeady (66 Jon Walters), Wes Hoolahan, James McClean.   Manager: Martin O'Neill

TURKEY: Onur Kivrak, Ömer Toprak, Gökhan Gönül, Hakan Balta, Caner Erkin, Nuri Sahin (84 Ishak Dogan), Ahmet Özek (70 Tarik Çamdal), Bilal Kisa (46 Ozan Tufan), Selçuk Inan (21 Oguzhan Özyakup), Hakan Çalhanoglu (63 Olcan Adin), Mevlüt Erdinç (81 Mustafa Pektemek).
Manager: Fatih Terim

Goals: Jon Walters (78) /
Ahmet Özek (17), Tarik Çamdal (75)

506.   31.05.2014
ITALY v REPUBLIC OF IRELAND   0-0
Craven Cottage, London
Referee: Michael Oliver (England)   Attendance: 22,879
ITALY: Salvatore Sirigu, Gabriel Paletta, Mattia De Sciglio, Matteo Darmian (88 Ignazio Abate), Leonardo Bonucci, Riccardo Montolivo (15 Alberto Aquilani, 37 Marco Parolo), Marco Verratti, Thiago Motta (62 Daniele De Rossi), Claudio Marchisio, Giuseppe Rossi (71 Alessio Cerci), Ciro Immobile (57 Antonio Cassano).   Manager: Cesare Prandelli

REPUBLIC OF IRELAND: David Forde, Stephen Ward, Alex Pearce, John O'Shea, Shane Long (73 Simon Cox), Séamus Coleman, Jeff Hendrick, Anthony Pilkington (59 James McClean), David Meyler (85 Paul Green), Aiden McGeady, Wes Hoolahan (67 Stephen Quinn).
Manager: Martin O'Neill

507.   07.06.2014
COSTA RICA v REPUBLIC OF IRELAND   1-1 (0-1)
PPL Park, Chester (USA)
Referee: RAUL CASTRO (Honduras)   Attendance: 7,000
COSTA RICA: KEYLOR Antonio NAVAS Gamboa (46 PATRICK Alberto PEMBERTON Bernard), MICHAEL UMAÑA Corrales, HEINER MORA Mora, GIANCARLO GONZÁLEZ Castro, ÓSCAR Esau DUARTE Gaitan, JÚNIOR Enrique DÍAZ Campbell, JOSÉ Miguel CUBERO Loría, CELSO BORGES Mora, MARCO Danilo UREÑA Porras (79 RANDALL BRENES Moya), BRYAN Jafet RUIZ González (74 CHRISTIÁN BOLAÑOS Navarro), JOEL Nathaniel CAMPBELL Samuels (86 DIEGO Geraldo CALVO Fonseca).
Manager: JORGE Luis PINTO Afanador

REPUBLIC OF IRELAND: David Forde, Richard Keogh, Stephen Kelly, Shane Duffy, Marc Wilson (40 James McClean), Glenn Whelan, Stephen Quinn (83 Simon Cox), Anthony Pilkington (68 Aiden McGeady), Paul Green (65 Jeff Hendrick), Robbie Keane (83 Wes Hoolahan), Kevin Doyle (70 Shane Long).   Manager: Martin O'Neill

Sent off: GIANCARLO GONZÁLEZ Castro (41)

Goals: CELSO BORGES Mora (64 pen) / Kevin Doyle (18)

Robbie Keane missed a penalty kick in the 67th minute.

508.   11.06.2014
REPUBLIC OF IRELAND v PORTUGAL 1-5 (0-3)
MetLife Stadium, East Rutherford (USA)
Referee: Baldomero Toledo (USA)   Attendance: 40,000

REPUBLIC OF IRELAND: David Forde, Stephen Ward (67 Stephen Quinn), Alex Pearce, Richard Keogh, Stephen Kelly (75 Simon Cox), David Meyler, Aiden McGeady (76 Kevin Doyle), Wes Hoolahan (64 Robbie Keane), Jeff Hendrick, Jon Walters (63 Shane Long), James McClean (67 Anthony Pilkington).   Manager: Martin O'Neill

PORTUGAL: RUI Pedro dos Santos PATRÍCIO, RICARDO Miguel Moreira da COSTA, Luís Carlos Novo NETO (66 Képler Laveran Lima Ferreira "PEPE"), RAÚL José Trindade MEIRELES (65 ANDRÉ Gomes Magalhães de ALMEIDA), JOÃO Filipe Iria Santos MOUTINHO, FÁBIO Alexandre da Silva COENTRÃO, WILLIAM Silva de CARVALHO, RÚBEN Filipe Marques AMORIM (81 MIGUEL Luís Pinto VELOSO), Silvestre Manuel Gonçalves VARELA (73 Adelino André Vieira de Freitas "VIEIRINHA"), CRISTIANO RONALDO dos Santos Aveiro (65 Luís Carlos Almeida da Cunha "NANI"), HUGO Miguel Pereira de ALMEIDA (66 HÉLDER Manuel Marques POSTIGA).   Manager: PAULO Jorge Gomes BENTO

Goals: James McClean (52) /
HUGO Miguel Pereira de ALMEIDA (3, 37), Richard Keogh (20 og), Adelino André Vieira de Freitas "VIEIRINHA" (77), FÁBIO Alexandre da Silva COENTRÃO (83)

509.   03.09.2014
REPUBLIC OF IRELAND v OMAN 2-0 (1-0)
Aviva Stadium, Dublin
Referee: Ilias Spathas (Greece)   Attendance: 14,376

REPUBLIC OF IRELAND: Shay Given (46 Rob Elliot), Stephen Ward, Alex Pearce, Richard Keogh, Anthony Pilkington (59 Aiden McGeady), David Meyler (86 Daryl Murphy), Darron Gibson (70 Glenn Whelan), Stephen Quinn, Wes Hoolahan (59 Robbie Keane), Robbie Brady, Kevin Doyle (59 Shane Long).   Manager: Martin O'Neill

OMAN: Ali Al Habsi, Saad Al Mukhaini, Abdul Salam Al Mukhaini, Hassan Al Gheilani (60 Ali Al Busaidi), Jaber Al Owaisi, Mohammed Al Siyabi (76 Hussein Al Hadhri), Raed Ibrahim Saleh (87 Mohamed Al Maashari), Qasim Said (60 Yaqoub Al Qasmi), Ahmed Al Mahaijri (60 Ali Al Jabri), Mohammed Al Masalami, Eid Al Farsi (81 Abzulaziz Al Muqbali).   Manager: Paul Le Guen

Goals: Kevin Doyle (20), Alex Pearce (81)

510.   07.09.2014   15th European Champs Qualifier
GEORGIA v REPUBLIC OF IRELAND 1-2 (1-1)
Boris Paichadze Dinamo Arena, Tbilisi
Referee: Kevin Blom (Netherlands)   Attendance: 22,000

GEORGIA: Giorgi Loria (46 Roin Kvaskhvadze), Ucha Lobzhanidze, Dato Kvirkvelia, Solomon Kverkvelia, Akaki Khubutia, Guram Kashia, Jaba Kankava, Murtaz Daushvili, Jano Ananidze (62 David Targamadze), Tornike Okriashvili (88 Levan Mchedlidze), Nikoloz Gelashvili.
Manager: Temur Ketsbaia

REPUBLIC OF IRELAND: David Forde, Marc Wilson, Stephen Ward, John O'Shea, Séamus Coleman, Glenn Whelan, Stephen Quinn (76 Robbie Brady), Aiden McGeady, James McCarthy (90+1 David Meyler), Jon Walters, Robbie Keane (75 Shane Long).   Manager: Martin O'Neill

Goals: Tornike Okriashvili (38) / Aiden McGeady (24, 90)

511.   11.10.2014   15th European Champs Qualifier
REPUBLIC OF IRELAND v GIBRALTAR 7-0 (3-0)
Aviva Stadium, Dublin
Referee: Leontios Trattou (Cyprus)   Attendance: 35,123

REPUBLIC OF IRELAND: David Forde, Marc Wilson, Stephen Ward (70 Robbie Brady), John O'Shea, David Meyler, Aiden McGeady, Wes Hoolahan (64 Kevin Doyle), Jeff Hendrick, Darron Gibson, James McClean, Robbie Keane (63 Daryl Murphy).   Manager: Martin O'Neill

GIBRALTAR: Jordan Perez (61 Jamie Robba), Scott Wiseman, Roy Chipolina (58 Yogen Santos), Joseph Chipolina, Ryan Casciaro, Liam Walker, Brian Perez, Aaron Payas, Jake Gosling, Rafa Bado (46 Robert Guilling), Lee Casciaro.
Manager: Allen Bula

Goals: Robbie Keane (6, 14, 18 pen), James McClean (46, 53), Jordan Perez (52 og), Wes Hoolahan (56)

512.   14.10.2014   15th European Champs Qualifier
GERMANY v REPUBLIC OF IRELAND 1-1 (0-0)
VELTINS-Arena, Gelsenkirchen
Referee: Damir Skomina (Slovenia)   Attendance: 51,204

GERMANY: Manuel Neuer, Jérôme Boateng, Antonio Rüdiger, Mats Hummels, Matthias Ginter (46 Lukas Podolski), Erik Durm, Julian Draxler (70 Max Kruse), Karim Bellarabi (86 Sebastian Rudy), Toni Kroos, Mario Götze, Thomas Müller.
Manager: Joachim Löw

REPUBLIC OF IRELAND: David Forde, Marc Wilson, Stephen Ward, John O'Shea, Glenn Whelan (53 Jeff Hendrick), Stephen Quinn (76 Wes Hoolahan), David Meyler, Aiden McGeady, James McClean, Robbie Keane (63 Darron Gibson), Jon Walters.   Manager: Martin O'Neill

Goals: Toni Kroos (71) / John O'Shea (90+4)

513. 14.11.2014   15th European Champs Qualifier
SCOTLAND v REPUBLIC OF IRELAND 1-0 (0-0)
Celtic Park, Glasgow
Referee: Milorad Mazic (Serbia)   Attendance: 59,239
SCOTLAND: David Marshall, Charlie Mulgrew, Grant Hanley, Steven Whittaker, Andrew Robertson, Russell Martin, Shaun Maloney, Scott Brown, Ikechi Anya (88 Darren Fletcher), Steven Naismith, Steven Fletcher (56 Chris Martin).   Manager: Gordon Strachan
REPUBLIC OF IRELAND: David Forde, John O'Shea, Richard Keogh, Séamus Coleman, Stephen Ward, Aiden McGeady, Jeff Hendrick (78 Robbie Keane), Darron Gibson (69 Stephen Quinn), James McClean, Shane Long (68 Robbie Brady), Jon Walters.   Manager: Martin O'Neill
Goal: Shaun Maloney (74)

514. 18.11.2014
REPUBLIC OF IRELAND v USA 4-1 (1-1)
Aviva Stadium, Dublin
Referee: Pawel Paczkowski (Poland)   Attendance: 33,332
REPUBLIC OF IRELAND: Shay Given (85 Rob Elliot), Alex Pearce, Ciaran Clark, Cyrus Christie, Stephen Quinn, Anthony Pilkington (64 James McClean), David Meyler, Robbie Brady, Anthony Stokes (59 Aiden McGeady), Daryl Murphy (77 Jeff Hendrick), David McGoldrick (77 Shane Long).   Manager: Martin O'Neill
USA: Bill Hamid, Alfredo Morales (65 Greg Garza), Fabian Johnson, Timothy Chandler (76 Jordan Morris), Geoff Cameron, Matt Besler, Mix Diskerud (76 Rubio Rubin), Alejandro Bedoya, Kyle Beckerman (88 Tim Ream), Chris Wondolowski (46 Bobby Wood), Jozy Altidore.   Manager: Jürgen Klinsmann
Goals: Anthony Pilkington (7), Robbie Brady (55, 86), James McClean (82) / Mix Diskerud (39)

515. 29.03.2015   15th European Champs Qualifier
REPUBLIC OF IRELAND v POLAND 1-1 (0-1)
Aviva Stadium, Dublin
Referee: Jonas Eriksson (Sweden)   Attendance: 50,500
REPUBLIC OF IRELAND: Shay Given, Marc Wilson, John O'Shea, Séamus Coleman, Robbie Brady, Glenn Whelan (84 Shane Long), Aiden McGeady (68 James McClean), James McCarthy, Wes Hoolahan, Jon Walters, Robbie Keane.   Manager: Martin O'Neill
POLAND: Lukasz Fabianski, Lukasz Szukala, Pawel Olkowski, Jakub Wawrzyniak, Grzegorz Krychowiak, Kamil Glik, Maciej Rybus, Slawomir Peszko (88 Michal Kucharczyk), Tomasz Jodlowiec, Arkadiusz Milik (84 Sebastian Mila), Robert Lewandowski.   Manager: Adam Nawalka
Goals: Shane Long (90+1) / Slawomir Peszko (26)

516. 07.06.2015
REPUBLIC OF IRELAND v ENGLAND 0-0
Aviva Stadium, Dublin
Referee: Arnold Hunter (Northern Ireland)   Att: 43.846
REPUBLIC OF IRELAND: Keiren Westwood (61 Shay Given), Marc Wilson, John O'Shea (71 Paul McShane), Séamus Coleman, Robbie Brady, Glenn Whelan (63 Harry Arter), Aiden McGeady, James McCarthy (46 James McClean), Jeff Hendrick, Daryl Murphy (56 Jon Walters), David McGoldrick (46 Kevin Long).   Manager: Martin O'Neill
ENGLAND: Joe Hart, Phil Jones, Chris Smalling, Gary Cahill (74 Phil Jagielka), Ryan Bertrand, Jack Wilshere (66 Ross Barkley), Raheem Sterling (66 Andros Townsend), James Milner, Adam Lallana (82 Theo Walcott), Jordan Henderson, Wayne Rooney (74 Jamie Vardy).   Manager: Roy Hodgson

517. 13.06.2015   15th European Champs Qualifier
REPUBLIC OF IRELAND v SCOTLAND 1-1 (1-0)
Aviva Stadium, Dublin
Referee: Nicola Rizzoli (Italy)   Attendance: 49,063
REPUBLIC OF IRELAND: Shay Given, Marc Wilson, John O'Shea, Séamus Coleman, Robbie Brady, Glenn Whelan (68 James McClean), James McCarthy, Wes Hoolahan (73 Robbie Keane), Jeff Hendrick, Jon Walters, Daryl Murphy (80 Shane Long).   Manager: Martin O'Neill
SCOTLAND: David Marshall, Charlie Mulgrew, Alan Hutton, Craig Forsyth, Matt Ritchie (46 Ikechi Anya), Steven Naismith (90+2 Christophe Berra), James Morrison, Russell Martin, Shaun Maloney, Scott Brown (85 James McArthur), Steven Fletcher.   Manager: Gordon Strachan
Goals: Jon Walters (38) / John O'Shea (47 og)

518. 04.09.2015   15th European Champs Qualifier
GIBRALTAR v REPUBLIC OF IRELAND 0-4 (0-1)
Estádio do Algarve, Faro-Loulé (Portugal)
Referee: Marijo Strahonja (Croatia)   Attendance: 5,393
GIBRALTAR: Jordan Perez, Jean Garcia, Roy Chipolina, Joseph Chipolina, Erin Barnett, Liam Walker, Jack Sergeant (85 Robert Guilling), Kyle Casciaro (61 Jake Gosling), Anthony Bardon, John-Paul Duarte (74 Michael Yome), Lee Casciaro.   Manager: Jeff Wood
REPUBLIC OF IRELAND: Shay Given, John O'Shea, Ciaran Clark, Cyrus Christie, Robbie Brady, Glenn Whelan, James McCarthy (70 Stephen Quinn), Wes Hoolahan (77 Aiden McGeady), Jeff Hendrick, Jon Walters, Robbie Keane (71 Shane Long).   Manager: Martin O'Neill
Goals: Cyrus Christie (27), Robbie Keane (49, 51 pen), Shane Long (79)

519.   07.09.2015   15th European Champs Qualifier
REPUBLIC OF IRELAND v GEORGIA 1-0 (0-0)
Aviva Stadium, Dublin
Referee: István Vad (Hungary)   Attendance: 27,200
REPUBLIC OF IRELAND: Shay Given, John O'Shea, Séamus Coleman, Ciaran Clark, Robbie Brady, Glenn Whelan, James McCarthy, Wes Hoolahan (75 James McClean), Jeff Hendrick, Jon Walters, Robbie Keane (46 Shane Long).
Manager: Martin O'Neill
GEORGIA: Nukri Revishvili, Ucha Lobzhanidze, Solomon Kverkvelia, Zurab Khizanishvili (81 Levan Kenia), Guram Kashia (76 Mate Tsintsadze), Aleksandr Amisulashvili, Giorgi Navalovski, Jaba Kankava, Valeri Qazaishvili (64 Giorgi Papunashvili), Tornike Okriashvili, Levan Mchedlidze.
Manager: Kakhaber Tskhadadze
Goal: Jon Walters (69)

520.   08.10.2015   15th European Champs Qualifier
REPUBLIC OF IRELAND v GERMANY 1-0 (0-0)
Aviva Stadium, Dublin
Referee: Carlos Velasco Carballo (Spain)   Att: 50,604
REPUBLIC OF IRELAND: Shay Given (44 Darren Randolph), Cyrus Christie, Stephen Ward (69 David Meyler), John O'Shea, Richard Keogh, Robbie Brady, James McCarthy, Wes Hoolahan, Jeff Hendrick, Jon Walters, Daryl Murphy (66 Shane Long).   Manager: Martin O'Neill
GERMANY: Manuel Neuer, Matthias Ginter (77 Karim Bellarabi), Jérôme Boateng, Mats Hummels, Jonas Hector, Ilkay Gündogan (84 Kevin Volland), Mario Götze (35 André Schürrle), Marco Reus, Mesut Özil, Toni Kroos, Thomas Müller.   Manager: Joachim Löw
Goal: Shane Long (70)

521.   11.10.2015   15th European Champs Qualifier
POLAND v REPUBLIC OF IRELAND 2-1 (2-1)
Stadion Narodowy, Warszawa
Referee: Cüneyt Çakir (Turkey)   Attendance: 57,497
POLAND: Lukasz Fabianski, Pawel Olkowski (63 Jakub Blaszczykowski), Grzegorz Krychowiak, Kamil Glik, Jakub Wawrzyniak, Lukasz Piszczek, Michal Pazdan, Krzysztof Maczynski (77 Lukasz Szukala), Karol Linetty, Robert Lewandowski, Kamil Grosicki (85 Slawomir Peszko).
Manager: Adam Nawalka
REPUBLIC OF IRELAND: Darren Randolph, Richard Keogh, Séamus Coleman, John O'Shea, Robbie Brady, James McCarthy, Jeff Hendrick, Glenn Whelan (58 Aiden McGeady), James McClean (73 Wes Hoolahan), Shane Long (55 Robbie Keane), Jon Walters.   Manager: Martin O'Neill
Sent off: John O'Shea (90+2)
Goals: Grzegorz Krychowiak (13), Robert Lewandowski (42) / Jon Walters (16 pen)

522.   13.11.2015   15th European Championships Qualification Play-offs
BOSNIA-HERZEGOVINA v REPUBLIC OF IRELAND 1-1 (0-0)
Stadion Bilino Polje, Zenica
Referee: Dr. Felix Brych (Germany)   Attendance: 15,260
BOSNIA-HERZEGOVINA: Asmir Begovic, Toni Sunjic, Emir Spahic, Mensur Mujdza (51 Ognjen Vranjes), Edin Cocalic, Ervin Zukanovic, Miralem Pjanic, Senad Lulic (88 Izet Hajrovic), Edin Visca (73 Milan Djuric), Vedad Ibisevic, Edin Dzeko.   Manager: Mehmed Bazdarevic
REPUBLIC OF IRELAND: Darren Randolph, Richard Keogh, Séamus Coleman, Ciaran Clark, Stephen Ward (67 Marc Wilson), Robbie Brady (86 Aiden McGeady), James McCarthy, Wes Hoolahan (60 James McClean), Jeff Hendrick, Glenn Whelan, Daryl Murphy.   Manager: Martin O'Neill
Goals: Edin Dzeko (85) / Robbie Brady (82)

523.   16.11.2015   15th European Championships Qualification Play-offs
REPUBLIC OF IRELAND v BOSNIA-HERZEGOVINA 2-0 (1-0)
Aviva Stadium, Dublin
Referee: Björn Kuipers (Netherlands)   Attendance: 50,500
REPUBLIC OF IRELAND: Darren Randolph, Séamus Coleman, Ciaran Clark, Richard Keogh, Robbie Brady, Wes Hoolahan (54 James McClean), Jeff Hendrick, Glenn Whelan (90+1 John O'Shea), James McCarthy, Jon Walters, Daryl Murphy (55 Shane Long).   Manager: Martin O'Neill
BOSNIA-HERZEGOVINA: Asmir Begovic, Ervin Zukanovic, Ognjen Vranjes, Emir Spahic, Edin Cocalic (46 Muhamed Besic), Sead Kolasinac, Edin Visca, Miralem Pjanic, Senad Lulic (80 Vedad Ibisevic), Haris Medunjanin (69 Milan Djuric), Edin Dzeko.   Manager: Mehmed Bazdarevic
Goals: Jon Walters (24 pen, 70)

524.   25.03.2016
REPUBLIC OF IRELAND v SWITZERLAND 1-0 (1-0)
Aviva Stadium, Dublin
Referee: Miroslav Zelinka (Czech Republic)   Att: 35,450
REPUBLIC OF IRELAND: Darren Randolph, Shane Duffy, Séamus Coleman, Ciaran Clark, Robbie Brady, Stephen Quinn (62 James McCarthy), David Meyler (62 Eunan O'Kane), Aiden McGeady (62 Jonathan Hayes), Shane Long (84 James McClean), Alan Judge, Kevin Doyle (26 Daryl Murphy, 78 Wes Hoolahan).   Manager: Martin O'Neill

SWITZERLAND: Yann Sommer, Fabian Schär, Ricardo Rodríguez (78 François Moubandje), Michael Lang (82 Silvan Widmer), Timm Klose, Granit Xhaka, Blerim Dzemaili (71 Shani Tarashaj), Valon Behrami (71 Gelson Fernandes), Haris Seferovic (62 Renato Steffen), Admir Mehmedi (71 Pajtim Kasami), Breel Embolo.   Manager: Vladimir Petkovic

Goal: Ciaran Clark (2)

525.   29.03.2016
REPUBLIC OF IRELAND v SLOVAKIA   2-2 (2-2)
Aviva Stadium, Dublin
Referee: Ola Nilsen (Norway)   Attendance: 30,217
REPUBLIC OF IRELAND: Rob Elliot (16 Darren Randolph), Stephen Ward (79 Jonathan Hayes), John O'Shea (46 Alex Pearce), Paul McShane, Cyrus Christie, Glenn Whelan, Eunan O'Kane (67 Anthony Pilkington), James McCarthy, Wes Hoolahan (73 Aiden McGeady), James McClean, Shane Long (46 Robbie Brady).   Manager: Martin O'Neill

SLOVAKIA: Matús Kozácik, Martin Skrtel, Kornel Saláta, Peter Pekarík, Dusan Svento (88 Lukás Tesák), Erik Sabo (64 Ondrej Duda), Marek Hamsík, Ján Gregus (74 Patrik Hrosovsky), Róbert Vittek (66 Adam Nemec), Miroslav Stoch (64 Róbert Mak), Stanislav Sesták (66 Vladimír Weiss). Manager: Ján Kozák

Goals: Shane Long (22 pen), James McClean (24 pen) / Miroslav Stoch (14), Paul McShane (45 og)

526.   27.05.2016
REPUBLIC OF IRELAND
v NETHERLANDS   1-1 (1-0)
Aviva Stadium, Dublin
Referee: ARTUR Manuel Ribeiro SOARES DIAS (Portugal)
Attendance: 42,438
REPUBLIC OF IRELAND: Darren Randolph, John O'Shea, Shane Duffy, Séamus Coleman, Bobbie Brady, Glenn Whelan (67 Darron Gibson), Stephen Quinn (67 Jeff Hendrick), Harry Arter (82 Eunan O'Kane), Jon Walters, David McGoldrick (76 Wes Hoolahan), Shane Long (67 James McClean). Manager: Martin O'Neill

NETHERLANDS: Jasper Cillessen, Joël Veltman, Virgil van Dijk, Jetro Willems, Jeffrey Bruma, Georginio Wijnaldum (82 Luuk de Jong), Kevin Strootman (70 Marco van Ginkel), Riechedly Bazoer, Quincy Promes, Vincent Janssen (75 Bas Dost), Memphis Depay (61 Steven Berghuis). Manager: Danny Blind.

Goals: Shane Long (30) / Luuk de Jong (85)

527.   31.05.2016
REPUBLIC OF IRELAND v BELARUS   1-2 (0-1)
Turner's Cross, Cork
Referee: Dejan Jakimovski (Macedonia)   Attendance: 7,200
REPUBLIC OF IRELAND: Shay Given (69 David Forde), Stephen Ward, Richard Keogh, Ciaran Clack, Cyrus Christie, David Meyler (75 Eunan O'Kane), Aiden McGeady (75 Callum O'Dowda), Jeff Hendrick, Darron Gibson (68 Wes Hoolahan), Daryl Murphy (68 Shane Long), James McClean (79 David McGoldrick).   Manager: Martin O'Neill

BELARUS: Sergey Chernik, Denis Polyakov, Aleksandr Martinovich, Maksim Volodko, Igor Stasevich (90+3 Pavel Nekhaychik), Mikhail Sivakov, Nikita Korzun, Sergey Kislyak, Aliaksandr Hleb (90+1 Sergey Krivets), Mikhail Gordeychuk (77 Sergey Politsevich), Nikolai Yanush. Manager: Aleksandr Khatskevich

Goals: Stephen Ward (72) / Mikhail Gordeychuk (20), Maksim Volodko (63)

528.   13.06.2016   15th European Champs Group E
REPUBLIC OF IRELAND v SWEDEN   1-1 (0-0)
Stade de France, Paris-St.Denis
Referee: Milorad Mazic (Serbia)   Attendance: 73,419
REPUBLIC OF IRELAND: Darren Randolph, Séamus Coleman, Ciaran Clack, John O'Shea, Robbie Brady, Glenn Whelan, James McCarthy (85 Aiden McGeady), Jeff Hendrick, Wes Hoolahan (78 Robbie Keane), Shane Long, Jon Walters (64 James McClean).   Manager: Martin O'Neill

SWEDEN: Andreas Isaksson, Mikael Lustig (45 Erik Johansson), Andreas Granqvist, Martin Olsson, Victor Lindelöf, Emil Forsberg, Sebastian Larsson, Kim Källström, Oscar Lewicki (86 Albin Ekdal), Zlatan Ibrahimovic, Marcus Berg (59 John Guidetti).
Managers: Erik Hamrén & Janne Andersson

Goals: Wes Hoolahan (48) / Ciaran Clark (71 og)

529. 18.06.2016   15th European Champs Group E
BELGIUM v REPUBLIC OF IRELAND 3-0 (0-0)
Stade Matmut-Atlantique, Bordeaux (France)
Referee: Cüneyt Çakir (Turkey)   Attendance: 39,493
BELGIUM: Thibaut Courtois, Toby Alderweireld, Thomas Vermaelen, Jan Vertonghen, Thomas Meunier, Axel Witsel, Kevin De Bruyne, Eden Hazard, Yannick Ferreira-Carrasco (64 Dries Mertens), Mousa Dembélé (57 Radja Nainggolan), Romelu Lukaku (83 Christian Benteke).
Manager: Marc Wilmots
REPUBLIC OF IRELAND: Darren Randolph, Séamus Coleman, Ciaran Clack, John O'Shea, Stephen Ward, Robbie Brady, Glenn Whelan, James McCarthy (62 James McClean), Jeff Hendrick, Wes Hoolahan (71 Aiden McGeady), Shane Long (79 Robbie Keane).   Manager: Martin O'Neill
Goals: Romelu Lukaku (48, 70), Axel Witsel (61)

530. 22.06.2016   15th European Champs Group E
ITALY v REPUBLIC OF IRELAND 0-1 (0-0)
Stade Pierre-Mauroy, Villeneuve d'Ascq (France)
Referee: Ovidiu Hategan (Romania)   Attendance: 44,268
ITALY: Salvatore Sirigu, Mattia De Sciglio (82 Stephan El Shaarawy), Angelo Ogbonna, Andrea Barzagli, Leonardo Bonucci, Alessandro Florenzi, Thiago Motta, Stefano Sturaro, Simone Zaza, Ciro Immobile (74 Lorenzo Insigne), Federico Bernardeschi (60 Matteo Darmian).
Manager: Antonio Conte
REPUBLIC OF IRELAND: Darren Randolph, Séamus Coleman, Richard Keogh, Shane Duffy, Stephen Ward, Robbie Brady, James McCarthy (77 Wes Hoolahan), Jeff Hendrick, Shane Long (90 Stephen Quinn), James McClean, Daryl Murphy (70 Aiden McGeady).   Manager: Martin O'Neill
Goal: Robbie Brady (85)

531. 26.06.2016   15th Euro Champs Round of 16
FRANCE v REPUBLIC OF IRELAND 2-1 (0-1)
Parc Olympique Lyonnais, Décines-Charpieu
Referee: Nicola Rizzoli (Italy)   Attendance: 56,278
FRANCE: Hugo Lloris, Patrice Evra, Adil Rami, Bacary Sagna, Laurent Koscielny, N'Golo Kanté (46 Kingsley Coman, 90+3 Moussa Sissoko), Dimitri Payet, Blaise Matuidi, Paul Pogba, Antoine Griezmann, Olivier Giroud (73 André-Pierre Gignac).   Manager: Didier Deschamps
REPUBLIC OF IRELAND: Darren Randolph, Séamus Coleman, Richard Keogh, Shane Duffy, Stephen Ward, Robbie Brady, James McCarthy (72 Wes Hoolahan), Jeff Hendrick, Shane Long, James McClean (68 John O'Shea), Daryl Murphy (65 Jon Walters).   Manager: Martin O'Neill
Sent off: Shane Duffy (66)
Goals: Antoine Griezmann (58, 61) / Robbie Brady (2 pen)

532. 31.08.2016
REPUBLIC OF IRELAND v OMAN 4-0 (3-0)
Aviva Stadium, Dublin
Referee: Demetrios Masias (Cyprus)   Attendance: 27,000
REPUBLIC OF IRELAND: Keiren Westwood (46 Darren Randolph), Ciaran Clark, Cyrus Christie, Marc Wilson, Robbie Brady (46 Stephen Ward), Stephen Quinn (65 Callum O'Dowda), Harry Arter, Glenn Whelan (46 Jeff Hendrick), Jon Walters, Shane Long (46 James McClean), Robbie Keane (57 Wes Hoolahan).   Manager: Martin O'Neill
OMAN: Faiyz Al Rushaidi, Abdul Salam Al Mukhaini, Nadir Mabrook, Salaah Al Yahyaei, Harib Al Saadi, Mohsin Al Khaldi (57 Eid Al Farsi), Hussein Al Hadhri (75 Hisham Al Shuaibi), Mataz Abd Raboh (57 Ali Al Busaidi), Mahmood Mabrook (46 Ahmed Al Mahajri), Raed Ibrahim Saleh, Abdulaziz Al Muqbali (87 Said Obaid Al Abdul Salam).
Manager: Juan Ramón LÓPEZ CARO
Goals: Robbie Brady (8), Robbie Keane (30), Jon Walters (34, 63)

533. 05.09.2016   21st World Cup Qualifier
SERBIA v REPUBLIC OF IRELAND 2-2 (0-1)
Stadion Rajko Mitic, Beograd
Referee: Viktor Kassai (Hungary)   Attendance: 7,896
SERBIA: Predrag Rajkovic, Jagos Vukovic, Antonio Rukavina, Matija Nastasic, Filip Mladenovic (77 Dusko Tosic), Branislav Ivanovic, Luka Milivojevic, Filip Kostic (82 Aleksandar Katai), Nemanja Gudelj, Dusan Tadic, Aleksandar Mitrovic (59 Andrija Pavlovic).   Manager: Slavoljub Muslin
REPUBLIC OF IRELAND: Darren Randolph, Stephen Ward (70 Stephen Quinn), John O'Shea, Richard Keogh, Séamus Coleman, Glenn Whelan, Jeff Hendrick (76 Daryl Murphy), Robbie Brady, Jon Walters, James McClean, Shane Long (90+2 Ciaran Clark).   Manager: Martin O'Neill
Goals: Filip Kostic (62), Dusan Tadic (69 pen) / Jeff Hendrick (3), Daryl Murphy (80)

534. 06.10.2016   21st World Cup Qualifier
REPUBLIC OF IRELAND v GEORGIA 1-0 (0-0)
Aviva Stadium, Dublin
Referee: Tony Chapron (France)   Attendance: 39,793
REPUBLIC OF IRELAND: Darren Randolph, Stephen Ward, Shane Duffy, Séamus Coleman, Ciaran Clark, James McCarthy, Jeff Hendrick, Robbie Brady (79 Glenn Whelan), Jon Walters, James McClean, Shane Long (90+4 John O'Shea).   Manager: Martin O'Neill

GEORGIA: Giorgi Loria, Solomon Kverkvelia, Guram Kashia, Otar Kakabadze, Giorgi Navalovski (89 Aleksandr Kobakhidze), Valeriane Gvilia, Murtaz Daushvili (90+3 Nika Kacharava), Jano Ananidze (73 Davit Skhirtladze), Valeri Qazaishvili, Tornike Okriashvili, Levan Mchedlidze. Manager: Vladimir Weiss

Goal: Séamus Coleman (56)

535.   09.10.2016   21st World Cup Qualifier
MOLDOVA v REPUBLIC OF IRELAND 1-3 (1-1)
Stadionul Zimbru, Chisinau
Referee: Jakob Kehlet (Denmark)   Attendance: 6,089

MOLDOVA: Nicolae Calancea, Veaceslav Posmac, Vitali Bordian, Vadim Bolohan, Igor Armas (36 Victor Golovatenco), Eugen Zasavitchi (61 Eugen Cebotaru), Alexandru Gatcan, Andrei Cojocari, Gheorghe Andronic (83 Eugeniu Sidorenco), Alexandru Dedov, Igor Bugaev.   Manager: Igor Dobrovolskiy

REPUBLIC OF IRELAND: Darren Randolph, Stephen Ward, Shane Duffy, Séamus Coleman, Ciaran Clark, Glenn Whelan, James McCarthy (80 David Meyler), Wes Hoolahan (86 Eunan O'Kane), Jon Walters, James McClean, Shane Long (63 Callum O'Dowda).   Manager: Martin O'Neill

Goals: Igor Bugaev (45+1) / Shane Long (2), James McClean (69, 76)

536.   12.11.2016   21st World Cup Qualifier
AUSTRIA v REPUBLIC OF IRELAND 0-1 (0-0)
Ernst-Happel-Stadion, Wien
Referee: Sergey Karasev (Russia)   Attendance: 48,500

AUSTRIA: Ramazan Özcan, Kevin Wimmer (78 Stefan Ilsanker), Florian Klein, Martin Hinteregger, Aleksandar Dragovic, Alessandro Schöpf (57 Louis Schaub), Julian Baumgartlinger, Marko Arnautovic, David Alaba, Marcel Sabitzer (73 Martin Harnik), Marc Janko.
Manager: Marcel Koller

REPUBLIC OF IRELAND: Darren Randolph, Shane Duffy, Séamus Coleman, Ciaran Clark, Glenn Whelan (24 David Meyler), Wes Hoolahan (78 David McGoldrick), Jeff Hendrick, Robbie Brady, Harry Arter, Jon Walters, James McClean (85 Aiden McGeady).   Manager: Martin O'Neill

Goal: James McClean (48)

537.   24.03.2017   21st World Cup Qualifier
REPUBLIC OF IRELAND v WALES 0-0
Aviva Stadium, Dublin
Referee: Nicola Rizzoli (Italy)   Attendance: 49,989

REPUBLIC OF IRELAND: Darren Randolph, Richard Keogh, Séamus Coleman (72 Cyrus Christie), Stephen Ward, John O'Shea, Jeff Hendrick, David Meyler (79 Aiden McGeady), Glenn Whelan, Shane Long, Jon Walters, James McClean.   Manager: Martin O'Neill

WALES: Wayne Hennessey, Chris Gunter, Ben Davies, James Chester, Ashley Williams, Neil Taylor, Joe Allen, Aaron Ramsey, Joe Ledley (72 Jazz Richards), Gareth Bale, Hal Robson-Kanu (46 Sam Vokes).   Manager: Chris Coleman

Sent off: Neil Taylor (69)

538.   28.03.2017
REPUBLIC OF IRELAND v ICELAND 0-1 (0-1)
Aviva Stadium, Dublin
Referee: Jakob Kehlet (Denmark)   Attendance: 37,241

REPUBLIC OF IRELAND: Keiren Westwood, Alex Pearce, John Egan (64 Andrew Boyle), Cyrus Christie, Aiden McGeady (73 Callum O'Dowda), Conor Hourihane (63 Eunan O'Kane), Jeff Hendrick (63 Stephen Gleeson), Jonathan Hayes (63 Daryl Horgan), Robbie Brady, James McClean (72 Shane Long), Kevin Doyle.   Manager: Martin O'Neill

ICELAND: Ögmundur Kristinsson, Ragnar Sigurdsson (53 Hólmar Eyjólfsson), Birkir Sævarsson (85 Vidar Ari Jónsson), Hördur Magnússon, Sverrir Ingason, Ólafur Skúlason (79 Arnór Smárason), Aron Sigurdarson (65 Orri Ómarsson), Aron Gunnarsson, Rúrik Gíslason (88 Ari Skúlason), Kjartan Finnbogason (72 Óttar Karlsson), Jón Bödvarsson.
Manager: Heimir Hallgrímsson

Goal: Hördur Magnússon (21)

539. 02.06.2017
MEXICO v REPUBLIC OF IRELAND 3-1 (2-0)
MetLife Stadium, East Rutherford (USA)
Referee: Ted Unkel (USA)   Attendance: 42.017
MEXICO: RODOLFO COTA Robles, DIEGO Antonio REYES Rosales, HÉCTOR Alfredo MORENO Herrera (46 OSWALDO ALANÍS Pantoja), CARLOS Joel SALCEDO Hernández (46 MIGUEL Arturo LAYÚN Prado), HÉCTOR Miguel HERRERA López (46 ORIBE PERALTA Morones), JORGE Daniel HERNÁNDEZ Govea, JESÚS Daniel GALLARDO Vasconcelos, JONATHAN DOS SANTOS Ramírez (59 ORBELÍN PINEDA Alvarado), JESÚS Manuel CORONA Ruiz (61 JAVIER Ignacio AQUINO Carmona), RAÚL Alonso JIMÉNEZ Rodríguez, CARLOS Alberto VELA Garrido (68 RAFAEL MÁRQUEZ Álvarez).   Manager: JUAN CARLOS OSORIO Arbeláez
REPUBLIC OF IRELAND: Darren Randolph, John Egan (64 Kevin Long), Shane Duffy, Cyrus Christie (73 Alan Browne), Richard Keogh, Conor Hourihane (64 Eunan O'Kane), Daryl Horgan (73 Stephen Gleeson), Callum O'Dowda, Daryl Murphy (64 Wes Hoolahan), David McGoldrick, James McClean.   Manager: Martin O'Neill

Goals: JESÚS Manuel CORONA Ruiz (16), RAÚL Alonso JIMÉNEZ Rodríguez (25 pen), CARLOS Alberto VELA Garrido (54) / Stephen Gleeson (77)

540. 04.06.2017
REPUBLIC OF IRELAND v URUGUAY 3-1 (1-1)
Aviva Stadium, Dublin
Referee: Craig Thomson (Scotland)   Attendance: 27,193
REPUBLIC OF IRELAND: Darren Randolph (46 Keiren Westwood), Stephen Ward, Kevin Long, Shane Duffy (61 Alex Pearce), Cyrus Christie, Glenn Whelan (46 Wes Hoolahan), Jeff Hendrick (74 James McClean), Jonathan Hayes (60 Aiden McGeady), Robbie Brady, Harry Arter, Jon Walters (61 Daryl Murphy).   Manager: Martin O'Neill
URUGUAY: ESTEBAN Néstor CONDE Quintana, Victorio Maximiliano "MAXI" PEREIRA Páez (63 FEDERICO RICCA Rostagnol), JOSÉ María GIMÉNEZ de Vargas, SEBASTIÁN COATES Nion, José MARTÍN CÁCERES Silva, MATÍAS VECINO Falero, CARLOS Andrés SÁNCHEZ Arcosa (46 NAHITAN Michel NÁNDEZ Acosta), EGIDIO Raúl ARÉVALO Ríos (46 ÁLVARO Rafael GONZÁLEZ Luengo), DIEGO Sebastián LAXALT Suárez (46 ALEJANDRO Daniel SILVA González), JONATHAN "URRETA" Matías Urretaviscaya da Luz, EDINSON Roberto Gómez CAVANI (13 CHRISTIAN Ricardo STUANI Curbelo).
Manager: ÓSCAR Washington TABÁREZ Sclavo

Goals: Jon Walters (28), Cyrus Christie (51), J. McClean (77) / JOSÉ María GIMÉNEZ de Vargas (38)

541. 11.06.2017   21st World Cup Qualifier
REPUBLIC OF IRELAND v AUSTRIA 1-1 (0-1)
Aviva Stadium, Dublin
Referee: David Fernández Borbalán (Spain)   Att: 50,000
REPUBLIC OF IRELAND: Darren Randolph, Stephen Ward (56 Daryl Murphy), Kevin Long, Shane Duffy, Cyrus Christie, Glenn Whelan (77 Aiden McGeady), Jeff Hendrick, Robbie Brady, Harry Arter (71 Wes Hoolahan), Jon Walters, James McClean.   Manager: Martin O'Neill
AUSTRIA: Heinz Lindner, Sebastian Prödl, Stefan Lainer, Martin Hinteregger, Aleksandar Dragovic, Valentino Lazaro, Florian Kainz (89 Michael Gregoritsch), Zlatko Junuzovic (79 Florian Grillitsch), Julian Baumgartlinger, David Alaba, Guido Burgstaller (75 Martin Harnik).   Manager: Marcel Koller

Goals: Jon Walters (85) / Martin Hinteregger (31)

542. 02.09.2017   21st World Cup Qualifier
GEORGIA v REPUBLIC OF IRELAND 1-1 (1-1)
Boris Paichadze, Tbilisi
Referee: Ivan Kruzlaik (Slovakia)   Attendance: 19,669
GEORGIA: Giorgi Makaridze, Solomon Kverkvelia, Nika Kvekveskiri, Guram Kashia, Otar Kakabadze, Giorgi Navalovski, Jambul Jighauri (75 Giorgi Chanturia), Valeriane Gvilia, Jano Ananidze, Valeri Qazaishvili (90+3 Davit Khotcholava), Giorgi Kvilitaia (85 Giorgi Merebashvili).
Manager: Vladimir Weiss
REPUBLIC OF IRELAND: Darren Randolph, Stephen Ward, Shane Duffy, Ciaran Clark, Cyrus Christie, Glenn Whelan (79 Daryl Murphy), Robbie Brady, Harry Arter (62 Aiden McGeady), Jon Walters, James McClean, Shane Long.
Manager: Martin O'Neill

Goals: Valeri Qazaishvili (34) / Shane Duffy (4)

543. 05.09.2017   21st World Cup Qualifier
REPUBLIC OF IRELAND v SERBIA 0-1 (0-0)
Aviva Stadium, Dublin
Referee: Cüneyt Çakir (Turkey)   Attendance: 50,153
REPUBLIC OF IRELAND: Darren Randolph, Stephen Ward (72 Callum O'Dowda), Shane Duffy, Ciaran Clark, Cyrus Christie, David Meyler (79 Conor Hourihane), Wes Hoolahan (62 Daryl Murphy), Robbie Brady, Jon Walters, James McClean, Shane Long.   Manager: Martin O'Neill
SERBIA: Vladimir Stojkovic, Jagos Vukovic, Antonio Rukavina, Nikola Maksimovic, Aleksandar Kolarov, Branislav Ivanovic, Luka Milivojevic, Nemanja Matic, Filip Kostic (72 Stefan Mitrovic), Dusan Tadic (81 Nemanja Gudelj), Aleksandar Mitrovic (80 Aleksandar Prijovic).
Manager: Slavoljub Muslin

Sent off: Nikola Maksimovic (68)

Goal: Aleksandar Kolarov (55)

544. 06.10.2017   21st World Cup Qualifier
REPUBLIC OF IRELAND v MOLDOVA 2-0 (2-0)
Aviva Stadium, Dublin

Referee: Bas Nijhuis (Netherlands)   Attendance: 55,800

REPUBLIC OF IRELAND: Darren Randolph, Stephen Ward, Shane Duffy, Ciaran Clark, Cyrus Christie, David Meyler, Wes Hoolahan (79 Aiden McGeady), Jeff Hendrick, Callum O'Dowda, Daryl Murphy (79 Harry Arter), Shane Long (83 Seán Maguire).   Manager: Martin O'Neill

MOLDOVA: Ilie Cebanu, Artiom Razgoniuc, Petru Racu, Alexandru Epureanu, Vitali Bordian, Artur Ionita, Alexandru Gatcan, Gheorghe Anton, Sergiu Platica (79 Vladimir Ambros), Radu Gînsari, Alexandru Dedov (55 Eugeniu Cociuc).   Manager: Igor Dobrovolskiy

Sent off: Alexandru Gatcan (90+2)

Goals: Daryl Murphy (2, 19)

545. 09.10.2017   21st World Cup Qualifier
WALES v REPUBLIC OF IRELAND 0-1 (0-0)
Cardiff City Stadium, Cardiff

Referee: Damir Skomina (Slovenia)   Attendance: 33,000

WALES: Wayne Hennessey, Ashley Williams, Chris Gunter, Ben Davies, James Chester, Aaron Ramsey, Joe Ledley, Andy King (65 Benjamin Woodburn), Joe Allen (37 Jonathan Williams), Hal Robson-Kanu (71 Sam Vokes), Tom Lawrence.   Manager: Chris Coleman

REPUBLIC OF IRELAND: Darren Randolph, Stephen Ward, Shane Duffy, Ciaran Clark, Cyrus Christie, David Meyler, Jeff Hendrick, Robbie Brady, Harry Arter (78 Glenn Whelan), Daryl Murphy (90+2 Kevin Long), James McClean.   Manager: Martin O'Neill

Goal: James McClean (57)

546. 11.11.2017   21st World Cup Qualifier Play-off
DENMARK v REPUBLIC OF IRELAND 0-0
Telia Parken, København

Referee: Milorad Mazic (Serbia)   Attendance: 36,189

DENMARK: Kasper Schmeichel, Simon Kjær, Andreas Bjelland, Peter Ankersen, Jens Stryger Larsen, Pione Sisto (72 Nicklas Bendtner), William Kvist, Christian Eriksen, Thomas Delaney, Nicolai Jørgensen, Andreas Cornelius (64 Yussuf Poulsen).   Manager: Åge Hareide

REPUBLIC OF IRELAND: Darren Randolph, Stephen Ward, Shane Duffy, Ciaran Clark, Cyrus Christie, Jeff Hendrick (90+3 Conor Hourihane), Robbie Brady, Harry Arter (88 Glenn Whelan), Callum O'Dowda, Daryl Murphy (74 Shane Long), James McClean.   Manager: Martin O'Neill

547. 14.11.2017   21st World Cup Qualifier Play-off
REPUBLIC OF IRELAND v DENMARK 1-5 (1-2)
Aviva Stadium, Dublin

Referee: Szymon Marciniak (Poland)   Attendance: 50,000

REPUBLIC OF IRELAND: Darren Randolph, Stephen Ward, Shane Duffy, Ciaran Clark (71 Shane Long), Cyrus Christie, David Meyler (46 Wes Hoolahan), Jeff Hendrick, Robbie Brady, Harry Arter (46 Aiden McGeady), Daryl Murphy, James McClean.   Manager: Martin O'Neill

DENMARK: Kasper Schmeichel, Jens Stryger Larsen (54 Peter Ankersen), Simon Kjær, Andreas Christensen, Andreas Bjelland, Pione Sisto, William Kvist, Christian Eriksen, Thomas Delaney, Yussuf Poulsen (70 Andreas Cornelius), Nicolai Jørgensen (84 Nicklas Bendtner).   Manager: Åge Hareide

Goals: Shane Duffy (6) / Andreas Christensen (29), Christian Eriksen (32, 63, 74), Nicklas Bendtner (90 pen)

548. 23.03.2018
TURKEY v REPUBLIC OF IRELAND 1-0 (0-0)
Antalya Stadyumu, Antalya

Referee: Slavko Vincic (Slovenia)   Attendance: 32,000

TURKEY: Volkan Babacan, Serdar Aziz (82 Kaan Ayhan), Gökhan Gönül, Hasan Ali Kaldirim, Çaglar Söyüncü, Emre Akbaba (69 Yunus Malli), Okay Yokuslu, Hakan Çalhanoglu (80 Irfan Can Kahveci), Mehmet Topal, Cenk Tosun (64 Enes Ünal), Yusuf Yazici (87 Alper Potuk).   Manager: Mircea Lucescu

REPUBLIC OF IRELAND: Colin Doyle, Séamus Coleman (63 Matt Doherty), Kevin Long, Shane Duffy, Conor Hourihane (69 Ciaran Clark), James McClean, Jeff Hendrick (80 Alan Judge), Alan Brown (68 David Meyler), Declan Rice, Seán Maguire (62 Shane Long), Scott Hogan (75 Daryl Horgan).   Manager: Martin O'Neill

Goals: Mehmet Topal (52)

549. 28.05.2018
FRANCE v REPUBLIC OF IRELAND 2-0 (2-0)
Stade de France, Saint-Denis
Referee: Georgi Kabakov (Bulgaria)   Attendance: 72,000
FRANCE: Steve Mandanda, Benjamin Mendy (63 Lucas Hernández), Samuel Umtiti (64 Presnel Kimpembe), Adil Rami, Djibril Sidibé (82 Benjamin Pavard), Blaise Matuidi, Steven N'Zonzi, Corentin Tolisso (77 Paul Pogba), Nabil Fekir (64 Antoine Griezmann), Olivier Giroud, Kylian Mbappé (77 Ousmane Dembélé).   Manager: Didier Deschamps

REPUBLIC OF IRELAND: Colin Doyle, Séamus Coleman, Kevin Long (80 Shaun Williams), Shane Duffy, Derrick Williams (82 Matt Doherty), Alan Brown (59 Harry Arter), Declan Rice, Jon Walters (59 David Meyler), Shane Long (70 Alan Judge), James McClean, Callum O'Dowda (70 Graham Burke).   Manager: Martin O'Neill

Goals: Olivier Giroud (40), Nabil Fekir (43)

550. 02.06.2018
REPUBLIC OF IRELAND
      v UNITED STATES 2-1 (0-1)
Aviva Stadium, Dublin
Referee: Andrew Dallas (Scotland)   Attendance: 32,300
REPUBLIC OF IRELAND: Colin Doyle, John O'Shea (35 Darragh Lenihan), Séamus Coleman, Kevin Long, Shane Duffy (77 Enda Stevens), James McClean, Jeff Hendrick (83 Harry Arter), Callum O'Dowda (89 Alan Judge), Declan Rice, Jon Walters, Graham Burke (58 Daryl Horgan).
Manager: Martin O'Neill

UNITED STATES: Bill Hamid, DeAndre Yedlin (70 Shaq Moore), Cameron Carter-Vickers (61 Tim Parker), Matt Miazga, Jorge Villafaña, Wil Trapp, Tim Weah, Tyler Adams, Weston McKennie (81 Joe Corona), RUBIO Yovani MÉNDEZ Rubin (77 Luca de la Torre), Bobby Wood (70 Josh Sargent).
Manager: Dave Sarachan

Goals: Graham Burke (57), Alan Judge (90) / Bobby Wood (45+1)

551. 06.09.2018   UEFA Nations League Group B4
WALES v REPUBLIC OF IRELAND 4-1 (3-0)
Cardiff City Stadium, Cardiff
Referee: Clément Turpin (France)   Attendance: 25,657
WALES: Wayne Hennessey, Ashley Williams, Ben Davies (81 Paul Dummett), Ethan Ampadu (67 Matthew Smith), Chris Mepham, Joe Allen, Aaron Ramsey, Tom Lawrence, David Brooks, Connor Roberts, Gareth Bale (75 Tyler Roberts).
Manager: Ryan Giggs

REPUBLIC OF IRELAND: Darren Randolph, Séamus Coleman, Stephen Ward (61 Enda Stevens), Ciaran Clark, Shane Duffy, Cyrus Christie, Conor Hourihane (57 Shaun Williams), Jeff Hendrick, Callum O'Dowda, Jon Walters, Callum Robinson (77 Daryl Horgan).
Manager: Martin O'Neill

Goals: Tom Lawrence (6), Gareth Bale (18), A. Ramsey (37), Connor Roberts (55) / Shaun Williams (66)

552. 11.09.2018
POLAND v REPUBLIC OF IRELAND 1-1 (0-0)
Stadion Miejski we Wroclawiu, Wroclaw
Referee: Boris Marhefka (Slovakia)   Attendance: 25,455
POLAND: Wojciech Szczesny, Arkadiusz Reca (72 Rafal Pietrzak), Kamil Glik (61 Jan Bednarek), Marcin Kaminski, Tomasz Kedziora, Jakub Blaszczykowski (81 Przemyslaw Frankowski), Grzegorz Krychowiak (73 Damian Szymanski), Karol Linetty, Rafal Kurzawa (46 Damian Kadzior), Arkadiusz Milik, Krzysztof Piatek (61 Mateusz Klich).
Manager: Jerzy Brzeczek

REPUBLIC OF IRELAND: Darren Randolph, Cyrus Christie (54 Matt Doherty), Richard Keogh, John Egan, Enda Stevens, Kevin Long, Callum O'Dowda (90 Alan Judge), Jeff Hendrick (54 David Meyler), Shaun Williams (73 Conor Hourihane), Callum Robinson (63 Graham Burke), Aiden O'Brien (81 Daryl Horgan).   Manager: Martin O'Neill

Goals: Mateusz Klich (87) / Aiden O'Brien (53)

553. 13.10.2018   UEFA Nations League Group B4
REPUBLIC OF IRELAND v DENMARK 0-0
Aviva Stadium, Dublin
Referee: XAVIER ESTRADA Fernández (Spain)
Attendance: 41,220

REPUBLIC OF IRELAND: Darren Randolph, Richard Keogh, Kevin Long, Shane Duffy, Cyrus Christie, Matt Doherty, Harry Arter (65 Callum Robinson), James McClean, Jeff Hendrick, Callum O'Dowda (46 Enda Stevens), Shane Long (83 Aiden O'Brien).   Manager: Martin O'Neill

DENMARK: Kasper Schmeichel, Simon Kjær, Mathias Jørgensen, Henrik Dalsgaard, Jens Stryger, Lasse Schøne, Thomas Delany, Martin Braithwaite, Yussuf Poulsen, Pione Sisto, Kasper Dolberg (79 Andreas Christensen).
Manager: Åge Hareide

554. 16.10.2018   UEFA Nations League Group B4
REPUBLIC OF IRELAND v WALES 0-1 (0-0)
Aviva Stadium, Dublin
Referee: Björn Kuipers (Netherlands)   Attendance: 38,321
REPUBLIC OF IRELAND: Darren Randolph, Richard Keogh, Kevin Long (75 Scott Hogan), Shane Duffy, Cyrus Christie, Matt Doherty, Harry Arter, James McClean, Jeff Hendrick, Aiden O'Brien (56 Shane Long), Callum Robinson (60 Seán Maguire).   Manager: Martin O'Neill
WALES: Wayne Hennessey, Ashley Williams, James Chester, Ben Davies, Joe Allen, Tom Lawrence, Harry Wilson (85 Chris Gunter), Matthew Smith (75 George Thomas), Connor Roberts, Tyler Roberts, David Brooks (87 Andy King).   Manager: Ryan Giggs
Goal: Harry Wilson (58)

555. 15.11.2018
**REPUBLIC OF IRELAND
    v NORTHERN IRELAND 0-0**
Aviva Stadium, Dublin
Referee: Slavko Vincic (Slovenia)   Attendance: 31,241
REPUBLIC OF IRELAND: Darren Randolph, Séamus Coleman, Shane Duffy, John Egan, Darragh Lenihan (84 Cyrus Christie), Glenn Whelan (36 Conor Hourihane), James McClean (66 Enda Stevens), Bobbie Brady, Jeff Hendrick, Callum O'Dowda (46 Ronas Curtis), Callum Robinson (66 Seán Maguire, 80 Scott Hogan).   Manager: Martin O'Neill
NORTHERN IRELAND: Bailey Peacock-Farrell, Jonny Evans, Craig Cathcart, Michael Smith (74 Jamie Ward), Steve Davis, Corry Evans (65 Paddy McNair), George Saville, Stuart Dallas, Jamal Lewis, Liam Boyce (71 Kyle Lafferty), Gavin Whyte (61 Jordan Jones).   Manager: Michael O'Neill

556. 19.11.2018   UEFA Nations League Group B4
DENMARK v REPUBLIC OF IRELAND 0-0
Ceres Park & Arena, Aarhus
Referee: Aliyar Agayev (Azerbaijan)   Attendance: 11,130
DENMARK: Frederik Rønnow, Andreas Bjelland, Mathias Jørgensen, Jonas Knudsen, Peter Ankersen, Lasse Schøne, Christian Eriksen (46 Lukas Lerager), Pierre Emile Højbjerg, Nicolai Jørgensen, Martin Braithwaite (78 Andreas Cornelius), Yussuf Poulsen (46 Christian Gytkjær).
Manager: Åge Hareide
REPUBLIC OF IRELAND: Darren Randolph, Séamus Coleman, Richard Keogh, Enda Stevens, Kevin Long, Shane Duffy, Cyrus Christie, Robbie Brady (66 Callum Robinson), Jeff Hendrick, Callum O'Dowda (80 Michael Obafemi), Aiden O'Brien (65 Ronan Curtis).   Manager: Michael O'Neill

557. 23.03.2019   16th European Champs Qualifiers
GIBRALTAR v REPUBLIC OF IRELAND 0-1 (0-0)
Victoria Stadium, Gibraltar
Referee: Anastasios Papapetrou (Greece)   Attendance: 2,000
GIBRALTAR: Kyle Goldwin, Joseph Chipolina, Jayce Olivero, Roy Chipolina, Louie Annesley (64 Adam Priestley), Liam Walker, Jack Sergeant, Anthony Bardon, Tjay De Barr, Anthony Hernandez (77 Alain Pons), Lee Casciaro.
Manager: Julio César Ribas Vlacovich
REPUBLIC OF IRELAND: Darren Randolph, Séamus Coleman, Richard Keogh, Enda Stevens, Shane Duffy, Matt Doherty (56 Robbie Brady), Conor Hourihane, James McClean, Jeff Hendrick, David McGoldrick, Seán Maguire (72 Harry Arter).   Manager: Mick McCarthy
Goal: Jeff Hendrick (49)

558. 26.03.2019   16th European Champs Qualifiers
REPUBLIC OF IRELAND v GEORGIA 1-0 (1-0)
Aviva Stadium, Dublin
Referee: Serdar Gözübüyük (Netherlands)
Attendance: 40,317
REPUBLIC OF IRELAND: Darren Randolph, Séamus Coleman, Richard Keogh, Enda Stevens, Shane Duffy, Glenn Whelan, Conor Hourihane, James McClean, Robbie Brady (74 Aiden O'Brien), Jeff Hendrick, David McGoldrick (81 Matt Doherty).   Manager: Mick McCarthy
GEORGIA: Giorgi Loria, Guram Kashia, Solomon Kvirkvelia, Davit Khocholava (65 Levan Kharabadze), Jaba Kankava, Nika Kvekveskiri, Vato Arveladze (73 Vako Qazaishvili), Otar Kiteishvili, Vako Gvilia, Giorgi Kvilitaia, Otar Kakabadze (85 Tornike Okriashvili).   Manager: Vladimír Weiss
Goal: Conor Hourihane (36)

559. 07.06.2019   16th European Champs Qualifiers
DENMARK v REPUBLIC OF IRELAND 1-1 (0-0)
Telia Parken, Copenhagen
Referee: Cüneyt Çakir (Turkey)   Attendance: 34,610
DENMARK: Kasper Schmeichel, Simon Kjær, Henrik Dalsgaard, Jens Stryger, Andreas Christensen, Lasse Schøne (72 Pierre Emile Højbjerg), Thomas Delaney, Christian Eriksen, Nicolai Jørgensen, Martin Braithwaite (65 Kasper Dolberg), Yussuf Poulsen.   Manager: Åge Hareide
REPUBLIC OF IRELAND: Darren Randolph, Séamus Coleman, Richard Keogh, Enda Stevens, Shane Duffy, Glenn Whelan, Conor Hourihane (82 Scott Hogan), James McClean, Robbie Brady (66 Alan Judge), Jeff Hendrick, David McGoldrick (88 Callum Robinson).
Manager: Mick McCarthy
Goals: Pierre Emile Højbjerg (76) / Shane Duffy (85)

560. 10.06.2019   16th European Champs Qualifiers
REPUBLIC OF IRELAND v GIBRALTAR 2-0 (1-0)
Aviva Stadium, Dublin

Referee: Radu Petrescu (Romania)   Attendance: 36,281

REPUBLIC OF IRELAND: Darren Randolph, Séamus Coleman, Richard Keogh, Enda Stevens, Shane Duffy, Conor Hourihane, James McClean, Jeff Hendrick, David McGoldrick, Scott Hogan (66 Seán Maguire), Callum Robinson (73 Robbie Brady).   Manager: Mick McCarthy

GIBRALTAR: Kyle Goldwin, Joseph Chipolina, Alain Pons (64 Ethan Britto), Jayce Olivero, Roy Chipolina, Louie Annesley, Liam Walker, Jack Sergeant, Andrew Hernandez (76 Ethan Jolley), Tjay De Barr, Lee Casciaro (9 Anthony Bardon).   Manager: Julio César Ribas Vlacovich

Goals: Joseph Chipolina (29 og), Robbie Brady (90+3)

561. 05.09.2019   16th European Champs Qualifiers
REPUBLIC OF IRELAND
   v SWITZERLAND 1-1 (0-0)
Aviva Stadium, Dublin

Referee: Carlos Del Cerro Grande (Spain)   Att: 44,111

REPUBLIC OF IRELAND: Darren Randolph, Séamus Coleman, Richard Keogh, Enda Stevens, Shane Duffy, Glenn Whelan, Conor Hourihane (82 Scott Hogan), James McClean, Jeff Hendrick, David McGoldrick (90+2 Alan Browne), Callum Robinson (58 Alan Judge).   Manager: Mick McCarthy

SWITZERLAND: Yann Sommer, Ricardo Rodríguez, Fabian Schär, Kevin Mbabu (90+4 Edimilson Fernandes), Nico Elvedi, Manuel Akanji, Granit Xhaka, Remo Freuler (90 Admir Mehmedi), Denis Zakaria, Haris Seferovic, Breel Embolo (86 Albian Ajeti).   Manager: Vladimir Petkovic

Goals: David McGoldrick (85) / Fabian Schär (74)

562. 10.09.2019
REPUBLIC OF IRELAND v BULGARIA 3-1 (0-0)
Aviva Stadium, Dublin

Referee: Tobias Welz (Germany)   Attendance: 18,259

REPUBLIC OF IRELAND: Mark Travers (76 Kieran O'Hara), Kevin Long, John Egan, Cyrus Christie, Alan Judge (59 Jack Byrne), Conor Hourihane (69 James McClean), Callum O'Dowda (76 Enda Stevens), Ronan Curtis (84 Jeff Hendrick), Alan Browne, Scott Hogan (60 James Collins), Josh Cullen.   Manager: Mick McCarthy

BULGARIA: Hristo Ivanov, Kristiyan Malinov (81 Georgi Terziev), Ivan Goranov, Anton Nedyalkov (59 Vasil Bozhikov), Kristian Dimitrov (80 Vasil Panayotov), Georgi Milanov (46 Ivelin Popov), Daniel Mladenov (68 Kiril Despodov), Simeon Slavchev, Georgi Pashov, Bozhidar Kraev, Nikolay Dimitrov (59 Wanderson Cristaldo Farias).   Manager: Krasimir Balakov

Goals: Alan Browne (56), K. Long (83), James Collins (86) / Ivelin Popov (67 pen)

563. 12.10.2019   16th European Champs Qualifiers
GEORGIA v REPUBLIC OF IRELAND 0-0
Boris Paichadze Stadion, Tbilisi

Referee: Marco Guida (Italy)   Attendance: 24,385

GEORGIA: Giorgi Loria, Gia Grigalava, Guram Kashia, Otar Kakabadze, Jimmy Tabidze, Jaba Kankava, Jano Ananidze, Tornike Okriashvili (79 Elguja Lobzhanidze), Vako Qazaishvili, Otar Kiteishvili (90 Giorgi Aburjania), Giorgi Kvilitaia (73 Levan Shengelia).   Manager: Vladimír Weiss

REPUBLIC OF IRELAND: Darren Randolph, Séamus Coleman, Shane Duffy, John Egan, Matt Doherty, Glenn Whelan, Conor Hourihane (90+3 Derrick Williams), James McClean, Jeff Hendrick, James Collins (79 Aaron Connolly), Callum Robinson (73 Alan Browne).
Manager: Mick McCarthy

564. 15.10.2019   16th European Champs Qualifiers
SWITZERLAND
   v REPUBLIC OF IRELAND 2-0 (1-0)
Stade de Genève, Lancy

Referee: Szymon Marciniak (Poland)   Attendance: 24,766

SWITZERLAND: Yann Sommer, Stephan Lichtsteiner (70 Remo Freuler), Fabian Schär, Ricardo Rodríguez, Nico Elvedi, Manuel Akanji, Admir Mehmedi (28 Edimilson Fernandes), Granit Xhaka, Denis Zakaria, Haris Seferovic, Breel Embolo (88 Renato Steffen).   Manager: Vladimir Petkovic

REPUBLIC OF IRELAND: Darren Randolph, Séamus Coleman, Enda Stevens, Shane Duffy, John Egan, Glenn Whelan, James McClean, Jeff Hendrick, Alan Browne, James Collins (46 Callum O'Dowda), Aaron Connolly (70 Scott Hogan).   Manager: Mick McCarthy

Goals: Haris Seferovic (16), Shane Duffy (90+3 og)

Sent off: Séamus Coleman (76)

565. 14.11.2019
REP. OF IRELAND v NEW ZEALAND 3-1 (1-1)
Aviva Stadium, Dublin

Referee: Robert Jenkins (Wales)   Attendance: 18,728

REPUBLIC OF IRELAND: Kieran O'Hara (66 Mark Travers), Kevin Long, Ciaran Clark, Derrick Williams (56 Callum O'Dowda), Lee O'Connor, Robbie Brady, Jack Byrne (63 Alan Judge), Alan Browne (66 Conor Hourihane), Josh Cullen, Seán Maguire (73 James Collins), Troy Parrott (63 Callum Robinson).   Manager: Mick McCarthy

NEW ZEALAND: Stefan Marinovic, Winston Reid (46 Bill Tuiloma), Liberato Cacace, Michael Boxall (74 Tommy Smith), Joe Bell, Chris Wood (76' Andre de Jong), Sarpreet Singh, Callum McCowatt (85 Elliot Collier), Ryan Thomas (74' Michael McGlinchey), Storm Roux (90+2 Tim Payne), Elijah Just.   Manager: Danny Hay

Goals: Derrick Williams (45), Seán Maguire (52), Callum Robinson (75) / Callum McCowatt (30)

566.   18.11.2019   16th European Champs Qualifiers
REPUBLIC OF IRELAND v DENMARK 1-1 (0-0)

Aviva Stadium, Dublin

Referee: Felix Brych (Germany)   Attendance: 51,700

REPUBLIC OF IRELAND: Darren Randolph, Matt Doherty, Enda Stevens, Shane Duffy, John Egan (46 Ciaran Clark), Glenn Whelan (82 Seán Maguire), Conor Hourihane (68 Callum Robinson), James McClean, Jeff Hendrick, Alan Browne, David McGoldrick.   Manager: Mick McCarthy

DENMARK: Kasper Schmeichel, Simon Kjær, Mathias Jørgensen, Henrik Dalsgaard, Jens Stryger, Lasse Schøne (84 Andreas Christensen), Thomas Delaney (13 Pierre Emile Højbjerg), Christian Eriksen, Martin Braithwaite, Yussuf Poulsen, Andreas Cornelius (33 Kasper Dolberg).   Manager: Åge Hareide

Goals: Matt Doherty (85) / Martin Braithwaite (73)

567.   03.09.2020   UEFA Nations League – Group B4
BULGARIA v REPUBLIC OF IRELAND 1-1 (0-0)

National Stadium Vasil Levski, Sofia

Referee: Manuel Schüttengruber (Austria)   Attendance: 0

BULGARIA: Georgi Georgiev, Petar Zanev (79 Plamen Galabov), Anton Nedyalkov, Strahil Popov, Kristian Dimitrov, Galin Ivanov, Georgi Kostadinov, Kristiyan Malinov, Todor Nedelev (83 Aleksandar Tsvetkov), Bozhidar Kraev, Spas Delev (76 Bircent Karagaren).   Manager: Georgi Dermendzhiev

REPUBLIC OF IRELAND: Darren Randolph, Enda Stevens, Shane Duffy, John Egan, Matt Doherty, James McCarthy (70 Robbie Brady), Conor Hourihane, Jeff Hendrick, Callum O'Dowda (74 Callum Robinson), Aaron Connolly, Adam Idah (77 Shane Long).   Manager: Stephen Kenny

Goals: Bozhidar Kraev (57) / Shane Duffy (90+4)

568.   06.09.2020   UEFA Nations League – Group B4
REPUBLIC OF IRELAND v FINLAND 0-1 (0-0)

Aviva Stadium, Dublin

Referee: Fabio Maresca (Italy)   Attendance: 0

REPUBLIC OF IRELAND: Darren Randolph, Enda Stevens, Shane Duffy, John Egan, Matt Doherty, Harry Arter, Robbie Brady, Callum O'Dowda (59 Callum Robinson), Jayson Molumby, Aaron Connolly (77 James McClean), Adam Idah (66 David McGoldrick).   Manager: Stephen Kenny

FINLAND: Lukás Hradecký, Juhani Ojala, Nikolai Alho, Daniel O'Shaughnessy, Leo Väisänen, Niko Hämäläinen (79 Jere Uronen), Tim Sparv, Robert Taylor, Glen Kamara, Teemu Pukki (90+1 Rasmus Karjalainen), Joel Pohjanpalo (63 Fredrik Jensen).   Manager: Markku Kanerva

Goal: Fredrik Jensen (64)

569.   08.10.2020   16th European Champs Qualifiers – Play-off
SLOVAKIA v REPUBLIC OF IRELAND 0-0 (AET)

Národný futbalový stadión, Bratislava

Referee: Clément Turpin (France)   Attendance: 0

SLOVAKIA: Marek Rodák, Peter Pekarík, Róbert Mazán, Denis Vavro (112 Norbert Gyömbér), Martin Valjent, Marek Hamsík, Jaroslav Mihalík (73 Lukás Haraslín), Albert Rusnák (86 Róbert Mak), Patrik Hrosovský, Juraj Kucka (86 Ján Gregus), Ondrej Duda (107 Róbert Bozeník).
Manager: Pavel Hapal

REPUBLIC OF IRELAND: Darren Randolph, Enda Stevens, Shane Duffy, John Egan, Matt Doherty, James McCarthy (61 Alan Browne), Conor Hourihane, James McClean (60 Robbie Brady), Jeff Hendrick, David McGoldrick (112 Shane Long), Callum Robinson (99 Callum O'Dowda).
Manager: Stephen Kenny

Penalties: 1-0 Marek Hamsík, 1-1 Conor Hourihane, 2-1 Patrik Hrosovský, 2-2 Robbie Brady, 3-2 Lukás Haraslín, Alan Browne (missed), 4-2 Ján Gregus, Matt Doherty (missed)

570.   11.10.2020   UEFA Nations League – Group B4
REPUBLIC OF IRELAND v WALES 0-0

Aviva Stadium, Dublin

Referee: Anasthasios Sidiropoulos (Greece)   Attendance: 0

REPUBLIC OF IRELAND: Darren Randolph, Enda Stevens, Kevin Long (25 Cyrus Christie), Shane Duffy, Matt Doherty, Conor Hourihane, James McClean, Robbie Brady (73 Daryl Horgan), Jeff Hendrick, Jayson Molumby (89 Josh Cullen), Shane Long (74 Seán Maguire).   Manager: Stephen Kenny

WALES: Wayne Hennessey, Ben Davies, Connor Roberts, Joe Rodon, Ethan Ampadu, Aaron Ramsey, Daniel James (77 David Brooks), Joe Morrell, Harry Wilson (67 Neco Williams), Matthew Smith (67 Dylan Levitt), Kieffer Moore.   Manager: Ryan Giggs

Sent off: James McClean (84)

571.   14.10.2020   UEFA Nations League – Group B4
FINLAND v REPUBLIC OF IRELAND 1-0 (0-0)

Helsingin Olympiastadion, Helsinki

Referee: Lionel Tschudi (Switzerland)   Attendance: 8,000

FINLAND: Lukás Hradecký, Paulus Arajuuri, Joona Toivio, Albin Granlund (86 Jukka Raitala), Jere Uronen, Tim Sparv, Robert Taylor, Pyry Soiri (46 Ilmari Niskanen), Glen Kamara (75 Rasmus Schüller), Teemu Pukki (81 Joel Pohjanpalo), Fredrik Jensen (86 Joni Kauko).   Manager: Markku Kanerva

REPUBLIC OF IRELAND: Darren Randolph, Enda Stevens, Shane Duffy, Matt Doherty, Dara O'Shea, Daryl Horgan (75 Ronan Curtis), Conor Hourihane, Jeff Hendrick (75 Adam Idah), Seán Maguire (53 Robbie Brady), Aaron Connolly, Jayson Molumby (83 Jason Knight).   Manager: S. Kenny

Goal: Fredrik Jensen (67)

1007.   12.11.2020
ENGLAND v REPUBLIC OF IRELAND 3-0 (2-0)

Wembley Stadium, London

Referee: Carlos del Cerro Grande (Spain)   Attendance: 0

ENGLAND: Nick Pope (46 Dean Henderson), Harry Maguire, Michael Keane, Tyrone Mings (64 Ainsley Maitland-Niles), Reece James, Jack Grealish (62 Phil Foden), Harry Winks, Mason Mount (73 Jude Bellingham), Jadon Sancho, Bukayo Saka, Dominic Calvert-Lewin (63 Tammy Abraham).   Manager: Gareth Southgate

REPUBLIC OF IRELAND: Darren Randolph, Shane Duffy, John Egan (14 Dara O'Shea), Cyrus Christie (61 Kevin Long), Matt Doherty, Daryl Horgan (61 Robbie Brady), Jeff Hendrick, Callum O'Dowda (61 James McClean), Alan Browne, Adam Idah (71 Ronan Curtis), Conor Hourihane (71 Jayson Molumby).   Manager: Stephen Kenny

Goals: Harry Maguire (18), Jadon Sancho (31), Dominic Calvert-Lewin (56 pen)

573.   15.11.2020   UEFA Nations League – Group B4
WALES v REPUBLIC OF IRELAND 1-0 (0-0)

Cardiff City Stadium, Cardiff

Referee: Petr Ardeleánu (Czech Republic)   Attendance: 0

WALES: Danny Ward, Ben Davies, Joe Rodon, Ethan Ampadu, Neco Williams, Chris Mepham, Rhys Norrington-Davies (62 Kieffer Moore), Daniel James, Joe Morrell, David Brooks (88 Tyler Roberts), Gareth Bale.   Manager: R. Giggs

REPUBLIC OF IRELAND: Darren Randolph, Kevin Long, Shane Duffy, Matt Doherty, Dara O'Shea (81 Callum O'Dowda), James McClean, Daryl Horgan (59 Jason Knight), Robbie Brady (82 Jack Byrne), Jeff Hendrick, Jayson Molumby (76 Conor Hourihane), Adam Idah (76 James Collins).   Manager: Stephen Kenny

Goal: David Brooks (67)

Sent off: Jeff Hendrick (90+4)

574.   18.11.2020   UEFA Nations League – Group B4
REPUBLIC OF IRELAND v BULGARIA 0-0

Aviva Stadium, Dublin

Referee: Lawrence Visser (Belgium)   Attendance: 0

REPUBLIC OF IRELAND: Darren Randolph, Kevin Long, Shane Duffy, Dara O'Shea, Conor Hourihane, Robbie Brady (80 Jack Byrne), Ryan Manning (87 Cyrus Christie), Daryl Horgan (67 Josh Cullen), Ronan Curtis (86 Troy Parrott), James Collins (87 Seán Maguire), Jason Knight.   Manager: Stephen Kenny

BULGARIA: Martin Lukov, Cicinho (60 Aleksandar Vasilev), Strahil Popov, Kristian Dimitrov, Galin Ivanov (61 Bircent Karagaren), Georgi Angelov, Aleksandar Tsvetkov, Kristiyan Malinov, Bozhidar Kraev, Dimitar Iliev (81 Denislav Aleksandrov), Spas Delev (61 Svetoslav Kovachev).   Manager: Georgi Dermendzhiev